Antique Metalware

ANTIQUES Magazine Library

Antique Metalware

BRASS, BRONZE, COPPER, TIN, WROUGHT & CAST IRON

Edited by James R. Mitchell

A Main Street Press Book

Universe Books   New York

Articles included in this volume, or excerpts from such articles, are printed as they appeared in the following issues of *The Magazine* ANTIQUES:

Part I: Cast-Iron Architecture on Beacon Hill in Boston, June, 1975; Cast-Iron Fountains in Vermont, April, 1949; Philadelphia's Ornamental Cast Iron, August, 1952; Charleston Ornamental Ironwork, May, 1970; Mobile Ironwork, September, 1967; The Ironwork of Old New Orleans, September, 1930; The Early Ironwork of Central Kentucky, May, 1948; Molded Iron in the Middle West, February, 1943; American Mid-Victorian Outdoor Furniture, June, 1959.

Part II: Decorative Cast Iron on the Virginia Frontier, March, 1972; Iron Furnaces in the Cumberland Valley, May, 1944; American Firebacks and Stove Plates, February, 1934; Some Early Andirons, October, 1941; The Whittinghams: Brassfounders of New York, April, 1957; Old Metal Fenders, April, 1939; The Franklin Stove, July, 1922; Franklin-Type Stoves, May, 1948; Box Stoves and Parlor Cook Stoves, November, 1948; Stovemakers of Troy, New York, January, 1973; Old-Time Foot Stoves, March, 1939.

Part III: American Tin Toys at the Abby Aldrich Rockefeller Folk Art Collection, December, 1976; The Little Toy Soldier, July, 1943; Toy Banks, October, 1926; The First Five Years of Patented Toy Banks, March, 1941.

Part IV: Keys for Collectors, August, 1948; Early Wrought-Iron Hardware: Spring Latches, August, 1954; Early American Stock Locks, August, 1970; Latch and Door Knocker, February, 1923; Early American House Hardware, I, August, 1923; Ready Reference for Furniture Hardware, III, August, 1927; Types of Wrought Iron Hardware Applicable to Early American Architectural Treatment, II, November, 1927; Types of Wrought Iron Hardware Applicable to Early American Architectural Treatment, III, December, 1927; An Eighteenth-Century English Brassfounder's Catalogue, February, 1931; English Hardware for American Cabinetmakers, November, 1931.

Part V: Surveyors' Equipment and the Western Frontier, September, 1970; Richard Patten: Mathematical Instrument Maker, July, 1959; Bits of Brass, January, 1972; Notes on Scissors, July, 1923; The Decorative Appeal of Hand Tools, February, 1965; The ABCs of Nails and Screws, March, 1949; English Bronze Wool Weights, December, 1963.

Part VI: On Weather Vanes, February, 1933; Weathervanes, March, 1951; Cushing and White's Copper Weather Vanes, June, 1976; The Fascinating Fire-Mark, December, 1923.

Part VII: French Antique Steel Furniture, August, 1960; French Tole, October, 1960; The Japanned Wares of Pontypool and Usk, July, 1937; Decorated Tinware, August, 1953; The Tinsmiths of Stevens Plains, Part I, July, 1939; The Tinsmiths of Stevens Plains, Part II, September, 1939; Decorated Tinware East and West, In Pennsylvania, September, 1954; Decorated Tinware East and West, In New Mexico, September, 1954; Pennsylvania Cooky Cutters, December, 1938; Cast-Iron Cooking Vessels, August, 1971; The American Copper Teakettle, April, 1966; Latten Spoons of the Pilgrims, March, 1952; Brass Tobacco Boxes, September, 1946.

Part VIII: The Village Blacksmith, June, 1955; Notes on Early American Brass and Copper, December, 1958; The Village Tinsmith, March, 1928; Coppersmithing in Early America, December, 1949; The Old Hardware of James Towne, January, 1941; Early Ohio Ironwork, July, 1936.

First Edition

Introductory material copyright © by James R. Mitchell.

Original articles copyright © 1922, 1923, 1927, 1928, 1930, 1931, 1933, 1934, 1936, 1937, 1939, 1941, 1943, 1944, 1946, 1948, 1949, 1951, 1952, 1953, 1954, 1955, 1957, 1958, 1959, 1960, 1963, 1965, 1966, 1967, 1970, 1971, 1972, 1973, 1975, 1976 by Straight Enterprises, Inc.

Library of Congress Catalog Card Number 77-70771

ISBN 0-87663-970-8, paper
ISBN 0-87663-298-3, cloth

Published by Universe Books
381 Park Avenue South
New York City 10016

Produced by The Main Street Press
42 Main Street
Clinton, New Jersey 08809

Contents

Introduction

To anyone who has studied the decorative arts, *The Magazine* ANTIQUES has long been a source of useful information. Unfortunately, as time passes the early issues become increasingly scarce and expensive. This volume brings together the most significant material on common, or non-precious, metals from the magazine in anthology form. At first it seemed sensible to organize the articles into sections on iron, copper, brass, steel, and tin plate. Upon further examination, however, it was found that such a division would not be as useful to the reader as one grouping the material according to the manner in which the metals were used. A number of the articles, for instance, discuss several of the metals or alloys as they are used in particular decorative forms.

Among the precious and non-precious elemental metals commonly used in the past are gold, silver, iron, copper, tin, lead, and mercury. The ancient rare, precious metals, gold and silver, are not common, hence, they are not considered in this anthology. Tin is the principal element in the alloy, pewter, which is the subject of a separate volume, *American and British Pewter,* in the ANTIQUES *Magazine Library* series. Mercury is the only metal which is liquid at ordinary temperatures and its chief use during the eighteenth and nineteenth centuries as a decorative element was in thermometers and barometers. Interestingly enough, there are no articles about these two forms in this book, even though their main working part is metal, because they are considered to belong to the furniture category. Lead, used in the past for window weights, bullets, and for the casting of occasional statues, also is not discussed. What remains, then, is a focus on the principal elemental metals, tin, copper, and iron. Copper and iron were used as single metals, with everpresent impurities, and were also alloyed with others. Three principal alloys—brass, bronze, and steel—are discussed here extensively.

Iron is not found as a free element in nature, but its ores were the most common metal mineral to be mined. Charcoal or coke, with limestone being used as a catalyst, are used in the process of smelting the ore in a blast furnace. Traditionally, the furnace was first charged with charcoal and after this had burned down, it was again charged with successive layers of ore, charcoal, and limestone. The charcoal or coke was once more set ablaze. As the coal burned, air was pumped through the furnace from the bottom as a blast. In the smelting of iron, it should be remembered that the ore does not melt in the heat but that a chemical reaction takes place. The ore is reduced with carbon to form free metal. The other unburnable parts of the ore and limestone remain as slag. Molten iron is heavier than molten slag so that the metal collects at the bottom of the furnace and the slag floats on top of it.

At the discretion of the furnacemen, the blast furnace was tapped at the bottom, permitting the molten iron to flow into sand molds in the casting floor at the base of the furnace. Kettles, pots, stove plates, and ingots of iron known as pigs (because the ingots were cast in the sand at right angles to the casting sprue and looked like baby pigs suckling a mother sow) were made in this way. After the castings cooled, the objects were removed from the sand molds, the sand cleaned off, the casting sprues broken off, and the object filed or finished for sale. Pig iron was the basic stock used for further operations such as making steel and wrought iron. Varying proportions of carbon were present in crude pig iron which affected the physical properties of the metal, such as its malleability. Further working of the metal made it much more useful.

Metallurgically, steel is a mixture of iron carbide and iron with a low carbon content. Prior to the late nineteenth century and the invention of the Bessemer process, steel was made either from wrought iron which was reheated in the presence of a carboniferous compound that formed blister steel or from pig iron which was broken into little pieces and placed in a crucible to melt. Extra carbon as well as other impurities were driven off by the heat as the pieces melted. The molten steel was poured from the crucible into an ingot mold, and the ingots were rolled or hammered to make various objects which were marked "cast steel." It should be remembered that such marking does not mean that the object was made by casting steel into a mold, but that the cast steel *method* was used to make the raw material. There is a very good possibility that many antique objects which are thought to be made of steel are actually made of finely finished wrought iron. Often people equate a finely finished smooth gray surface with the term steel, and a rough black surface with the term iron.

Copper occurs freely in nature as a metal and was so known by the Indians of North America who made projectile points from it. The best source of the metal was once found in the Keweenaw Peninsula of Upper Michigan, but Indians traded in the commodity throughout the continent. The metal has many uses as an element in making alloys with other metals in which copper is the smaller part. For example, it is used to harden silver which is too soft to use or work in a pure state. It serves the same function with tin to make the alloy pewter. Traditionally, when copper is the major element and tin is the minor one, the resulting alloy is called bronze. Similarly, when the minor ingredient is zinc with copper the major element, the alloy is called brass. Sheet copper was used to make teakettles and other vessels in colonial America. The material was either imported as rolled sheets or they were hammered out by hand from copper smelted in the Colonies. Copper, like iron, is reduced with carbon although a catalyst such as limestone is not needed to assist the chemical reaction.

Although copper was used in sheet form, brass and bronze do not lend themselves readily to rolling or hammering. The two alloys are melted in a crucible and then cast in sand molds like cast iron. An object such as an andiron column is cast in two parts and these are later soldered together with a yellow solder called spelter. The brass or bronze object is then filed, sanded, and polished before it is offered for sale. Spelter is also used to solder the parts of a copper vessel together.

Another type of metal discussed in this anthology is tin plate. To be strictly accurate, one should really call the material tin-plated sheet iron. The final two words of the term, however, are understood and are usually not mentioned. Tin plate is made by rolling iron into thin sheets which are plated by dipping them into molten tin. The plating is very thin and gives the iron a shiny surface as well as protecting it from corrosion. Metals other than iron react with oxygen in the air in the presence of moisture to form a thin layer of corrosion on the surface which protects the interior from further action. Iron, however, reacts with oxygen in the presence of moisture to form rust, and this process does not stop when the surface is rusted. It continues until the corrosive action has completely destroyed the metal. Certain types of iron smelted with charcoal rather than with coke, which has a sulfur content, are not as liable to rusting. The best way found to prevent any rust is to coat iron with a protective layer of some other material such as tin.

Tin plate offered many possibilities to early craftsmen because it could be easily bent, pressed, cut, and soldered to form different useful items, especially for the home. The newly-made object was as shiny as new pewter or silver plate. Some tinware is left unadorned, but the overwhelming majority of it has been decorated in some manner. Beginning in the mid-eighteenth century the vogue for Japanned tin plate in the style of oriental lacquerwork became established. This was a decorative technique which involved the use of black coatings such as asphaltum which were painted and gilded in lacquer colors. Work so executed was relatively inexpensive (especially when compared with Oriental lacquerwork objects) and large quantities of such tinware were made and sold in Europe, England, and North America.

The primary common metals and the ways in which they were processed could be discussed endlessly. As with other areas of the decorative arts, an understanding of basic methodology and technical change is absolutely essential. Collectors in every field should be encouraged to pursue these fundamental concerns with the thoroughness of the scientific investigator.

The articles in *Antique Metalware* form a primer or handbook on a wide variety of subjects, and are written in a non-technical vein. Underlying all of the findings, however, is a basic understanding of metal technology. The value of the ANTIQUES material lies in its diversity. There have been individual books on many of these categories of metalwork, but nowhere has there been such a variety of authoritative articles assembled between two covers.

Attitudes towards scholarship in the field of antiques have changed over the years. From a simple description of collections and objects in catalogue fashion, we have moved to a treatment of a subject which is as thorough as possible concerning the making of the objects and their makers. Since 1922, when ANTIQUES was first published, specialists have studied and written about the objects of their love and devotion with considerable skill and understanding. Their efforts are of considerable benefit to us today.

I Architectural Iron

There are nine articles in this section which have been arranged so that the reader moves from New England, to Philadelphia, through the South, and into the Midwest. The final article is Joseph T. Butler's "American Victorian Furniture," a subject with more than a regional focus. While part of his article is concerned with iron furniture, over half of it is devoted to wood and cane.

Through a reading of these articles one is reminded that architectural iron was used in all parts of the United States, not just in Charleston or New Orleans, as is popularly believed. Even in those areas which had no iron production, the raw material was either acquired and fabricated in a foundry or the finished product was shipped in from specialty houses in one of the early industrial centers. One factor which made such heavy, long distance shipping possible was an expanding rail transportation system, a network of iron lines.

In almost all the articles, the authors point out that the principal architectural iron used in America was cast iron made in foundries. Despite this fact, such ornamental ironwork is still commonly called wrought iron. A skilled craftsman such as a blacksmith can forge wrought iron objects but the intricate, naturalistic cast ornament of the mid- to late-nineteenth century, popularly styled Victorian, was beyond the resources of the average smith whose principal tools were a battery of hammers and an anvil and whose raw materials were rod and bar stock.

Cast-iron architecture on Beacon Hill in Boston

BY ROBERT MACKAY

AMONG THE earliest advocates of cast iron in architecture were Isaac Ware, John Nash, Sir Robert Smirke, and Robert and James Adam. As early as 1756 Ware observed that "cast iron is very serviceable to the builder and a vast expense is saved in many cases by using it; in rails and balusters it makes a rich and massy appearance."[1] However, the major credit for popularizing cast iron must go to Robert Adam, who found it particularly applicable to his delicate motifs, especially when mixed with other materials. His influence on the design of railings is evident in Lewis Nockalls Cottingham, *Smith and Founder's Director* of about 1823, the first pattern book for ornamental ironwork to affect the design of the surviving cast-iron architecture on Beacon Hill and its immediate environs (see Fig. 7).

The combination of cast and wrought iron apparent in English ornamental ironwork in the late eighteenth century cannot be found on Beacon Hill until about 1805, when cast-iron ornaments began to appear on wrought-iron fences. The urn finial on the wrought-iron fence of the second Harrison Gray Otis House (Fig. 1) is typical of the simplicity of the early cast-iron decorative devices.[2]

Ironically, the first complete cast-iron railings and balconies often imitated wrought-iron patterns as, for example, in the side balcony at 45 Beacon Street and in the first-floor window guards of the second Harrison Gray Otis House (see Fig. 1).[3] With time, however, cast ornamentation came into its own as architects and founders realized that the material was economical and permitted a degree of articulation that could not be achieved with other substances. Asher Benjamin, in *The Architect or Complete Builder's Guide* of 1839, included plates of cast railing patterns noting "that cast iron is produced in most parts of this country, and at a cost so low as to place it within the reach of all, the great amount of its yearly consumption and the facility with which it may be wrought into the most beautiful shapes, render it an object worthy of attention here."[4]

While Nathaniel Bradlee, George Dexter, Edward Shaw, Richard Upjohn, Solomon Willard, and other architects active on Beacon Hill are known to have designed their own fence patterns,[5] builder's and founder's guides seem to have been the primary source of motifs for cast-iron railings, particularly during the second quarter of the century. Cottingham's *Smith and Founder's Director*, Thomas

Fig. 1. 85 Mount Vernon Street, Boston. The cast-iron urn finial topping the wrought-iron fence is typical of the simplicity of early cast decoration. The window guards in the background are cast imitations of a wrought-iron pattern. *Photographs are by Richard Cheek.*

Fig. 2. 41 West Cedar Street, Boston. The Greek revival pattern of the cast-iron railing is taken from Plate 60 of Asher Benjamin's *Practice of Architecture* (see Fig. 5).

Fig. 3. 2 Joy Street, Boston. The design of the cast-iron railing is taken from Plate 60 of Benjamin's *Practice of Architecture* (see Fig. 5).

U. Walter and J. Jay Smith's *A Guide to Workers in Metal and Stone* (1846), and above all Benjamin's *Practice of Architecture* (1833) and *The Architect or Complete Builder's Guide* have left their imprint on Beacon Hill's streets. A recent survey I conducted of cast-iron railings, balconies, and architectural decoration there revealed that seven of the thirty designs that could be found at more than one location[6] were from Benjamin's guides (see Figs. 2-6).

The finest example of a Cottingham design is the handsome fleur-de-lis fence between 69 and 83 Mount Vernon Street (Fig. 7) that is drawn from two of the plates in his *Director*. Cottingham's greatest contribution to the ironwork on Beacon Hill, however, was undoubtedly his influence on Benjamin and Walter, for a number of the Americans' motifs show a resemblance to Cottingham's.

Curiously, what may be Boston's finest cast-iron railing pattern is the work of an unknown designer. The double-anthemion motif (Fig. 8) was probably first applied to iron by Robert Adam and was in turn reinterpreted by a host of neoclassicists. The problem of attributing it brings into focus the iron founders themselves, many of whom must have designed their own fence patterns. Regrettably, the whole story will never be known, for the founders did not mark their products and even the foundry pattern catalogues, which must have existed in great numbers, have all but disappeared,[7] leaving us with only occasional advertisements illustrated with woodcuts to link designs and manufacturers.

13

Fig. 4. 69 Bowdoin Street and vicinity. The design for this scintillating series of stoop railings was taken from Plate 54 of Benjamin's *The Architect or Complete Builder's Guide* (see Fig. 6).

The Boston city directory does not differentiate between "Founders" and "Iron Fence Builders" until 1848 (the *Boston Almanac* makes the distinction a year later), but it is possible to trace certain fence founders back through the decades since they were earlier listed as blacksmiths and whitesmiths. Ebenezer Weeman and Daniel Safford may have been the first founders in Boston to specialize in fences. Weeman started out in 1818 on Green Street in the West End and is recorded at several other locations before settling at 16 Merrimac Street in 1830, where he

remained for thirty-seven years. Although associated with George Jones in the 1820's, he spent the greater part of his long career without a partner. On the other side of the city, Safford never seems to have left Devonshire Street, where he was also first listed in 1818. Known as the Daniel Safford Company from 1836 to 1850, his foundry later became Smith and Lovett's Universal Iron Works, which was still functioning at the turn of the century. Also recorded in the directories are the founders George W. Adams (w. 1838-1849), Joseph R. Bryant (w. 1841-1853),

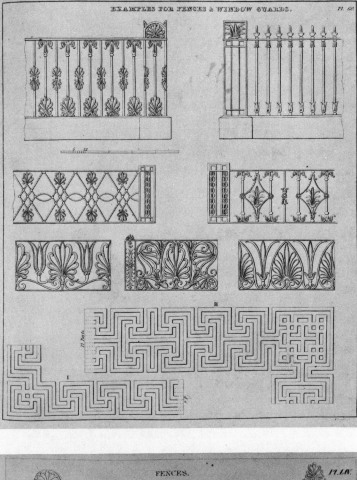

Fig. 5. Plate 60 from Asher Benjamin's *Practice of Architecture* (New York, 1833).

and Sidney Patch (w. 1840-1868), who must also have contributed to Beacon Hill's ornamentation. It is conceivable that Daniel D. Badger, who in later years was to change the face of downtown New York with his prefabricated cast-iron façades, also manufactured railing in Boston during the 1830's. Listed in partnership with W. P. Hart on Cross Street near Commercial from 1830 to 1832, Badger moved to the corner of Fulton Street the following year, where he was listed in partnership with Isaiah Wadleigh. In the 1839 directory Badger and Wadleigh were at 2 Union Street in the employ of A. Richardson and Company, saw makers. In the 1840's Badger was alone at 7 Haverhill,[8] but in 1848 "The Daniel D. Badger & Co." moved to 42 Duane Street in New York, across from the iron manufactory of his well-known competitor James Bogardus.

As mid-century approached and acanthus and anthemions began to go out of fashion, most of Beacon Hill's cast iron was already in place. Thus the overly ornamented, two dimensional, design-board creations of the mid-Victorians are not as numerous there as they are in other parts of Boston. It seems as if the material at mid-century was always asked to masquerade as something other than itself; on Beacon Hill in this period, every newel post seems to sprout from an iron bud and the simple footscraper of the Federal period is transformed into a bone held aloft by two standing dogs. In England an agitated Pugin observed:

It is impossible to enumerate half of the absurdities of modern metalworkers; but all these proceed from the false notion of disguising instead of beautifying articles of utility. How many objects of ordinary use are rendered monstrous and ridiculous simply because the artist, instead of seeking the most convenient form, and then decorating it, has embodied some extravagance to conceal the real purpose for which the article has been made![9]

This excessiveness and deception must have been as instrumental in giving cast iron a bad name in Boston as it was elsewhere, for in the 1860's and 1870's wrought iron began to reassert itself in the city. With some noteworthy exceptions, the age of cast iron in Boston was over by the late 1870's.

For those who may be inspired to do further research on cast-iron ornamentation, I offer a few suggestions. First, be extremely cautious when dating railings and objects,

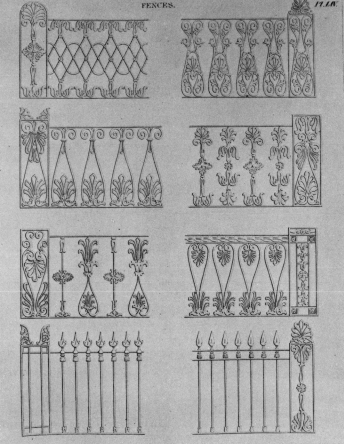

Fig. 6. Plate 54 from Asher Benjamin's *The Architect or Complete Builder's Guide* (Boston, 1839).

Fig. 7. 69-83 Mount Vernon Street, Boston. The pattern of the cast-iron fence is drawn from Plates 30 and 33 in the second edition of Lewis Nockalls Cottingham's *Smith and Founder's Director* (London, 1824).

for while it is evident that certain houses (both individual and row) received their iron accessories at the time of construction, most of the ironwork was added later. For instance, the fences shown in Figure 7 were probably made about 1831 when the houses were built, whereas a similar fence running from 8 to 20 Louisburg Square must have been a joint project of the residents at a later date, since those buildings went up over a five-or six-year span. A second problem is the astounding longevity of certain patterns. The railing at 11 Chestnut Street, for example, was still being cast at the outset of World War II. Finally,

even the smallest, ornamental devices have a story to tell. Footscrapers are a study in themselves, not to mention balconettes, or window-box protectors. A recent survey of balconettes in London conducted by Felicity Ashbee revealed 160 varieties. Four varieties can be found on Beacon Hill, the most picturesque of which is located at 126 Myrtle Street.

Cast iron bound row houses and blocks together in a way that had not been possible before its introduction. At its best (Fig. 9) it can still offer some of the most impressive examples of outdoor art to be found in Boston.

[1] John Gloag and Derek Bridgwater, *A History of Cast Iron in Architecture* (London, 1948), p. 116.

[2] Perhaps the finest example on Beacon Hill of composite cast- and wrought-iron work is the latticework arrangement surrounding the oriel window at 57 Beacon Street. It forms a semitransparent veil that mirrors the arched shapes of the façade below.

[3] Harold Kirker, in *The Architecture of Charles Bulfinch* (Cambridge, Massachusetts, 1969), p. 159, attributes the design of the window guards to Bulfinch himself and states that "he apparently used it only once again, in the third Otis house. . . ."

[4] Asher Benjamin, *The Architect or Complete Builder's Guide* (Boston, 1839), p. 47.

[5] The only surviving architect's rendering of a Beacon Hill fence that I know of is George Dexter's 1837 sketch of a pale that was to extend between 63 and 67 Mount Vernon Street. Only the gateposts at those addresses resemble the Dexter rendering, which is now at the Boston Athenaeum.

[6] Row houses built concurrently with similar cast-iron fixtures were considered as a single location.

[7] A Boston catalogue issued by Chase Brothers, c. 1856, includes illustrations of fancy gates, railings, and hitching posts. When last recorded it was in the possession of Marjorie Smith of Taneytown, Maryland.

[8] A catalogue entitled *Illustrations of Iron Architecture* published by Badger's firm in 1865 states that the founder was in Boston in 1842 and 1843.

[9] Gloag and Bridgwater, *A History of Cast Iron*, pp. 206, 208.

Fig. 8. 4 Louisburg Square. The source for the graceful double-anthemion design of the cast-iron railing has not been discovered. The spiraling flagstaff holder is actually the tongue of an open-mouthed serpent.

Fig. 9. 61 Mount Vernon Street, Boston. This massive cast-iron gate must be considered one of the outstanding examples of outdoor art in the city.

CAST-IRON FOUNTAINS
IN VERMONT

By RUTH ROBINSON

Miss Robinson, a pupil of the late Philip L. Hale of Boston, works by choice for the most part with pen and ink and wash. She provided the pen-and-ink illustrations for Albert Jay Nock's Journey Into Rabelais' France.

IN VERMONT SEVERAL SUMMERS ago I became interested in the number and variety of cast-iron fountains that are still in use there. These vestiges of nineteenth-century landscape decoration showed marked differences in design and proportion, in the water jets and the paint used to protect the iron.

In quest of these fountains I traveled pretty well over the state. I found twenty-six, only two of which were the same in design. Of these one was four feet high, the other much larger and differently painted. That sufficient interest is still taken in most of these fountains to keep the iron protected is most satisfying; the paint used, however, is sometimes unbelievably ruinous to their charm. Sometimes, but not always, the fountain was used in a cast-iron pool which added greatly to the decorative effect. Frequently when a cement pool was used it appeared to be a replacement; there were evidently more iron basins originally than now are about. There are also fountains where no basin is needed, such as one, for instance, placed in a small pond filled with pink water lilies.

Only a few of these fountains were marked. Those few had on them the plate of the Mott Iron Works of Mott Haven, New York. In going over the history of the Mott company, I learned that it was the custom for architects or individuals to assemble a fountain as they wished, choosing the base, basins, and ornaments from the catalogue. Only when a fountain was ordered as a whole did the company mark it. It is evident that the Vermont fountains were mostly chosen by individuals, which explains their variety. All twenty-six that I found were represented as a whole or in parts in the old catalogues of the Mott Iron Works. In the catalogues of Fisk, however, and of Janes and Kirtland, the two big contemporary concerns making ironwork, many of the same designs also appear.

The *swan* was the first fountain the Mott Company put out, in 1860. A few years before this A. J. Downing in his book *The Theory and Practice of Landscape Gardening*, while arguing the beauty of the water jets of Europe and the possibilities of building fountains in this country, gave as an example of a "simple but lovely fountain" a cut of the *swan*, as later made by Mott.

In 1858 Janes and Kirtland produced a copy of the cast-iron fountain in the Place de la Concorde in Paris for the city of Savannah, Georgia, so it would seem that they were ahead of Mott in building fountains.

In the world of fountains the cast-iron variety is not the most beautiful. At the height of their popularity in the 1870's, however, they fitted into their ornate period with a good deal of character.

Although I have sketches of the *boy with the boot*, the *girl with the fish*, the *girl and boy under the umbrella*, a *stork* from a doctor's front dooryard, and others that would be remembered, I have chosen from my collection the nine here illustrated as the best to exemplify what interested me in the cast-iron fountains of Vermont.

Little information is available about the artists who worked with the conventional patterns of the cast-iron industry and from them evolved the fountains that are found today in the quiet cemeteries and towns of Vermont. One wonders who the persons may have been who designed the calla lilies, who made the water jets play like grasses about the walking ewer carrier, or planned the water to drip like tears upon the kneeling figure of a woman.

SWAN FOUNTAIN at Hyde Manor, Sudbury.

FOUNTAIN in West Rutland Cemetery.

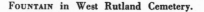

FOUNTAIN in the cemetery at Waterbury.

WELL-PROPORTIONED FOUNTAIN at New-
fane, painted white.   *Left*

FOUNTAIN in private grounds at Cuttingsville, with an unusually handsome cast-iron pool basin.   *Right*

GAILY PAINTED fountain, with red and
green trim, at the side entrance to
Bennington Cemetery.   *Below, left*

FOUR-FOOT FOUNTAIN
in a small park in
Brandon, painted dark
green.

SLOW-DRIPPING WATER contributes to the
effect of this fountain in Cuttingsville
Cemetery, painted bronze.

*Illustrations from wash drawings
by the author.*

THIS FOUNTAIN in a remote cemetery
near Bristol is an example of poor
choice in assembling the parts. The
calla lilies deserve better support than
the heavy base, and the basins are too
widely spaced.

19

Philadelphia's ornamental

Woodcut of a railing which can still be seen in many places, from *Godey's Lady's Book (1853)*.

Railing design, from catalogue of Variety Iron Works, York, Pennsylvania *(c. 1850-1860)*.

ARCHITECTURAL ACCESSORIES of ornamental cast iron came as a boon to the builder of the mid-nineteenth-century. Victorian home owners, in revolt against the classic severity of the Federal period, were eager for elaboration of their premises, and the recent introduction of ornamental cast iron provided an inexpensive means of achieving an elaborate effect. The city residence could now be fitted with an elegant floriated balcony, or with one of Gothic tracery. If the location permitted, the house might have a verandah—or several of them, superimposed in gallery fashion, as was common practice in New Orleans. A more restrained use of the material consisted of an intricately detailed railing surrounding a tiny grass plot in front of the house, with a huge ornamental cast-iron urn in the center. Fancy cellar window guards, footscraper, and handrail were standard trimming. Cast-iron fountains played gently in the gardens of the more impressive mansions, and ornate cast-iron chairs were dotted about under the shade trees on the lawn.

In *Fashion and Famine*, a novel written in the 1840's by the then very popular author, Mrs. Ann Sophia Stephens, there is a description of a cottage of that day in New York City. In prose quite as arabesque as the ironwork she is describing, Mrs. Stephens sets forth the Victorian ideal of a residence: ". . . one of those miniature palaces—too small for the very wealthy, and too beautiful in its appointments for any idea but that of perfect taste, which wealth does not often give. The front, of a pale stone color, was so ornamented and netted over with the lace work of iron balconies and window gratings, that it had all the elegance of a city mansion, with much of the rustic beauty one sees in a rural dwelling. A little court, full of flowers, lay in front, with a miniature fountain throwing up a slender column of water from the centre of a tiny grass plot, that, in the pure dampness always raining over it, lay like a mass of crushed emeralds hidden among the flowers. The netted ironwork that hung around the doors, the windows, and fringed the eaves, as it were, with a valance of massive lace, was luxuriously interwoven with creeping plants."

In the United States as well as in England, ornamental cast iron began to be used in quantity beginning in the 1840's, not only as architectural ornament but also in cemeteries. The Victorian cemetery burgeoned with ex-

amples of the current taste for it. All the symbols of loss and mourning were immortalized in iron on the plot enclosures: the broken rosebud, the reversed torch, the weeping willow, the lyre, the heart, the mourning angels.

A great deal of the ornamental cast iron in the United States, and also in Canada, came from Philadelphia—and in particular from the firm of Robert Wood, later to become Wood and Perot. Robert Wood, founder of The Philadelphia Ornamental Iron Works, was born in 1813 and apprenticed when quite young to a blacksmith. In 1839 he set up in business, with but one helper, producing wrought-iron window guards, awning posts, and railings. For the next ten years he listed himself as "Robert Wood, blacksmith, Ridge Road below Spring Garden Street." His business expanded steadily and, after the appearance of his first catalogue showing ornamental cast-iron products, he set himself down as "Robert Wood, Iron Rail Foundery and Manufacturing." So rapidly had his reputa-

cast iron

BY FRANCES LICHTEN

tion grown for fine design and workmanship that, by mid-century, his small shop had expanded into a plant employing three hundred hands. In 1857 he was joined by Elliston Perot, an accomplished designer of cast iron. The firm of Wood and Perot existed until the death of Elliston Perot in 1865, when it became Robert Wood and Company; it seems to have gone out of business around 1881.

That this firm was a notably progressive one is evidenced by the fact that, around 1849, or a little earlier, a free catalogue was issued, advertised as "Wood's Portfolio of Original Designs of Iron Railings, Verandahs, Settees, Chairs, Tables, and other Ornamental and Architectural Iron Work." Today, when free catalogues are an everyday matter, such an event would occasion no comment whatsoever, but at the time the catalogue appeared, the very idea was such a novelty that it created quite a stir. The appearance of this handsome folio, says a writer in 1858, "issued gratuitously by this house, containing engravings and designs to be executed in cast iron, such as never before had been equalled, and the impulse that was then given to decorative art has been felt in all parts of our country. Most of the cemeteries

and squares throughout the whole country are adorned with work executed in Philadelphia; and every city, probably every town in the Union contains some specimen of our manufacturers' skill and taste."

From time to time Wood and Perot re-issued their magnificent catalogue. An edition brought out in 1862 refers to it as "A Portfolio of Original Designs of Ornamental Iron Work of Every Description." In 1864, Wood and Perot are still claiming "that their variety of patterns exceeds that of any similar establishment in the country."

To this they add—and a touching reminder it is of the Civil War—that "among the new designs added to their list will be found many suitable for military purposes."

These catalogues of Wood and Perot's are now rarities, most of them having probably disintegrated. I have seen two copies of these handsome folios of lithographed drawings. They furnish incontrovertible evidence that a great many of the cast-iron balconies, galleries, and railings which add so much to the visual charm of New Orleans and other southern cities were made in Philadelphia. By 1858, in fact, the firm of Wood and Perot had established a branch in New Orleans called Wood, Miltenberger & Company, where they maintained a large showroom as

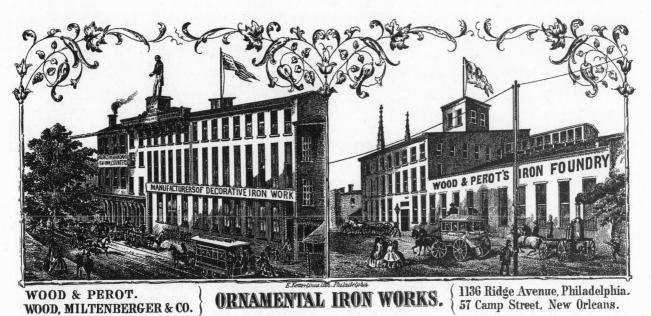

Lithograph showing Wood and Perot's Iron Foundry, from *Philadelphia and Its Manufactures* by Edwin T. Freedley (1858).

21

Detail of morning glory, one of the naturalistic motifs sponsored by Wood and Perot. *Photograph by Hans Burkhard.*

well as shops for finishing work manufactured in Philadelphia.

The most casual stroll today through the Victorian sections of Philadelphia will reveal many of the identical railings and balconies which have been featured so romantically in stories and pictures of New Orleans and the old South. Here, however, the galleries and balconies which have managed to survive the decades and the house-wrecker must be looked for at the rear of city houses, where they served for porches upstairs as well as on the first floor. In the older suburban sections of Philadelphia they were used, as elsewhere, as verandahs.

There were many who were extremely critical of the use of ornamental cast iron as an adjunct to architecture. The Victorian supporters of functionalism considered that ornamental cast iron served no purpose but to "make a big show." Followers of Ruskin decried it because it was mechanically produced. But cast iron also had its defenders. One such, an American architect, stated his position in 1859: "I would use iron as a decorative language, and as such, take pleasure in its practical uselessness."

The average Victorian, untroubled with aesthetic scruples, frankly doted on ornamental cast iron in all its variations and manifestations. It was an uncritical love. Sarah Josepha Hale, the editor of *Godey's Lady's Book,* decided that her readers should learn something about it. In 1853, she led off the July issue with an article entitled *A Day at the Ornamental Iron Works of Robert Wood,* as one of a series called *Everyday Actualities.* In presenting such a series in a woman's magazine, Mrs. Hale was doing something new. She was introducing to her gentle public, which was nationwide, the wonders of the industrial age. Through this particular article, her readers could learn the steps in manufacturing which went into the making of their grape-patterned verandahs, or about

View of salesroom of John B. Wickersham, New York manufacturer of ornamental cast iron, in 1854.

IRON WAREHOUSE OF JOHN B. WICKERSHAM, NO. 312 BROADWAY, NEW YORK.

the processes by which the cast-iron Newfoundland dog on their lawn came into being. The article took up all the technicalities of pattern-making, molding, and casting.

A great deal of the design of cast iron was Renaissance in character, but the designers did not ignore the new taste for the Gothic, or the growing trend toward the rustic and the naturalistic. The much-publicized "corn-fence" in New Orleans is an example of the extremes to which the naturalistic was carried: interlaced corn stalks, foliage, and leaves form the design of the railing, while the posts have pumpkins for bases and bundles of corn stalks for shafts, with a cluster of ears of corn as finials.

The pirating of competitors' designs was general practice, and it is amusing to note that despite its claims of "original designs" the firm of Robert Wood was not always above it. This practice was commented on by two commissioners sent over from England in 1853 to report on the American ornamental iron products shown at the New York Crystal Palace. They noted that while castings "are made in large quantities in New York, Boston, Philadelphia, and other large cities, these are usually copies or adaptations of similar work made in this country [England]."

Robert Wood was unusually progressive for his time in having his own pattern-making department. In his day pattern-making was usually a free-lance profession. Some of the patterns took weeks to carve in wood, and since they were costly affairs they were planned so that they could be put to many uses. A pattern designed as a railing, for instance, might serve equally well as a window guard, or various units might be combined (none too harmoniously sometimes) to form large gates, verandahs, or summer houses. Robert Wood's patterns were valued at several hundred thousand dollars, and were housed in a fireproof building. He had a lithographed drawing

Gate for cemetery plot, produced at Wood and Perot's Foundry. Symbols include the weeping Cupid, the reversed torch, the discarded laurel wreath, and the poppy of sleep. *Index of American Design, National Gallery of Art.*

made of every article he manufactured, and these prints formed the basis of his handsome catalogues.

It is difficult to assign pieces to specific manufacturers, since free-lance pattern makers often sold the same design to various firms. Furthermore, designers had no scruples whatever about copying each others' patterns. Here in Philadelphia I have seen two different copies of a design which appeared originally in Wood and Perot's catalogues. The original is distinguished for its delicacy and grace of modeling. In the copies the modeling is vulgarized, both in feeling and in execution.

Another difficulty in assigning a piece to a particular manufacturer results from a practice common to the trade. Whenever a firm went out of business, its patterns were always bought up by other manufacturers. Therefore, even though an article may be stamped with a firm's name (though few of the early pieces were), this is no guarantee that the design was first created by or for that firm. Wood and Perot designs are duplicated, for instance, in many of those issued by the Variety Iron Works of York, Pennsylvania. This firm was founded in 1840, and in 1860 became E. G. Smyser's Sons, which in its turn became Smyser-Royer Company. We can only conclude that at some time in its existence the firm in York, Pennsylvania, must have acquired quite a few of the patterns of the Philadelphia firm.

There were many firms manufacturing ornamental cast iron in Philadelphia; seventeen were listed in 1858—a number which fell off to eleven in 1864. But there was none with such a reputation for "tasteful elegance" as that of Robert Wood.

Second-story rear verandah in Philadelphia, showing one of Wood and Perot's designs. *Photograph by Hans Burkhard.*

Charleston ornamental ironwork

BY ALSTON DEAS

CHARLESTON ORNAMENTAL IRONWORK is justly celebrated, and still exists in profusion in the older portion of the city, despite the toll exacted by earthquake, hurricane, fire, and, during the Civil War, prolonged bombardment. A few excellent pre-Revolutionary examples remain, a large number dating from the late eighteenth and early nineteenth centuries, and a greater number still from the prosperous period of the 1820's to the 1860's. A good many gates of less importance but creditable design, executed in later years, are also still to be seen; these date, in general, from the 1870's to the 1930's.

It appears unlikely that any wrought iron of artistic quality was executed prior to the fire of 1740, which wiped out most of the original city. When new houses of a more ambitious character began to replace those that had been destroyed, there began to be a demand for decorative ironwork, and this was to increase until the years immediately preceding the Revolution. With the stabilization of business following the conclusion of that struggle, many fine new buildings were erected and adorned with good ironwork in the new taste.

An advertisement of one James Lingard, "Smith and Farrier," which appeared in the *South Carolina Gazette* for May 21 and 28, 1753, informs the public that he makes "all kinds of scroll work for grates and stair cases." The fine section of railing shown in Figure 1 may well date from this

Fig. 1. Wrought-iron railing, probably 1750's.
Perhaps the earliest example of such work extant.
*Charleston Museum;
photographs by Louis Schwartz.*

Fig. 2. Portal gates of St. Philip's Church, c. 1772-1775. Design copied from part of the communion rail in St. Michael's Church, purchased in London in 1772.

period. For many years it occupied a space between two buildings of relatively modern origin on King Street, but it had obviously been salvaged from a structure of far earlier date. It is perhaps the oldest example of finished design and workmanship in Charleston.

There was never an attempt in Charleston to emulate the elaborate work of the great smiths of England, France, and Germany. Such an effort would have overtaxed the facilities and the ingenuity of local artisans, but the basic designs of the European smiths were adapted with thoroughly satisfactory results. At least one pattern book survives in the collection of the Charleston Library Society, published by W. and J. Weldon in "Holborn, near Chancery Lane," London, in 1765, and there may well have been others. Also available as a model was the handsome little communion rail purchased in London in 1772 which still graces St. Michael's Church. Almost certainly the design of the portal gates of St. Philip's Church (Fig. 2) derives from a panel of this rail, as does the central element of a balcony originally at 87 East Bay and now on the house at 84 South Battery.

Except for the gate of the Miles Brewton House, shown in ANTIQUES for April 1970 (p. 560), that of St. Philip's western churchyard (Fig. 3), across the street from the church, is the only important one now remaining which is believed to be of the pre-Revolutionary period. It is of unusual design, with sturdy, severely plain upper and lower structural members and a delicately beautiful central panel of scrolls, husks, and twisted leaves. It probably dates from about 1770, the date of the wall it adjoins.

Contemporary records chronicle the activities of two prominent Charleston smiths of the period, Tunis Tebout and William Johnson, but we learn more about them as participants in the Revolutionary struggle than as ironworkers. Either one of them may well have made this gate, or, for that matter, the fine step and landing rail of the John Edwards House (Fig. 4), or the lantern standards of the South Carolina Society hall (Fig. 5).

These lantern standards were not made as an adjunct of the present building, which dates from 1804. It is clear that the stair railings have been cut off at the lower end, and these standards substituted for the original terminals. They are, indeed, a good deal earlier than the building, and were probably salvaged from a demolished edifice of some importance.

After the Revolution, balconies similar to those then in vogue in England appeared in Charleston in considerable numbers (Fig. 6). The scrolled vertical uprights supporting the upper rail were frequently decorated with cast lead rosettes. Ornamental panels at the center, occasionally balanced by panels on either side, relieved the monotony of an uninterrupted row of uprights, particularly in the larger balconies.

At the same time many worth-while gates and fences of a dignified, restrained style were erected. These bore little resemblance to the multiscrolled, imposing gates of the nineteenth century. Attractive lunettes, used in arched passageways and over entrances to carriage houses and other outbuildings, enjoyed considerable favor (Fig. 7).

The ironwork particularly identified with Charleston in the minds of most visitors is that created in abundance between about 1820 and 1860. Several of the Charleston ironworkers of this period were German, one at least was a Scot, and one is presumed from his name to have been Italian. The best known, and perhaps the most prolific, was Christopher Werner, the son of a carriage maker of Muenster in Westphalia. Born on April 13, 1805, Werner probably first

Fig. 3.   Gateway of the western churchyard of
St. Philip's. Probably c. 1770, the date
of the building of the wall.

Fig. 4. Step and landing rail of the John Edwards House, 1772.

Fig. 5. Lantern standards of the South Carolina Society hall; 1760's, probably salvaged from a pre-Revolutionary structure.

Fig. 6. Balcony at 83 East Bay, typical of the period 1800-1810. Ornamental central panel, and cast lead rosettes on uprights.

Fig. 7.   Lunette used over entrance to a carriage house
in Elliott Street, now demolished; probably c. 1790.
Charleston Museum.

Fig. 8.   Gateway from the William Aiken house;
probably 1830-1840.
One of a pair, with 83-foot fence,
made by Christopher Werner (1805-1875).
Originally on upper King Street, now bordering
the grounds of the Gibbes Art Gallery.

became acquainted with ironworking in his father's shop.
He received a good education, emigrated from Germany to
escape military service, and was naturalized as an American
in Charleston on December 10, 1839. Establishing himself
at first in the carriage business, he soon expanded his activities to include blacksmith, wheelwright, and foundry work,
subsequently limiting his principal activities to the forging, as
well as casting, of iron. His shop at the corner of State and
Cumberland Streets, with all of its equipment, was destroyed
in the great fire of 1861. During the Civil War, his operations were directed chiefly toward the making of military
equipment. Afterward, until his death in 1875, he resumed
the production of gates and fences.

Two outstanding examples of Charleston ironwork generally conceded to have been produced in Werner's shops
are the William Aiken fence (Fig. 8) and the gateway of
Hibernian Hall (Fig. 9). The first originally adorned the
grounds of William Aiken's residence on upper King Street.
It was moved a few years ago to its present position along
the western border of the grounds of the Gibbes Art Gallery, where it shows to considerably better advantage than
it did in its rather cramped original setting. The handsome
fence is eighty-three feet long, and there is a pair of lofty
matched gates. The second example of Werner's work, the
gateway of Hibernian Hall, is an even finer and better-pro-
portioned creation although more limited in scope. It occupies a prominent position on Meeting Street, where the
entire focus is on the beautiful gateway itself, and the fence
is essentially functional in design.

Fig. 9.   Gateway of Hibernian Hall,
incorporating the Irish harp, probably 1840-1845;
by Christopher Werner.

Mobile ironwork

BY MARGARET ROSE INGATE, *President, Historic Mobile Preservation Society*

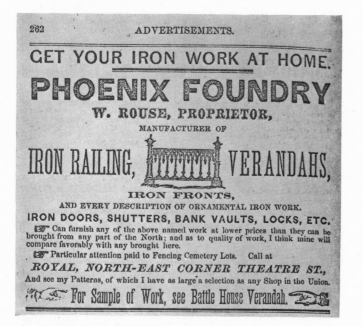

From Henry Farrow & Co.'s *Directory of the City of Mobile*, 1871.

Over the years, we have published in ANTIQUES a fair amount about decorative ironwork in America. Two excellent surveys—Mary Willis Shuey's *The Ironwork of Old New Orleans* (September 1930, p. 224) and Kathleen Yerger Johnstone's *Iron as Ornament* (June 1944, p. 308)—concentrate on the stylistic development of ornamental wrought and cast iron and the history of their use in the old South, but give little information about their makers. Mrs. Ingate's research on makers of Mobile ironwork enables her to fill in some of the missing names. *Ed.*

ON BEING ASKED what he was looking at, a casual viewer of the decorative ironwork on one of Mobile's old buildings would probably reply "wrought iron, of course"—and he would probably be wrong. While there are lovely examples of wrought iron in Mobile, cast iron is much more common. The basic difference is that wrought iron was forged by hand, while cast iron was made in molds. Wrought iron came earlier and its charm persists in a few remaining balconies, a gate or two, and an occasional remnant of fence in a cemetery. Designs are simple, and each piece has a neat, finished look. Although cast iron is often more ornate than this earlier type of work, it is never as delicate.

Cast iron became popular in Mobile about the middle of the nineteenth century, as cotton brought greater affluence to the city. It was used architecturally and for garden benches, fountains, and ornaments. Some strap iron—flat beaten strips—with rosettes of cast iron had been used as early as the 1840's and may still be seen today, but the very ornate, intricate cast designs came into use as the prosperity of the city increased. New houses were embellished with ironwork as a matter of course, and many owners of old brick town houses added porches and verandas or galleries with elaborate cast-iron railings and posts.

Some ornamental iron found in Mobile was

The wrought-iron balcony extending across almost the entire front of 50 South Franklin Street is extremely simple and delicate. It is original to the structure and is thought to be the work of a local blacksmith. The Egyptian doorway and recessed entrance are typical of Mobile town houses of the 1840's and are seen frequently in the older parts of the city. The building, owned by Dr. Frank England, is presently used as his office. *All photographs are by Thigpen.*

Mausoleum and fence of cast iron with the name plate of Robert Wood's foundry attached. One of two in Magnolia Cemetery, this is the *Family Tomb of Hope H. Slatter.* The other example, almost a duplicate of this, has no foundry plate or mark.

256 State Street, in the De Tonti Square Historic District, was built in 1857 by Carey Butt. It changed hands twice before it was purchased in 1897 by Dr. T. H. Frazer, whose daughter Alice still resides there. The ornamental cast iron on the front and east wing was acquired by Dr. Frazer at time of purchase from Augustus Kling's Home Industry Foundry. The Kling residence is directly behind this one and the rear yards adjoin, with a friendly gate between.

imported from France, as that on the Bunker-Moraques residence at 157 Monroe Street is said to have been. America lagged behind England and other European countries in the production of ornamental cast iron and this probably accounts for the importation of some of the earlier examples. However, ships brought men as well as materials, and skills and techniques from abroad were soon learned. To the traditional European designs, geometrical and classical, Southern metalworkers added a number of their

own. These were inspired by nature, and in Mobile grape clusters, tendrils, and leaves, and the acorn-and-oak-leaf pattern were favorites. Manufacturers of ornamental cast iron borrowed patterns and designs from each other freely, so it is almost impossible for us now to assign a specific design to a specific maker.

Although there are no clues to the identities of the earliest local makers of ornamental iron, city directories published as early as 1837 enable us to draw up a preliminary list of makers from that date on. Directories for 1838, 1840, 1841, and 1857 to 1868 are not available, but the information presented here was culled from those for all the other years between 1837 and 1900. By 1837 there were at least two iron foundries in Mobile: James Curry & Co. and I. D. Spear. These firms and blacksmiths by the dozen advertised decorative ironwork in the city directory for that year. Many smiths combined such work with other trades; for example, William Hutchinson, who in 1839 owned an oyster saloon at 219 Dauphin Street, advertised, "Will keep on hand fresh oysters, day and night," and "also, at the same place [carry] on . . . sheet iron manufacturing." Others did "shipsmithing" and "bell hanging." In addition

This cast-iron gate has wrought scrolls at the bottom. Originally it was the entrance to the residence of Murray Forbes Smith, whose daughter Alva first married William Vanderbilt and later O. H. P. Belmont. The gate was removed in the early 1930's when the house, built in the 1840's, was demolished. It now admits visitors to Dr. Earl Wert's Springhill Avenue property.

Cast-iron cemetery gate in the popular weeping-willow-and-lamb design; J. Lang, Maker and Mobile are molded into the upper frame of the gate, and *1861* appears on the small scroll above. *Historic Mobile Preservation Society.*

One of a pair of cast-iron benches bearing the mark John Lang, Mobile on the center back of the seat. This one is in the garden of Mrs. A. B. Tissington Jr.; the other is in Catholic Cemetery.

to professional blacksmiths, numerous slaves learned to use the anvil and hammer, and probably some of the few examples of wrought iron remaining in Mobile are their work.

McGuire and Fry's *Mobile Directory* of 1837 lists some black- and whitesmiths. The term "whitesmith" was used to refer to a worker in tin or other "white" metals, or, as here, to a skilled worker in iron who finished pieces forged by a blacksmith or created decorative ironwork —as opposed to horseshoeing and other commonplace tasks. One of the two foundries in the 1837 directory, James Curry & Co., listed Audley H. Gazzam as blacksmith. Gazzam appears in the directories through the years in this and related occupations. James Curry also worked over an extended period; in 1844 his shop, then known as the Jefferson Foundry, was operated with Robert E. Redwood on St. Anthony Street between Water and Royal Streets. In 1852 I. D. Spear, the other of the two 1837 foundries, was in business at the same address, 112 Water Street, but his shop was now known as the Phoenix Foundry.

In 1855 Skates and Gazzam were making ornamental cast iron at the Mobile Foundry. Apparently Skates later organized his own shop, as a listing appears in city directories of 1861 for Skates & Co. at Magnolia and State Streets. Skates and Gazzam's Mobile Foundry site, the southeast corner of State and Water Streets, was used by a number of foundries.

Benjamin D. Roberts was advertising ornamental cast iron in 1861. He maintained a shop on Conti Street near two other foundries, John Lang and the Home Industry. Roberts' full-page advertisement in the city directory represented him as a "Manufacturer of Plain and Ornamental iron railing . . ." Most of the foundries were clustered within three or four blocks of the Mobile River, where they could readily meet the needs of ships calling at the port.

John Lang, advertising in the 1869 directory, is the only Mobile foundryman of the nineteenth century whose marked work has been found. He employed the young German immigrant Augustus Kleng as a "finisher." Kleng, who later spelled his name Kling, had come to Mobile in 1866. He worked as a blacksmith, first in his own small shop, and later, after leaving Lang, at the Home Industry Foundry on Conti Street in partnership with John Meyers. Kling's Home Industry was in operation well into the twentieth century. Much beautiful work still to be seen in Mobile is attributed to the firm, but there are no records to authenticate any of it. According to local and family tradition, a bench and chair in the grape-and-leaf motif are the Home Industry's original designs. Some of these iron seats still exist, and today both are being widely copied in aluminum.

Another firm listed in the 1869 directory was C. W. Gazzam Sr.'s Mobile Foundry at State and Magnolia Streets. This was near the site of Skates and Gazzam's Mobile Foundry (listed in 1855)

Residence of Mrs. Charlie Bell White, 205 Church Street. This house, in Church Street East Historic District, was built before 1840. In the 1850's it was connected by a recessed iron balcony to the adjoining house to the west (now demolished), and the two were known as the "mother-daughter" houses. The curved steps and the cast-iron ornament on the porch are believed to have been added when the houses were joined. The grillwork at top and base of the columns is unusual.

and the same site as that of Skates & Co. (listed in 1861). In 1871 the same address is given for the Gulf Foundry Co., owned by C. W. Gazzam and J. F. Jewett. Jewett had been in business two years before as J. F. Jewett & Co., blacksmiths.

Much of the marked iron now in Mobile came from the foundry of Wood & Perot, later Robert Wood & Co., in Philadelphia (see ANTIQUES for August 1952, p. 112, for an article on this firm and its wares). Vessels from northern ports called regularly at Mobile, and the iron was shipped south from various centers by water. We are indebted to Daniel Geary, an indefatigable salesman for Robert Wood, for enabling us to identify a number of pieces: two of his ledgers covering the period 1866 to 1873, now in the Historic

Cast-iron gates of the Basilica of the Immaculate Conception. The diocese, earliest on the Gulf, was established in 1704, and the present edifice was erected in 1833. There are no marks on gates or fence, which encloses the entire block, but church archives reveal an 1860 order to Messrs. Wood, Miltenberg & Co. of New Orleans for gates and a fence fitting this description—with the proviso that the entire work should not cost more than $5,000. There are gates on all four sides and massive square columns at each corner.

This design, a graceful combination of fruits and flowers, is seen frequently throughout the city in railings and fences, but none of the examples is marked. As far as I know, its earliest use is in Magnolia Cemetery, where it encloses a plot in which the latest tombstone is dated 1848. The example pictured is in front of a house on Government Street presently used by the Junior Chamber of Commerce as an information center. It was built in 1860 and is situated on ground that was granted by the French in 1748 to Mme. De Lusser, widow of a French soldier killed in 1736. *City of Mobile.*

Mobile Preservation Society, contain orders for a wide variety of ornamental iron, giving descriptions, prices, and names of customers (see the cover of this issue, and p. 321). Geary was also a prolific letter writer, and his letters (these, too, are now owned by the society) give interesting side lights on the happenings of the times.

Geary's advertisement appears in 1869, and that he was a keen competitor is indicated by William Rouse's advertisement in the same directory: he admonished Mobilians, "Get your iron work at home." Rouse was an experienced ironworker, and he is listed as blacksmith in the directories from 1837 on.

In 1871 Rouse was calling his firm the Phoenix Foundry (this was entirely separate from I. D. Spear's Phoenix Foundry). In the directory for that year his advertisement called the attention of one and all to an example of his work, the veranda of the Battle House, largest and most important hotel in the city and well known throughout the state and along the Gulf Coast. Daniel Geary's correspondence indicates that he made great efforts to obtain this commission and that he was bitterly disappointed to lose it.

Thomas S. James was another well-known Mobile agent for a Northern manufacturer of ornamental iron, Chase Brothers of Boston. His advertisement appears in the directories for 1858, but no marked Chase iron has been found in Mobile. However, a fence with an arched gateway, marked by Chase and dated 1854, was found by Mary Wingfield Scott in Petersburg, Virginia (*Richmond Times Dispatch Magazine,* December 24, 1939). There are in Mobile two unmarked fences with arched gateways, which bear the same acorn-and-leaf design as that of Chase's Virginia example.

Much of Mobile's old ornamental iron has disappeared: some has been thrown on the scrap heap, much has been destroyed by careless workers and vandals, and still more has gone to other cities, to be enjoyed by collectors or copied by manufacturers. Despite these deplorable losses, Mobile iron may still be seen embellishing many houses and gardens throughout the historic districts. And in more modern sections old fences, gates, and railings lend warmth and character to stark twentieth-century buildings.

A simple wrought-iron fence from the side yard of Augustus Kling's North Jackson Street residence. The rosettes or daisies at top, center, and base are of cast iron. This was almost certainly made by Kling's Home Industry Foundry.

Cast-iron fountain, one of three on the campus of Springhill College. The base is marked W. J. FISK CO., DANBURY, CONN. College records disclose that it was installed in 1870.

City Hall, built in 1857-1858, was originally a market. A series of arches like this one on two sides of the building are ornamented with delicate wrought iron. Four double carriage entrances to the inner courtyard have this same light lacy work at the tops of their arches (see ANTIQUES, March 1964, p. 309, Fig. 28).

The Ironwork of Old New Orleans

By Mary Willis Shuey

Some day Antiques expects to see a revival of architectural cast iron. Southern cities are full of examples of work in this material, and summer colonies of Southern folk are said to have brought the vogue for it to New York before the Civil War. But to study the development of the decorative use of iron in this country, it is necessary to visit New Orleans. A glimpse of what may be found there is given in this article. For the accompanying illustrations, Antiques is specially indebted to the Newcomb College School of Art and its generous director, Ellsworth Woodward. — *The Editor.*

A TRIP through the Vieux Carré, or through the Garden District of New Orleans, brings home the phrase, "The City of Iron Lace." In these old sections of the city we find ironwork — both wrought and cast — to be the most important decorative element in the local architecture; for, though the buildings are almost severely plain, they are alluringly veiled in delicate lace — lacy galleries, balconies edged with lace, strips and festoons of lace to the very roofs. The slender columns that support the galleries are wreathed with threadlike designs of iron, and ingenious little brackets support the lighter burden of balconies — Spanish and just window size. The elaborate cast-iron galleries that jut out over the sidewalks and stretch across entire house fronts are marks of the Americanization of New Orleans, so the French say. But French, Spanish, and American New Orleans all contribute their own patterns to the infinite variety of the city.

Climate and the mode of living in early days were probably responsible for the extensive use of ironwork. The houses of the Vieux Carré, the French city, laid out by Bienville in 1718, accommodated business establishments on the ground floor, with family quarters above. The merchant had his store below his home; the doctor dwelt above his office, and the banker above his bank. The old walls of brick and stucco rose straight from the *banquette*, or pavement, over which the upper galleries extended. At one side of the store or office, a paved passageway led through an arched entrance from the street to the inner court of the house, and at the rear rose the slave quarters, built in tiers of two and three stories.

A sharp contrast is observable between the severely simple ironwork of the lower, business floor, and the more elaborate screening of the home above. From the street rise slender iron colonnettes, perfectly plain; but, once the family level is reached, the taste for ornamentation is given free rein.

Ask someone, offhand, and you will be told that all the ironwork in New Orleans — or at least in the Vieux Carré — is wrought. On the contrary, there is a good bit of cast iron to be found throughout the city, and the iron of the Garden District is almost all cast. The wrought iron dates back to the time of the Spanish occupation (*1766–1803*), and is the only Spanish touch remaining in a city that, under Spanish rule, and even through American days, remained essentially French. Much of it owes its Spanish character to the gracefully designed gates and balcony rails of the Cabildo, which has left traces of its influence again and again, in both wrought and cast iron, throughout the city.

The old Cabildo, or town hall of Spanish days, destroyed by the fire of 1788, was reërected in 1795. The present gates were a

Fig. 1 (above) — St. Peter Street Balconies (*c. 1810*)
Wrought-iron balconies of graduated depth are the early heritage of Spanish tradition in New Orleans

Fig. 2 (centre) — Wrought-Iron Gate of the Cabildo (*1795*)
About 1803, the Spanish arms of the lunette were supplanted by the present sunburst and thirteen stars

Fig. 3 (right) — A Royal Street Passage (*1820–1830*)
Wrought-iron gates still jealously guard the privacy of the inner courtyards of some of the Vieux Carré houses

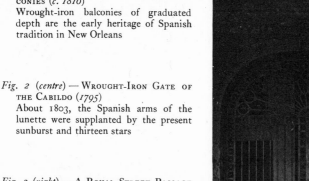

Figs. 4–11 — EXAMPLES OF WROUGHT IRON (*c. 1795–1830*)
The pattern of wrought-iron balustrades, delicately silhouetted against white stuccoed walls, was the chief decorative feature of old New Orleans homes

Fig. 12 — CAST IRON AT ITS BEST (*1846*)
The design of the ironwork on the Pontalba buildings is elaborate but highly refined casting, in which much of the spirit of the old wrought ironwork survives

Fig. 13 — TYPICAL CAST IRON (*c. 1840*)
Perhaps inevitably the cheaper process of casting put an end to wrought iron for general architectural use. These arboreal designs are characteristic of the period

part of the Spanish building, and originally bore the Spanish arms, for which, after the American occupation, the stars of the thirteen Colonies were substituted. Several other changes have been made. Legend has it that General Butler broke up part of the gates during his never-to-be-forgotten stay in New Orleans. The General's reputation in New Orleans is so black, however, that any damage in that region would be attributed to him.

But the oldest locally made wrought iron in New Orleans is to be found in the Ursuline Convent, erected *1727–1734*. Its hinges and other hardware were beaten out by slaves — "*brute* Africans," the records say. Here we find no attempt at ornament; nor does skilled slave labor appear in New Orleans until the insurrections in San Domingo and the West Indies (*1791*) drove a number of French Creoles to New Orleans, and, with them, their faithful and frequently highly competent slaves, who turned out very creditable ironwork. Some railings, however, were imported from France and Spain. Certain authorities maintain that brass knobs and square brass bolts on railings always denote foreign work, while the true New Orleans wrought iron invariably has balls and ornaments of lead.

When the notable pirates Jean and Pierre Lafitte were not pirating, they ran a peaceful blacksmith shop; and some of New Orleans' loveliest wrought-iron balconies and grilles are attributed to them. Indeed, the figures of the Lafittes haunt the Vieux Carré, as their exploits colored the period from 1805 to 1815. True, they were pirates, but they had no lack of sound sense and loyalty. The story goes that, in Jean Lafitte's blacksmith shop on Chartres Street, the fate of New Orleans was really decided; for it was here that the redoubtable buccaneer reached an agreement with Andrew Jackson. And so, when the memorable Battle of New Orleans was fought, January 8, 1815, Lafitte and his five hundred Barataria pirates came to Jackson's aid, and saved the day.

Look through old directories and you will find, with the addresses: Devault, *forgeron*; Malus, *forgeron*; Marre, *forgeron*; Rouli, *forgeron*; Urtubise, *forgeron*; Pelane, *forgeron*. They were specialists all, and each had his favorite design which he wrought with peculiar adeptness and a fine flourish. Pelane, it is said, tapered the rods of his balustrades like blades of grass, bent them into graceful scrolls, and wove them into slender, pointed arches. The balcony on the Waldhorn Building, at Canti and Royal Streets, is his. Ironworkers say that at least eight heatings were required for each scroll — and the scroll is repeated many times. The names of popular patterns sound like those of old coverlet designs: *the arrow, the leaves, the widow's mite, the diamond, the grape, the shell, the acorn,* and *the tulip.* In other designs, feather motives are very carefully executed. Along St. Peter Street, many of the galleries run continuously across the fronts of adjoining buildings, and are broken only by inner guard rails, which divide each domain from its neighbor. These grille partitions, protected as they are against invasion by bristling spikes, are often most original in pattern. They are assignable to the years between 1800 and 1820.

In the ironwork of the more pretentious houses, monograms were

Fig. 14 — AN ADMIRABLE DESIGN (*c. 1840*)
The men who carved the wood models for much of the mid-century cast iron were sculptors of no small ability. Witness this balustrade, which is equally effective against open sky or wall, and is sufficiently bold and simple in treatment to be impressive even to the distant view

extensively used — the initials woven repeatedly through the design. The monogram fashion extended well into the cast-iron era, which dawned in New Orleans in the late 1820's. By 1840, cast iron had superseded the finer, but more costly, hand-wrought decorations. Several well-known foundries, which had previously manufactured the machinery used for sugar-making, turned their attention to fancy casting. Of these, the Leeds Iron Works and the Shakespeare Iron Works were two of the best known, and they employed the most skilled craftsmen in wood and metal who could be brought from France. Until 1861, these foundries did excellent work; but, during the Civil War, they concentrated on war supplies, and never again returned to their earlier peace-time occupation.

The finest cast-iron work in New Orleans, however, came from abroad, to adorn the façades of the Pontalba Buildings, and, with the recurring monogram *A. P.* in delicate tracery of metal, to perpetuate the names of Almonaster and Pontalba. It was Don Almonaster who built the Cabildo and the Presbytere. Quite as much to his credit, he was the father of a beautiful daughter, Micaela, among whose many suitors were plain John McDonogh and another person no less august than one Joseph Xavier Celestin Delfair de Pontalba, son of the Baron Pontalba. New Orleans residents will tell you that Micaela favored the poor young Scotchman, but that parental pressure forced her into marriage with the grandee, who promptly carried his bride to France. After that nothing was left for the slighted John but to grow very rich, as he did, and to devote his money to erecting schoolhouses. And over the door of each building he carved his name in large letters, so that it might be remembered when the names of Almonaster and Pontalba had been forgotten. He was doomed to a second disappointment. In 1846, the Baroness Pontalba returned to New Orleans, piled up her famous mansion block, and hung it, fore and aft and roundabout, with iron balustrades, made in France, and repeating in every panel the twined initials of Almonaster and Pontalba. It is still one of the sights of the city; but no one ever hunts up a McDonogh school to view either its architecture or its inscription.

The houses of the Garden District show many varieties of New Orleans cast iron. Theirs is the era of the Greek revival, when the names of New Orleans streets no longer recalled the prowess of local celebrities, but reflected the contemporary pseudo-intellectualism by honoring Melpomene, Terpsichore, Calliope, Dryades. The city had moved out, and the Garden District was the choice of all who wanted space and gracious living. Most of the houses were of brick, either painted or covered with smooth plaster and screened with iron galleries. Likewise, they were set in squares or half squares of ground, and surrounded with ornate iron fences, which grew larger, more imposing, and more extraordinarily ornate with each new house. Along Prytania Street today, stretches an almost unbroken line of cast-iron fences, varying from five to eight feet in height, and displaying almost everything that can be done in cast iron, from simple straight-line patterns to garlands of flowers and fruit, tall stalks of sugar cane, and the full glory of ripening corn.

Cast-iron figures were a part of the gardens of the times. Today ancient fountain statuary of strange contour and oddly disposed avoirdupois turns up at auctions and is bid in for old-fashioned gardens. It includes iron ladies who forgot to count their calories, cupids, angels, gargoyles — tastes varied.

The gates of the old courtyards are still in use, and, while many of the Vieux Carré houses are now apartments and their

Figs. 15 and 16 — IRON SCULPTURE (*c. 1840*)
Almost humorously Victorian: and yet who, today, would remove these back-to-nature designs, symbolic of rural repose and of the corn and sugar cane whence Louisiana derived its wealth, as well as of the ease and grace of life that wealth made possible

Fig. 17 (below) — CAST-IRON COLUMN (*1860*)
Relic of a cast-iron building made in Holly Springs, Mississippi, erected and riveted together in New Orleans before the Civil War, and incontinently burned to the ground before completion. Fortunately this fine column was saved

courts dedicated to tea-room libations, there remain some inner shrines whose privacies are jealously guarded. The wrought-iron lamps that hang in these courtyard passages are always enticing; and today New Orleans is keeping them, instead of selling them as it did a few years ago. But some of the old wrought-iron balconies have gone East and West — to adorn who knows what houses.

And incidentally, do you know the difference between a gallery and a balcony? Many persons do not. A gallery is supported from the ground by columns; while a balcony rests on brackets, and is usually a small affair. Balconies may extend the length of a building, however; it is the manner of support that determines the designation.

From the standpoint of direct craftsmanship, I surmise that we must award the palm for highest merit to early wrought iron. Cast iron has not yet fully recovered from the stigma of being a product of the industrial era — which, perhaps because it has brought the world so much that is desirable in the way of creature comfort, and so little that is estimable in art, is generally viewed with disesteem. Nevertheless, the work of the molder is by no means to be despised. Upon it, during mid-Victorian days, was expended an exceptional degree of skill, patience, and true artistic genius. And nowhere is this fact better exemplified than along the enticing thoroughfares of New Orleans.

THE EARLY IRONWORK OF CENTRAL KENTUCKY

And Its Role in the Architectural Development

By CLAY LANCASTER

Clay Lancaster has written widely, for ANTIQUES *and other publications, on the architecture of the South, especially that of Kentucky. In our Kentucky issue of November 1947, his subject was the state's architectural firsts. In the present article he traces the development of one of Kentucky's architectural embellishments — its ironwork.*

THERE is still a popular, but mistaken, conception that the early wrought iron of the South is to be found in or near Charleston, and that the later cast iron is in New Orleans, and that the remaining Southern communities are practically devoid of either. But Lexington, in the heart of Kentucky, 500 miles from both Charleston and New Orleans, has examples of ironwork similar to each.

The first ironwork to make its appearance beyond the Alleghenies was building hardware. Some of the early locks bear the plates of English makers, others of locksmiths in the East, the latter usually stamped IMPROVED after the manner of good Yankee salesmanship. Even after the burning of brick became a common practice, iron fittings and window glass were the two building commodities not locally produced. Not until the latter 1780's did the metal industry take root in central Kentucky, and it soon became one of the thriving enterprises. Wrought iron made its appearance before cast, since it requires less equipment. Some of the first decorative ironwork came from the same men who shod horses; but most artisans preferred to feel their distinction from menial laborers. The man who shod horses was called a *blacksmith*, whereas the man who created objects of iron to be seen and admired was a *whitesmith*, as was the smith who worked in silver. In 1792 a Lexington firm offered for sale "BARR IRON assorted, SMITH'S ANVILS and VISES, CASTINGS." Thus the whitesmith could purchase at home the implements and materials necessary for his craft; and "castings" suggests the beginning of the rivalry between wrought and cast work.

The 1806 city directory for Lexington lists the name "Sam Wilkerson, whitesmith," and a dozen years later there were the names of four men of that occupation. One of these, Thomas Studman, had announced in 1809 that he did all kinds of "Whitsmith's work," including "all sorts of plain and ornamental Railings, Grates, Iron Doors, for fire proof buildings, Screws of different kinds and Smith's work in general."

Wrought-iron railings and fences dating from the beginning of the nineteenth century are often quite beautiful, and it is unfortunate that so few of them have survived. The contemporary John Hunt and Thomas Bodley houses, facing one another across Gratz Park in Lexington, had iron fences set into stone slabs circumscribing the little front yards. Only the fence of the latter remains, composed of plain, upright bars fastened to an upper and lower horizontal rod, enhanced by small rosettes, with cast anthemia affixed to alternate vertical points (*Fig. 1*). The Bodley house also had a pair of fancy hitching screens of the same period and style that stood at the curb; but these have been removed to the safety of the walled garden.

About the earliest establishment in Kentucky with facilities for casting was the Bourbon Furnace, probably located in the vicinity of Paris (Bourbon County), and in operation in 1794 (*The Kentucky Gazette*, June 14, 1794). A few years later its proprietors claimed that their castings were "equal in quality, and superior in workmanship, to any . . . imported into this state." Much that they produced was used for cooking or heating equipment; but staple architectural pieces found a steady market, and special types were made to order.

The foundry begun by Joseph Bruen in Lexington in 1816 was to be in operation for over half a century, with large production. In the 1838–1839 *MacCabe Directory of the City of Lexington*, it was described as follows:

There is . . . an Iron Foundry . . . carried on by Steam Machinery. The building is of solid brick, measuring 160 feet in length. It was erected in 1830, and furnishes this [Fayette] and adjoining counties with most of their iron. The metal used is chiefly imported from Pittsburgh and the Red River and Maria Forges. The establishment employs about 25 hands, and sells 100 tons of wrought iron per year. The capital invested is near $80,000. The building was erected by Mr. Joseph Bruen, an enterprising citizen, who still continues to superintend the business of the establishment.

Bruen ran the plant until his death in 1848, after which it was continued by members of the family, finally passing into other hands. During the latter part of the Bruen régime, a larger structure than the 1830 building was erected for the foundry, and the old one then became a machine shop. An iron store was run in connection with them. John McMurtry, a later owner and manager of the Bruen works, gained quite a reputation as an inventor, which is significant in that the technical skill developed through

FIG. 1 — WROUGHT-IRON gate and fence of the Thomas Bodley house, Gratz Park, Lexington (*c. 1816*).

FIG. 2 — DETAIL of the rotunda stairway of the Kentucky State House, Frankfort (*1827–1829*). Architect: Gideon Shryock.

Fig. 3 — Upper Portion of Southern National Bank, Main Street, Louisville (*1837*). Architect: Gideon Shryock.

Fig. 4 — Plate 26, Minard Lafever, *The Beauties of Modern Architecture* (New York, 1835).

making the parts for the inventions would result in increasingly finer architectural ironwork as well.

Wrought iron was most in use in the early Georgian architectural style in Kentucky. Nails, shutter guards, strap and HL hinges, and the bar of iron spanning the fireplace opening to hold in place the brick or stone voussoir of the chimney, were typical applications. Cast iron was represented by five-pointed stars, showing against the face of a wall, and fastened to the ends of the tiebeams. Some of the Shaker "family" residences at Pleasant Hill had iron handrails to the outside stairs (see ANTIQUES, November 1947, p. 344).

It is generally agreed that the first Greek Revival building west of the Allegheny Mountains was the Kentucky State House (*1827-1829*) designed by Gideon Shryock (ANTIQUES, July 1945, p. 35). The hexastyle Ionic portico of this Frankfort edifice is admired as an aesthetic attainment; but the double stone stairway, self-supporting, and built on the principle of an arch in a circular wall, is remembered as a remarkable structural achievement — and its simple iron railing accentuates the straightforwardness of its construction (*Fig. 2*). Charles Shryock, son of the architect, tells us that for this building, "A convict, an expert blacksmith, did the iron forging, the most important of which was the iron band around the springing stones of the brick arch of the dome." Thus, iron actually held together a most important feature of Kentucky's former capitol.

About 1837, Gideon Shryock planned the Southern National Bank (now the Credit Association Building) on Main Street in Louisville (*Fig. 3*). The stone façade was inspired by a design of Minard Lafever, published as plates 25 and 26 in his *The Beauties of Modern Architecture* (1835) (*Fig. 4*). Many times the scale of the Lafever design, Shryock's façade was modified in its proportions, and redesigned into a flat, linear pattern sympathetic to a cast technique for the crowning device.

In New Orleans, balconies are the distinguishing feature of the Vieux Carré, and after 1800 these galleries were quite common. From New Orleans, about 1810, came Mathurin Giron, the famous confectioner and *pâtissier*. In the mid-thirties, M. Giron undertook to have his own building erected on Mill Street, Lexington, the second floor of which contained rooms for supper parties. The 44-foot railing that enhanced the upper gallery resembled the earliest type found in New Orleans, composed of latticework bars with Roman rosettes at the intersections, above which were horizontal rails filled with guilloches reversely whorled at either end. The strict repetition of the lattice was relieved by three squares with radial designs of cast iron, and four panels with strips twisted into figure eights (*Fig. 5*). This continuous railing pattern was adapted to every conceivable type of central Kentucky porch or stairway barrier, straight or curved. Although it is American Greek Revival in period, it is early

eighteenth-century English in feeling, and traceable to Romanesque ironwork of the ninth and tenth centuries.

Like the railings, fences about city lots were essentially nettings of wrought bars, fastened together with cast ornaments in typical Empire fashion. But the cast pieces became larger and more complex, and more prominent in the design scheme. Silhouette, basrelief classic urns or lyres sometimes interrupted the geometrical pattern of a fence, and floral shapes were to follow a bit later. The posts for these fences were hollow castings with pagoda-roof heads, or square skeletal towers composed of contemporary decorative elements (*Fig. 7*).

Nowhere are attic window grilles more prevalent than in Kentucky. Elsewhere, they were often inserted at regular intervals in the frieze of the entablature (ANTIQUES, May 1946, p. 307; May 1947, p. 327); in Kentucky, they were usually beneath the entablature, or under the simpler cornice, as the case may be (*Fig. 6*). Flat-façaded houses contiguous to the street — possibly individualized by a recessed doorway — with grilled attic windows

Fig. 5 — The Confectionery of M. Giron, Mill Street, Lexington (*c. 1837*). This old photograph shows the south half of the building, the portion that has been razed. *Photographer unknown.*

FIG. 6 — DETAIL of the George Bowyer house, South Upper Street, Lexington (*1847*). Architect: John McMurtry. Typical iron window grille. Wood consoles and cornices are prototypes of forms usually cast during the next decade.

FIG. 7 — WROUGHT AND CAST fence and gates to the house on High Street, Lexington, remodeled for Stephen Swift during the early 1840's. House demolished. *Photographer unknown.*

are typical town residences in the heart of the state, especially in Frankfort. The grilles of the Greek era are very much alike in this region; and one meets with this same window guard from Maine to the Gulf. At least two dies were struck of the one pattern, for the size varies by a few inches. The elements are equivalent to a design for a cast railing from Asher Benjamin's *Practice of Architecture* of 1833 (Pl. 30). The center motif is the Peloponnesian clustered anthemion, and to the right and left are scrolled swirls. Ubiquitous in Kentucky, they probably were cast there, the original impression having been taken from an imported archetype.

Later in the epoch of revived Greek architecture, ancient architectural embellishments became requisite, and the desire for marble temple antefixes was appeased with iron open-relief rakings similar to the attic-window grilles. Interior cornices and the relief bands about sunken ceiling panels were molded of plaster; but since this material was impractical for use outside, it was replaced by iron. Egg-and-dart, and bead-and-reel could

be purchased by the yard at the foundry shops. The favorite order for porticoes of the late forties and fifties was the Corinthian. Whereas the earlier Doric and Ionic capitals were usually wood, the later campaniform capitals garnished with acanthus leaves were, with few exceptions, of cast iron. Some specimens in Fayette County have a magnificent, sculpturesque projection, such as those of the Charles Innes house (*1854*) on the Russell Cave Road (*Fig. 8*).

The zenith of Kentucky architectural ironwork meant for visual enjoyment might be considered to have been reached about mid-point in the century. Iron was used to throw emphasis on openings, such as window frames with Greek "ears" or hoods over entrances that sometimes attained the dimensions of good-sized porches (*Fig. 9*). Indoors, the marbleized iron mantel was introduced; sometimes it was harmonious with other Greek features, and sometimes not.

Before the strictly post-and-lintel Greek had fully supplanted the Georgian style of architecture in Kentucky, the Gothic Re-

FIG. 8 — DETAIL of the Charles Innes house, Russell Cave Road, Lexington (*1854*). Architect: John McMurtry.

vival had appeared. The depressed Federal fanlight was succeeded by the soaring lancet. Such a break in idiom required an entirely new set of motifs, not just a modification of the old. Compound colonnettes replaced fluted columns, barge-boarded gables replaced narrow raking boards or pediments, crenelations replaced entablatures; and instead of anthemia there were watercress foliations. Floral forms were raised from capitals and panels to parapets and pinnacles. Special casting was required for the conspicuous fittings of the Gothic Revival.

One of the earliest buildings to use Gothic motifs was a strange admixture of the ancient and medieval, Saint Peter's Catholic Church, erected on North Mulberry Street (North Lime) in 1837 by the young Lexington builder, John McMurtry. Like the first Hellenic building west of the Alleghenies, this earliest Gothic building made use of iron — in the "spire pole" and "Irish crown" at the base of the conical spire.

In 1852 McMurtry conceived the castellated villa, Ingleside, on the Harrodsburg Road. This was for Henry Boone Ingels, son-in-law to Joseph Bruen, and the intermediary manager of the foundry between Bruen and McMurtry. With casting facilities so convenient, the architect availed himself of them, designing pointed turrets with crockets and finials to be placed upon the square piers flanking the principal entrance bay (*Fig. 10*). And cast-iron drip molds supported the foot-and-a-half-thick walls, bridging the wide doorway opening or narrower windows. Excepting, possibly, the band about the springing stones of the dome of the Shryock State House, iron in Kentucky had never before served a purpose so structural. The chimneypieces in the drawing room and parlor were of stone; but the other rooms had marbleized iron mantels about each fireplace, of the type sold by Mr. Ingels at his downtown stand.

During the summer of 1855, the Bruen Foundry was operated by John McMurtry, and a short while after this he became the owner. That an architect should conduct his own forge and foundry was to have a direct bearing upon the use of iron in the local architecture. Gothic peaks similar to those of Ingleside went on the McMurtry gateway to the cemetery in Paris, and a Lexington store front of three floors was built, in the pointed style, entirely of cast iron and glass (*Fig. 11*). The store was built for the

FIG. 9 — SAYRE COLLEGE, Lexington, built as a private residence in 1846. Railings are original. Enlarged as Sayre Female Institute, 1855–1860, at which time the cast-iron porch was added.

partnership of Craig, Elliott and Company, and beginning May 2, 1857, an engraving of this Gothic structure appeared among the advertisements in the *Lexington Observer and Reporter*, which dates it as a building of the mid-fifties. Modillions and consoles beneath the existing topmost cornice (the parapet, like the show windows, having been removed) are enough like those of the George Bowyer residence, known to have been built by McMurtry in 1847, to warrant McMurtry as the designer of the business house too. As at Ingleside, acutely pointed windows were above more obtuse arches, and the drip molds also were very much alike. A large percentage of the iron pieces facing the building were flat plates;

FIG. 10 — DETAIL OF INGLESIDE, on Harrodsburg Road near city limits, Lexington (1852). Architect: John McMurtry.

FIG. 11 — Cast-Iron Store Fronts in Lexington. To the right is the upper part of the Craig, Elliott and Company façade (*c. 1857*); to the left, Melodeon Hall (*c. 1877*). *Unless otherwise noted, photographs are by the author.*

but the hoods, cornices, and capitals, and the various parts of the complex parapet had to be cast each for its appointed place.

During the second half of the nineteenth century, Americans attempted a cosmopolitanism in the design of their buildings. They liked to think of it as a revised Renaissance, but the architects knew that they were devising new forms as much as they were combining old, and this eclecticism encouraged the use of iron. The prevalent mistake was in accepting aggregate accumulation for aesthetic attainment. Too often an otherwise legitimate design was stifled naively beneath a conglomeration of ornament.

The Eclectic Period was the Age of Iron in many ways. It was the period of the iron convenience. The beginning of contemporary plumbing and heating brought with it iron bathroom fixtures and iron furnaces. Rooms were filled with iron furniture — beds, tables, chairs, benches, stools, hall stands, and umbrella racks — and many foundries produced some of these articles in six or seven different designs, which could be ordered through illustrated catalogues. The children were amused by mechanical iron toys. Iron posts had heads of dogs or horses with hitching rings in their mouths; and hitching posts acquired the forms of gaily painted jockeys or stable boys. Ornamental garden pieces represented life-size deer, dogs, or lions; and grotesque faces leered from pedestaled urns. Water splashed over cast-iron fountain figures. Hinged iron caskets for the dead were the shape of Egyptian mummies swathed in loose cloth pulled up about the arms folded on the chest; a removable plate permitted a glimpse at the face of the deceased through an oval of glass. Attached architectural ironwork kept abreast of these things, maintaining much of the same plenteous spirit.

As one walks along the streets of Lexington today he comes upon front fences from Springfield and Kenton, rakings from Philadelphia, weather vanes from Pennsylvania, and entire business façades consisting of stacks of Corinthian or composite columns, or superimposed arcades, from Pittsburgh or Cincinnati, many of the latter on earlier buildings that had been remodeled. Habitually, these were quantitative rather than qualitative. Only lightning rods seem sensible — to ground the lightning attracted by so many extrorse iron points! These embellishments impress rather than delight the eye; they are architectural frosting in lieu of nourishment. The development of ironwork, decoratively, came to a standstill. The design of castings degenerated to the point where it was the haphazard combination of the ornaments of more creative epochs. Here was the decease of early architectural ironwork in Kentucky — in America, for that matter. What was to come later belongs to our own day.

MOLDED IRON IN THE MIDDLE WEST

A New Material in a New World One Hundred Years Ago

By JOHN ALBURY BRYAN

WHEN the middle west's cultural development began to flower, the whole country was being flooded with art reproductions. Lithographs and steel engravings satisfied the average yearning for pictures; mass production was beginning in some furniture factories; and cast iron was available at a considerably lower price than wrought iron to those who sought ornamentation for the exterior of their houses or for their lawns.

Late in the 1830's ironworkers in this part of the world organized themselves into companies or foundries for the making of cast-iron balconies, railings, urns, and other embellishments. Each company had a patternmaker, who had to be a woodcarver since most of the patterns were then made of mahogany or walnut. Then there was a moldmaker, who formed the molds of sand; and finally there were the men who understood the firing of iron, temperature control, and so on. It meant a coöperative effort, contrasted to the method of the age-old blacksmith who was a lone wolf by comparison. The newspapers of St. Louis carried rather lengthy comments whenever ironwork of unusual design from one of those foundries made its appearance on the streets of the rapidly expanding city; and local capital that had formerly been heavily interested in the fur trade turned with enthusiasm to the new iron industry for a generous part of its investments.

Among the first products advertised by the local foundries were ornamental grates. The *Daily Evening Gazette* in St. Louis, for the year 1839, carried an announcement by Bridge & Rayburn that they had a complete stock of those useful and decorative articles. Figure 1 illustrates an example found in the old home of Adam Lemp, built about 1840 near Second and Elm Streets — a part of the area recently cleared of buildings by the National Park Service in preparation for the Jefferson National Expansion Memorial. This grate has been saved for future display in the proposed Museum of American Architecture within the confines of the Memorial, along with many other objects of iron, wood, and stone salvaged from that site.

The general run of balconies and fences during the 1840's was of a modified gothic character, such as the balcony across the parlor windows of the Robert Campbell house, which is still standing at Fifteenth and Locust Streets in St. Louis. This house was not built until 1851, but stock designs of ironwork were still made at that time from the molds erected in the previous decade. These continued in favor until about 1855, when the wave of enthusiasm for the Italianate style of architecture called for heavier designs in railings and all other decorative details *(Fig. 2)*. Precedent was found in the cast-bronze work of the Italian Renaissance, with the rinceau as the favorite motif.

The town houses carried more ironwork than did most of the "Lake Como" villas that dotted the countryside adjacent to St. Louis. However, the most famous of those villas, Selma Hall, has cast-iron balconies on its four-story square tower, besides railings and urns on the terrace overlooking the river (see article by Charles van Ravenswaay on page 70).

The decade 1850-1860 saw the first attempts at formal landscaping of public parks and cemeteries in the trans-Mississippi country. By that time St. Louis manufacturers had received the elaborate catalogue issued by the International Exhibition held at the Crystal Palace in London during the summer of 1851. A careful study of that publication will show that the ironwork of the middle west was more conservative in its ornamentation than that of mid-Victorian England. Perhaps the outstanding contribution of the St. Louis foundries, from the standpoint of design, was in the garden benches, especially those made at the establishment of Shickle, Harrison & Company *(Fig. 3)*.

By 1862 the iron dome on the St. Louis Courthouse was completed; and the entire block, or Courthouse Square, was enclosed with a high fence of cast iron

FIG. 1 — GRATE FROM THE HOME OF ADAM LEMP, NEAR SECOND AND ELM STREETS, ST. LOUIS. *Now in the Museum of American Architecture, Jefferson National Expansion Memorial, St. Louis.*

FIG. 2 — A GOOD EXAMPLE OF ADAPTATION OF ITALIAN RENAISSANCE MOTIFS. Balcony panel that formerly adorned a bay window on the William Morrison house, southeast corner of 17 and Locust Streets, St. Louis, which was built in 1858 and razed in 1933. *Photograph by Adolph Felder.*

easily. The most highly prized possessions among thousands of pioneer home-owners in Nebraska, Colorado, and Utah were the St. Louis stoves, bearing the imprint of Bridge & Beach or Giles Filley on one or more parts (*Fig. 4*). Their profuse ornamentation was a delight to the children who lived through the bleak winters in rather scantily furnished homes during those early years of the far west's development. One of the most amusing stove designs from this period has the top molded to resemble a mansard roof, complete with dormers and fancy shingles (*Fig. 5*).

The architectural iron companies located in Cincinnati, St. Louis, and Chicago enabled the majority of the cities and towns in the Mississippi Valley to flaunt something of a more metropolitan air by means of fluted columns, bracketed cornices, and heavily encrusted arcades, molded in imitation of the patterns that had once lent distinction to Athens and Rome (*Fig. 8*). Better still, they reduced the fire hazards for growing cities that had not had time to provide adequate fire-fighting equipment. The same foundries that cast heavy Corinthian columns for banks and warehouses also made verandas in trellis patterns, often with entwining grapevines, wistaria, or roses — all cast to look as much like the natural growth as possible (*Fig. 6*). The Sturtevant-Ebaugh house at Beardstown, Illinois, is perhaps the best surviving example in the middle west of a two-story veranda in iron. It dates from 1866.

The Cincinnati foundry of Miles Greenwood & Company had its Corinthian columns in place as far west as St.

FIG. 3 — BENCHES MADE BY SHICKLE, HARRISON & CO., ST. LOUIS (*c. 1868*). *A*, (*above*): The bas-relief panel represents a special adeptness in handling the medium of cast iron. Now lacquered sea green, with pad of bronze green leather. *Owned by the author; photograph by Hardin Walsh, Index of American Design*. *B* and *C*, (*below*): When Henry Shaw, English-born hardware merchant, gave his adopted city, St. Louis, the park which he named "Tower Grove," he provided fifty cast-iron benches at a cost of $9,000. Only three are left today. Each is 7 feet long. Gothic detail seemed to be especially fascinating to the designers in the middle west, whereas in Philadelphia and Baltimore Greek ornament was generally favored. *Now in the grounds of the Superintendent's house, Tower Grove Park, St. Louis; photographs by G. Vietor Davis.*

(ANTIQUES for July 1942, p. 41, shows a rare old view of the St. Louis Courthouse, taken in 1868). Just after the close of the Civil War the thirty-acre Lafayette Park in St. Louis was enclosed with a massive iron fence, cast from designs submitted by Francis Tunica in a city-wide architectural competition. That fence is still in service, but the one around the Courthouse was taken down about 1896.

As for the practical side of the story of molded or cast iron, products of the stove manufacturers of this region had as much to do with the early winning of the west as any others. Certainly the cities and towns between the Mississippi River and the Pacific Coast could not have grown so rapidly without the help of cooking and heating stoves. These were easily installed in the balloon-frame houses, and could be moved from one mining town to another very

FIG. 4 — COOK STOVE MADE BY BRIDGE & BROS., ST. LOUIS (*1853*). *Courtesy A. G. Brauer Supply Co., St. Louis; photograph by Adolph Felder.*

Joseph, Missouri, about the time that John Brown was carrying on his bloody warfare just across the Missouri River in Kansas. The St. Louis foundry owned by the Pullis Brothers was another establishment that gave architectural dignity to the early banks, courthouses, and hotels over an area more than five hundred miles west of the Mississippi. These facts show the rapidity with which the use of cast iron in architecture spread across the land when we remember that the first building in the United States to use iron in all its main parts was erected as late as 1842, in Boston, by Daniel Badger.

An indication of the widespread popular interest in those men who had advanced the use of iron was shown in the action of the citizens of Ford County, Illinois, in 1859. They voted to change the name of their county seat from Prospect City to Paxton in honor of Sir Joseph Paxton, the architect of the great exhibition palace of iron and glass that London first gazed upon in 1851.

At present many of the cast-iron objects illustrated in this article face the prospect of being thrown into the furnace to meet the demands of warfare. So it is fortunate that a magazine devoted to the study and preservation of American antiques should preserve at least the record of these works, which represent midwestern America of the nineteenth century as truly as anything in the realm of painting, sculpture, or cabinetwork.

FIG. 5 (*above*) — A "FIREPLACE STOVE" OF THE GENERAL GRANT ERA. So called because the front doors were made to slide from the center, allowing the blazing fire to lend its cheer to the room. Note the amusing mansard-roof top. Made at Quincy, Illinois, about 1868 by Comstock, Castle & Company. *Photograph by Bryan Campbell.*

FIG. 6 (*right*) — RESIDENCE OF THE COMMANDANT, U. S. ARSENAL, ST. LOUIS. Built in 1840; razed in 1918. Its broad verandas gave a fine view of the Mississippi River. *Photograph by Doctor Robert H. Fuhrman.*

FIG. 7 (*below*) — A CAST-IRON VERSION OF THE TWENTY-THIRD PSALM. Gate to the cemetery lot of the Felker family at Vienna, Missouri. *Photograph by Hardin Walsh, Index of American Design.*

FIG. 8 — CAST-IRON ARCADE OF THE MERCHANTS BANK BUILDING. Built in 1858 at the northwest corner of First and Locust Streets, St. Louis. Thomas W. Walsh, architect. The building was razed in 1940. *Photograph by Lester Jones.*

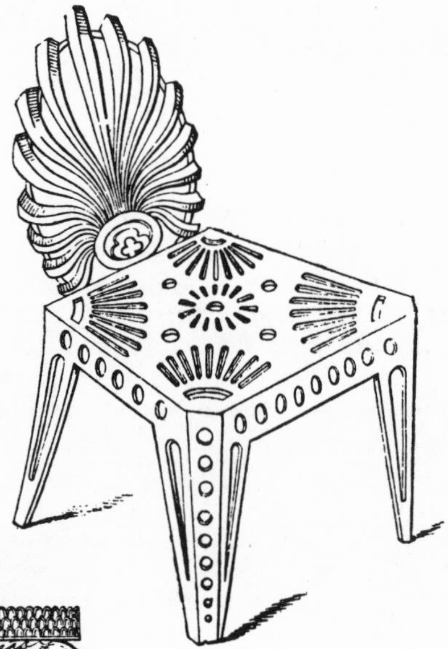

Fig. 1.
"Etruscan" chair; cast iron.
From J. C. Loudon's
*An Encyclopedia of Cottage,
Farm & Villa Architecture
& Furniture;*
London, 1833.

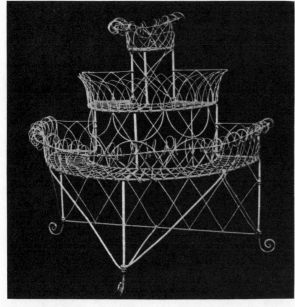

Fig. 2.
Twisted-wire flower table,
designed by John Reynolds.
From *The Official Descriptive
and Illustrated Catalogue of the
Great Exhibition of 1851.*

American mid-Victorian

WHILE THE NINETEENTH CENTURY did not originate outdoor furniture, it did produce this specialized type in far greater quantity and diversity than its predecessors. The eighteenth-century romantic gardens of England and the Continent had, indeed, often combined exotic garden seats with a variety of rustic grottoes, Egyptian obelisks, Chinese umbrellas, Greek garden houses, and Gothic ruins. Charles Middleton's *The Architect and Builder's Miscellany* (London, 1799) contains a variety of designs for such garden structures, and a plate picturing six garden seats intended for use in the romantic garden of which one is "rustic" (made of natural wood), one Gothic, one Chinese, two classical, and the other a novel combination of Chinese and classical motifs. Such designs were intended to be executed by hand, with details and combinations of motifs left to the ingenuity of the craftsman, but with the industrial advances of the nineteenth century it became possible to mass-produce outdoor furniture for popular use.

J. C. Loudon's *An Encyclopedia of Cottage, Farm & Villa Architecture & Furniture,* published in London in 1833, shows an iron chair cast in two pieces (Fig. 1). The writer noted that this chair could be widely available and that:

When carved work, or much ornament, is to be executed in furniture, cast iron will always be found cheaper than wood, even though a small number only of the article were wanting.

Metal was one of the materials most frequently used for nineteenth-century outdoor furniture, and in addition to cast iron, twisted wire was very popular. *The Official Descriptive and Illustrated Catalogue of the Great Exhibition of 1851* (Crystal Palace) illustrated a flower table

Fig. 3.   Twisted-wire plant stand, probably Continental,
c. 1850. *Elinor Merrell.*

Fig. 4.   Cast-iron chair in the rococo taste.
From A. J. Downing's *The Horticulturist* (1857).

outdoor furniture

BY JOSEPH T. BUTLER, Curator, Sleepy Hollow Restorations

by John Reynolds of New Compton Street in this material (Fig. 2); the table top was supported by three serpents, and the entire ensemble must have been graceful and airy. Suites of this furniture included chairs, settees, benches, stools, tables, and elaborate plant stands (Fig. 3).

By the middle of the century American periodicals and manuals of taste often recommended cast-iron furniture for its beauty, durability, and cheapness. *The Horticulturist*, a periodical founded by Andrew Jackson Downing and devoted to good taste in the garden and home, showed representative pieces of cast-iron furniture in the issue for October 1857. One of these was a chair (Fig. 4) in the rococo taste, combining grapes and leaves in an asymmetric pattern in back and legs. Still more asymmetric was a "rustic" bench which simulated natural, untrimmed branches; this was made by the foundry of J. W. Orr in New York (Fig. 5). Another bench (Fig. 6) showed an interesting combination of Gothic and rococo details; one very similar to this design appears in Figure 7. Several urns and flower stands shown in the same section were labeled as products of Robert Wood of Ridge Avenue in Philadelphia. Downing said that metal outdoor furniture should be painted a dark color—either black or slate.

Another type of outdoor furniture extremely popular at the time was made of cane (sometimes called rattan or wicker). One of the taste manuals concerned with this type of furniture was Gervase Wheeler's *Rural Homes*, published in New York in 1852. The cane or rattan used was the highly durable stem and tendril of a climbing palm found in the East Indies. The frames for pieces of seat furniture were made from white oak or hickory,

Fig. 5. "Rustic" cast-iron bench. *The Horticulturist* (1857).

Fig. 6. Cast-iron bench with Gothic and rococo detail. *The Horticulturist* (1857).

Fig. 7. Cast-iron bench with Gothic and rococo detail. *Sleepy Hollow Restorations.*

47

Fig. 8. Group of rattan furniture. From Gervase Wheeler's *Rural Homes;* New York, 1852.

Fig. 9. Wicker settee in the Chinese taste. *Rural Homes.*

Fig. 10. Intricately braided wicker armchairs. *Rural Homes.*

carefully selected for straightness of grain. This was steamed and bent into the desired shapes and the cane was split when it was tied onto the frames. The cane was imported into New York via Antwerp, Bremen, and Rotterdam, and its fashioning into utilitarian articles employed many people.

Wheeler stated that between three and four hundred boys at the House of Refuge in New York were thus occupied, and that in the Bloomingdale section of the city and in the suburbs a group of Germans employed at least two thousand girls in their rattan manufactories. However, neither of these was the most extensive manufacturer of wicker objects: Wheeler gave that title to Messrs. J. & C. Berrian of 601 Broadway. One of Wheeler's illustrations of the Berrian furniture showed a selection of rattan pieces accompanied by the following description:

The articles grouped together in our illustration exhibit a sofa, arm-chair, rocking-chair, and foot-bench; the sofa, from the pointed termination of its curves approaching to the Gothic principle of construction, and hence suitable to a building in that style; and the other pieces, from their symmetrical and rectilinear and spherical lines, adopted to an Italian or any other description of finish but the strictly Gothic.

Indeed, the romantic taste, as in the eighteenth century, did not limit itself to the Gothic and Italian influences. Included by Wheeler was a settee in the Chinese style (Fig. 9):

Another style of sofa or settee is shown, which, from its peculiar Chinese character, is very pleasing. It is made of the cane in its solid form—in such a shape generally styled "bamboo"—and is originally a pattern of Chinese manufacture. For a hall or an old-fashioned and quaint-looking sitting room it is very suitable. In congruity with this is a pattern of great elegance, and character; this has a pleasing blending of the curved and angular lines, and appears to me to show a very successful treatment of the material.

Two additional chairs (Fig. 10) were shown which were noteworthy for their use of intricately braided rattan, and many other objects, such as fire screens, swing seats, work stands, and flower stands, were illustrated. In addition, J. & C. Berrian's *Catalogue of Housekeeping Articles*, which dates from the 1850's, states that infants' chairs, high chairs, knife and spoon baskets, and clothes hampers, were available. Wheeler highly recommended the use of rattan in furniture because of its "durability,

Fig. 11.   Rustic wooden bench, c. 1865.
Litchfield (Connecticut) Historical Society.

elasticity and great facility of being turned and twisted into an almost endless variety of shapes."

A third type of mid-nineteenth century outdoor furniture was that constructed from tree branches or roots combined to form a natural seat. A. J. Downing, who favored the rustic and picturesque in both gardens and interiors, showed in his *Cottage Residences* of 1844 a rustic bench closely similar to an example made twenty years later (Fig. 11). He stated that "rustic seats, placed here and there in the most inviting spots, will heighten the charm, and enable us to enjoy at leisure the quiet beauty around." To create such a piece of furniture, branches were chosen and arranged so that they would naturally form the contours of the piece (Fig. 12).

The Horticulturist of 1858 carried two articles on rustic furniture. The simplest of these were stools fashioned from forked branches for supports with slabs of wood for the seat (Fig. 13), and much care and attention was sometimes lavished on the combination of the elements into a useful whole. This furniture was recommended for interior as well as outdoor use.

In cottages this description of furniture is very appropriate. In summer bowers, piazzas, and near or in garden walks, it is pleasant to see, if not to rest on, such objects, which have an "expression of purpose" about them satisfactory to the mind. Under a fruit tree, an easy seat is proper and comfortable. Every agricultural laborer is more or less accustomed to the use of tools, and it is surprising how a little use in the adaptation of the materials at hand increases one's facility in such work. An old apple or pear orchard furnishes capital materials; all that is required for their construction is a saw, an axe, a gauge, and a few nails. The requisite skill is possessed by every man of ordinary intelligence; the taste grows by its exercise.

The creation of rustic furniture was not, however, limited to men. Catherine Beecher and Harriet Beecher Stowe in *The American Woman's Home* of 1869 illustrate a stand for flowers (Fig. 14) made from roots which have been scraped and varnished, and suggest that this type of activity be carried on in the home by women.

These three types of outdoor furniture—metal, cane, and rustic wood—seem to be typical of mid-nineteenth-century America; but even a casual study of the examples illustrated makes it clear that all three hark back to an earlier romantic tradition of the bizarre, the exotic, and the picturesque.

Fig. 12.
Rustic stools fashioned from forked branches.
The Horticulturist (1858).

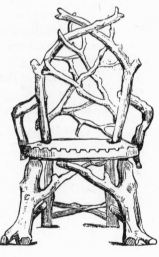

Fig. 13.   Rustic armchair.
The Horticulturist (1858).

Fig. 14.   Rustic plant stand; from *The American Woman's Home* (1869), by Catherine Beecher and Harriet Beecher Stowe.

II Heating, Fireplaces, Andirons, etc

In primitive societies fire was used in the open, but as civilization progressed people learned that fire can be more efficiently used if it is contained. Even when fire is set in a fireplace with a chimney, however, about 90% of the heat is lost. Containing the heat in a stove retains more of it for use, and beginning in the eighteenth century iron was considered the best material for stoves.

The first two articles in this section are concerned with early iron smelting furnaces in Virginia and Cumberland County, Pennsylvania. The history of these furnaces is given along with illustrations of them and of their products such as five- and ten-plate stoves, firebacks, andirons, and other articles made of cast iron. The next four articles discuss objects used in open fireplaces such as screens, fenders, andirons, firebacks and stove plates. One of the articles is of particular interest and concerns the Whittinghams, brassfounders of New York City. More examples of their andiron work survive today than that of any other maker. The following four articles deal with two varieties of stoves: those associated with Benjamin Franklin's name and inserted in the fireplace, and the box type which stood in a room and was connected to the chimney by a stovepipe. The last article discusses all the little portable gadgets used to carry heat into such unheated places as churches as well as beds.

Modern central heating is certainly more efficient and less troublesome than old-fashioned methods, but the remnants of our present progressive age certainly will not be as charming or interesting to future generations as those surviving for us today. Ironically, the iron stoves perfected in the nineteenth century are now enjoying a comeback, especially in rural areas. As alternative heating devices, they can provide a remarkably inexpensive means of reducing one's ever-escalating natural gas or fuel oil bills.

Decorative cast iron
on the Virginia frontier

BY JOHN BIVINS JR., *Curator of collections, Old Salem*

AMONG THE numerous Southern decorative arts which have received relatively little recognition in print, cast iron is a rewarding field for students of early industries. Unfortunately, early Southern cast iron has not survived in any quantity despite its durability: many fine decorated stove plates and firebacks have been carried away as scrap in the endless cycle of reclamation that is part and parcel of the modern manufacture of steel and iron.

Although the South never equaled the iron output of the North, several Southern furnaces, particularly in Virginia, did produce significant amounts of bar iron and castings. One of these eighteenth-century operations was Marlboro Furnace in Frederick County, Virginia, about twelve miles from Winchester. The only remains of this establishment visible today are a ruined mill and a small limestone dependency; this is in marked contrast to the scene an eighteenth-century visitor would have beheld. Spread over an area of "not more than 50 rods," or 275 yards, was a two-story stone manor house surrounded by dependencies including three barns, a stable "50 feet long, 22 wide," a kitchen, washhouse, springhouse, bathhouse, and "three separate apartments" for use as dining rooms "for workmen of different descriptions." The furnace itself was surrounded by a "casting house, pot-house, bellows-house, and ware-house," in addition to the forge, which had "two hammers and four fires." Other industrial buildings were a large gristmill, a sawmill, a smithy, and a distillery. A countinghouse, fish pond, fountain and fountain house, and a neat hexagonal icehouse completed the picture. Surrounding the site was timber "sufficient for . . . lasting supply," which was of no little importance in operating a blast furnace. Not far to the east lay ore beds which yielded iron "excelled in quality by none in America, either for castings or bar-iron . . ." (Isaac Zane broadside, "To Be Sold or Rented, etc.," March 4, 1791. Coates and Reynell Papers [MS], Historical Society of Pennsylvania; hereafter cited as C&R Papers, HSP).

Master of this impressive establishment was Isaac Zane Jr., whom Philip Vickers Fithian described in 1775 in his *Journal* as

a Man of the first Rank here, both in property & Office— He possesses the noted Malbrow Iron-Works, six Miles from this Town [Stephensburg, now Stephens City]—He has many Slaves, & several valuable Plantations—he is, with Regard to Politicks, in his own Language, a "Quaker for the Times. . . ."

Indeed, Zane's "several valuable Plantations" were to occupy some thirty-five thousand acres in three counties before his death in 1795. His "Office" at the time included membership in the Virginia House of Burgesses, where he had become friends with Thomas Jefferson and James Madison. He was also a colonel in the Shenandoah militia and a magistrate of the district.

Isaac Zane was raised in the conservative mercantile Quaker milieu of Philadelphia; his father had risen to wealth from the ranks of the numerous house carpenters in that city (*Pennsylvania Gazette*, June 25, 1767, No. 2009, Supplement). In 1767 young Isaac, with the financial help of his father and several other Philadelphia merchants, bought into a furnace establishment which had been built near Winchester by Lewis Stephens around 1760 (correspondence, C&R Papers, HSP; Frederick County, Virginia, deed books). Partners in Zane's venture were John Hughes, Samuel Potts, and John Potts Jr., all of Philadelphia (*ibid.*), but Zane shortly bought them out in order to operate the furnace on his own. The huge capital outlay required for this purchase forced Zane to assume a considerable burden of debt, which he was never able to shake off; he remarked later to his

Fig. 1. Remains of an iron furnace known in the Winchester, Virginia, area as the Taylor furnace; evidently this was the same as that which Zane called "Marlbro Old Furnace" in a description of his estate.

Fig. 2. The five-plate Wedding stove.
Mercer Museum.

Fig. 3. Front plate, Wedding stove;
24¼ by 19¾ inches.
Mercer Museum.

Fig. 4. Side plate, Wedding stove;
23¹⁵⁄₁₆ by 27⅜ inches.
Mercer Museum.

brother-in-law John Pemberton that "the dictates of . . . Honor to render to every man his due has been a heavy shadow to the Sun shine of my Happiness . . ." (Isaac Zane to John Pemberton, undated letter of early 1780's; C&R Papers, HSP).

Such problems, however, did not seem to cloud the early years at Marlboro. Zane happily set about acquiring an impressive personal estate. He patronized several prominent artisans in Philadelphia, including Joseph and Nathaniel Richardson, from whom he bought such niceties as "pincushion hoops and chains," "silver porringers," and "6 table spoons" (C&R Papers, HSP) to please the lady whom Fithian described as Zane's "kept & confessed Mistress," Elizabeth McFarlane. Other articles in the Zane manor very likely from Philadelphia shops included "1 Pier Looking Glass . . . value £50," and "eight day Clock £18," as well as a thirty-shilling "patent Lamp" and "1 Mahogany knife case with 2 doz^n large knives." Zane's household boasted a half-dozen "beds and furniture," which might have been from the shop of Benjamin Randolph, whom Zane's father patronized frequently (Benjamin Randolph bill to Isaac Zane Sr., 1768-1769; C&R Papers, HSP). Numerous pieces of walnut furniture, listed in the estate inventory of 1795 (C&R Papers, HSP) and possibly made for Zane in Winchester, included such items as two desks-and-bookcase, both £9, one of them "well mount^d"; two "double leaf'd falling walnut Table[s] 1.16.0," "a neat plain walnut Table 16/," a "double Book Case of walnut Cost 50/mak^g." Numerous other pieces including tables, chests, and chairs were also of walnut, but a dressing table and a "Chair of ease" are not identified as to their respective woods.

Zane had purchased William Byrd III's library for £2,000 in 1778, but by the time of his death he had disposed of all but four hundred volumes to reduce some of his debt, which had increased heavily during the Revolution. In all, Zane's personal estate amounted to upwards of £5,000 (*ibid.*), over and above his considerable real estate holdings.

Zane relied on the furnace for financial support. In 1772 a new furnace was built closer to better ore beds, and despite the enormous task of moving the entire operation nearly six miles east, Zane was able to report to John Pemberton by December 1772:

we have far exceeded expectation of what I thought could be done in one Summer, to Say, after so hard a Winter, & a late Spring, to Build a large Strong furnace, & all its appurtenances, make 40 Tons open Castings 16 Tons pott ware, keep the forge going & leave off in a little time with 120 Tons piggs in store . . . (Zane to Pemberton, December 10, 1772; C&R Papers, HSP).

To keep the furnace "& all its appurtenances" in blast, Zane had in his employ woodcutters and colliers to supply charcoal, patternmakers and potters to supply casting patterns, carpenters and joiners to repair the buildings and make wooden implements, foundrymen to supervise the running of castings and pigs, and hammermen to convert the pigs into wrought iron in the chafery. Probably more than a hundred men were employed in the operation, many of whom lived on the premises.

The principal output of Marlboro, as of most other American furnaces, was bar iron which had been converted from pig iron in the chafery, and a good deal of it was shipped to England through such factors as William Allason of Falmouth on the Rappahannock (William Allason Papers, Virginia State Library). Shipment of iron from Marlboro to the Virginia ports was neither easy nor cheap, however, since there was no direct navigational link.

John Pemberton handled vendues of bar iron in Philadelphia and on numerous occasions also arranged for the sale of castings in that city (Zane Correspondence; C&R Papers and Pemberton Papers, HSP). Zane evidently limited his Philadelphia consignments to utilitarian ware such as pots, kettles, Dutch ovens, mortars and pestles, and the like, as the following advertisement from the *Pennsylvania Gazette* for April 5, 1770, indicates:

To be SOLD cheap for cash, by John Pemberton, A FEW TONS OF BAR IRON, and a parcel of neat CASTINGS, consisting of large, middle sized, and small pots; and some bake plates. . . .

Zane's own inventory proves an excellent guide to production: of the cast ware, pigs and utilitarian or "kitchen" ware constituted the bulk of the items run at the casting floor. Of these, pots and kettles were the most numerous and pots ranging in size from two to ten gallons were regularly run, along with kettles of eleven- and seventeen-gallon capacities. To make the clay molds for these items, Zane had purchased expensive pewter patterns (estate inventory of Marlboro; C&R Papers, HSP). Also listed in an inventory (estate inventory of Marlboro; Frederick County Superior Court Will Book I, pp. 224-305) were skillets and Dutch ovens in several sizes as well as salt pans and teakettles; "waggon boxes," which were the bearings used in wagon wheels, were another product. Flatware included hatter's irons, bridle rings, ladles, and flatirons.

Production at Marlboro during the Revolution was no small undertaking, since Zane had contracted to make swivel guns and one-, four-, and six-pounder howitzers, in addition to round shot up to twenty-four-pounder shot. Many orders came from the new state government and because of the general economic crisis during the period Zane was not paid for much of what he supplied.

More interesting to students of ironware are the decorated pieces cast at Marlboro. Patterns for these listed in Zane's inventory are a good guide to what was produced:

1 Franklin Stove pattern	£6.0.0
1 10 plate Stove do.	6.0.0
1 £4 open do. Mahogany Carv'd	4.0.0
1 do. do. do. more plain 40/	2.0.0
1 £5 open do. plain	2.0.0
1 £3 pipe ditto	3.0.0
1 £3 open do. Mahogany Carv'd	3.0.0
1 do. do. do. plain	1.10.0
1 £3 pipe do. plain	1.10.0
1 Fairfax Arms back wall plate pattern	8.0.0

Mentioned in a second inventory was a pattern for "Dog Irons." Cast andirons from this period are rare today, but surviving examples seem to follow rococo patterns. (An example at Old Salem has a straight upright surmounting a round boss with the date *1775* in relief, and cabriole legs terminating in scroll feet. The maker is unknown.)

In November of 1772, Zane mentioned to Pemberton that he was running "Near 10 Tons Stoves" (C&R Papers, HSP) in a week's time, and as we see from the inventory, these consisted of Franklin stoves, "pipe" or six-plate stoves, ten-plate stoves, and "open" or five-plate jamb stoves. Nothing is known at this time about the appearance of Zane's Franklin stove or of the ten-plate stove, but the five-plate stoves were generally of normal Germanic configuration, aimed at the large German population in the Shenandoah Valley.

A patternmaker by the name of James Calhoun evidently made patterns for at least two jamb stoves for Zane; Calhoun was later associated with Westham Foundry in Richmond (Westham Foundry information courtesy Harold Gill, Colonial Williamsburg). Three decorated five-plate stoves have been identified with Marlboro; two of these were recorded by Henry C. Mercer in his pioneering *Bible in Iron*. Parts of these three stoves are in the Mercer Museum in Doylestown, Pennsylvania; other pieces of the same stoves are in private collections and in the Museum of Early Southern Decorative Arts.

Illustrated in Figure 2 is a five-plate stove, missing only the left plate, which depicts what is referred to in the second edition of Mercer as the Wedding Fable. The front plate of this stove (Fig. 3) is Pennsylvania German in nature, showing the actual betrothal ceremony with angels hovering protectively overhead. The side plates (Fig. 4) are more interesting, in that their design was drawn from a fable well known to eighteenth-century Germans. Although the message is not fully understood today, the fact that the stove is dated 1768, a leap year, may be important in interpreting this scene. According to ancient custom the woman was to wear the pants during leap year, but here the man has put his breeches out of reach and stands by derisively as the women try futilely to bring them down by ringing hand bells. Something of a parallel to this stove plate is a Krebs fraktur illustrated in Number 64 of *Fraktur-Writings or Illuminated Manuscripts of the Pennsylvania Germans* by Donald A. Shelley (Allentown, Pennsylvania, 1961).

The design of the Wedding stove, like that of the other five-plate stoves cast at Marlboro, is composed of primitive rococo elements and two-dimensional human figures very characteristic of other German-American art, such as fraktur. The carver of Zane's five-plate stove patterns, however, seems to have taken little interest in the endless

Fig. 5. Side plate, five-plate Peace stove; 20⅝ by 22¼ inches. *Mercer Museum.*

Fig. 6. Front plate, Peace stove; 20½ by 17½ inches. *Mercer Museum.*

repetition of geometric and architectural devices which characterizes many Pennsylvania stoves. His rather clumsy attempt at foliated scrollwork, in combination with the stiff movement of the figures, creates a sense of primitive baroque. The heavily molded corner rims, however, have the same medieval precedents as contemporary Pennsylvania stoves. The top and bottom plates for this stove are undecorated except for an ogee-molded lip; in their original state, a rounded tab at the front edge of both plates (now missing in Fig. 2) was drilled to take a long threaded bolt which held the stove together. The front of such stoves was often lifted off the floor with bricks or a specially cut stone.

Of clearer decorative precedent is a Zane five-plate stove with a Biblical design. The German inscription on the side plate (Fig. 5) is from Isaiah 11: 6, 7, identified in the bottom right corner of the casting. It reads, in translation, *I look for a better time, when all strife shall cease [and when] cows and bears shall feed together [and] the wolves shall dwell with the lambs.* The front plate (Fig. 6) bears the inscription (in translation) *Every one shall live without fear under his own vine and fig tree,* taken from Micah 4: 4. This plate is decorated with two fig trees, one with a vine, and is unmistakably marked ISAAC ZANE. Assuming that the Wedding stove was made from a "Mahogany Carv'd" pattern, this stove may have been the one that Zane noted in the inventory as an open stove, "more plain." Certainly this small stove is much less elaborate than the Wedding stove—even its corner rims are plainer—but the nature of its forthrightly stated message makes it particularly interesting. The date 1773 is one of the latest known on an American five-plate stove; it was not long after this that six- and ten-plate stoves completely took over in popularity.

The third stove with Marlboro association is repre-

Fig. 7. Front plate, five-plate Birds stove; height 21 inches. *Mercer Museum.*

sented in a fragmentary manner. The plate (Fig. 7; number 24443 in the Mercer Museum) is identified simply as the Birds of 1769; both corner rims are broken. Recently an identical front plate complete with rims, as well as broken top and bottom plates, was found near Winchester along with the remains of a Wedding stove. Both stoves had come from the same early building. In addition to this strong regional tie, the Birds plate almost certainly was carved by the same hand as the Wedding plates; the resemblance is especially strong in the details of the scrolls. Presumably, patterns for both these stoves were carved by Calhoun.

No complete six- or ten-plate stoves from Marlboro are known, but three identical side plates from six-plate stoves have been found in the neighborhood of Woodstock, Virginia, some fifteen miles south of the site of Marlboro Furnace. These plates (Fig. 8) are elaborately decorated in the chinoiserie manner with complex interlacing C and S scrolls surmounted by a figure which appears to be a Buddha holding a branch of the Bo Tree. Although the source for this formal design is unknown, it was probably taken from some eighteenth-century design book known to specialist carvers of the period. The highly artistic carving on this elegant plate is similar in feeling to that on Philadelphia Chippendale furniture, and it is likely that the pattern came from that city. The plate may be strongly attributed to Marlboro, but definite proof will have to wait until a marked front plate is found.

By far the most interesting casting associated with Marlboro Furnace is from the "Fairfax Arms back wall plate pattern" (Fig. 9), for which Zane noted in 1795 that he had paid £8. A memorandum filed in the Pemberton papers sheds interesting light on the origin of the pattern:

Recd 12 moth 20th 1770 of John Pemberton Eight pounds for the carving the Arms of Earl of Fairfax for a Pattern for the Back of Chimney sent Isaac Zane jr.
Bernard & jugiez

The specialist carvers Nicholas Bernard and Martin Jugiez operated a "Looking-Glass Store" in Philadelphia, "In Walnut-street, between Front and second-streets, and next Door to Mr. Claypoole's." There they offered "All Sorts of Carving in Wood or Stone, and Gilding, done in the neatest Manner—"(*Pennsylvania Gazette*, January 6, 1763).

It is not known what prompted Zane to have this baronial pattern cast; perhaps his reason was simply that the Fairfax family was highly respected in colonial Virginia. One of these firebacks remains at the site of Belvoir, the Fairfax estate, which may or may not indicate that the family originally commissioned the massive casting. Its impressive size (it weighs nearly three hundred pounds) and crisply carved design assure the Fairfax fireback a place among major American castings.

The production of cast iron at Marlboro continued for less than ten years after the Revolution. Although Zane remained active in state politics, his health began to fail in the early 1790's. He had made repeated attempts to sell his furnace complex during the 1780's, hoping to relieve himself of the considerable debt connected with it, but it was left to his sister Sarah Zane to worry about the disposal of the huge estate. At the time of Zane's death in 1795, the works were "completely out of repair," not even fit to be rented (Alexander White

Fig. 8. Side plate, six-plate chinoiserie stove; 22 by 27¼ inches.
Museum of Early Southern Decorative Arts; photograph by Bradford L. Rauschenberg.

Fig. 9. The Fairfax fireback; 31¾ by 34 inches.
MESDA; *Rauschenberg photograph.*

to Sarah Zane, September 12, 1795; C&R Papers, HSP). The Marlboro estate was not settled until 1812, and the furnace was never again put into blast. Zane's earlier furnace, which he referred to as Marlboro Old Furnace, was purchased by a member of the Bean family and was evidently producing iron until sometime in the early nineteenth century. This operation was subsequently taken over by the Taylor family of Frederick County; a ten-plate stove of about 1820 in the Old Salem collection is marked A. P. TAYLOR FREDERICK.

IRON FURNACES IN THE CUMBERLAND VALLEY

The Story of the Ege Family

By LENORE EMBICK FLOWER

IRON MANUFACTURE in Pennsylvania was "big business" in the second half of the eighteenth century, flourishing in spite of the difficulties raised by the English Acts of Trade which became law in 1750. The Act for Colonial Manufacture at that time required that iron furnaces in the Colonies produce nothing more pretentious than crude pig iron, which was to be transported in English vessels to the mother country and sold back to the colonists in the form of manufactured implements. But the rapid growth of the iron industry in the Scotch-Irish Cumberland Valley attests the disregard of these acts, and is significant of political as well as commercial "straws in the wind." The contribution of the industry to Colonial life and advancement was real and important.

Virtually all the furnaces of the region produced the same type of wares. Stove plates and hearth backs were perhaps the most ambitious as well as the most decorative. Other products were cranes of many sizes, fire hooks, tall and squatty kettles for use on the open hearth, dippers, Dutch ovens, and numerous and sundry implements for farm and forest. All too many of the latter have vanished.

"Fire dogs," as iron andirons were called in the section, were made for use in dining rooms and bedrooms, brass andirons serving for more formal rooms. These fire dogs are of various designs and are prized as collectors' items (*Fig. 1*). From about

FIG. 1 — FIRE DOGS WITH FLAME-SHAPE TOP. Found in furnace worker's cabin near Carlisle Furnace, Pennsylvania. *From the author's collection.*

FIG. 2 — TEN-PLATE STOVES. Right, marked *GEORGE EGE MOUNT HOLLY IRON WORKS*. Eagle decoration on top surrounded with 17 stars; on front a trumpeting figure. *From the Pennsylvania State Museum.* Below, marked *Peter Ege Pine Grove.* Finely cast with unusually delicate design. *From the Hamilton Historical Society, Carlisle.*

1790 for thirty or forty years, the ten-plate stove (*Fig. 2*) was popular and at its zenith carried the craftsman's decorative skill to new heights in iron. Even as late as twenty years ago, many of these stoves, which are still admirable for heating, were to be found, but virtually none are to be purchased now.

As early as 1748 tradition credits the erection of the first forge in the Cumberland Valley—at Mt. Holly Springs, without benefit of land warrant from the Proprietaries. But it was the erection in 1762 of the Carlisle Iron Works at Boiling Springs that drew many men of capital from eastern Pennsylvania, as the rich veins of manganese, magnetic, and iron ores lured them with evanescent visions of wealth. The furnace built there in the midst of dense forest growth had in its favor the interest of the Penn's secretary, the Reverend Richard Peters of Philadelphia, who in 1762 acquired title to the first 2,000 acres of virgin timber which abounded along the Valley's South Mountain.

From 1764 to 1768, the four Morris brothers, John Armstrong, and Robert Thornburg of Philadelphia, with Francis Sanderson of Carlisle, were owners of the plant; the two latter acted as managers. From this period three stove plates of a possible set of five for a jamb stove are known (*Fig. 5*). They are of the same size and design as in the Stiegel plates of the same decade, and show similar floral arrangements, darts, twisted columns, and so forth. They are also very like those made by the Stevenson Mary Ann Furnace in York County. The similarity of the stove plates turned out in all of these furnaces in the period supports the thesis of earlier iron historians that one designer was responsible for all of them. Ironworkers and ore miners were itinerants, and it is probable that designers traveled from furnace to furnace.

Of all the ironworkers of the region, perhaps the Eges were the most important. The saga of their family deserves its own chapter in the history of the Pennsylvania iron industry. In 1772, Michael Ege I, younger brother of George Ege of Berks County, who was the owner of Charming Forge, became one of the partners of the Carlisle Iron Works. He had first served under the tutelage of William Henry Stiegel and his brother George, and completed his apprenticeship at the Spring Forge, York County, now Spring Grove. There he married and thence he came to Boiling Springs.

By 1786 he had become sole owner of the Carlisle Iron Works. His skill, in large degree, was developed in his son, Michael Jr., to whom the works passed in 1815 when the elder Michael died. On the death of Michael Jr. in 1827 the plant began to decline; the estate passed to his minor son, Peter F. Ege, who lost the works in 1859.

The first Michael, however, increased his holdings, and in 1793 at sheriff's sale acquired a furnace at Mt. Holly Springs erected in 1785 by Stephen Foulk and Stephen Cox Jr. Another son of Michael's, George, inherited this plant at his father's death, but it did not continue long as an iron foundry, being later converted for papermaking.

During the Revolutionary War the forges at Boiling Springs and Mt. Holly were used to make cannon and other munitions by artificers who knew iron as skilled blacksmiths. Most prominent of these was William Denning, who is said to have made the first cannon in Pennsylvania at the Mt. Holly Forge, where, according to tradition, Denning melted the brass buttons of his uniform as he stood before the heat of the open forge. The last ironmaster at the Carlisle Iron Works of Boiling Springs, the late J. C. Bucher, found buried on the estate an old cannon barrel bearing the inscription *A. Carr fecit 1785,* perhaps the last of Revolutionary models *(Fig. 9)*.

FIG. 3 — HEARTH BACK WITH NAME CARLISLE. Lettering and proportion good. *From the Pennsylvania State Museum.*

In 1795 Michael Ege erected the Cumberland Furnace near Huntsdale which passed to his two daughters when his estate was settled. Its success was short-lived and the furnace was not rebuilt after 1854 when it was "blown out" in production.

But it was with his purchase of the Pine Grove Furnace that Michael Ege Sr. reached the height of wide authority and great wealth. By it he became sole possessor of four furnaces and two forges, and had undisputed rights to about twenty-five contiguous miles of mountain tracts of virgin timber and rich ore deposits.

The site of Pine Grove Furnace, when purchased from the Proprietaries in 1762, had been notable only for this rich timber acreage. Not even the astute ironmaster, George Stevenson, who owned the land for ten years, suspected its potentialities as a furnace site. In 1773 he sold the land to Jacob Simeon, with its "mills, dams, and races, buildings, etc.," who nine years later "improved land on the south side of the 150 acre tract whereon a furnace is now erected— by the name of Pine Grove Furnace and a mine hole sunk to supply said furnace." The purchasers of the furnace were Michael Ege and Joseph and Thomas Thornburg, who later sold a part of their interest to a resident manager, John Arthur, of Virginia.

Michael became sole owner of Pine Grove in 1803. His eldest son, Peter Ege, inherited it on the father's death in 1815, and in 1830 added Laurel Forge with six fires, a run-out, and trip hammer. Pine Grove iron of this period is of much beauty and the ten-plate stoves and decorative hearth pieces are the joy of collectors *(Figs. 6 and 10)*.

Reverses caused Peter Ege to lose Pine Grove in 1833. In 1844, following a few years of varied ownership, the furnace became the possession of William Watts, who owned

Photographs by M. W. Eddy.

FIG. 6 *(below)* — STOVE PLATE FROM PINE GROVE FURNACE. Graceful stork design. The products of this plant are today much in demand for their beauty. *From the Pennsylvania State Museum.*

FIG. 4 *(above)* — CARLISLE FURNACE STOVE PLATE. Not dated, but said by tradition to bear face of one of the Eges. *From the Bucher collection.*

FIG. 5 *(left)* — STOVE PLATE. One of three similar examples known. Dated *1764,* and marked *Carlisle Furnace* and *Thornbrug Ansland*; the latter names evidently designated Thornburg and Sanderson, owners of the plant. It is like one made by Stiegel, and also one at Stevenson and Thompson's Mary Ann Furnace. *From the Hamilton Historical Society.*

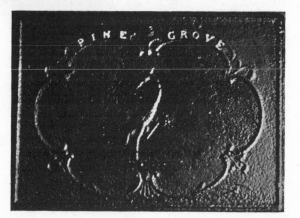

it for some twenty years with profit to himself and the community. In April 1864, Watts sold the 25,000 acres to William G. Moorehead for $225,000; in November of that year the new owner sold the plant for $1,500,000 to the South Mountain Iron Works, a stock company.

The last year of the Civil War gave the furnace its peak valuation. Following the depression of the 1870's, the property sold in 1877 for $100,000 with mortgage of $150,000. The last purchaser of the site was the State of Pennsylvania which bought the works in 1913 for $29,827.

In the old days the social life of any of these furnaces centered about the "Big House," home of the ironmaster. The lady of the Big House dispensed not only all the culture known at the works, but needed medicines and care as well. The Big House was the hospitable center for much visiting from friends, and the master and lady of the community usually found time to know intimately the sorrows or joys of the workers, who looked to them for both employment and ministrations. The Big House at Boiling Springs, built by Michael Ege Sr. about 1795, is a beautiful example of all such houses and is fortunate to have preserved many of its memories with the last mistress of the ironworks, Mrs. J. C. Bucher, who still occupies the home.

The house has a mahogany stairway, easy of ascent, with sweeping balustrades and deep well, some tiled fireplaces, and fine old woodwork of the period. Although twice remodeled, it looks the stately part of the Big House, standing

FIG. 7 — IRON UTENSILS. The handle of the dipper, dated *1762*, has an interesting heart-shape extension where it joins the bowl. The branding iron is marked *S.Fine*. Probably made in the Cumberland Valley. *From the Bucher collection, Boiling Springs, Pennsylvania.*

FIG. 8 (*above*) — IRON COOKING POTS. Probably made at one of the Cumberland Valley furnaces. *From the Hamilton Historical Society.*

FIG. 9 (*left*) — IRON CANNON BARREL. Dug up on the Carlisle Iron Company Estate, Boiling Springs. Marked *A. Carr fecit 1785*. From the Bucher collection.

FIG. 10 (*below*) — FIREPLACE INSET. Peter Ege Pine Grove. From the collection of Mr. and Mrs. John Capiello.

historian and student of social democracy.

Cumberland Valley iron items are still to be found in its environs, in isolated localities, and at country sales. Speedily added to collections are pots that once hung from cranes, fire dogs of sturdy construction and individualistic design, and varied utensils. Farmers have unearthed stove parts or fire backs that were once the adjuncts of a mansion house.

Because charcoal iron has its own soft beauty of finish, it will always be sought. Everything that went into its construction was honestly done. In each piece lives again the labor of the ore miner, the woodcutter, and the charcoal burner of the mountains, the furnace and forge man, teamster and bosch man of the settlement, craftsman, molder, and designer—each a symbol of America and her beginnings.

at the top of seven graded terraces high above the lake. A door from the service terrace leads directly into the ironmaster's study. This made the ironmaster easily accessible, without use of the "front door," to a man coming from ore mine or furnace in grimy clothes.

A similar Big House was built in Pine Grove in the 1790's for Peter Ege—perhaps when he married Jane Arthur, daughter of the one-time resident manager. Destroyed by a spark from a locomotive in the 1860's, it was rebuilt later along similar lines, but today under Pennsylvania state ownership is in dilapidated condition.

The furnace, too, is in ruins. But the old charcoal iron with its soft luster, the forge, the old bosch whose very angle of declivity was a closely guarded secret, the social structure of the community, the racial background of its workers, and the patriarchal position of the ironmaster, afford a study interesting not alone to the lover of antiques but also to the

American Firebacks and Stove Plates

By WALTER A. DYER

Note. The following article makes no pretense of being anything other than a reminder of the alluring aspects of early cast iron. The material, including the illustrations, will be found more amply and scientifically presented in the late Henry C. Mercer's invaluable monographs, *The Decorated Stove Plates of the Pennsylvania Germans* (*1899*) and *The Bible in Iron* (*1914*), both now out of print. Doctor Mercer's later volume includes an extended bibliography, to which, however, should now be added Charles S. Boyer's *Early Forges & Furnaces in New Jersey* (*Philadelphia, 1931*), a work affording several demonstrations of the distinguished designs in cast iron produced outside of Pennsylvania during the late 1700's and early 1800's. ANTIQUES believes that the art of cast iron, sadly neglected of late years, deserves to be revived. That event is, however, likely to be postponed until the discovery of some economical process by which the metal may be rendered rustless without impairment of its essential texture and native color. — *The Editor.*

AMONG the most interesting products of the early American ironworkers — and iron forging and casting constituted one of the earliest of our colonial crafts — are the flat plates, crudely cast in relief designs, which once served as firebacks and stove plates. Dating from the middle of the seventeenth century to the end of the eighteenth, these represent a distinct phase in the early development of American art industries. It is unfortunate that the names of the artists who created the designs have been lost, though the manufacturers are, in many cases, known. Despite their primitive character, these designs are often highly imaginative and not infrequently reveal a fine quality of artistic balance and decorative effect, as well as no little narrative ingenuity.

The making of these iron plates was a relatively simple process. The patterns were first carved in wood. They were then pressed into wet sand, which took the exact imprint of the wood model. Into the mold thus prepared molten iron was poured. When the metal cooled, the result was a cast-iron plate bearing precisely the design carved in the wood, albeit with some imperfections, and lacking the sharpness of modern casting. To this very roughness and softness of outline much of the charm of the old plates is due.

American iron manufacture dates back to the founding of the Massachusetts Bay Colony, three hundred years ago. About 1630, to repeat a fairly well-known bit of history, one Thomas Hudson of what is now Lynn, Massachusetts, discovered bog iron ore in a marsh near the ford of the Saugus River, a few miles north of Boston. Presently

Fig. 1 — PICKERING FIREBACK (*dated 1660*)
According to tradition, cast at Saugus, Massachusetts. Probably from an English pattern. The spindle decoration recalls applied ornament on wooden chests of the period. A similar fireback occurs in the collections of the Society for the Preservation of New England Antiquities, Boston

Fig. 2 — FIREBACK: THREE GRACES (?) (*dated 1697*)
A wainscot design. Doctor Mercer quotes authority for ascribing this fireback to Holland and for calling it *The Goddesses*, identifying them as Pallas, Juno, and Venus. Note that firebacks have pedimental tops, which distinguish them from contemporary stove plates.
Figures 1 and 2 from the Essex Institute, Salem

a furnace and foundry were erected by Joseph Jenks of Lynn. Charcoal was the fuel used, and, so far as is known, the first casting was an iron pot made in 1642. It was Jenks who, in 1652, is said to have cast the dies for the famous pine-tree shillings. A few years later, what is believed to be the first American fireback was, presumably, cast by Jenks at Saugus.

Late in the seventeenth century, bog ore was discovered in New Jersey and Pennsylvania. Still later, iron mines were worked. Forges, foundries, and furnaces were established in Pennsylvania, Maryland, New Jersey, and elsewhere. By the middle of the eighteenth century eastern Pennsylvania had become the centre of the iron industry.

It was in Pennsylvania that most of the early decorated stove plates were cast; but these were preceded in point of time by firebacks. The fireback, chimney back, or fire plate had been in common use in England, Holland, Flanders, France, and Germany since the fifteenth century. In America the original idea and the general form were at first derived from England rather than from the Continent, though the later plates found in Pennsylvania show distinct German and Dutch influence. Firebacks were in use in England up to the middle of the eighteenth century, and seventeenth-century examples are often quite elaborate, displaying armorial, pictorial, and conventional designs.

The roaring fires maintained in the fireplaces of early days were something of a menace. The mortar in which the surrounding stones or bricks were set was liable to crumble and permit the flames to work through. The iron fireback was employed to protect both brick and mortar. Usually a fairly thick, decorative piece of cast iron, it stood upright against the masonry at the back of the fireplace. Rarely it was flanked by side pieces.

Since the first firebacks cast in this country were apparently produced in New England, they followed English patterns, sometimes plain, but more often ornamented with coats of arms in relief, or floral and conventional motives. They were oblong in form, being somewhat taller than wide. The earlier examples usually had the top corners beveled; later ones are finished with a semicircular cresting with supporting devices quite Dutch in character. In many instances they resemble the gravestones of the period.

Most of the American firebacks now in existence were made after 1725; but a few seventeenth-century specimens, reputed to be of native production, may be seen in Massachusetts museums. One, in the old Pickering house at Salem, bears the initials P. I. A., and the date *1660*. It is supposed to have been made by Jenks at Saugus for

Fig. 3 — Fireback: Cavalier and Prisoners
Below the prancing steed, a band of roped prisoners, under escort. The allusion is probably inexplicable. Form suggests chair back of Regency period — even to the upholstery nails. Costume of about 1740. Probably a Continental European casting, second quarter of the eighteenth century. Doctor Mercer places it slightly later.
From the Essex Institute

John and Alice Pickering. Many of the American firebacks bore conventional designs, but some were pictorial in character.

While it is perhaps fair to assume that their casting was usually accomplished in this country, it does not necessarily follow that the more elaborate and skilfully composed designs were originated here, or that their carved wood patterns were locally executed. The similarity between many so-called American firebacks and known examples abroad is so close as to argue that not a few wood patterns were imported from abroad, or, perhaps, that direct recasts were made from imported cast-iron examples.

While firebacks from Pennsylvania are far rarer than stove plates, a number of the former survive. They are all eighteenth-century products. One venerable specimen, bearing the initials I.L. and the date *1728*, is believed to have been made at Durham Furnace for James Logan of Stenton, Pennsylvania. German influence is evident in the ornamentation of most of these Pennsylvania firebacks and of their near relatives, the stove plates.

With the introduction of the stove and the grate, after 1740, firebacks began to pass out of fashion, although they continued in some use throughout the century and were probably manufactured up to the time of the Revolution. One example, made in New York, bears the initials A.T. and the date *1767*.

Often confused with the fireback, but easily distinguished therefrom, is the stove plate. The stove plate is a slab of cast iron, about two feet square and half an inch or more thick. If decorated, it was once the side or end piece of a five-plate or six-plate stove such as came into use for heating and cooking in some sections of the country between 1740 and 1760. Of these stoves perhaps some little description is desirable in advance of any discussion of their plates.

The five-plate jamb stove, or wall-warmer, was a boxlike, wood-burning affair whose design was borrowed from European sources. Some American stoves of this type may have been made in New York and New Jersey, but the great majority of them must be ascribed to Pennsylvania. They were constructed of five rectangular cast-iron plates, clamped together, leaving one side, or end, open for the admission of fuel. This open portion might be connected with the fireplace in an adjoining room, whence the stove could be fed with hot embers

whose smoke would roll back into the common chimney. In some instances, the stove was thrust directly into a disused fireplace. In this position its front projected sufficiently to radiate a genial heat; but fueling the contraption from the rear must have been an awkward performance. The five-plate stove is described by Benjamin Franklin as "fixed so that you may put the Fuel into it from another Room or from the Outside of the House." Franklin used the term "German stove" to designate this device. The plates forming the front, sides, and occasionally the top, of five-plate stoves were usually ornamented in relief.

Obviously the five-plate stove presented

Fig. 4 — Fireback: The Highlander (?) (*dated 1767*)
Doctor Mercer pictures a clearer casting of this same design, in which he identifies the Falstaffian figure, somewhat unconvincingly, as a "Highlander." The style of ornament is earlier than the date. Hence the casting may have been done in New York from a wood pattern carved abroad.
From the Metropolitan Museum of Art

problems of installation and operation. Hence about the middle of the century, the six-plate stove was introduced. This apparatus was closed on all sides and was provided with a fuel door, a bottom draft, a smoke pipe, and, eventually, a small oven. Instead of being almost cubical, like the five-plate stove, the six-plate stove began to assume an oblong shape, its length being greater than its width, so that only the end plates were approximately square. When the oven opening intruded upon one of these plates, only one full-sized ornamental stove plate was used.

A typical six-plate stove of the later period consists of plates seven eighths of an inch thick, held together by long rods. It stands fairly high on cast-iron trestles. The box measures three feet long, two feet high, and a little over a foot wide. The whole contrivance weighs nearly five hundred pounds. A semicircular flat hearth extends below the fuel door and draft; the smoke hole occurs in the top near the front; and a small oven with a door appears at one side.

However, it is not the old stoves, themselves, that interest antiquaries and collectors, so much as the decorative plates of which they were constructed. Most of the original stoves have long since been broken up or have fallen apart; but their scattered individual plates have been resurrected from such strange places as drains, culverts, pigpens, chimney tops, and doorsteps. To the late Dr. Henry C. Mercer of Doylestown, Pennsylvania, is due the credit not only for pointing out the artistic merits of these old plates but also for discovering and preserving dozens of specimens, and for unearthing our present information about them. Most of Doctor Mercer's extensive collection has

Fig. 5 — Fireback: Adam and Eve (*dated 1770*)
Despite the flanged edges suggestive of a stove plate, Doctor Mercer believes this to be a fireback probably cast in America from a German original. He feels that the pattern was cut locally in wood; but there is a curious suggestion of plaster in the surfaces and in the scraped treatment of edges.
From the Essex Institute

Fig. 6 — Stove Plate: Cain and Abel (*dated 1741*)

Doctor Mercer ascribes the casting to the Durham Furnace in Bucks County, Pennsylvania. The face of the iron clearly reveals the ridges made by the boards constituting the original wood pattern. It is difficult to believe that a design so anciently traditional in character was prepared in this country, even by an imported craftsman. However, the casting is, no doubt, local.

From the Pennsylvania Museum of Art

Fig. 7 — Stove Plate: David and Jonathan

All the *N*'s of the inscription face in the wrong direction. This, with the crude cutting of the pattern, suggests a Pennsylvania German adaptation or copy of a foreign original. A careful comparative study might reveal the sources of some of these compositions in mediæval manuscript illustrations.

From the Pennsylvania Museum of Art

Abel, the Miracle at Cana, the Temptation of Joseph, Adam and Eve, the Woman of Samaria, the Tenth Commandment, the Golden Calf, the Death of Absalom, David and Goliath, Samson and the Lion, Samson and Delilah, David and Jonathan, Abraham and Isaac, the Flight into Egypt, the Pharisee and the Publican, Elijah Fed by the Ravens, and the Widow's Cruse of Oil.

As has been said, the plates not infrequently bear the name of the manufacturer or his furnace, or both, together with the date. Thomas Rutter, of the Colebrookdale Furnace, Berks County, appears to have been one of the leading iron-founders. Others were Daniel Udree of Oley in the same county; John Potts at the Warwick Furnace in Chester County; Henry William Stiegel at Elizabeth Furnace in Lancaster County; and Thomas Maybury at Hereford Furnace in Berks County. Other furnaces which may be mentioned were Coventry Furnace, Reading Furnace, Mary Ann Furnace, Carlisle Iron Works, and the prolific Durham Furnace.

been lodged in the Bucks County Historical Society Museum; but good plates may be found also in the Pennsylvania Museum of Art in Philadelphia, the Metropolitan Museum of Art in New York, the Essex Institute in Salem, and elsewhere.

As already remarked, the antiquary will find his chief interest in the ornamental designs on the old Pennsylvania plates. Cast in relief, in the same manner as the firebacks, they have the same softness of line due to time and the process of their making. For the most part they are fairly elaborate: crude but vigorous, quaintly primitive in type but imaginative and boldly handsome. Some are pictorial, presenting scriptural, legendary, symbolic, or mythological motives; some bear conventionalized patterns, in which the familiar tulip frequently recurs. Often the date of manufacture appears, sometimes the name of the maker or his furnace, and, not infrequently, a legend, motto, or scriptural quotation, usually in German.

Of the conventionalized patterns one of the most popular shows two round-arched panels, with a heart in one and a tulip in the other. Of the heart-and-tulip combination the variations are almost infinite. Another favorite was the tree of life, which was later borrowed for the jambs of the Franklin stove.

Pictorial subjects may be divided into Biblical and secular. The latter include St. George and the Dragon, the Dance of Death, the Wedding, the Wheel of Fortune, the Family Quarrel, the Wedding Dance, and the Prussian Grenadiers. A much larger number, however, are of Biblical import: such as Cain and

Probably the most famous of the Pennsylvania ironmasters of the latter half of the eighteenth century was "Baron" Stiegel, who made a fortune as an iron founder and went bankrupt in the attempt to make glass. Stiegel came to this country from Germany in 1750, and in 1752 married Elizabeth, daughter of one of the wealthiest ironmasters, Jacob Huber of Brickerville, Lancaster County. In 1757 Stiegel bought the

Fig. 8 — Stove Plate: St. George and the Dragon (*dated 1746*)

A pattern within the capability of a local wood carver, and, whatever its source of inspiration, representing Pennsylvania German workmanship.

From the Pennsylvania Museum of Art

Fig. 9 — Stove Plate: The Horseman (*dated 1756*)

Doctor Mercer discusses this design and its variants. Despite Renaissance reminiscences in the frame, doubtless, in all respects, a local Pennsylvania product.

From the Pennsylvania Museum of Art

property from his father-in-law and erected a new and larger works, which he called Elizabeth Furnace. Here he employed about seventy-five men. By 1760 he was one of the most prosperous ironmasters in Pennsylvania. He bought a half interest in Charming Forge in Berks County, thus swelling the army of his employees to nearly three hundred. In 1762 he erected his glasshouse at Manheim, and, though he continued his iron business, his primary interest shifted to the new industry. The story of his extravagant and flamboyant manner of living and his downfall is too familiar to need repetition.

Stiegel stove plates are rare, but a few have been preserved in private and museum collections. One bearing the date *1769* carries the words *H. W. Stiegel Elizabeth Furnace*, besides a portrait in a wreath, and Masonic emblems in the lower corners. The portrait is a classic profile in low relief and has been thought to represent either George III or some other historic or legendary personage. For the most part, however, Stiegel confined his designs to variations of the heart-and-tulip motive with the double arch, bearing his name and that of his furnace.

As the six-plate stove was developed and elaborated, acquiring oven and fuel doors and other appurtenances, and becoming somewhat smaller in size, it eventually acquired ten plates — the extra four constituting an interior oven. To quote Doctor Mercer: "The whole construction is that of the six-plate stove, with the exception that an internal rectangular oven is inserted in the stove box, over the fire, consisting of four thin cast iron plates, fitted with interior channels (and coinciding with the openings of the oven in both side plates), so made as to permit the heat of the fire to pass entirely around the oven and to leave the stove through the smoke pipe set in the front end of the top plate. The front plate is perforated with a fuel door below, and a small door for cleaning the soot above the oven. The bottom plate has the hearth extension, as in the six-plate stove, and the stove is bolted together generally with three, sometimes with five, vertical outside bolts, in the fashion of the older stoves. . . . This stove was not an American invention, but had long been known and used in Europe." Stoves of this kind continued in use for close to a century. They were, in fact, manufactured as late as 1840. American stoves usually had oven doors on both sides.

With the passing of the years, the ornamental designs of their cast plates became sharper, more mechanical and conventional — less imaginative and interesting. The oldest and crudest plates, from the five-plate stoves, are probably the most valuable; but the collector's interest is bound to centre more or less on the subject matter and treatment of the decorative design.

SOME EARLY ANDIRONS

By F. GORDON ROE

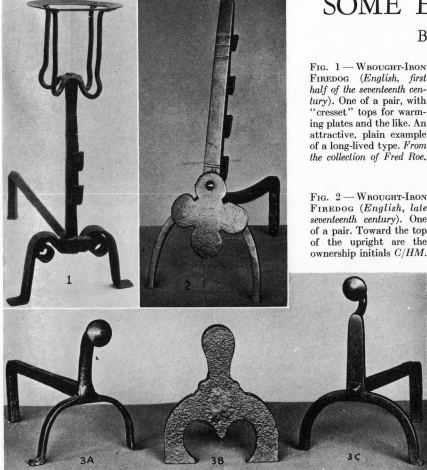

FIG. 1 — WROUGHT-IRON FIREDOG (*English, first half of the seventeenth century*). One of a pair, with "cresset" tops for warming plates and the like. An attractive, plain example of a long-lived type. *From the collection of Fred Roe.*

FIG. 2 — WROUGHT-IRON FIREDOG (*English, late seventeenth century*). One of a pair. Toward the top of the upright are the ownership initials *C/HM.*

FIG. 3 — ENGLISH ANDIRONS. *A* (*eighteenth century*) and *C* (*seventeenth century*), both of Sussex iron, are types frequently encountered. *C* is an unusually well-finished specimen, many others being coarsely fashioned. *B* inclines in character to the 1500's, though ascribed to the later 1600's. *Figures 2 and 3 from the Victoria and Albert Museum (G. Russell Davies bequest).*

not really eliminate the andiron. The terminal supports of dog-grates are nothing more than an adaptation of the firedog principle, used to raise a fire basket instead of directly supporting and retaining the fuel. Moreover, the fire-iron supports on many old-fashioned fenders are descendants of the andiron (see ANTIQUES, April 1939, p. 178).

While these derivatives replaced andirons to a certain extent, the latter remained in active service here and there in country places, bridging the gap till modern times brought about a revival. This revival was due to the growth of interest in antiquities, and to the recently renewed popularity of the hearth fire. Andirons have ever filled more than a purely functional capacity. Says Fuller's *Worthies* (1662): "The iron doggs bear the burthen of the fuel, while the brazen-andirons stand only for state" (*N.E.D.*). And from Prynne (1661) we have: "The little Creepers, not the great Brass shining Andirons, bear up all the wood, and heat of the fire" (*N.E.D.*). Thus a well-furnished hearth might have more than one pair of firedogs, fulfilling different purposes. Not, of course, that all "brazen-andirons" were merely for show. Many were certainly intended for use, and it may be noted that their horizontal fire bars, turned down as a foot at the rear, are always of iron.

Besides dogs of cast brass, or of silver, enameled metal, or, much later, of ormolu, many were fashioned in iron with brass ornaments. When my remote kinsman, Christopher Roe, made his will in 1650, he listed "one paire of Iron copirons with brasse." The terms firedogs and "copirons," or "cob-irons," though not always synonymous, were at this date virtually interchangeable; cob-irons seem to have become equivalent to *andirons furnished with spit hooks*. I assume, therefore, that Christopher Roe's "copirons" were what are sometimes called "spitdogs," of wrought iron with a finial or other adornment of brass.

The pair of iron dogs of which one is shown in Figure 1 demonstrates in a more than usually pleasing manner some noteworthy features characteristic of the first half of the 1600's. These dogs are equipped with hooks to support spits, and are crowned with cuplike devices capable of supporting plates or jugs of liquor to warm by the fire. Perhaps intentionally, the pendent loops of the cups are useful for hanging up things like ember tongs. Many "cupdogs," however, lack this droopy looping, their cups curving more smoothly to the standard. If not invariably present, these cups remained popular through much of the seventeenth century. I have heard of a pair of such dogs being made in the third quarter of the nineteenth century, not as pseudo-antiques but for actual country use, simply because the type was serviceable. They were, however, copies from an old pair.

Toward the end of the seventeenth century, many of the plainer dogs ceased to have any pronounced cresting. Spit hooks continued as a frequent feature, sometimes attached to the front of the standard, sometimes on the back (*Figs. 2, 5, 6*), sometimes movable (*Fig. 4C*). Many andirons never possessed this feature, and differentiation is carried to a fine point by distinguishing firedogs from spitdogs.

ANDIRONS, or firedogs, vary considerably in detail, but their basic construction, as well as their function, has remained essentially the same throughout the ages. When fashioned for use on a hearth in the center of a room, andirons consisted of a horizontal bar supported by an upright at each end. But for the wall fireplace, one standard was eliminated, and the horizontal bar was simply bent down at the end to form a foot.

One exception to this rule is an interesting pair of andirons, given by the late J. H. Fitzhenry to the Victoria and Albert Museum in London, which have no uprights whatever. They are cast, in iron, as couchant dogs, with heraldically elongated bodies. Dating from the 1500's, and of Flemish manufacture, they are literally "firedogs." A canine element rarely occurs in andiron design, and may have little to do with the origin of the term.

Some pre-Roman andirons of double-ended type, excavated in England, have uprights crested with representations of horned oxen heads, but do not differ essentially in construction from many andirons of vastly later date. Indeed, their arched bases are comparable with those of more recent specimens, such as Figures 4A and 4C.

From the Middle Ages on, andirons were plentifully employed In *Ville de Paris*, Sauval notes that the *chenets* (andirons) of the royal chambers were of wrought iron; four pairs were made for the queen's rooms in the Louvre, the smallest of which weighed forty-two pounds, and the heaviest one hundred and ninety-eight pounds (quoted in *Some Account of Domestic Architecture in England*, 1859). When the grate appeared, long afterward, it did

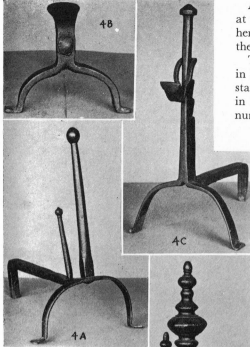

A type of andiron characteristic of the later seventeenth century had a disc decoration at the junction of upright, legs, and fire bar. Figure 2 is a nice example of this type, but here, instead of the more usual roundel or roundels, is a quatrefoil, wrought of iron, like the dog.

Though of the 1700's, Figure 5B allies itself to a type of scroll-topped andiron familiar in late gothic times. Many late seventeenth- and eighteenth-century firedogs have their standards curled over at the top, as in Figure 3A and C — types frequently encountered in England, and here represented in good Sussex iron. Both types were made in large numbers, and each has its charm, though the fact that the finial of Figure 3C is thrown forward on a C-scroll instead of a plain curve makes it somewhat the more decorative. Another variation is seen in Figure 4B, in which the curve is rearward.

The andiron of Figure 3B has been assigned to the late 1600's, though the form of the base has distinctly a sixteenth-century character. On the other hand, some simple types, such as Figure 3A, became traditional and continued to be made over a lengthy period.

The uncurved standard persisted, as in Figure 4A and C, and more elaborately as in Figures 5 and 6. While the dogs of Figure 6, which are of wrought iron with brass finials, give a bright and attractive effect, my preference is for the bolder lines of Figure 5A, which is of cast iron. Note that the lower part of its baluster has a distinct affinity with candlestick design of the second half of the seventeenth century (see Figure 4, page 315, ANTIQUES, June 1938).

Whether as hearth ornament or grate support, a form of firedog with boldly molded members, much heavier than Figure 5A but not unrelated to it, was made till a late date. Other late andirons exhibit a revival of Jacobean motifs. Many examples, of cast iron, tell their period clearly; but we are reaching a time when free copies or actual reproductions of the antique were making an appearance. I have seen very good examples of later renaissance types in brass, fashioned without the slightest idea of deception, in the second half of the nineteenth century. It must never be forgotten that reproduction is not a completely new craft.

Those bent on making their finds "in the rough" — picking up their andirons from the hearth — should not jump to the conclusion that the date of a fireplace is necessarily that of its hearth furniture, or *vice versa*. The effect may be venerable, but the dates may vary a lot either way.

FIG. 4 (*above*) — ENGLISH ANDIRONS (*eighteenth century*). Representing various types. *A* and *B* of Sussex iron. *C* has a movable spit hook. *From the Victoria and Albert Museum (A and B, G. Russell Davies bequest; C, formerly in the F. A. Crisp collection).*

FIG. 5 — ENGLISH ANDIRONS (*eighteenth century*). *A*, cast-iron, from first half of the century; note robust form, and similarity of baluster to contemporary candlestick design. *B* has spit hooks at back. *From the Victoria and Albert Museum (A, formerly in the Shoppee collection; B, G. Russell Davies bequest).*

FIG. 7 (*below*) — ANDIRONS FROM VARIOUS SOURCES (*mainly of late seventeenth and eighteenth centuries*). *A* and *C*, of brass and iron; *B*, iron with brass knob; *D* (French), ormolu and bronze; *E*, gunmetal and iron; *F*, iron; *G*, iron with gunmetal finial. *From Pratt & Stair.*

FIG. 6 — WROUGHT-IRON FIREDOG WITH BRASS FINIAL (*English, eighteenth century*). One of a pair. Compare with Figure 5A. *From the Victoria and Albert Museum.*

BY GEORGE H. KERNODLE AND THOMAS M. PITKIN

The Whittinghams:

brassfounders of New York

Andirons with engraved scenes on the plinths, marked R. WITTINGHAM / N.YORK. *Ginsburg and Levy.*

IN ENGLAND DURING THE EIGHTEENTH CENTURY, with coal rapidly replacing wood as fuel, brass-fronted coal grates became the most important item of fireplace gear; but in this country andirons continued to be the dominant item. Certainly as early as the last quarter of that century a separate type of andiron had come into being here, and there is seldom any question of its nationality. Regardless of the maker, American andirons can usually be recognized by characteristics as distinctive as those that identify New England blockfront chests, Philadelphia lowboys, and Baltimore Hepplewhite furniture.

Along with John Clark, James Davis, and Paul Revere (all of Boston), and some others (including at least one Philadelphia maker), Richard Whittingham of New York and his sons belonged to a group of artist-craftsmen who set the style for fine American andirons in the early Federal period. Brass andirons imprinted with the mark *R. Wittingham / N.York* are highly regarded by collectors to whom quality and good taste mean something more than the satisfaction of owning "signed" pieces. There is no question that the name of the maker was

Richard Whittingham—father or son—but there is some doubt as to whether both men used the mark, and there is very little information about their business activities.

Both Whittinghams were of English birth. The father was born in 1747 or 1748, and became a brassfounder at Birmingham, the great English center of the craft. He migrated to the United States with his wife, four sons, and two daughters, landing in Philadelphia on September 22, 1791. Soon after his arrival he became a citizen, but his son Richard, then fifteen years old, preferred to remain a British subject, with all the restrictions that involved, until he was an old man.

A promising offer of employment was made to Whittingham shortly after he reached America. He was among the craftsmen (mostly English immigrants) recruited to take part in The Society for Establishing Useful Manufactures, a project in which Secretary of the Treasury Alexander Hamilton was actively interested. The society, which was incorporated in New Jersey, is noteworthy as a pioneer industrial corporation, but its manufacturing ventures were unsuccessful; operations at

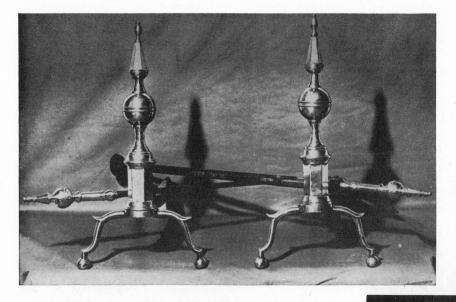

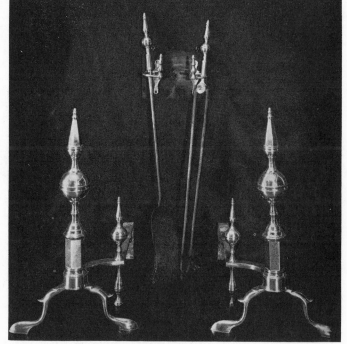

Firesets with marked andirons. Left, marked R. WITTINGHAM / N.YORK. *Mrs. Lawrence J. Ullman.* Below, marked J. DAVIS / BOSTON. *Collection of Edward M. Bostick.* An interesting example of design copying. The legs of the Whittingham andirons would suggest that maker even if there were no marks, and each edge of the center band on the finials is beaded, while that detail on the Davis 'irons has no beading. The log-rests of this pair (square in cross-section) also differ from those of the Davis andirons, which are broad and flat with movable lugs—a New England detail. Some of the other features, most noticeably the spikes of the finials, are almost identical and not in the Whittingham manner.

its Passaic Falls site were discontinued in 1796, and even in the early part of 1795 craftsmen were beginning to leave the unfinished mills where textile and hat manufactures had been planned. Whittingham is mentioned in the society's records as a poor but "very usefull and deserving mechanic" who asked for relief on account of debts owed to him for making machinery; he was to be paid off in "such part of the Machinery" as was "not of importance to the Society."

Whittingham then settled in New York. He first appeared in the *New York Directory* in 1795 as "Richard Whittingham, brassfounder," on Henry Street. He evidently depended for success on this listing in the *Directory* and on his growing reputation, for no advertising has been found in contemporary newspapers. Described in a brief biographical sketch as "no mere artisan, but a man of reading and extended information," he soon gained recognition in his field.

Under the British mercantilist system such copper ore as was mined in the Colonies was usually sent to England for refining, and coppersmiths and brassfounders had to depend for raw material on the expensive imported rolled copper or on alloys from broken bells, old cannon, and other discards. This accounts for the scarcity of colonial brass artifacts, and probably explains our high percentage of early iron andirons with brass finials —here brass could be used sparingly but effectively. It also suggsts that articles made of bell-metal (a reddish alloy of copper and tin) in this period are likely to be American. After the Revolution sheet copper became increasingly important. The sheathing of ships with it was an established practice, and the same material was used for stills and various household utensils. Scrap copper was combined with zinc, in a recently-developed process, to make brass. Until about 1800 brass was usually worked by casting, although rolled brass had been developed in England and was coming into use here. British mills continued as the source of most new sheet copper until Paul Revere and his son built the first American rolling mill at Canton, Massachusetts, in 1801.

Eager to make the most of their pioneering venture, the Reveres petitioned Congress in 1807 for a duty of seven and a half per cent on imports, and in this matter the paths of Whittingham and Revere crossed. In a rare instance of concerted action "the copper smiths and braziers of New York and Philadelphia" joined to file protests, or "memorials," against the petition, and that of

the New York group was signed "Richard Whittingham and others." After consideration by a Congressional committee the Revere petition was denied, and copper remained on the free list.

As Whittingham's sons grew up they became associated with the foundry, and most of them later set up their own shops. Isaac was listed in the *New York Directory* as a brassfounder as early as 1800, and Joseph, Charles, and Benjamin appeared as independent craftsmen in the period 1825-1835. Richard Whittingham, Jr., was first listed in 1810. By 1818 he had evidently taken over his father's business, for in that year he was listed as a brassfounder at his father's last foundry address, 95 Henry Street, and the elder Whittingham was listed as without occupation. A patent-medicine testimonial signed by the elder Whittingham that appeared in the New York *Commercial Advertiser* in 1819 indicated that he had been in poor health for some years; and on September 13, 1821, soon after returning from a visit to his old home in England, the father died.

The younger Richard Whittingham is described as a conscientious man, quiet and reticent. "While thoroughly

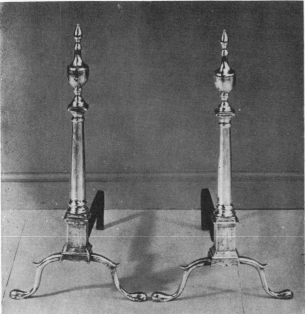

Marked R. WITTINGHAM / N.YORK. *Mrs. Lawrence J. Ullman.*

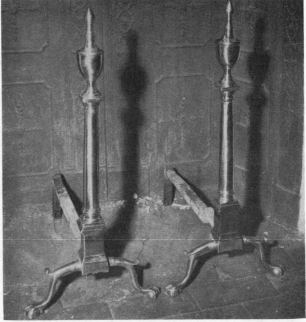

Unmarked. *Robert E. Lee Foundation.*

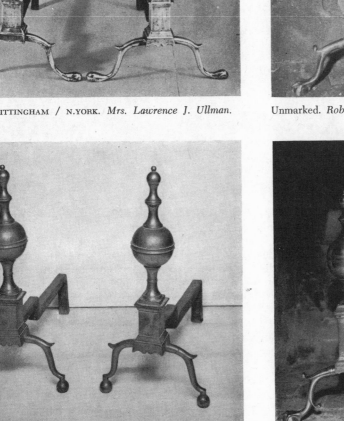

Marked R. WITTINGHAM / N.YORK. *Joe Kindig, Jr.*

Unmarked. *Collection of Mr. and Mrs. Andrew Parker.*

Comparison of the unmarked examples on the right of this group with their marked prototypes on the left strongly suggests an attribution of "Whittingham type" for the unmarked 'irons.

informed with regard to all that concerned his business," his son's biographer states, "his chief interests were outside of it." He was deeply religious, an ardent collector of books, and a material contributor to the library of the General Theological Seminary. According to the records of Trinity Church Parish he was married on January 4, 1805, to Mary Ann Rollinson, daughter of the engraver William Rollinson. Rollinson, whose stipple engraving of Alexander Hamilton executed in 1805 is one of the most important American historical portraits, had come to New York from Birmingham in 1789. It is of course purely conjecture to suggest that he may have executed the engraved landscapes and commemorative scenes which are uncommon, if not unique, features of some Whittingham andirons.

Some of the brassfounders copied from each other, and many unidentified makers copied single details from those who marked their wares. These practices make it difficult to attribute unmarked 'irons to a particular maker; but there are details characteristic of most marked Whittingham andirons, and when unmarked 'irons combine two or more such elements they may be conditionally accepted as of "Whittingham type." Well-formed sturdy legs with short spurs and large ball feet are such features, and they may have originated at the Whittingham foundry. Another typical element (though not invariably found) is the large ball with a broad concave center band beaded along both edges, supporting a contoured finial. The squared plinth base is valanced like a simple cupid's bow along its lower front edge. These elements, in combination with square plinths treated in the distinctive Whittingham manner, characterize 'irons which may be accepted as of "Whittingham type" whether they are stamped or not. With less certainty,

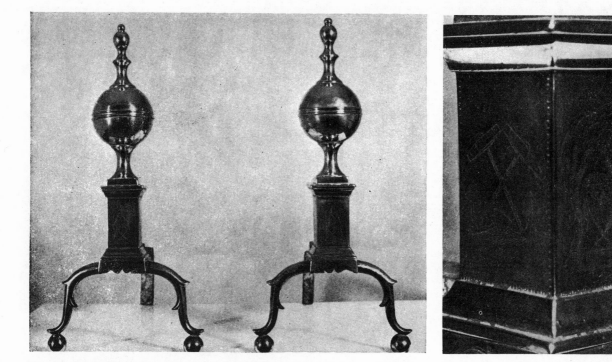

Unusual engraved pair of marked Whittingham andirons with distinctive Whittingham features. *Collection of Mr. and Mrs. T. M. Williams.*

some unmarked andirons with round or hexagonal plinths and with finials and feet in the Whittingham manner may be conditionally given such an attribution.

It seems certain that the Whittinghams made fireplace equipment other than andirons, and perhaps a wide variety of brass goods which may have included lighting devices. Some of the larger articles may bear marks, so obscure as to be discovered only by careful examination. American fire tools of that time came in pairs (shovel and tongs), and even single items marked by any maker are extremely rare. Marked Whittingham fire tools are hardly to be expected but would be interesting finds.

The *Digest of Manufactures* (1823) lists eight firms in New York County using brass in various products, including one making "Iron and brass goods of all kinds" and using "a machine for cutting open work for brass fenders." Sheet-brass fenders dating from about 1820, with punched-out designs, are generally suspected of being English, but here is evidence that fenders of that type and time were being made in this country also. The "machine" is not identified with the Whittingham foundry, but since we know that the elder Whittingham had built machinery it is possible that his foundry was a source of these late fenders—machine-pierced, with straight fronts and rounded corners.

As with objects produced by craftsmen in several other fields, fine American andirons reached a peak of artistry about 1800, lingered briefly there and, gradually shorn of ornament, started the slow descent toward the strictly functional. Later pairs of unmarked 'irons with only one Whittingham characteristic are plentiful; but it may never be possible to classify them beyond the surmise that they were made by some member of the Whittingham clan.

Careful cleaning, close scrutiny, and tedious comparison of related details will be necessary if anything is to be done to classify old fireplace equipment. Trial attribution based on related techniques has gone far toward identifying American antiques in many categories. Some such system based on individual and regional characteristics may be useful in classifying unmarked American andirons.

Andirons marked R. WITTINGHAM / N.YORK., with round plinths unusual in the work of this maker. *Colonial Williamsburg, Inc.*

OLD METAL FENDERS

By F. GORDON ROE

FOR practical purposes, the history of unattached fenders for the fireplace begins in the second half of the seventeenth century. For previous ages, hearths had no such protection. They might be raised above the floor or flush with it; they might even be enclosed by some sort of built-in curb; but the conception of a movable fender was slow in fruition. Firedogs generally sufficed to keep burning logs in place, especially when the ash was carefully banked; but though coal was in use long before independent fenders were thought of, that gaseous fuel was partly responsible for their invention. It does not follow that all early movable fenders were used for coal fires, though they were to become more closely associated with coal than with any other fuel. But whoever first burned coal in a "cradle" raised from the hearth unwittingly did something to prepare the way at long last for the fender. The higher the grate, the more risk there is of hot cinders shooting out into the room. For this reason the fender was developed from a strip of metal to the more familiar three-sided retainer. Yet fire baskets or grates, in one form or another, survive from periods well before fenders were known.

Perhaps the Great Fire of London in 1666 had some effect in preparing the public for fenders, but the first use of "fender" (in this sense of the word) noted in the *New English Dictionary* is as late as 1688 (*Fig. 1*). MacIver Percival found references to fenders in an auction catalogue of 1703 (*Old English Furniture and its Surroundings, 1920, pp. 69–70*). In 1710, as the *N. E. D.* reminds us, Dean Swift alludes to "a mouse within the fender to warm himself." As the eighteenth century progressed, fenders were made in increasing numbers, though it is difficult to find examples of earlier date than about 1730–1740.

An early form of fender is without ends, merely stripped across the base of the fireplace opening (*Fig. 2*). This type should be carefully noted, as inexperienced observers may make the mistake of dismissing such pieces as defective. However, as strip fenders continued to be made throughout the eighteenth century, the type is not necessarily indicative of early date. Ornament and general style must be taken into account. Later eighteenth-century strip fenders are often bow-fronted or otherwise shaped, representing an intermediate type between the straight strip and the three-sided fender. But as the latter had at that period already made its appearance, we must beware of a too superficial system of classification.

Note, as to fenders with ends: not until a late period was the projection more than quite shallow. The fender stood well *within* the forward spread of the hearthstone, and laterally covered scarcely more than the actual fireplace opening. Deep movable fenders or curbs, with a spread sufficient to inclose the three sides of the hearth, are comparatively modern.

During the eighteenth century, steel or brass were the usual metals for fenders. Others occur, not excepting iron, but not until the next epoch did the iron fender really come into its own. Decorative motives coincide with contemporary taste; piercing and engraving are freely employed. Designs are elegant, especially in earlier examples. Disklike feet are sometimes attached to the outside of the fender to prevent it from pitching forward: a feature not always found, but traceable through various types up to modern times. Straight feet *inside* "floorless" fenders also occur (*Fig. 3, b*). Some examples have a narrow "floor" on the inside to keep them erect (*Fig. 2*).

The lightness and grace that characterized the best eighteenth-

FIG. 1—DETAIL OF BRASS FENDER OF THE EARLY TYPE
(*English, second half of seventeenth century*)

A finely ornamented example, in the Miniature Room at Ham House, Surrey — Ham, where Lady Lauderdale's ghost has been said to walk and scratch at the paneling.
Photograph by courtesy of the Victoria and Albert Museum

FIG. 2 — ENGLISH "STRIP" FENDERS (*eighteenth century*)
Pierced and engraved. *a*, brass, showing Adam influence. *b*, steel, perpetuating an earlier type. This example has a narrow "floor" within it to keep it erect.
From the Victoria and Albert Museum

FIG. 3 — ENGLISH "STRIP" FENDERS (*second half of eighteenth century*)
An early form of fender, without ends. *a*, steel, pierced and engraved in contemporary decorative motives. *b*, brass, c. 1730. Pierced and engraved in characteristic leaf scrolling and exotic birds. Note disklike feet for holding fender upright; straight feet are likewise attached to the back.
From the Victoria and Albert Museum

century work are apparent in the piercing and engraving of steel fenders of the period (*Figs. 2 and 3*). Classical urns and griffons in contemporary examples show Adam influence. But piercing does not stop with such conventional devices: figures, such as Neptune in his chariot, may be encountered. Infinitely varied in ornamental details, eighteenth-century fenders reflect the elegant taste of the period (*Fig. 4*).

Yet the early nineteenth century produced fenders that one might be proud to possess. The conscious classicism of the Empire expressed itself in certain modish examples, elaborately designed and executed in a faultless technique. Mixed materials might be employed, the mingling of, say, blackened metal, bright steel, and *ormolu* creating a rich effect. Ordinary steel or brass fenders continued to be freely made in designs showing, at first, a direct continuity from later eighteenth-century types. Perforated sheet-iron fenders appeared, usually painted green. One comfortably solid type, common in brass or steel in the earlier part of the nineteenth century, is here represented, for variety's sake, in a famous etching by George Cruikshank for Dickens' *Oliver Twist* (*Fig. 6*). Mrs. Corney's parlor, as portrayed, was distinctly of the lower-middle-class sort, and some of her furniture was quite old-fashioned, but her fender was of a type popular enough, if not necessarily new.

One scarcely associates the fender shown in Figure 5 with the fashionable world. In my young days, a plainer version, part bright steel, stood before most kitchen ranges, though I suppose that more modern methods of cooking have now largely ousted it. Presumably the fender dates from the early nineteenth century. The top is boxed with pierced metalwork for the dual purpose of retaining cinders and serving as a trivet. The circular foot in front is a common characteristic of the type. Though perfectly illustrating all salient features, Figure 5 is photographed from a brass toy less than eight inches long.

Steel and brass fenders continued, but by the middle of the nineteenth century the cast-iron variety had become firmly established. I illustrate this period freely. So many fenders of the time have come down to us that it is well to establish a basis for judging them. Few Victorian fenders of this sort "mix" with any period but their own, but they take their place effectively in an appropriate setting.

For clarity, I have selected examples from a manufacturer's

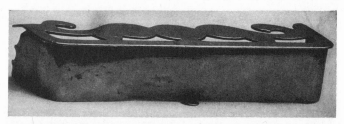

FIG. 5 — TOY FENDER OF BRASS (*early nineteenth century*)
Though slightly less than 8 inches long, perfectly illustrates a type of kitchen fender. Full-size examples often occur in steel. Top is boxed with pierced metal. Note circular foot. *From the author's collection*

FIG. 6 — "MR. BUMBLE AND MRS. CORNEY TAKING TEA"
Illustration by George Cruikshank for *Oliver Twist*, reproduced from the first (separate) edition of the novel (*1838*); originally appeared in *Bentley's Miscellany* for February 1838; plate later reworked and considerably darkened. Shows Bumble the Beadle taking tea with Mrs. Corney, matron of the workhouse where Oliver was born. Note the brass fender, a lowly but popular type of the early nineteenth century

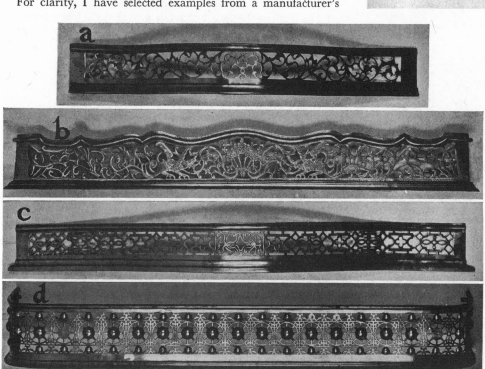

FIG. 4 — ENGLISH STEEL FENDERS (*eighteenth century*)
Showing variety in form and decoration. Brass examples of similar type occur in equally varied styles, illustrative of the elegant taste of the eighteenth century. Compare the elaborately interwoven design of *b* with the restrained geometric patterns of *c* and *d*.
From the Pratt & Stair collection

pattern book in the Victoria and Albert Museum. Many of the plates are signed by W. Kilner of Sheffield, who flourished about 1850. These designs were carried out in iron, but similar examples are found in other materials. Let us call one prevalent type the "rod"; its dominant feature is one or more circular-sectioned bars with a finial at each end, rather like old-fashioned curtain poles (*Fig. 7*). Other designs illustrated speak for themselves; but note in Figure 7 how Victorian designers utilized Gothic motives and emulated the *chinoiseries* of the previous century.

Two examples shown in Figure 7 offer special provision for accommodating fire irons. Fire-iron rests were known much earlier, when they sometimes surmounted the fronts of fenders, indicating a different disposition of the hearth implements. But fire-iron standards in the returns of fenders, whether incorporated or detached, may be classed as descendants of the old firedogs.

Many fenders were shown at the Great Exhibition of 1851, and two or three are illustrated in the official catalogue. Hoole, Robson and Hoole, of Sheffield, displayed "Burnished steel fenders, with metal and or-molu mountings. Bronzed fender, with steel mountings. Dead or sprung steel fenders, with stamped burnished steel ornaments. Bronzed, black, and cast-iron fenders" (*Catalogue*, Vol. II, *p. 609*). Among other exhibitors of fenders were the celebrated Coalbrook Dale Company (examples in steel, bronze, and *ormolu*); Robertson, Carr and Steel, Sheffield, (brass, "some with burnished steel"); Mapplebeck and Low, Birmingham; Yates, Haywood and Co., Rotherham, Yorkshire, and London, who combined "the appliances of science . . . and the palatial character of the middle ages"; and the following with London addresses: William Pierce; William Samuel Burton ("Registered ornamental fenders"); Featham, Miller and Sayer; Tupper and Carr ("Galvanized fenders") (*Figs. 9 and 10*).

Wire fenders invite special discussion. In the United States, such fenders have been claimed as exclusively American, at least in origin. In one of the last letters I received from the late Homer Eaton Keyes, former Editor of Antiques, he asked my opinion in this matter. Mr. Keyes, whose knowledge of American antiques was vast, had "no question that such screens were made in the late 1700's and early 1800's in this country, but of course a great many fenders were imported from abroad" — as indeed they still are.

Now, here is a problem that needs careful handling. As a *terminus a quo*, Mr. Keyes' dating is a fair enough approximation of origin. Most old types I have examined hark back in design to that period, though examples may be actually of later construction. But this question of nationality is more difficult. Particular types of wire fender may be specifically American; but wire fenders have been well known in England for some time. Much older folk

FIG. 7 — FENDER DESIGNS (*c. 1850–1860*)
From the pattern book of an English ironfounder. *a and b*, supplied in sizes from 3 feet 10 inches to 5 feet, plate signed by the engraver, *W. Kilner, Eng. Sheff c*, pseudo-Elizabethan, doubtless popular at time of Shakespeare tercentenary, 1864, and earlier; *sizes*, 3 feet 10 inches to 6 feet. *d*, reflecting gothic revival. *e*, in Victorian *chinoiserie*. *f*, the sofalike ends and (*g*) the curved rests at each end, provide accommodation for fire irons. *h*, low and relatively unadorned. *i*, of medium height, elaborately scrolled; *sizes*, 4 feet to 5 feet 6 inches. *j*, high, architectural in character, forming a close-woven barrier between fire and room; *sizes*, 2 feet to 4 feet 8 inches.
From the Victoria and Albert Museum

than I can remember them as commonplaces of their youth; but I need not leave it at that. Writing of later Georgian fenders in England, MacIver Percival mentions those of "iron wire with a brass rail" (*op. cit., p. 150*).

There seems to be a virtual relationship between these wire devices and the ordinary metal fenders with vertical slits which were common in England from the latter part of the eighteenth century. But wire for fireplace use was also known. When Mrs. Philip Lybbe Powys visited Buckingham House — later Buckingham Palace — in 1767, she remarked "in every chimney a lacquered wire fire-board," which passed heat without sparks and was "really ornamental" (H. Clifford Smith: *Buckingham Palace, 1931, p. 87*). From such fireboards, wire fenders could easily develop. A pair of fenders in the Soane Museum, though not of wire, shows kinship with wire fenders. The items have brass tops and bases, but the intervening space is filled with diamond-patterned trellis, cast in what looks like bronze. They probably date from about 1825–1830. In the breakfast parlor of the Soane Museum remain a true wire fender of the short kind, and a wire fire screen of similar type, the latter hooking to the grate. The fender has a steel top rail and base, though the base is raised on

FIG. 8 — ENGLISH FIRE GUARDS

a, wire fender of simple mesh; more or less modern, but of traditional type. *Height*, 12 ¼ inches. *b*, wire guard (*nineteenth century*). Straight strands with swags at top. *Height*, 24 inches. *c*, steel guard (*1870's*). This guard, made for nursery purposes, never had wire filling. *Height*, 28 ½ inches. *From the author's collection*

FIG. 9 — "PIERCE'S CHASED OR-MOLU FENDER" (*c. 1850–1860*)

Enameled cast-iron fender, "in the enriched style of the period," as the manufacturer, William Pierce of London, described it in the official catalogue of the Great Exhibition of 1851 (*Vol. II, p. 605*)

brass knob feet. The screen has brass top and base rails. In both cases, the wire filling is of vertical strands, curved to archlike intersection at the top, doubtless inspired by the Gothic revival. Another type I have observed has vertical strands, uncurved, but perhaps relieved with a slight frieze of wire scallops, suggesting severely simplified Adam swags (*Fig. 8, b*). Wire mesh is also found, though, in my experience, mainly in later or modern examples. Wire-mesh fenders are still being produced (*Fig. 8, a*). Structurally, most wire fenders and guards conform to type. The frame is often of iron and the top rail of brass, or covered in ribbon brass. The base may be floored with sheet iron, usually flat but sometimes shelving in the center toward the fireplace.

Wire fenders were, and perhaps are, made in two heights, short and tall. Some are difficult to date with precision. Types became traditional, but the Soane examples were presumably bought between 1812 and 1837, and are useful items to remember. Figure 8, *c*, known in England as a "fire guard," has served in at least two generations of nurseries. Incidentally, I note that Thomas Henry Fox, 44 Skinner Street, London, showed "Brass wire hangings, fire guards," at the 1851 Exhibition (*Catalogue*, Vol. II, *p. 597*).

Reproductions of eighteenth-century fenders in steel or brass have been made for some time, and built-up pieces are not unknown. Some of the older reproductions are puzzling, and may be recognized only by the trained and observant eye. There is really no satisfactory way of explaining in print how such pieces may be detected. One must learn the look of them, and that can be done only by experience. But good old fenders are to be found and deserve to be sought. No modern invention has yet succeeded in ousting these hearthside furnishings from human affection.

FIG. 10 — "BURTON'S NAUTILUS REGISTER-STOVE" (*c. 1850–1860*)

With "fender and chimney piece for the same." The proud product of William Samuel Burton, "Inventor and Manufacturer" of 39 Oxford Street, London. Shown at the Great Exhibition of 1851 in London, and illustrated in the official catalogue (*Vol. II, p. 620*)

Note. I wish to express special thanks to the Director of the Victoria and Albert Museum for permission to illustrate a number of items in that institution; likewise to Messrs. Pratt and Stair, and to C. Reginald Grundy. *F. G. R.*

The Franklin Stove

By W. W. KENT

TRAVEL is full of surprises. To ride all of a gray day in a slow train through evergreen forests relieved by rocky meadows, giving now and then glimpses of seaboard towns backed with blue water, bobbing dorys, and picturesque lobster pots piled on the edge of sandy beaches, and to arrive at night at an inn, is, to be sure, not particularly surprising. When, however, on such an October jaunt as this through Nova Scotia, it was discovered that the inn, though in a small village, was well kept by a competent, kindly host; that its office, with low ceiling and open-wood fire, had an old-time air of English hospitality and peaceful cheer, belated and chilled travellers were, at least, pleased. And some of them, observing that the fire was burning in an unusually handsome Franklin stove, resplendently ornamented with acanthus leaves, gleaming brass discs and polished rail (Fig. 1), indeed, began to be surprised. Moreover, this inn possessed two Franklin stoves, the second presiding over a cosy parlor just above the office, and, unlike most wayside inn parlors, no sooner did any one take a seat within it, than a maid came and lighted a fire, if one were not already

Fig. 1 — FRANKLIN STOVE (*early nineteenth century*)
Observe the finely patterned brass rail across the top and the well turned finials. *Courtesy, Mrs. Manning.*

blazing. This fire too, was built always of scrub pine and smelt of the North. (Fig. 2.) This second open stove bore on its front the name of the makers, forgotten long ago, in Philadelphia, and he who runs close enough may read it any day in the Lovett House parlor.

Encounter with these two pieces brought again to mind some questions: Why have most states of our Union lost their Franklin stoves? Why do we generally design, in their stead, a hole in a brick or stone chimney breast? Why have the old open stoves persisted in many parts of Nova Scotia and Canada? Finally, were our ancestors in the States indebted to Franklin alone for the delightful innovation of ornamental, cast iron, open stoves and their cheerful atmosphere, or is the obligation to be divided?

Fig. 2 — FRANKLIN STOVE (*early nineteenth century*)
This and previous illustration from the Lovett House, Chester, N. S. *Courtesy, Mrs. Manning.*

By some persons most of these questions can be answered as soon as asked; but the last one required of me some research. In so far as I can determine from browsing on the verbiage of earlier writers, Benjamin Franklin had to do with the so-called Franklin stove to the following extent. In 1678, according to Shuffrey's delightful book, *The English Fireplace*, a new form of fireplace was built in England for Prince Rupert. The Prince evidently felt the coal pinch, as we do today, and saw that too much smoke and heat went rapidly up the old perpendicular flue. So a bricklayer, named Bingham, devised a better fireplace. It was made, with a view to consuming more of the smoke and retaining longer the heat, by hanging a baffle-plate, hinged at the junction of its upper and lower halves, in the flue in the rear of and above the grate. When the upper half was pulled forward, the smoke and heat passed down the flue under the baffle-plate and up the flue behind it. When the upper half was swung back, the smoke and heat went through the opening so made, and, as usual, directly up the flue. This device evidently seemed to Mr. Bingham, and probably to the Prince and others, to retain the heat longer in the fireplace and to consume more smoke when the top of the plate was pulled forward, as was done after the fire had begun to burn well.

In 1711 two Frenchmen, Nicolas Gauger and DuBois, an architect, designed a fireplace with a *soufflet* or blower in the hearth, which, when open, increased the draft by taking in air under the hot iron bottom of the fireplace. Their model also included a caliduct, or zig-zag square sectioned iron pipe, which took in fresh air from outside and passed it around stationary baffle-plates set in different levels of the caliduct, as it traversed the back of the fireplace, and finally discharged the heated air into the room.

These two improved fireplaces must have been known to Franklin, as will be seen by referring to any drawing of his model, which shows that he combined the two ideas in his newer "Pennsylvania Stove" in 1742. This was an open stove of cast iron, intended to save fuel and to increase the warming of rooms. Wood was its fuel, but its improvement over the earlier stoves lay in the fact that the heat of the fire reached both front and back of the fresh-air caliduct by passing through the flue, which was built down to the hearth level behind the caliduct and then was turned and built perpendicularly up. Franklin also made a flue-cleaning door, or vent, above the fire in the soffit of the fireplace opening, but did not show how to clean out the turn or bottom of the flue at the fireplace level,—which seems a defect that could be overcome by some one today.

Figs 3, 4 — PATTERNS FOR FRANKLIN STOVES OR GRATES (*1790-1810*)
Carved white pine patterns for Franklin stove castings. Of very thin wood, carved and glued to templates on the back. *The Author*.

Franklin did not have his stove made for sale by, or for, himself; nor did he patent it, perhaps because he realized how the earlier principles of the Frenchmen were embodied in it. But he gave the model to Robert Grace, a friend, who cast and sold the stove or its parts. The idea was pirated in England by an ironmonger (J. Durno, Schuffrey thinks probable), who altered it by making the air chamber of brick and by placing a register in the only cast iron part retained, so that the heat could be controlled from the room. Durno also adapted it, for the English trade, to burn coal instead of wood.*

We see, therefore, that the open stove for wood and coal was improved by successive borrowings and betterings of others' ideas. Such is the story of most inventions. A modern heating and ventilating grate has long been made and

*All this is made more lucid by reading *Franklin's Memoirs*; and also J. Durno's *Description of a New Invented Stove*; W. Glossop's *Stove Maker's Assistant*, of 1772, and other accounts, but especially Schuffrey's, *The English Fireplace*, published by B. T. Batsford, London. The latter is very wisely and fully illustrated, with excellent drawings and photos and quotes interestingly from the various available writings on the subject.

Fig. 5 — FRANKLIN STOVE (*early nineteenth century*)
At Fort Anne, Annapolis Royal, N. S. *Courtesy, L. M. Fortier, Esq*

sold in New York, which, as I recall it, improves on the English and Franklin models; and there are others. We all know of Latrobe and the Baltimore Heater. It is an ugly duckling in appearance, "but it can swim darned well," for it is a great heater, practically and economically.

Count Rumford (Benjamin Thompson), of Concord, N. H., about 1798 condemned Durno's theories in general, and, possibly after suffering from a smoky flue, deprecated the bends and irregularities therein which attend Franklin's and other inventions. Back to the straight, old unimpeded English flue of Prince Rupert's time he went, except for an improved throat and interior shelf. He devised a fireplace and flue system which led us, alas, into the worship of brick open fireplaces. He abandoned iron work for all but the grate, and made an improved back, sides, and throat, and a straight flue calculated at a sectional area of from one-eighth to one-tenth of the fireplace opening area, as I recall it. These ideas all work well together and are followed now by the best designers, but they would also succeed with a Franklin fire frame or open stove. Therefore, while praising Rumford for the latter ideas, I cannot help blaming him (although a distant connection) for depriving us of our cast iron, open stove of some form at least; for although brick may radiate more heat, and may outlast iron, the gain in efficiency is not worth the æsthetic loss of the stove. Indeed, most of Rumford's principles may be incorporated in a brick set fire frame.

Franklin's name was probably connected with his stove during the time when Robert Grace cast and sold it, and with the American modifications of it, if not with the English also, until even the mere fire frame, with or without a raised hearth on iron legs, and

Fig. 6 — FRANKLIN STOVE (*mid-nineteenth century*)
At Fort Anne. An odd mixture of Rococo and Gothic styles. *Courtesy, L. M. Fortier, Esq.*

Fig. 7 — FRANKLIN STOVE (*early nineteenth century*)
Empire style; of date similar to those shown in *Figs. 1 and 2.*
At Annapolis Royal. *Courtesy, James P. Lynch, Esq.*

without any purely Franklin ideas incorporated, is now dignified by his name. Certain old American farmhouses today contain these frames, with brick hearths built on the floor level, but possibly the raised iron hearth has, in these cases, been lost. The idea in the raised hearth was that of keeping the fire from the floor, radiating more heat and bringing the fire further out into the room than would be possible with a brick hearth at the floor level.

That Franklin had much to do with the development of the ornamental part of the cast iron fire frame and back, I cannot believe. A strong Adam influence is seen in many of them and later ones show the Empire influence. The hob grate appears to have suggested the need of ornamental side pieces and back, when more metal was added to the ancient brick and stone form, of which the origin goes back to the cave dwellings.

The ornamental patterns or forms for the mould in casting were usually made of quite thin, clear, white pine bent to the form of the desired curve by attaching templates to the backs. (Fig. 3.) They were delicately and well carved. Sometimes small brass-headed tacks and nails were driven in to save the labor of carving small bosses. Beads or fillets and lead castings of other repeated ornaments were attached for the same reason. Such lead repetitions on a colonette are seen in the illustration (Fig. 4.)

No one would do less than praise Franklin for his invention of a new stove, because it is largely due to his work that all similar stoves and frames came into such general use in America. But we must not forget that the term "Franklin Stove" is a misnomer when applied to a hearthless, backless fireframe with no part especially due to Franklin's inventive genius. Many such frames were of other men's design, and some came from England, I believe, or were inspired by English designs.

If you visit Nova Scotia and go the round of the south shore to Chester and Halifax, and then, of the north shore, back to Digby or Yarmouth, it is well worth while to stop at lovely Annapolis Royal and visit Fort Anne. There is another good inn in Annapolis, filled with fine old mahogany and china, and a trip out to South Milford and the hospitable house of Thomas at the head of the Liver-

pool Lakes, will explain why Albert Bigelow Paine wrote *The Tent Dwellers* there. But better than pursuing the lakes and their big trout and ancient rock inscriptions, now deciphered as Indian legendary art; better than hunting rare hooked rugs on farmhouse floors, is it to stand on the ramparts of Fort Anne, where French and English fought and fell, see the yellow tide surge up the river, driven from far away Fundy, and wander through the old garrison house with courteous Mr. Fortier, whose charge it is. Here hang the colored coats of arms of the famous French nobles of early Port Royal's history, before the English took it and

Fig. 8 — FRANKLIN STOVE (*early nineteenth century*)
Empire style. Shows finely executed grape-vine pattern. Altogether an exceptional piece of casting. Compare previous and succeeding illustrations. At Annapolis Royal. *Courtesy, B. B. Hardwick, Esq.*

changed it to Annapolis Royal, and here are excellent so-called Franklin stoves. There are yet more of them in the houses of various citizens of Annapolis, who admire and very sensibly use them with an almost reverent spirit, which hesitates to abandon the certain good of the old for the uncertain value of the new. (Figs. 4, 5, 6, 7, 8.)

In the States are many old fire-frames lying in the shops. Such a frame, without the iron hearth, which came into my possession quite accidentally, but whose ornamentation is quite unusual, is illustrated. (Fig. 10.) The extensive modeling of the acanthus is excellent and so is its location on the metal. The ball finials are of brass. It represents beautiful design and fine casting.

Another worth-while example (Fig. 11) is still, I think, to be seen in Hyannis, and bears on its front the name of the maker, H. H. Stimpson, Boston. It is a fine stove and deserves a place in a country house. The queer little andirons have left it and gone to some owner unknown to me, but the courteous owner of the stove is Mr. Carroll. Of these irons as harmonious accompaniments of an iron open stove I would say more, as I know of only one other pair in existence. They came from the ancient attic of a house torn down in Brewster, Mass., years ago. Though bereft of their former abode they are still lifelike to the point of animation. Evidently they are English and came, perhaps, from one of those ancient foundries, such as that in the parish of Waldron, Sussex, whence came other andirons of similar form, direct descendants of Elizabethan designs.*

In a splendidly built and beautifully panelled small house on Cape Cod, the birthplace of a famous sea captain, I once saw a so-called Franklin fire-frame with acanthus and grape ornament on side half-columns. Above these were brass discs and above these brass ball finials. All the house was doomed to destruction:

Fig. 9 — Franklin Stove (*early nineteenth century*)
Similar to *Figs. 7 and 8*, but not so well modelled or cast. Well turned finials. Feet should be compared with those of *Fig. 8. Courtesy, James P Lynch, Esq.*

the stove and panelled parlor with its recessed window seats, rare in small country houses two hundred years old. No one could contemplate such desecration unmoved. I began by bargaining for the parlor panelling and Franklin stove (for it would not do to take the stove away from its old-time association with such fine woodwork), and I ended by purchasing even the windows, sash, jambs, seats and architraves, which brought also the mouldings of the eaves outside. And now all these are again associated under one roof, as of old, although, unfortunately, not in their former relative positions. However, when I see the old Franklin stove-frame, safe from the junkman's clutch; and reflect that many may yet sit before its cheerful blaze, the rescue seems well worth while. The only regret that lingers is that I could not have acquired the entire house, repaired its weakened timbers and mouldings and so preserved

Fig. 11 — Franklin Fire Frame with Old English Andirons
Made by H. H. Stimson, Boston. Frame of same period as *Fig. 10*. Andirons much more ancient *Courtesy Carroll Co., Hyannis, Mass.*

the beautiful old structure, with its little parlor only seven feet high, as a shrine intact for the Franklin fire-frame which had bestowed such animation and genial warmth on hundreds who once knew its hospitality.

*Mr. Shuffrey gives an illustration of two at Penshurst Place, Kent, England (page 138).

Fig. 10 — Franklin Fire Frame
No iron hearth appears here. The piece suggests very early nineteenth century work, both in type of design and in the extreme refinement of the casting. The influence of wood carving on this is evident. *Studio, Frances Adams Kent, Orleans, Mass.*

FRANKLIN-TYPE STOVES

By JOSEPHINE H. PEIRCE

Josephine Halvorsen Peirce (Mrs. Frank Dana Peirce) of Leicester, Massachusetts, has been collecting stoves and information about them for twelve years. She is manager of the Worcester Better Business Bureau, and besides has written columns and feature articles for many publications.

ON FEBRUARY 1, 1745, the *Boston News-Letter* advertised the "New Fashion Fireplaces or Stoves from Philadelphia," and announced as "Just published, an account of the New-invented Pennsylvania Fireplace." This was Benjamin Franklin's contribution to heating — not really a stove, but a cast-iron fireplace in which he combined two improvements in heating which had been devised in Europe. From the fireplace built in England for Prince Rupert he appropriated the descending flue; from the French fireplace of Nicolas Gauger he borrowed the caliducts and the soufflet or blower in the hearth. The open fire burned on an iron hearth, and the smoke rose in front of a hollow metal back, passed over the top and down the other side where it entered the flue by a curved channel at the level of the hearth.

In his autobiography, Franklin wrote:

Having, in 1742, invented an open stove for the better warming of rooms, and at the same time saving fuel, as the fresh air admitted was warmed in entering, I made a present of the model to Mr. Robert Grace, one of my early friends, who, having an iron furnace, found the casting of the plates for these stoves a profitable thing, as they were growing in demand. To promote the demand, I wrote and published a pamphlet, entitled *"An Account of the new-invented Pennsylvanian Fire-places"* &c. This pamphlet had good effect. Governor Thomas was so pleased with the construction of this stove, as described in it, that he offered to give me a patent for the sole vending of them for a term of years: but I declined it from a principle, which has ever weighed with me on such occasions, viz. *That, as we enjoy great advantages from the inventions of others, we should be glad of an opportunity to serve others by any invention of ours; and this we should do freely and generously.*

An ironmonger in London, however assuming a great deal of my pamphlet, and working it up into his own, and making some small changes in the machine, which rather hurt its operation, got a patent for it there, and made, as I was told, a little fortune by it. . . The use of these fireplaces in very many houses, both here in Pennsylvania, and the neighboring states, has been, and is, a great saving of wood. . .

The pamphlet mentioned that some improvements in fireplaces had been made by lowering the breasts and narrowing the hearth, but even so, rooms were drafty, and it was Franklin's contention that not only was fuel wasted, but that many people caught colds, and many diseases resulted from the colds. He even thought it might be safer to sit in the street, and quoted the old Spanish proverb:

If the wind blows on you through a hole
Make your will, and take care of your soul.

Although these stoves were considered an improvement over previous heating devices, the amount of heat they gave is indicated in a letter from Philadelphia to the *Boston Evening Post*, printed July 17, 1749. Speaking of a summer heat wave, the writer said, "How warm our Stove-Rooms seem in Winter! And yet the highest they ever raised my thermometer was to 56 degrees."

The first Franklin stoves were intended to be set inside an open fireplace, already built, but the size and shape of the stove rarely coincided with the brick opening, and the space had to be filled in. Then too, the original idea of the smoke outlet on the bottom had to be changed, because of difficulties with the draft. Not all chimneys were suited to the down-draft principle, so the smoke outlet was shifted first to the lower part of the back plate, then to the upper part, and finally to the top. The importance of installing the fireplaces correctly is suggested by a news item in the *Boston Gazette* for December 22, 1747:

On the 11th Instant early in the morning a Fire broke out at Mr. Pierpont's House near the Fortification, occasioned by the Heat of the Iron Hearth on one of the Newly invented Fireplaces, whereby the Floor was set on Fire; the people being in Bed, perceived a great Smoke, got up and happily discover'd and timely Distinguished [*sic*] the Fire.

Because of Franklin's generosity in sharing his stove idea, furnaces everywhere made them, boldly using their own names. Dealers, too, would order stoves in quantity with their names cast in the metal. Some were known as fireplaces; others were simply called stoves: all were of the open-front variety. The sides below the hood of the early models were quite straight; later they were made with a flare to throw more heat into the room.

The oldest known Franklin, a modification of the original pattern, made probably about 1750, is in the Bucks County Historical Society Museum, at Doylestown, Pennsylvania. This has a wide hood which keeps smoke from entering the room, and is decorated with a sun face and sixteen rays which are surrounded by branching leafage, and streamers with the motto *Alter Idem*. This decoration is the one described by Franklin in verse, on the last page of his pamphlet:

A second Self or Another the Same
by a Friend
Another sun! 'tis true, but not the SAME
Alike I own, in Warmth and genial Flame
But, more obliging than his elder Brother,
This will not scorch in Summer like the *other*
Nor when sharp *Boreas chills our shivering Limbs*
Will *this Sun* leave us for more Southern Climes
Or in long Winter Nights, forsake us here,
To cheer new Friends in tother Hemisphere;
But faithful still to us, this *new Sun's* fire
Warms when we please, and just as we desire.

DURING THE LATE 1700's classic motifs were in vogue for mantel ornament. The frieze or hood on this stove is in the prevailing style, with garlands and urns inside a beaded border. The stove must have smoked, for the sheet-iron shield is a much later addition. Originally in the Haven House, Portsmouth, New Hampshire. *Courtesy Portsmouth Historical Society.*

1948

The first patent for a "Franklin Stove" by that name was taken out in 1816 by James Wilson of Poughkeepsie, New York. A feature of his design was the thirteen stars symbolic of the thirteen original states. Later he made it seventeen, and again used twenty stars. Some of his earlier stoves were topped with a sheet-iron dome for radiating the heat. Later ones had elaborate claw feet and fine brass rails.

Franklin was a name that had public appeal, and after this patents were taken out for Franklin Fireplace Stoves, Pipe Franklin Stoves, Open Franklin Stoves with Andirons, Closed Franklin Stoves with Doors, Fold-door Franklin Stoves, Slide-door Franklin Stoves, Ben Franklins, and so on. There were also the many Cooking Franklin Stoves, and the Franklin Reflectors whose radiating surfaces were increased by circulation of the smoke behind and below the fire.

The decorative motifs cast in the frieze and side plates of Franklin stoves are usually an index to their date, for they followed the style trends of their time. In the later 1700's classic ornament on the hood reflected the Adam influence in garlands and urns within a frame of fine beading. After the Revolution, conventional rosettes were replaced by small profiles of Washington and Franklin; the eagle and stars, and patriotic mottoes like *Be Liberty Thine* were introduced. With the nineteenth century Franklin stoves, like furniture and architecture to which they were related, were embellished with such Empire expressions as acanthus leaves, grapes and vines, sheaves of wheat, rope twists.

New improvements in heating devices appeared rapidly in the 1800's but fireplace stoves, with variations, continued in demand almost throughout the century. Then, as now, people liked the sight of the open fire.

PROFILES of Benjamin Franklin and George Washington decorate this Franklin stove (*c. 1795*). *Courtesy Metropolitan Museum of Art.*

EARLIEST OF THE WILSON PATENTS, the first taken out for a "Franklin Stove," in 1816 at Poughkeepsie, New York. Thirteen stars surround the eagle. The dunce-cap dome, which added a great deal of heat to the room, has brass collar and finial. The brass fender did not originally belong on the hearth. Wrought-iron feet are riveted in. The stove is 29 inches wide, 25 inches deep, and 65 inches to the top of the finial. *Courtesy Henry Ford collection, Edison Institute, Dearborn, Michigan.*

No. I SIZE, made by Bridge, Beach & Co., St. Louis (*c. 1854*). The harvest motif, with cornstalks and trailing vines, betrays its mid-western origin. The opening is 21 inches wide, 13 inches deep, 19½ inches high. *Courtesy Mrs. Eleanor C. Ingalls, Corvallis, Oregon.*

TYPICAL of James Wilson's decorative designs is the eagle surrounded by stars. This has seventeen stars, so was made sometime after 1817. The heating dome has a brass collar and the knobs are brass. The long pipe also adds more heat to the room. The stove was for years in a law office in Brinley Hall, Worcester, Massachusetts, built in 1836–7. After the building was demolished in 1895 it was moved to the home of Charles M. Thayer. *Courtesy of Mrs. Thayer.*

A SIMPLE and dignified Franklin in an attractive setting. *Courtesy Mrs. John F. Bicknell, Worcester, Massachusetts.*

A HANDSOME FRANKLIN STOVE with acanthus-leaf decoration is the C. (Charles) Postley patent of 1815, made in New York. The pierced brass top rail, brass bosses, and knobs give it elegance. The opening is 27 inches wide, 25 inches high, and the stove is 38 inches wide overall. This stove was purchased before 1820 and placed in a house in North-field, Massachusetts, by Captain James White, where it stood until about fifty years ago, when it was brought to Leicester by his great-granddaughter. It is still in the possession of the family. *Courtesy J. Sidney Whittemore, Leicester, Massachusetts.*

BOX STOVES
AND PARLOR COOK STOVES

By JOSEPHINE H. PEIRCE

The chapter on Franklin stoves from Mrs. Frank Dana Peirce's forth-coming book on stoves appeared in ANTIQUES *for May 1948. We here present material from another chapter. In addition to collecting information on stoves, Mrs. Peirce is manager of the Worcester Better Business Bureau.*

EVIDENCE SHOWS that stoves in the form of a box were used by early New England settlers, and records state that stoves were cast at the Lynn furnace in 1647. Box stoves were mentioned in Judge Sewall's diaries from 1701 to 1707, and were advertised in the first Boston newspapers in 1723. None of them can be found today, because many that existed at the time of the Revolution were turned in then for scrap and the remainder at various times later when the price of iron went up.

In Pennsylvania some of the iron plates which formed the stoves of the German settlers, and a few complete stoves, have been preserved in museums. Designs in these castings were of Biblical subjects, from original German patterns. They were the earliest type of box stoves, known as jamb stoves, made of five iron plates, like a box with one end open. The open end was set through a hole in the wall into a fireplace in another room. Usually the stove was in the living room (known as a stove-room)

and the fire in the kitchen fireplace, which served for both cooking and heating. As the wood in the fire burned down, the hot embers were shoveled through the jamb into the stove, while the smoke escaped back into the fireplace chimney.

Six-plate stoves, known as Holland stoves, draft stoves, or wind stoves, stood away from the wall and had a smoke-pipe and draft or fuel door. These stoves, common in Norway, Sweden, and Holland in the seventeenth century, became popular in New England. The six-plate stove was also the "best seller" of the nineteenth century and varied from 14 to 40 inches in length, with larger sizes for public buildings.

In another type the firebox was cast in one piece. About 1780 the Shakers started making this kind, and in order to get more heat they used stovepipes which made several turnings before entering the chimney. By 1840 someone had conceived the idea of having two flues from the stove itself, with a horizontal connecting piece from which a pipe led to the chimney. These became known as two-column stoves and burned wood or charcoal. This type opened a new field for designers, who used fruit and flower motifs, as well as pure baroque and Greek revival styles. Between the two columns, on top of the fire chamber, there was a hole with a cover, which could be removed to give a place for a teakettle.

Thus from the box stove developed the parlor cook stove "constructed in such a manner as to recommend it to the notice of those wanting a neat and convenient stove for the sitting room, and one which at the same time possesses capacity to do the cooking for a small family in the most economical manner." By 1850 the parlor cook stove had become a very handsome piece of furniture.

BOX STOVE (*c. 1750*), with the firebox cast in one piece. The bottom casting extends to form the hearth, and the wrought-iron feet are riveted into the base. The door is cast, but other small parts are wrought. Stoves of a similar design were made and used later by the Shakers. *Courtesy Lawrence B. Romaine.*

THREE-LEGGED box stove made at Plymouth, Vermont, in 1839, sometimes referred to as a *Mayflower* stove because of the decoration. It was common to advertise box stoves by the name of the design — *Rising Sun, Tropic* (with a few palm trees), and so on. *Courtesy Lawrence B. Romaine.*

Box Stove with grape design similar to that on contemporary pressed glass (*mid-1800's*). *Courtesy Mrs. Eleanor Hudson Welch.*

Two-Column Stove, 44 inches high, made by J. H. Shear, Albany, New York, in the 1840's, with sharp, fine castings. The center ornament may be removed when the boiling hole is needed for a teakettle. *Courtesy Gilbert M. Tucker.*

"Little Cod," a box stove 12 by 18 inches wide, of the type used by fishing vessels of the Grand Banks for cooking and heating. Made by the Charles Fawcett Manufacturing Company, Limited, of Sackville, New Brunswick. *Courtesy Mrs. Benjamin B. Snow.*

Four-O'clock Stove, intended for use in bedrooms, where a fire was lighted at four o'clock to take the chill off the room before bedtime. Made at the Tyson Furnace, Plymouth, Vermont, and purchased in 1844 by John Titus, who took it with his bride to Holden, Massachusetts. It is still used by his granddaughter, Mrs. L. C. Hamill. No. 1 size, length, 15 inches.

Parlor Cook Stove in the Victorian manner, camouflaged to appear as an elegant piece of furniture. The central cartouche depicts a pioneer hero disarming an Indian of his tomahawk, while the heroine, tied between two trees, looks on. The removable vase which tops the stove is made to hold a vial of perfume with which to dispel cooking odors. Beneath the hinged top are two boiling holes. Either coal or wood may be used, and elaborate flues carry the heat around the oven. Height, 35½ inches. *Author's collection.*

Stovemakers of Troy, New York

BY JOHN G. AND DIANA S. WAITE, *New York State Board for Historic Preservation*

THE CITY OF TROY, founded shortly after the Revolutionary War, rapidly grew into a major commercial and industrial center. Its Yankee founders quickly took advantage of the cheap water power and the city's strategic location at the head of navigation on the Hudson.

Goods being shipped overland between New England and the West were ferried across the Hudson at Troy, and the city developed into the hub of an excellent system of waterways. It became the eastern terminus of the Erie Canal which opened a waterway to the Great Lakes in 1825. The Champlain Canal, which emptied into the Hudson at Waterford just north of Troy, provided a water route to Lake Champlain and Canada. Also just above Troy, at Cohoes, the Mohawk River cascades into the Hudson. The first railroad to serve Troy was chartered in 1832, and by 1840 others were being constructed to Boston, New York City, Schenectady, and points west. By 1875 railroad lines radiating from Troy in all directions provided cheap transportation for both raw materials and finished products, just as the canals had half a century earlier.

The founding of Rensselaer Polytechnic Institute in 1824

"for teaching the physical sciences with their application to the arts of life" also encouraged Troy's development as an industrial center. It was the first engineering school in the country, and during the nineteenth century it provided much of the leadership and technical expertise for local industries.

The manufacture of iron goods was one of the earliest and most important of Troy's many industries. The Albany Rolling and Slitting Mill, built by John Brinckerhoff and Company on the Wynantskill in 1807, later became Corning, Winslow and Company, and under that name made the armor plates for the ironclad *Monitor* during the Civil War. Also located along the Wynantskill was the famous Burden Iron Company, founded in 1809, which produced large quantities of horseshoes and railroad rails. The Bessemer process for the conversion of pig iron into steel was first employed in the United States at the Winslow, Griswold and Holley Company in Troy in 1865.

Coal from the anthracite region of northeastern Pennsylvania was shipped to Troy inexpensively first along the Delaware and Hudson Canal and later on the Delaware

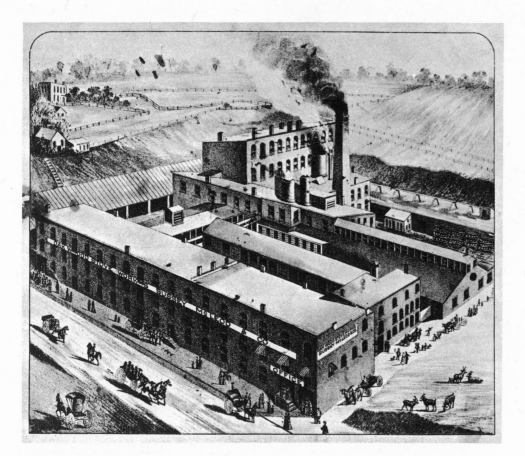

Bird's-eye view of the Oakwood Stove Works, Troy, c. 1880. (From the catalogue of *Bussey, McLeod & Co. Stoves,* Troy, 1880, p. 2.) *Metropolitan Museum of Art.*

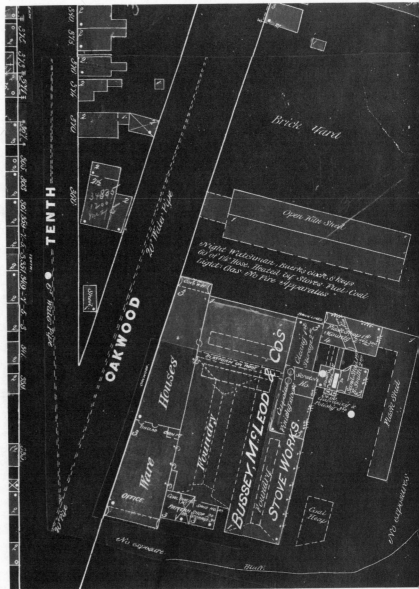

Plan of the Oakwood stove works. The works were at the junction of Oakwood Avenue and Tenth Street and were operated by the firm of Bussey, McLeod and Company. The works were begun c. 1863 and were in use through 1916. Although it was one of Troy's largest stove foundries, only a few of the buildings on this plan have survived. (From *Insurance Maps of the City of Troy, New York, Including West Troy and Green Island,* New York, 1875, with later corrections added by hand, Pl. 2.) *New York State Library.*

Parlor stove manufactured by the firm of Johnson, Geer and Cox, which was in business from 1840 through 1845. *Antique Stove Museum, Hoosick, New York; photograph by John G. Waite.*

and Hudson Railroad. The pig iron for the foundries also came by barge and rail from Pennsylvania and Vermont, from Columbia and Dutchess counties in the Hudson Valley, and from Clinton and Essex counties in the Adirondacks. Limestone for flux was readily available from the Hudson Valley, as were ample deposits of fine molding sand. The finished products were shipped by water and by rail to consumers all over the United States and Canada.

Troy became one of the greatest American centers for the production of cast-iron stoves. They were cast there occasionally during the first two decades of the nineteenth century, but they were not made in quantity until the 1830's and 1840's when changing architectural tastes created a greater demand for stoves and improved transportation made it possible to ship them economically. During this period the first companies were established which produced only stoves, rather than a wide variety of cast-iron items as had usually been the case before.

The taste of the 1850's and 1860's dictated that stoves be decorative as well as functional, and Troy foundries

An example of the ornate parlor stoves produced in Troy during the 1840's. This stove was patented in 1844 and manufactured by John Morrison at the Green Island Foundry. *Antique Stove Museum; Waite photograph.*

Parlor stove, patented in 1845, and manufactured by P. Low and Company, which began business in 1844 and was succeeded in 1845 by the firm of Peter Low. *Antique Stove Museum; Waite photograph.*

This ornate Gothic revival parlor stove was patented in 1847. Called "J. Wager's Patent," it was probably manufactured either by the firm of Wager and Pratt (1847-1848) or Wager, Pratt and Company (1849-1851). *Antique Stove Museum; Waite photograph.*

Two sizes of the Ilion parlor stove patented in 1853 and manufactured by Wager, Richmond and Smith. *Antique Stove Museum; Waite photograph.*

The Castle Stove was patented in 1853 and manufactured by George W. Eddy, who was first listed as a stove manufacturer in 1852. It was one of a number of architecturally inspired parlor stoves manufactured in Troy during this period. *Antique Stove Museum; Waite photograph.*

responded by producing large quantities of iron stoves in virtually every popular architectural form and style. Stove production declined during the 1870's but revived during the 1880's when many companies began manufacturing furnaces for central-heating systems. Several new firms were established to meet the demand for furnaces but most of them were short lived.

After 1890 both stove and furnace production in Troy declined rapidly, and by 1920 only two companies remained in business. Among the reasons for this decline was the failure of Troy companies to keep pace with technological developments in heating and cooking; another factor was the general decline of Troy as an iron and steel center as the Great Lakes iron ranges were opened and Pittsburgh and Midwestern cities came into prominence as steel-making centers.

The Troy stove companies were founded by men of varied backgrounds. Some had been tinsmiths, merchants, or carpenters; others became managers after learning the foundry business as molders, stove mounters, furnacemen, or pattern makers. Some of the early manufacturers began business as stove dealers. Evidence suggests that the two functions were closely related. Some manufacturers, for example, became dealers and then returned to manufacturing.

Many of the stove companies were family owned and operated. Often company names and partners changed every few years. James Wager, for example, who was described by the *New York Times* in 1872 as "the oldest stove manufacturer in the United States," was a principal in twelve different firms during a career which began in 1838. It was not uncommon for several different stove companies to be located at one foundry, and companies often moved from one foundry to another, sometimes trading foundries with other stove firms.

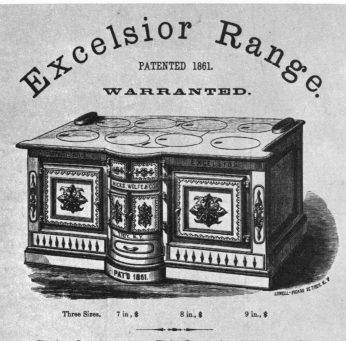

The Excelsior Range, patented in 1861, was manufactured by Hicks, Wolfe and Company, a firm which was in operation from 1859 through 1866. *New York State Library.*

This store front at 15 First Street was erected in 1863 for the First National Bank of Troy. Cast-iron columns and carved-brownstone elements are combined to reflect the patriotic sentiments manifested in the city during the Civil War. The columns were cast by Starbuck Brothers, who made store fronts for a number of other Troy buildings during this period. Usually cast iron was used only on the first-floor façade. *Waite photograph.*

Some companies manufactured only stoves, while others made stoves only intermittently while also producing such things as plows, hollow ware, laundry irons, machinery, steam engines, railroad-car wheels, architectural ironwork, glass tiles bound in cast iron for sidewalks and steps, and cast-iron store fronts. Because of the abundance of iron foundries, a number of Troy's buildings, including private houses, were constructed with architectural ironwork that ranged from railings and window lintels to ground-floor store fronts and entire façades.

Although the stoves and other cast-iron products changed

This small parlor stove, Onward No. 2, was patented in 1865 and manufactured by Fuller, Warren and Company, the city's largest and most important stove works. Established c. 1828 as L. Stratton and Son, the firm continued in business until 1932 as the Fuller and Warren Company, manufacturing a large variety of stoves, ranges, and furnaces. *Antique Stove Museum; Waite photograph.*

According to the manufacturers, Daniel E. Paris and Company, the design of the Mansard Parlor Cook Stove was perfected in 1869-1870 at a cost of $11,000 and was patented in 1871. Referring to the four mica windows on the front of the stove, the catalogue noted that "the windows being upright on a sloping surface, like the new Mansard or French Roof to buildings (whence the name), the effect is most beautiful, making the room bright and cheerful, and when desired these windows can be opened, thus making an Open Fire-place still more cheerful." (From the catalogue entitled *Mansard Cook, Mansard Parlor Cook, and Dome Reservoir, Made by Dan'l E. Paris & Co., Troy, 1871.*) *Metropolitan Museum of Art.*

with manufacturing technology, the foundries themselves remained remarkably unaltered. The stove companies that survived into the twentieth century used the techniques and sometimes even the buildings of the earliest Troy foundries.

Most of the stove works in Troy had cupola furnaces, although some had air furnaces. Both types were used to melt down pig iron rather than to reduce ore to iron. Before being remelted each load of pig iron was tested to determine the percentages of silicone, sulphur, and manganese it contained. The mixtures were closely controlled so that the castings would be tough, durable, smooth, and free from imperfections.

A cupola was a vertical, cylindrical furnace, several stories high. At its lowest level was a layer of burning bed coke on which were piled alternating layers of pig iron and coke, with limestone used as a flux. The cupola was fed through the top, and the molten iron was drawn from the bottom.

The air furnace consisted of a covered bed on which coke and pig iron were fired together. A grate at one end and a chimney at the other assured a constant draft of air over the bed. A door permitted the puddler to skim slag from the surface of the molten metal with an iron bar known as a rabble. The air furnace was not as practical as the cupola furnace in producing iron for stove components because it required more coke than the cupola and could melt less pig iron. It was also much more difficult to use because the constant draft of air during the heating process would cause the iron to "burn," or oxidize, in places. This problem did not arise in the cupola furnace because

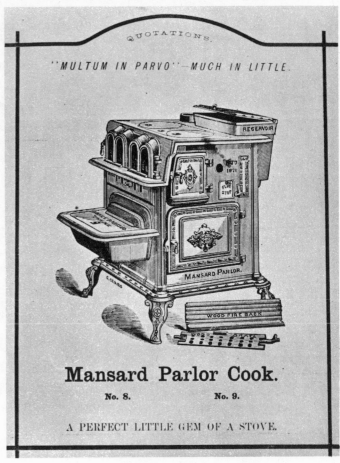

QUOTATIONS.

"MULTUM IN PARVO" — MUCH IN LITTLE.

Mansard Parlor Cook.

No. 8.   No. 9.

A PERFECT LITTLE GEM OF A STOVE.

the iron was continually maintained at a high temperature. The iron produced in an air furnace was stronger and could be drawn more readily, but these characteristics were not critical in stove manufacturing.

The molten iron was taken from the furnace in ladles of about forty-pounds' capacity to the molding room, a large open space often two or three stories high lighted by monitor windows and skylights. The castings were made in molding boxes known as flasks, which held a mixture of fine sand and moistened clay that acted as a binder. The mold for one face of the casting, called the drag, was formed by packing tempered sand around the wooden pattern at the bottom of the rectangular drag until the drag was filled. A bottom board was then placed over the drag and the whole mold inverted. Very carefully the pattern was removed and the impression in the sand checked for accuracy. The mold for the other face of the casting, called the cope, was formed in the same way, inverted, and clamped over the drag. The molten metal was then poured into the combined mold through funnel-shape openings in the cope called sprues.

After the casting was made, it was shaken out of the mold and the sand was returned to the molder for reuse, often being dried in a small furnace. The molding process required much judgment and skill. It was necessary to pack the sand into cope and drag very carefully. If it were too loose, the casting would not form correctly. If too tight,

the gases would not escape and the casting would be damaged.

The castings were then taken to the finishing and mounting rooms, where they were machined and assembled. This step also required much skill because if the joints were not absolutely tight, the stoves would not operate properly. Near the finishing and mounting rooms were the cleaning rooms and machine, blacksmith, tinsmith, and enameling shops. Power was usually provided by steam engines, although water power was used in some of the early stove works.

After the stoves were completed, they were blackened, crated, and taken to salesrooms or warerooms to await shipment. Although in some cases the sales- and warerooms were located at the foundry, most companies also maintained commercial buildings on River Street in the center of the Troy business district.

The *New York Times* for February 12, 1872, described the wide variety of stoves for sale in Troy during the 1870's: "A man who cannot suit himself with a stove in walking along River street, Troy, must be one of those creatures—too often to be met—impossible to please. He could pick and choose between baseburners, self-feeders, gas-consumers, patent bakers, hot closets, reservoirs, and a hundred other sorts." From River Street the stoves were shipped astonishing distances. An account written in 1891 listed some of their exotic destinations: "Llamas have

Manufactured by Fuller, Warren and Company, this J. A. Lawson's Fire-Place Furnace known as the Splendid originally heated an entire three-story wing of a Troy townhouse. The wing was erected about 1881. The furnace is dated 1878 on the top and has a plaque dated 1880 bolted on near the bottom, apparently indicating the year of manufacture. Sheet-metal pipes located on either side of the furnace behind the mantelpiece opening were connected to flues which conveyed warm air to the upper stories. The slate mantelpiece, painted to imitate marble, was probably manufactured by one of several Troy mantel works in operation during that period. *Authors' collection; Waite photograph.*

carried them [Troy stoves] across the Andes to the farther coast of South America, camels to the shores of the Black Sea, and ships to Northern Europe, Turkey, China, Japan, and Australia."[1]

To tap the ever-expanding market in the western part of the United States during the 1860's and 1870's, a number of Troy stove companies opened salesrooms and warehouses in Chicago while others constructed foundries in Chicago and other Midwestern cities. Iron stoves were manufactured in Troy to burn bituminous coal and prairie hay, which was the only fuel available in the West.

Related industries also developed in Troy. One of these was the production of the wooden patterns that were impressed into the molding sand. The shops which produced the patterns provided them to out-of-town as well as local stove manufacturers. Other related industries were the manufacturing of stove linings and firebrick.

A number of Troy residents were prominent inventors of stoves, and many of the patents they held were granted during the 1840's when the business developed rapidly. The most famous of Troy's inventors was Philo Penfield Stewart (1798-1868). As a young man he went to Mississippi to be a missionary to the Choctaw Indians, but later he settled in Elyria, Ohio, and helped to found Oberlin College. In 1836 he invented the celebrated "P. P. Stewart Summer and Winter Cooking Stove" in New York City. Moving to Troy about 1837, Stewart arranged for Starbuck and Company and later Fuller, Warren and Company to produce stoves of his design. These were so successful that Fuller, Warren and Company still advertised Stewart stoves and ranges in the twentieth century.

[1]Arthur James Weise, *Troy's One Hundred Years, 1789-1889*, Troy, 1891; p. 269.

A checklist of Troy stovemakers.

THIS LIST INCLUDES only stove manufacturers once located within the nineteenth-century boundaries of Troy. There were many others in the neighboring communities of Green Island, Lansingburgh (now part of Troy), and West Troy (now Watervliet). Many companies that manufactured stoves were also listed at one time or another as retail stove dealers, and frequently we found it difficult to differentiate between manufacturers and dealers. Dates were determined from a wide variety of sources including business directories, census records, patents, trade catalogues, county records, nineteenth-century newspaper accounts, and business histories. Where two reliable sources differ about a date, we have given both with a slash between them. It should be remembered that a date cast on a stove may indicate when the design was patented rather than when it was manufactured.

Anthony, Davy and Company, 1845-1849
Atwood and Cole, 1844-1845
Atwood, Anson, 1841-1843
Atwood, Cole and Crane, 1846
Burdett, Paris and Company, 1868
Burdett, Potter, Smith and Company, 1869-1870
Burdett, Smith and Company, 1871-1916
Burdett, Smith and Company Inc., 1917-1936
Burtis and Company, 1891-1893
Burtis and Mann, 1883-1890
Bussey and McLeod, 1863/64
Bussey and McLeod Stove Company, 1882-1898
Bussey, E., and Company, 1863
Bussey, McLeod and Company, 1865-1882
Buswell and Durant, c. 1859-1866
Buswell, Durant and Company, 1867-1871
Cahoone, Norton and Company, 1867
Church, H. and H. S., 1871-1876
Church, H. S., 1877-1883
Clark, Keeney and Company, 1850
Cole and Crane, 1847
Cole, S., and Company, 1850-1852
Cole, Spencer, 1848-1849
Co-operative Foundry [Co-operative Iron Founders Association], 1867-1873
Co-operative Stove Works, 1879-1891
Corse and Company, 1879-1881
Cottrell [Cotrel], Samuel, 1835
Cox and Church, 1863-1864
Cox, Church and Company, 1865-1870
Cox, Warren, Morrison and Company, 1854

Davy and Cotrel, 1840
Davy and Cure, 1860
Davy and Lape, 1861
Davy, Anthony and Phillips, 1850-1851
Davy, Ingraham and Phillips, 1852-1857
Davy, John T., 1841-1844
Dickerman, J. E., 1877-1883
Dunham, A. T., and Company, c. 1846-1853
Eddy and Company [Eddy, Charles and Company], 1857-1868
Eddy and Corse, 1869
Eddy, Charles, 1847/48-1856
Eddy, Corse and Company, 1870-1878
Eddy, George W., 1852-1875
Empire Stove Works, 1895-1905
Fales, A. B., 1872-1907
Faye and Company, 1849-1853
Faye, Josiah C., 1854-1863
Fayerweather, Joseph H., 1845-1846
Fellows, J. and A., 1835-1840
Fellows, John P., before 1829-1848
Filley, Marcus L., 1859-1891
Fuller and Warren Company, 1881-1932
Fuller, Warren and Company, 1859-1881
Fuller, Warren and Morrison, 1855-1858
Geer and Bosworth, c. 1846
Geer and Company, 1857-1859
Geer, Chaffey and Company, 1853
Geer, Chaffey and Richmond, 1851-c. 1852
Geer, Gilbert, 1847-1850
Geer, Wager and Company, 1838-1839
Giles, Henry G., 1866

Giles, Henry G., and Son, 1867-1879
Giles Stove Company, 1879-1886, 1889-1890
Gold Coin Stove Company, 1899-1916
Gould, J., and Company, 1881-1882, 1884-1887
Greene, C. O., 1874-1884
Henderson, Frank, 1902-1915
Henderson, J. C., 1877-1890
Henderson, J. C., and Company, 1891-1901
Hicks and Wolfe, 1867-1877
Hicks, George W., 1854-c. 1856
Hicks, G. W. and E. J., c. 1857-1858
Hicks, Wolfe and Company, 1859-1866
Howell and Company, 1860, 1862
Howell, Martin R., 1857-1859
Hoyt and Wynkoop, c. 1892-1895
Hoyt, James B., 1896
Hyde, James R., 1854-1896
Ingraham, A., and Company, 1871-1874
Ingraham, A. and W. H., 1868-1870
Ingraham and Phillips, 1858-1862
Ingraham, Phillips and Company, 1863-1867
Johnson and Cox, 1846-1849
Johnson and Geer, 1834-1840
Johnson, Cox and Fuller, 1850-1853
Johnson, Elias, 1854-1857
Johnson, Geer and Cox, 1840-1845
Keeney, Felton and Company [Felton, Keeney and Company], 1851
Keep, William J., and Company, 1876-1879
Keep, W. J., 1880-1881
Lape, Ten Broeck, and Lape, 1884
Lee and Smith, c. 1855-1857
Lee, James, 1858-1862
Low and Hakes, 1854-1855
Low and Hicks, 1847-1853
Low, P., and Company, 1844
Low, Peter, 1845-1846
Mahony, M[ichael], 1880-1883
Mallary and Ingalls, 1854, 1859-?
Mallary, Ingalls and Tibbits, 1855-1858
Mann, Herbert R., 1891
McClellan and Company, 1876
Mohawk and Hudson Manufacturing Company, 1876-?
Morand and Clark, 1864
Morrison and Colwell, 1863-1872
Morrison and Manning, c. 1836-1837, 1841-1843
Morrison and Tibbits. 1849-1854
Morrison, James Jr., 1860-1862
Morrison, James Jr., and Company, 1859
Morrison, John, 1844-1847
Morrison, John, and Son, 1848
Mosher Heating Company, 1904-1910
Mosher Manufacturing Company, 1901-1903
Mosher, M. J., 1888-1893
Mosher, M. J., and Company, 1900
Mosher, M. J. and M. R., 1894-1899
Munsell and Thompson, 1860
Munsell, Thompson and Munsell, 1859
Newberry, Filley and Company, 1854-1858
Nutt and O'Brien, 1860-1862
Nutt, James E., and Company, 1856-1859
O'Brien, John, and Son, 1863-1866
Palmer and Hicks, 1869-1876
Palmer, C. W., 1865-1868
Palmer, Peter A., and Company, 1857-1864
Paris, Daniel E., 1869-1870
Paris, Daniel E., and Company, 1871-1891
Paris Manufacturing Company, 1888-1893
Paris, Merritt E., and Company, 1876-1881

Pease, Keeney and Company, 1848-1849
Phillips and Clark, 1884-?
Phillips and Clark Stove Company, 1890-1916
Phillips, George H., and Company, 1868-1883
Potter [Charles E.] and Company, 1871-1882
Potter [Louis] and Company, 1859-1862
Potter and Paris, 1862-1865
Potter, L., 1858
Potter, L., and Company, 1853-1857
Potter, Paris and Company, 1866-1867
Quackenbush, John H., 1872/73-1876
Richardson, Jonathan, 1867-1880
Riley and McConihe, 1864
Riley, McConihe and Hay, 1863
Sanders and Wolfe, 1854
Sanders, Wolfe and Warren, 1855
Shavor and Henderson, 1869, 1873-1876
Sheldon and Greene, 1862-1869, 1873
Sheldon, Greene and Company, 1870-1872
Skinner, Gould and Company, 1875-1881
Smith and Sheldon, c. 1855-1857
Smith, Sheldon and Company, 1858-1861
Standley and Son, 1881-1882
Starbuck and Gurley, 1823-1829
Starbuck Brothers, 1854-1884
Starbuck, N., and Son, 1835-c. 1846
Starbuck, N., and Sons, 1829-1835
Starbucks and Gurley, 1821-1823
Stewart, William, 1884
Stowe, F. H., 1882
Stratton, Alexander M., c. 1835-c. 1839
Stratton, L., and Son, c. 1828-1833
Stratton, R. M., and Company, ?-1829
Swett, George W., 1894
Swett, George W., and Company, 1886-1894
Swett, Quimby and Company, 1852-1869, 1883/84-1885
Swett, Quimby and Perry, 1869-1883
Tibbits and McCoun, 1860-1862
Tremere and Lape, 1862-1864
Tremere, James A., 1859-1860
Troy Architectural Iron Works and Foundry, 1884-1892
Troy Co-operative Company [Troy Co-operative Foundry], 1874-1878
Union Foundry Company, 1869-1871
Van Hagen, J., and Sons, 1886-1904
Van Hagen, John E., 1902-1904
Velsey and Chase, 1883
Velsey, C. M., 1888
Velsey, C. M., and Company, 1884-1887
Viall, House and Mann, 1849-1851
Victor Stove Company, 1882-1888
Wager and Dater, 1844/45-1847/48
Wager and Fales, 1860-1867
Wager and Fox, 1856-1858
Wager and Pratt, 1847/48-1848
Wager, Fales and Company, 1868-1871
Wager, Fox and Company, 1859
Wager, James, c. 1840-1844/45, 1855, 1872
Wager, Pratt and Company, 1849-1851
Wager, Richmond and Smith, 1853-1854
Wager, Smith and Company, 1852
Wager Stove Company, 1873-1878, 1886, 1889, 1895-1896, 1898-1902
West Side Foundry Company, 1894-1906
Wilcox, Morand, Keep and Company, 1863
Wolfe and Warren, 1856-1858
Wolfe Stove Company, 1878-1882
Wood, W. H., Foundry Company, 1885-1897

OLD-TIME FOOT STOVES

By LURA WOODSIDE WATKINS and EVAN W. LONG

Note. The following article is an amalgamation of two articles on the same subject, independently submitted by the authors. — *The Editor.*

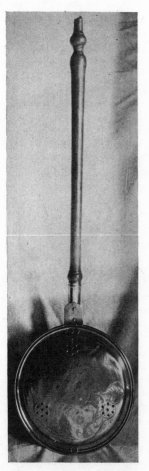

FIG. 1 — BRASS WARMING PAN

Made by William C. Hunneman of Boston (*1769-1856*), an important manufacturer of metal wares large and small. The lid of this pan is slightly pierced and elaborately engraved. Handle broken. A pewter warmer by William Will of Philadelphia is illustrated in Kerfoot's *American Pewter*, Figures 25 and 80

FIG. 2 — BRASS WARMING PAN

Lid pierced with only 12 holes as against 21 in the preceding example. Engraving more formal and correspondingly less interesting. The turned handles of these pans are often very handsome

FIG. 3 — EARLY FOOT STOVE FROM CONNECTICUT (*c. 1800*)

Constructed of wood, with ventilating holes arranged in a decorative pattern. The front panel may be lifted to permit ingress of a tray of hot coals. A form of stove too likely to catch fire.
From the collection of Lura Woodside Watkins

FROM ancient times various types of portable heater have been dedicated to warming the extremities of humankind. Some of these contrivances harbored burning substances such as charcoal or oil; others merely conserved and distributed the heat of bricks, stones, boiling water, or lumps of iron, whose temperature had been raised by contact with fire before they were placed in their appropriate containers.

The Japanese favored a pocket stove curved to fit the person and utilizing a slow-burning charcoal composition. In China devices for heating feet and hands were made of pottery covered with basketwork and filled with hot coals. These efficient braziers afforded twenty-four hours of relative comfort. In the latter part of the sixteenth century metal spheres with screw caps were filled with hot water to serve as hand warmers. The Ashmolean Museum, in Oxford, England, owns an object which an old booklet describes as "a brazen ball to warm ye nunnes hands."

In England from the fifteenth century to the nineteenth the warming pan, a lidded metal basin to be filled with hot coals and wielded by means of a long handle of wood or iron, occupied a place of honor by the kitchen fireplace. It was the housewife's pride to keep the lid of this pan — ordinarily of brass or copper — so brightly polished that its luster rivaled that of the near-by flame. And as she polished she could pause and refresh her virtue by reading the pious exhortations often engraved around the rim of the lid. In his diary for 1669 Pepys mentions a "noble silver warming pan" that had just been presented to him. A warming pan of pewter, the work of William Will, is pictured in Kerfoot's *American Pewter* (*Figs. 25 and 80*). From England the warming pan came to this country with the early settlers who used the instrument chiefly to mitigate the midwinter anguish of diving into a cold and clammy bed. The pierced or engraved copper or brass lid gave coppersmith and brazier opportunity to display their artistic skill. Among household furnishings bed warmers were important enough to warrant their frequent mention in wills. In the probate records for the Massachusetts county of Essex from 1635 to 1681, warming pans appear almost as frequently as any other item.

The foot stove probably had its origin as a lamp, or as a pan of embers or burning charcoal, placed beneath a footstool. From this beginning the once separate parts were combined, apparently in Shakespeare's time, into a single portable unit. Howard G. Hubbard reports that in 1594 Hugh Platte, at Lincoln's Inn, London, wrote:

> Warming pinnes, or froes, are put into thin cases, and those cases wrapped in linnen baggs, to serve to heat beds, and to cast one into a kindly sweat. The like device is used in conveying such iron pinns into hollow boxes of wood, first lined inwardly with metal, either to laye under their feete when they write, or studie, in cold weather, or in their coches to keep their feete warm.

Although as already noted warming pans are frequently mentioned in early inventories, we find no references to the use of foot stoves among the first American colonists. The lack of these conveniences must be attributed to pioneer conditions, since foot warmers were commonly used in the 1600's by the people of the Low Countries, and the settlers must have been familiar with them. The Dutch *genre* painters, who portrayed so many household accessories in their compositions, have left ample evidence that the *stoof* was a recognized necessity. In at least three of his pictures Jan Steen, who died in 1679, introduced the familiar wooden box with tin lining and iron "pinn" (*Twelfth Night*, *The Sick Girl*, and *The Doctor's Visit*). This type of stove was introduced into America by the Dutch colonists, and handsome examples decorated with carving and piercing may occasionally be found.

The New English Dictionary quotes a writer in *Harper's* for 1883 who speaks of "charcoal to put in the little foot warmers used by all womankind in Dutch churches." This may be not quite correct. Charcoal and red embers from the fireplace are not the same thing, and burning charcoal liberates dangerous fumes unsafe in close or crowded churches and homes.

A simpler variety of stove, also betraying Dutch influence, was made in Connecticut (*Fig. 3*). This wood-enclosed stove resembles the pierced tin form, except that its door slides up instead of swinging on hinges. It has no lining of metal or other protection against the heat of the coal pan.

The Dutch also made foot stoves of elaborately ornamented brass. One specimen, dated *1733*, combines repoussé and openwork ornament, employing the familiar tulip for motive. It is round instead of rectangular.

Such contrivances were common in England and America by the early eighteenth century. In 1716 the playwright Gay wrote, "The Belgian stove beneath her Footstool glows." History records that, in 1744, the First Church in Roxbury lost its third edifice as a result of fire caused by foot stoves. Thereafter their use in the building was prohibited. One shudders to think of that chill New England meetinghouse in zero weather, when even the comfort of warm feet was denied the suffering congregation! In 1748, David Blasdell, the Amesbury clockmaker, made two stoves for the tithing men, receiving one pound four shillings for his labor. He was typical of the handy artisan of his time, for he not only worked on clocks, but also made and repaired augers, andirons, steelyards, and gunlocks, repaired tin and brassware, made nails, shod horses, molded spoons, forged ironwork for vessels, made tow combs, sold groceries, dry goods, meat, and wood, and operated a

FIG. 4 — CARVED WOOD FOOT STOVE (*eighteenth century*)

Either a Holland example or of Dutch inspiration

cider mill. No doubt the majority of handwrought foot warmers were made by local tinkers possessed of similar universal capabilities. The demand for foot stoves was large, and since their making involved no serious difficulties almost every smith must have tried his hand at the job. Not improbably such stoves were piled on the wagons of countless Yankee peddlers, as a regular item of merchandise to be distributed among habitations in the wilderness.

In the eighteenth century, the early form of the word — *stow* — was often heard. We find that Agnes Lobdell of Boston, reporting her losses by the fire of 1760, lists "1 Tin Stow" worth two pounds and five shillings. Easter Tinkom mentions "1 Stow & frame"; Rachel La Mottee, "Stove & pan," at three pounds ten shillings; and Jonathan Mason, "1 Tin Stove & Case."

Evidently the tin stove had come into its own in New England by this time, and its popularity continued for another century. The usual type of the early 1800's is a wooden frame with turned corner posts, enclosing a pierced tin container for the iron or tin fire pan. Glowing embers from the fireplace provided the heat, which radiated through the small openings, bathing in a genial warmth the pedal extremities that rested on the barred frame above. The punched decoration is, of course, the interesting feature of this type of stove. Hearts, circles, and geometric designs predominate. The four pictured examples in Figure 5 are representative. They are for individual use. The stove at the right was carried to service in Bradford, Massachusetts, about 1830. On many a Sunday its owner filled it with hot coals at the old house on the corner of Salem Street, the first home of Bradford Academy, where members of the congregation were supplied with fresh fuel before church began.

Figure 6 illustrates two somewhat larger stoves that may conceivably have been enjoyed by two persons at once. The unusual round example has a wooden top with large openings for radiation, tin sides, and a round coal pan. A family-size affair, similar to the square one shown in Figure 6, is owned by Miss Eleanor Hudson. It is fully four times as large as an individual foot stove

FIG. 5 (*below*) — METAL STOVES IN WOOD FRAMES (*first half of nineteenth century*)

A safer form than that of Figures 3 and 4. The woodwork merely constitutes a frame for a tin box within which a pan of coals may be placed. The example at the left is from Ohio and displays more elaborate piercing than most New England stoves of the period. The ap-

proximate date of stoves of this type may be judged by the character of the turned corner posts. In none of the stoves here illustrated do the turnings display any such refinement of proportions and elaboration of members as would indicate eighteenth- or even very early nineteenth-century craftsmanship. The example at the right is known to have been used in the 1830's. The one at the left was taken to the Western Reserve by settlers from New England.

Left, from the Ohio State Archeological and Historical Society; others from the collections of Eleanor Hudson and Lura Woodside Watkins

and was probably placed in the center of the pew, where father, mother, and the children could share its genial outgiving of warmth. This Gargantuan heater is illustrated in Figure 15.

FIG. 6 — TWO FOOT STOVES (*second third of nineteenth century*)
The unusual cylindrical example at the right has a perforated wooden top to prevent the user's feet from scorching. The example at the left displays a cratelike wood frame devoid of decorative embellishment.
From the collection of Eleanor Hudson

An amusing contrivance, which should have a bail, although it was never equipped with a frame, is the stove heated by a whale-oil burner shown in Figure 8. The lamp, once lighted, was slipped into a cunningly shaped opening and was fastened in place by a movable strip of tin. To prevent too great a concentration of heat, the top of the box is fitted with an air chamber in the form of an inverted dome that insures proper distribution of warm air. This peculiar device was found in Connecticut, where ingenious Yankees often turned their wits to inventing and patenting such contraptions, in spite of their questionable practicability.

A combined lantern and foot stove, manufactured by Francis Arnold, of Middle Haddam, Connecticut, was exhibited at the New York Exposition of 1853. It might well have been the affair shown in Figure 9. It will be seen that a whale-oil burner provides both light and heat. Windows on the front and sides and a substantial handle for carrying make the box a veritable lantern. When the upper section is tipped back on its hinges, a sloping surface, nicely carpeted, with a ledge for resting the heel of the shoe, is revealed.

In fact, at various times foot stoves intended to serve a multitude of collateral purposes came on the market. In England, in 1781, a patent was issued for a heater with an earthenware case for the purpose of warming beds, dishes, plates, and feet in carriages or in churches. An 1846 patent covers a combination foot and bed warmer and a potato roaster.

At the Philadelphia Centennial in 1876 an English firm exhibited a pottery device to be filled with hot water and placed in boots for the purpose of drying and heating these intractable articles of footwear. That any of these all too ingenious inventions were actually manufactured and marketed may be doubted.

While the warming pan was the chief instrument for preheating the old-time bed, the more compact foot stove was requisitioned for long winter drives and for counteracting the Sabbath chill of unheated churches, where the rule of four-hour services was not relaxed in deference to Boreas. Prior to 1825 the adequate heating of churches or other places of public assembly was hardly thought of. Even in 1840 only the larger houses of worship were equipped with sizable coal or wood stoves. In an attempt to afford the congregation at least some foot comfort, dogs were frequently permitted to enter the church and to lie across their master's feet, while in some churches a fur robe tacked to the seat might be wrapped around the nether

FIG. 7 — ALL-METAL FOOT STOVE (*first half of nineteenth century*)
Made in Pennsylvania and exhibiting characteristically elaborate piercings. The absence of a wood frame fails to constitute proof that the stove was not originally equipped with such a safeguard

FIG. 8 — OIL-BURNING FOOT STOVES (*1830–1850*)
Left, of wood lined with tin and equipped with a lamp.
From the Bucks County Historical Society, Doylestown, Pennsylvania.
Below, pierced tin stove, heated with a whale-oil lamp. A device within the stove evenly distributes the heat. Found in Connecticut.

From the collection of Lura Woodside Watkins

limbs of the shivering worshipers. In some localities, during the noontime intermission in the preaching the congregation would repair to a near-by house for luncheon. Such a refuge was often erected specially for the purpose and was known as the "Sabbaday house." It appears to have been little more than a shed with horse stalls at one end and a large fireplace at the other. From the latter shrine the assembled folk would select fresh embers for their foot stoves before repairing to the sanctuary and enduring the second installment of the sermon. The hardier, and perhaps more devout, souls viewed foot stoves as crass material substitutes for the celestial fires which should have been kindled solely by the hortatory friction of the sermon. But certain it is that most of the women and even some of the men, whatever their spiritual reliance upon the parson, preferred to plant their feet firmly on a diminutive but cozy heater. Watson, in his *Annals (1842)*, says that the more prudent and feeble women carried foot stoves to church with them. Howells, writing in *Longman's Magazine* in 1882, mentions "the foot stove which one of his congregation carried to meeting and warmed his poor feet with."

Even the small comfort yielded by the foot stove was declared unhealthful by an English writer of 1818, who in a discourse on the art of preserving the feet observes, "Our English travellers should always be on their guard against the use of feet stoves." Even in those days, apparently, America was a materialistic land of creature comforts.

Various other means of warming the feet, either at home or abroad, were resorted to in olden days. One of the commonest was a large slab of soapstone that could be heated in the fireplace and then placed, well wrapped, in bed or carriage. Iron handles for lifting it were inserted in holes bored in the soft stone *(Fig. 11)*. A smaller version was dedicated to warming and drying cowhide boots *(Fig. 12)*. Hot-water bottles proved comfortable on long journeys, and to that end they were shaped to fit the feet pressed against them *(Fig. 14)*. They are a product of the mid-nineteenth century and were made in mottled Rockingham ware both at the Bennington works and at some of the smaller potteries in New England. The same kind of bottle was turned out at Portland, Maine, in stoneware washed with dark-brown slip. Some specimens marked *J. T. Winslow, Portland, Me.* will be found. The elongated stoneware bottle of Figure 14 represents a type of foot warmer used until quite recently. Earlier containers of the same shape were made in gray stoneware and in glazed redware.

Home-contrived substitutes for special hot-water containers were many. Often the family cider jug was requisitioned. A hot

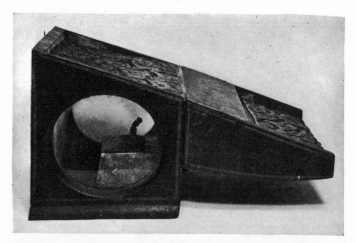

FIG. 9 — COMBINATION LANTERN AND STOVE (*c. 1850*)
A double-service device, equipped with whale-oil lamp. Closed, it serves well as a portable lantern spreading its beams in three directions. Open, it affords a carpeted rest for chilled feet.
From the collection of Eleanor Hudson

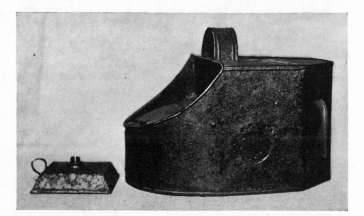

FIG. 10 — COMBINATION FOOT WARMER AND CARRIAGE LANTERN (*c. 1830–1850*)
Another double-service device, capable of heating and lighting simultaneously if placed under the front seat of a vehicle. Made of tin, with wire ventilator at side; equipped with whale-oil burner.
From the collection of Mrs. Bertram K. Little

FIG. 11 (*left*) — SOAPSTONE FOOT WARMER (*nineteenth century*)
Heated in the fireplace or oven and wrapped in wool cloths, these soapstones remained at least tepid for several hours.
From the collection of Eleanor Hudson

FIG. 12 (*right*) — BOOT DRYER (*nineteenth century*)
To be heated and dropped into the leg of the short boots worn by many men until the late nineteenth century.
From the collection of Lura Woodside Watkins

brick wrapped in cloth was a frequent companion of slumber or of a sleigh ride. A crude but efficient means of heating a bed was to employ a log of green wood about eighteen inches long and nine inches in diameter. This log was heated either in front of the fireplace or in the kitchen oven, then wrapped in cloth. A family in eastern Pennsylvania reports that a log, christened "Uncle John," served thus faithfully for twenty-five years prior to the advent of the rubber hot-water bag and electric pad.

Men and women may come and go, but, if legend may be trusted, cold extremities have been the lot of humankind at least since Noah's day. No doubt they will continue forever to be a plague exorcisable only by close personal contact with an appropriate talisman. But though there is greater potency in today's electric pad than in all the metal and earthen heaters employed by our ancestors, the old-time devices possess certain mystical powers that no mechanical ingenuity can duplicate. Even when stone cold, they can still warm the heart — a capability denied to their modern rivals even when their temperature has been raised to the boiling point.

FIG. 13 — CARRIAGE OR SLEIGH FOOT WARMER (*mid-1800's*)
Earthenware with warm chocolate-brown glaze. Metal screw cap and brass-mounted thermometer. Probably made at Zanesville, Ohio.
From the Krantz collection

FIG. 14 (*below*) — HOT-WATER FOOT RESTS AND A STONEWARE BED WARMER (*c. 1850*)
From the collections of Mrs. John O. De Wolf, Eleanor Hudson and Lura Woodside Watkins

FIG. 15 — FAMILY-SIZE FOOT STOVE
This tin-and-wood heater was carried to church or meetinghouse, where the whole shivering family could enjoy its comforting warmth on a winter's day. It is four times the size of the largest of the individual foot stoves. A number of these distributed through the church would compensate for the absence of central heating. Some communities maintained "Sabba-day houses" where during the noon intermission the congregation could eat lunch and replenish the fuel in their foot stoves, before the afternoon session.
From the collection of Eleanor Hudson

III Toys

In this section all of the articles deal with mass-produced toys which were a product of manufacturing methods introduced during the nineteenth-century Industrial Revolution. Tin toys were made from sheet iron which had a thin coating of tin on both sides to prevent rusting. Both toy soldiers and toy parts were cast in molds. Parts were stamped or pressed out, assembled, and painted. The soldiers were usually one-piece affairs which were decorated by painting to represent the desired military unit.

Tin toys are probably the smallest intricate objects made from metal, and among the most attractive. Extremely durable, they are relatively free of sharp edges, and when painted, present a picturesque appearance not to be duplicated in any other medium. Their appearance is not unlike that of much fine Japanned ware, and special decorators were hired to paint the toys in bright and charming colors.

American tin toys
at the Abby Aldrich Rockefeller Folk Art Collection

BY JUDITH BLOOD

TIN-TOY MANUFACTURERS were working in the newly industrialized United States as early as 1830, and were particularly successful during the third quarter of the nineteenth century. The collection of tin toys at the Abby Aldrich Rockefeller Folk Art Collection provides a useful index to the tin-toy trade in America during this period, as it includes wares produced by nearly every factory manufacturing tin clockwork and pull toys between 1830 and 1880.

Tin-toy making in America began as the logical outgrowth of the manufacture of tin household goods. As early as 1740 Edward Pattison (or Patterson) and members of his family who had emigrated from Ireland were tinsmiths in the Connecticut River valley. However, it was not until the introduction of sheet-tin manufacturing in America about 1815 that the tin industry became widespread.[1] By 1820 at least five tin factories were operating in and around Berlin and New Britain, Connecticut, where the Pattisons had first worked.

Toys were made from sheet tin in several ways. Parts were cut from the sheet and either soldered or clamped together by metal tabs which formed an extension of each part; or each half of a toy, cut from a sheet, was hammered into a mold and then soldered or clamped together. The toys were painted after they were assembled.

It was the Philadelphia firm of Francis, Field and Francis (also known as the Philadelphia Tin Toy Manufactory after

1848) that first realized the potential of wholesaling tin toys.[2] In 1853 they advertised themselves as purveyors of, among other tin objects, "Japanned Ware and Tin Toys in Great Variety. . . ." The company produced an astonishingly complete line of miniature household furnishings, as well as an impressive array of toy vehicles (see Fig. 1). It seems obvious from its advertisements between 1840 and 1855 that the company sold its toys wholesale to both large urban retailers and small village storekeepers. In addition, after about 1850 expanded trade led to the advent of jobbers who, as middlemen, controlled the distribution of toys from manufacturer to retailer. In order to prevent retailers from ordering directly from the manufacturer jobbers often required that neither toy nor packaging disclose the name of the maker. Large-scale manufacturers added to the confusion by becoming jobbers themselves and by frequently selling parts of toys to other companies. In the case of simple pull toys the physical characteristics of the animals or human figures and the ornamentation of the platforms are usually the best clues to the maker.

By 1850 the clockmakers and tinsmiths of Connecticut had become masters of design and were producing a great variety of imaginative and attractive tin toys. Thanks to the extensive research of the late Edith F. Barenholtz, much is known about the particularly inventive Connecticut toymaker George W. Brown, who was apprenticed to a clock-

Fig. 1. Horse and wagon made by Francis, Field and Francis (also called the Philadelphia Tin Toy Manufactory), Philadelphia, 1830-1850. Painted tin; length 9½ inches. The black decorations painted freehand on the white wagon and on its orange japanned roof emphasize the early date of this toy. Stenciled decorations were applied to later tin toys. The discrepancy in size between the driver, in his yellow suit and black boots and cap, and his hollow white horse in black harness indicates a whimsical lack of concern for proportion among early toy manufacturers. The tin wheels are orange. The semicircular tin wire that connects the horse's left legs prevented the hooves from catching as the toy was pulled along.

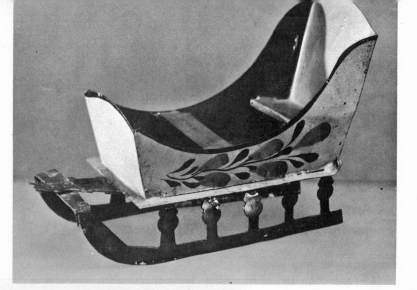

Fig. 2. Sleigh made by J. Spencer, New York City, 1832-1850. Painted tin; length 6¼ inches. A round paper label printed *J. Spencer, Maker, New York,* indicates that this vibrant yellow sleigh with green runners and a red interior was made before jobbers prohibited the marking of toys with the manufacturer's name. Spencer was making tin and wooden toys in New York as early in 1832, and continued to work until 1850. The freehand red and black floral design, repeated on the other side and on the back of the sleigh, is typical of motifs found on toys manufactured between about 1830 and 1850.

Fig. 3. Broadway and Fifth Avenue omnibus, made by George W. Brown and Company or Stevens and Brown Manufacturing Company, Cromwell, Connecticut, 1856-1880. Painted tin and cast iron; length 7¾ inches. This yellow tin omnibus with green cast-iron wheels is drawn by two white tin horses and is driven by a coachman dressed in black and white. The red stenciled floral and leaf and geometric designs exhibit a liveliness typical of American folk decorations. Powered by a clockwork mechanism attached to the rear wheels, the omnibus must have been profitable for the company, as it is illustrated in both *The George Brown Toy Sketchbook* (Pl. 12) and in the 1872 price list issued by the American Toy Company, the jobbers for Stevens and Brown in New York City.

Fig. 4. Horse in a hoop made by George W. Brown and Company or Stevens and Brown, 1860-1880. Painted tin and cast iron; diameter 7½ inches. The hollow tin white horse is mounted by a cast-iron pin through the base of its mane to parallel tin bars that are soldered to a red and white tin hoop. Although hoop toys containing horses, dogs, and children were originally introduced by George W. Brown and Company or Stevens and Brown, Hull and Stafford's showroom catalogue of the late nineteenth century displays two sizes of horses in hoops, indicating either that they manufactured imitations or that they acted as jobbers for the George Brown or Stevens and Brown horses in hoops.

Fig. 5. Water wagon made by Hull and Stafford, Clinton, Connecticut, or Stevens and Brown, 1869-1885. Painted tin and cast iron; length 16½ inches. This bright blue water wagon is harnessed to a pair of hollow tin horses which appear to trot when the small cast-iron wheels revolve. The horses resemble those made by Stevens and Brown. Water wagons identical to this one appear in a Hull and Stafford jobbers catalogue and in the 1872 price list of the American Toy Company. The Hull and Stafford water wagon is shown with a driver; the American Toy Company's, without one.

Fig. 6. Locomotive Cuba, made by George W. Brown and Company or Stevens and Brown, 1856-1880. Tin, cast iron, and wood; length 10¼ inches. The red tin body and yellow tin cab of this locomotive are combined with a wooden front end, base, and smokestack. The stenciled decoration is black and gold and the cast-iron wheels are orange. The engine is powered by a clockwork mechanism. This locomotive is illustrated in *The George Brown Toy Sketchbook* (Pl. I, Fig. 2), where it is called the Union. In the American Toy Company price list of 1872 a different locomotive appears twice under the names General Grant and New York.

Fig. 7. Victorian cottage bank made by George W. Brown and Company or Stevens and Brown, 1856-1880. Painted tin; height 6¼ inches. Three black chimneys and profusions of gingerbread painted gold adorn this red-roofed, yellow cottage. It has black stenciled windows and door, and is mounted on a yellow platform. Banks in various cottage designs, reflecting architectural fancies of the period, were popular items in the Brown line. This example is illustrated both in *The George Brown Toy Sketchbook* (Pl. 29), and in the later American Toy Company catalogue of 1872. The banks sold at wholesale for $10 per dozen complete with lock and key.

Fig. 8. Two-horse buggy made by Hull and Stafford or the Union Manufacturing Company, Clinton, Connecticut, 1856-1885. Painted tin and cast iron; length 9½ inches. These white tin horses with distinctive scalloped manes are harnessed in red and black to a red tin buggy decorated with traces of a floral pattern stenciled in gold paint. The tin hood is collapsible. The cast-iron wheels are black.

maker in Forestville, Connecticut, before founding George W. Brown and Company in 1856. During the 1860's, in addition to making toys and clocks, Brown developed a thriving business in lamp burners which he sold to the Bristol Brass and Clock Company in 1868. The next year George W. Brown and Company merged with J. and E. Stevens of Cromwell, Connecticut, adding a line of clockwork and nonmechanical tin toys to the cast-iron toys and banks which had made Stevens' reputation. *The George Brown Toy Sketchbook,*[3] presumed to be a working catalogue of George W. Brown and Company's and Stevens and Brown's production between the 1860's and early 1870's, is an invaluable source of Brown's designs and an index to contemporary taste in toys. The Broadway and Fifth Avenue omnibus shown in Figure 3 corresponds to Plate 12 in the sketchbook, while the locomotive Cuba shown in Figure 6 appears as Plate I, Figure 2 in the sketchbook (where the locomotive is called the Union). Some of the designs capture the romantic elements of Andrew Jackson Downing's Gothic revival architecture. A case in point is Plate 29, which depicts a variety of banks, including the one shown in Figure 7.

Many of George Brown's designs were unique to his company, but many others were widely copied by other firms as well. Stevens and Brown also sold parts to other firms, including the Union Manufacturing Company of Clinton, Connecticut. Sometime in the early 1870's Union was absorbed by the newly founded firm of Hull and Stafford, another Clinton company, which probably continued to purchase parts from Stevens and Brown. Stevens and Brown stopped production in 1880, but many of the tin toys made by them and by George W. Brown and Company survive as timeless examples of good design in playthings.

The Merriam Manufacturing Company of Durham, Connecticut, advertised in its 1856 price list that a five per cent discount would be given for cash transactions. Tin horses on wheels, such as the one illustrated in Figure 9, sold at wholesale for $18 per gross. By 1886 Merriam was selling not only to Macy and Company in New York and John Wanamaker in Philadelphia but also to large stores in Chicago, St. Louis, and other Midwestern cities. The firm often sold its distinctive horses to Edward R. Ives of Bridgeport, Connecticut, which specialized in clockwork toys and trains, and achieved its greatest success in the 1870's and 1880's.

Althof, Bergmann and Company, located at Park Place and Church Street, New York City, issued a catalogue in 1874. In it they called themselves "Importers of Toys and Fancy Goods," and pointed out that "we pay particular

Fig. 9. Horse on wheels made by the Merriam Manufacturing Company, Durham, Connecticut, 1856-1885. Painted tin and cast iron; length 6½ inches. The gilded hollow tin horse with a painted red saddle and black harness, hooves, and eyes is soldered to an embossed green tin base which is attached to four cast-iron wheels. The flowing mane, single ear, and long tail are characteristic of horses made by the Merriam Manufacturing Company. They are often found on carts and wagons made by Edward R. Ives of Bridgeport in the 1870's.

Fig. 10. Horse on wheels made by Hull and Stafford or the Union Manufacturing Company, 1856-1885. Painted tin and cast iron; length 7 inches. This hollow tin horse is painted white with a red girth and a black harness, and is mounted on a green tin base which has four cast-iron wheels. While a description of the Hull and Stafford horse on wheels would nearly match the Merriam toy shown in Fig. 9, the distinctive physical features of the horses differentiate the two makers.

Fig. 11. Horse on wheels made by Althof, Bergmann and Company, New York, 1867-1885. Painted tin; length 14¾ inches. This brown horse has a black mane and tail. The red saddle and gold girth are applied. The wheels are cast iron. Such well-delineated toys and unusual details set Althof, Bergmann products apart from the other pull toys made between 1867 and 1885, the years Althof, Bergmann was in business.

attention to avoid all sharp edges and corners'' in their tin toys. Unfortunately they did not list any prices. Some Althof, Bergmann toys imitated those of other American manufacturers (*cf.* Figs. 3 and 13), but most of their line is European in feeling (Figs. 11, 12).

At the end of the nineteenth century the number of American firms making toys dwindled in the face of inexpensive imports from Germany, where toymakers were applying the technique of lithography to the decoration of toys.

---

[1] Inez and Marshall McClintock, *Toys in America* (Washington, D.C., 1961), p. 88.

[2] See ANTIQUES for December 1934, pp. 210-211. Francis, Field and Francis was founded in 1830.

[3] The original catalogue is in the collection of Bernard Barenholtz. A facsimile edition, edited and with an introduction by Edith F. Barenholtz, was published by the Pyne Press, Princeton, New Jersey, in 1971.

Fig. 12. Girl with cow made by Althof, Bergmann and Company, 1867-1885. Painted tin and cast iron; length 9¾ inches. Her brown hair shaded by a flat-brimmed yellow hat, this hollow tin girl walks beside an alert brown cow. The girl is dressed in red and white, and both figures are mounted on a green tin base which has cast-iron wheels.

Fig. 13. People's Line omnibus, made by Althof, Bergmann and Company, 1867-1885. Painted tin and cast iron; length 14 inches. This clockwork omnibus is similar in design to the George W. Brown omnibus shown in Fig. 3. Althof, Bergmann and Company's 1874 catalogue offered this bus in four sizes, ranging from 10½ to 21 inches long. In this version the precariously perched coachman dressed in red drives a yellow bus stenciled in red. It is pulled by two horses painted gold with red harnesses. The wheels are cast iron. A wire leading from the front axle to the front of the harness can be moved to determine the direction the toy takes in motion.

Fig. 14. Girl on a velocipede, possibly Stevens and Brown, 1870-1880. Tin, cast iron, fabric, and composition; length 11 inches. The doll on this black cast-iron tricycle has a composition head and torso, legs and arms made of strips of tin, and molded tin hands and feet. Her eyes, hair, and mouth are painted, and she wears brown and white trousers and a brown worsted jacket trimmed with lace. The tin sheet that covers the clockwork mechanism is painted red. The 1872 American Toy Company catalogue illustrates a similar toy which sold at wholesale for $24 per dozen, and was advertised as being "a source of amusement equally to the child and adult."

Fig. 15. Locomotive Rocket and open car, made by James Fallows and Sons, Philadelphia, 1890-1895. Painted tin and cast iron; length 8 inches. The locomotive is made of molded and soldered tin painted red, black, and yellow, with the name stenciled on both sides and a star embossed on the front end. The open car hooked to the engine is stamped-and-soldered tin painted green. All the wheels are cast iron. The simplicity of design and appealing clear colors of this toy were characteristic of the quality of toys made in Philadelphia between 1830 and 1900.

THE LITTLE TOY SOLDIER

Invincible in Peace: Invisible in War

By ROSEMARY MORSE HOPKINS

FOR NEARLY TWO CENTURIES, the toy soldier has held sway, rivaled only in recent days by the airplane, in the play and imagination of countless small boys in many countries. He has been to them, in their youth, a symbol of gallantry, courage, and patriotism which has doubtless proved a lasting model for their later bearing in life as well as in battle. As Waterloo was won on the cricket fields of England, so probably were the seeds of other victories sown when

miniature armies were manoeuvered upon the playroom floor. In time of war, the little lead soldier has given his all, the very lead from which he might have been cast going, instead, into bullets. In time of peace he reappears, to inspire another generation to deeds of valor. Of the vast armies of toy soldiers manufactured over the years, most have fought their last campaigns and disappeared into oblivion. Fortunately, however, an appreciable number of veterans have assembled in

FIG. 1 — KNIGHTHOOD IN FLOWER. An armored man and horse, 4 inches high, and a knight on foot. Both were cast flat, in lead, with movable arms and visors, and brilliantly colored, with careful detail. Made by Bisold, in Nuremberg, probably in the late 1860's or early 1870's, though similar types are attributed to about 1820, and were once among the playthings of a young French nobleman. They are from an original set of twelve. The name of the maker appears in relief on the base of but one, as seems to have been the custom.

FIG. 2 — MOUNTED SOLDIERS. Cast flat, in lead; overall height, 4⅜ inches. Brightly painted on both sides, with faces and front of uniforms on one surface, and backs on the other. From a set of six mounted officers, all differently uniformed, made probably *c.* 1850-1860, though this type also is attributed to an earlier date. On the base of one figure appears in relief the name of the maker, *SCHILDKNECHT*.

All illustrations from the author's collection.

FIG. 3 — A MILITARY BAND. In the uniform of a French regiment of the Second Empire; moustache and imperial of Louis Napoleon type. Height 1⅞ inches; cast solid, with removable heads. From a boxed set of 30 pieces, including a mounted general and staff, and a company of infantry. The set was probably made in France just prior to the Franco-Prussian War.

FIG. 4 — RICHMOND LIGHT INFANTRY BLUES. The officer and eleven of the rank and file are molded solid, but thin; height, 2¾ inches. The set, cast in 1893, commemorated the one hundredth anniversary of this famous Virginia regiment, in continuous existence since May 10, 1793. In 1861 the "Blues" joined, as Company E, the First Regiment of Virginia Volunteers, Army of Northern Virginia.

collections, to be regarded as items of paramount interest by truly serious-minded grown-ups.

The toy soldier was known to the ancients, as testified by examples in lead and pottery, and in later years cast in silver, to become another sport for kings. But it was not until after the military exploits of Frederick the Great, in the second half of the eighteenth century, that it became universally popular as a plaything. The manufacture, in quantity, of these toys developed in Germany, probably originating in Nuremberg about 1760. Competitors soon began production throughout northern Germany, and from numerous shops in cities in that region lead soldiers, beautifully designed and executed, supplied a wide market. However, the esthetic and commercial precedence remained in Nuremberg. There, early in the nineteenth century, Ernst Heinrichsen introduced the so-called "Nuremberg scale," establishing standard sizes for the mounted and unmounted figures. This scale was more or less generally adopted, though the specimens in the accompanying illustrations show that not all manufacturers conformed to it. I know of boxed sets of lead soldiers extremely popular with French children of fifty years ago, in which the pieces of unmounted men were not over an inch in height.

Nor did the German manufacturers always excel in the artistry of the product, as is so often claimed; some of the French pieces of 1880-1890 are unsurpassed. Au Paradis des Enfants on the Rue de Rivoli, for example, had in the late 1880's piles of little oval boxes, looking like miniature butter tubs, which one little boy known to me spent hours examining, trying to stretch his allowance to cover as many as possible. Each box contained a complete battle scene from historic campaigns, such as the Zulu War, the French in Indo-China, and so on. A blue and white label on the cover indicated the contents. A small box could be bought for 1 fr. 75, and a larger set for 2½ francs. The sets were of very small figures, flat, painted on both sides, very generous in number, and packed in layers separated by tissue. Anyone who has shared the experience of this little boy will recall the thrill of unveiling each layer and revealing the pieces in all their brilliance and promise of exciting play.

The little men shown in the accompanying illustrations are from the author's collection and, while a few of them are of the type played with by Junior on the nursery table, the majority are of grandfather's day or earlier. In time their ranks will be augmented by toy veterans of World War II.

FIG. 5 — SEVEN STRAGGLERS. From as many different sets (c. 1880-1895). *Left to right:* (1), Leading the file, the oldest veteran in the group, a French zouave, cast solid, though very thin, 2 5/16 inches high. (2), A figure evidently intended to represent an American infantryman, cast flat, with movable left arm, so that his musket may be brought from "left shoulder arms" to a semblance of "carry arms." (3), A type of tin soldier, not lead, formed by halves cast hollow and joined, representing a Prussian infantryman, 2⅜ inches high. (4), A zouave, or Turko, of the French army, one of a set of 30-odd pieces, embracing zouaves, infantry of the line, and *chasseurs-à-pied,* together with a general and other mounted officers. As the general in this instance was in the likeness of General Boulanger, the set is rather definitely dated as of the 1880's. The set was made in Paris and demonstrates, by accuracy in detail and artistry in modeling, the superiority of French manufacturers. (5), An officer in full-dress summer uniform, consisting of gray coat with tails, white trousers, white spiked helmet, strongly suggesting that he might have been made to portray an officer of the Seventh Regiment, New York National Guard. The little boy who originally owned the piece, now a mere lad of sixty-four years, insists that it was purchased, with others of the set, on the Island of Jersey, about 1891. There may be some other lad, however, who definitely recalls the occasion for the commemoration of which such sets were made, at the instance of New York's famous Seventh. The figure is molded solid, with removable head, standing 2⅝ inches. (6), A sailor of the Royal British Navy, wearing regulation straw hat and beard. Although his miniature Lee-Metford rifle has gone, he still wears his cartridge-box and knife bayonet. (7), A sturdily constructed Highlander, who once carried a rifle at "shoulder arms," but, like the sailor, he has misplaced it.

FIG. 6 — MUSIC AGAIN. Leading (*at right*) are four musicians of a British foot regiment, with spiked helmets and scarlet coats; height, 1 13/16 inches. Cast solid, with removable heads (c. 1880). Following them is a drummer, one of a set of six, in the uniform of a British foot regiment of about 1826, although the piece was made in France, possibly as late as 1920. Cast hollow; height, 2¾ inches. This figure is rare in that the drumsticks are carried in the right hand and are not in use on the drum, as usually molded. Next is a drummer in the uniform of an Austrian foot regiment of the period of the Napoleonic Wars, made in France following the first World War. Cast solid, of lead, 2¼ inches tall. Behind him marches a very spirited bass drummer, of a British foot regiment, made by the English firm, Britain, Ltd., whose hollow-cast lead soldiers, depicting many of the British regiments as well as those of other countries, became universally popular some twenty years ago. This figure is 2⅜ inches in height. Bringing up the rear of the procession are three bandsmen of one of the British regiments of guards, in scarlet tunics and fur busbies. These are solid cast, stand 2⅜ inches in height, and date about 1890. The ten figures in this group readily show that no scale, Nuremberg or other, has been adhered to by manufacturers.

Fig. 1 — ALLURING MECHANISMS

No child could long hesitate between the enticements of taffy and the joy of seeing Sambo swallow the penny instead. Sambo would get the penny, or a mule would kick it into safe-keeping.

Toy Banks

By WILLARD EMERSON KEYES

Illustrations from the collection of David Moskowitz

TO whom is the world indebted for the child's savings bank? Could it have been Benjamin Franklin, that man of many inventions, whose maxims designed for the encouragement of thrift are among our most familiar quotations? Or was it some later and humbler genius — an ironfounder, perhaps, seeking profits from a by-product during a dull season? May it not be that the toy was naturally suggested by the founding, in 1816, of the first chartered banks for savings, or by the strife over the United States Bank in Andrew Jackson's time? It is impossible to say; for, by their very nature, these little receptacles for vagrom pennies were not precisely toys, nor were they a child's necessaries like pattens and copper-toed boots.

There is no literature of the depositories for children's savings. Patient search fails to bring to light the story of their origin. Such meager information as we possess indicates that they made their appearance not much, if any, earlier than the middle of the last century. At any rate, none of the banks pictured here bears positive evidence of having existed previous to the Civil War. The oldest obtainable catalogue of toy manufacturers that lists children's banks bears no date, but, from certain obscure allusions in it to the Peace Jubilee in Boston, we may infer that it was published about 1870.*

It is certain, however, that toy banks, at any rate of a simple design, were plenty, long before the Peace Jubilee. There are persons now living who recall, in all their vivid brightness, scattered golden days in that tragic time of the conflict between the States, when the war-drums still were throbbing; and, distinct in the picture, standing out clearly in the recollection of the cluttering furniture of the old sitting room, is a little cast-iron bank. Perhaps this object reposed on the mantel — the carved, white marble mantel of mid-Victorian years — the mantel which never knew the glow of a cheerful blaze upon the hearth beneath. Perhaps it rested on the whatnot in the corner, facing those delirious forms in sable haircloth and tortured black walnut which seemed to the eyes of their generation to establish a standard of beauty in household furniture that should endure to be the envy and despair of all posterity to come; but it was there — childhood's penny bank.

During the long months of the child's year, the toy bank accumulated its hoard of pennies — gifts and rewards and payments. At Christmas time it disgorged its treasure, but only by a tedious process of shaking and tilting and twisting, until the coins slipped, one by one, out of prison to pursue again their adventurous course through a wilderness of pockets.

Such toy banks of the commoner sort were patterned on the large square mansions which had been built out of fortunes made by privateering in the War of 1812. Each

*In this catalogue is an illustration of the Chronometer Bank — A Novelty in Toy Banks — and this description: "The coin, put in at the top is deposited in the vault below, and a mechanical device indicates the number deposited. The upper index contains the numbers from 1 to 10; the lower from 10 to 100. This is supposed to be the work of Father Time, represented in the Medallion as

endeavoring to turn a cent into a dollar, suggesting that the accumulation of wealth is the result of the proper employment of Time and Money."

Fig. 2 — WILLIAM TELL BANK

This is an accurate bit of cast iron mechanism. A coin placed on William Tell's crossbow seldom fails, when the spring is released, to shoot over the boy's head and into the castle.

devices, not differing greatly from those made use of in some of the banks in this collection in Philadelphia. There may be small doubt that a sinister purpose lurked back of this scheme of fashioning miniature banks in the shape of toys. A youngster could be lured into a habit of thrift utterly foreign to his nature by his unappeasable curiosity to see the thing work. It was worth a penny or a nickel — worth foregoing what the coin would buy — to watch William Tell shoot the cash over the head of his little, trusting son into the dark tower behind, or to see Pat's pig flirt it with his hoof into the grinning open mouth of his master.

edifice was surmounted by a cupola, and above the blind door, over which ran the inscription *Bank* or *Savings Bank*, appeared the slit through which the coins found sanctuary. In the Sunday School libraries of that period, side by side with Harry Castlemon's enthralling romances of *Frank on a Gunboat* and *Frank on the Prairie*, were ranged stories of hardened fathers who crept at midnight into the chamber of an innocent little son or daughter, emptied the cherished toy bank which stood upon the shelf and carried off the contents to propitiate the Demon Rum. The special tragedy of such occurrences lay in the fact that the child had invariably fallen asleep while formulating the high resolve of taking the money from the bank, next morning, to buy physic for a mother on the brink of dissolution from consumption, or halitosis, or other fatal malady.

The Statue of Liberty Bank, the U. S. Grant Bank, the Flatiron Building Bank, tell their own story of date. The others may be of almost any period. A connoisseur in the manufacture of iron small wares might be able to judge from their style, or from some occult marks legible to him alone, when these specimens passed through the foundry. But though we have connoisseurs in old furniture and old fabrics, old coins, old jewelry, and old tableware, no man has yet made a name for himself as an authority on toy banks and their beginnings.

Still, though we lack positive evidence in the matter, some of a negative character not lightly to be thrown out of court is to be found in Jacob Abbott's neglect to mention the toy bank in either the *Rollo Books* or the *Fran-*

Among the toy banks in the collection here partly illustrated are some of an ingenious mechanism, which might be expected to supply a clue to the time in which they flourished.* But mechanical toys have been found in the tombs of the Pharaohs and the Caesars. Archimedes amused himself by constructing them. They were operated by springs, triggers, tumblers, and various balancing

*The William Tell, Tammany, Pat and His Pig, and other early patent marks of the 1870's and 1880's.

Fig. 3 — TWO MECHANICAL BANKS

In the first, Judy holds a tray on which the coin is placed. At the pressing of a lever, Judy swings to the right, slipping the coin into an aperture at the rim of the bank, while Punch delivers a blow on his wife's head with his club. Patented *1884*. The *Tammany Bank* at the right drops a coin placed on the right hand into a slit concealed by the left arm. Patented *1873*.

conia Stories. These tales for the edification of early Victorian childhood are a mine to the antiquary who wishes to inform himself as to the domestic manners of Americans in the days before the railroad. They describe in minute detail the contents of rooms — household utensils, furniture, playthings, tools. It seems a pretty safe conclusion, that if the toy bank had existed in Jacob Abbott's time, he would have arranged that Rollo possess one, if only to suggest a lecture on thrift delivered by the impeccable Jonas.

We should behold Rollo, succumbing to a moment of terrible temptation and buying a penny whistle — a trifle dear to a boy's heart, but of no use in acquiring merit or obtaining salvation — a bauble, soon to be tired of and thrown away — a clear example of money squandered. We should learn that Rollo might have spared himself much agony of mind if he had put the money into his little toy bank, as Jonas had counseled while the small boy was still deliberating, torn between duty and the lyric lure of the whistle.

Nor is it clear that Rollo ran across any savings banks during his memorable visit to his Uncle George in Cambridge — a scene from Rollo's history that Jacob Abbott strangely overlooked — a scene depicted by another and, alas, a distinctly frivolous hand. From this the reader gains the impression that Rollo's Uncle George was a wastrel, not interested in any savings bank, toy or otherwise.

Jacob Abbott would have described the adventure in loftier style. He would have shown Rollo upon his return home from Cambridge forgetting even to kiss his mother in his eagerness to deposit in the toy bank on the whatnot the remnant saved from his allowance of expense money, thereby bringing a watery gleam of approval to the bleak countenance of his father, Mr. Holliday. But that is mere surmise; we find no mention of the toy bank in the tales of Jacob Abbott, though we are told of trundle-beds, wheelbarrows, crickets, knives, this, that, and the other. The inference is reasonable, is it not, that there was no such

thing as a toy bank at the time Jacob Abbott was writing — in the thirties and forties, not far from a century ago?

The collection of toy banks here in part illustrated is remarkable for its variety; remarkable also in showing how large a place these objects have filled in that world of unconsidered trifles upon which so much of the world's labor has been expended, even from the day when the patriarch Noah made the first miniature Ark to amuse his grandchildren Tubal and Magog and Arpachshad and to fix in their minds the great event in which he had been chief actor.

The fact that these toy banks have attracted the attention of a collector is significant.

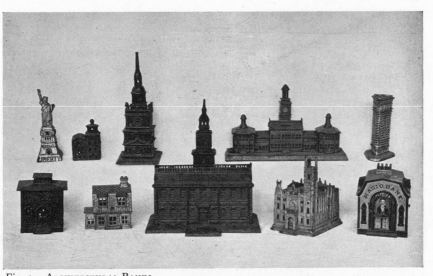

Fig. 4 — ARCHITECTURAL BANKS
Buildings, imaginary and historical; Independence Hall, the Statue of Liberty, and the Flatiron Building are all clearly recognizable.

It implies that a familiar companion of our childhood is passing; has, perhaps, definitely passed from the ken of the present-day juvenile. Not so many years ago an ingenious Yankee doomed the old-fashioned toy bank by his invention of a nickel cylinder affair, in which a coin once slipped was securely locked until nine more followed it, when the lot were automatically released. And now a paternal government, through the medium of the public school, has taken over the functions of small banks of all kinds. The children take their pennies, nickels, and dimes to the school-teacher. The money is collected and the lump is deposited in a grownups' institution where it earns interest. The capital and increment are returned to the pupils at the beginning of vacation or a little before Christmas.

Thus another of the old familiar things, cherished in memory, goes the way to oblivion. The toy bank, which once occupied an honored place in the sitting room now gathers dust in a dark corner of the attic until by incredible fortune it is sought out by a collector, in whose hands it acquires interest, if not dignity, as a survival of a lost art or a departed custom. And, possibly, among the toys thus saved from ash-can and junk-heap there may, here and there, be one fashioned by a cunning workman — a specimen not only unique but marked by some artistic excellence. Far stranger things have happened.

THE FIRST FIVE YEARS OF PATENTED TOY BANKS

By H. BLAIR HULL

Note. This article was prepared largely at the instance and with the assistance of the late Norman Sherwood of Spring Lake, New Jersey, whose knowledge of old mechanical toy banks was extensive and of long standing. He submitted Mr. Hull's article to ANTIQUES and the Magazine regrets that he did not live to see it published. With the manuscript he sent the following introductory notes:

"While Blair Hull is a comparatively new name in the bank collecting field, its owner makes up for relative inexperience in enthusiasm and in thoroughness. He is peculiarly fitted for the special study he has undertaken — namely, patent research in the field of toy banks, mechanical and otherwise. When introduced to his work I had no idea of its importance. My initial skepticism soon changed to genuine interest and then to a deep appreciation of the real contribution he has been able to make in a comparatively short time to our knowledge of the whole subject. I had always depended for information about toy banks upon advertising dodgers, leaflets, trade catalogues, house organs, and jobbers' catalogues, plus what I could learn directly by investigating the still-existing foundries, their history and traditions. Now that Blair has come along to do this job of patent research, a whole new avenue of information is opened. I feel very appreciative, and very grateful for the opportunity given me to collaborate, to a certain extent, in the good work. The best I can wish for Blair Hull — and for every other enthusiastic collector — is that he may find all the rare mechanical banks which his research discloses as having existed."

FIG. 1 — HALL'S EXCELSIOR BANK. Patented December 21, 1869, by John Hall, Watertown, Massachusetts, inventor. Marked *Halls Excelsior* on front; constructed of cast-iron parts, wood figure, wood table, paper arms. It is operated as follows: when doorbell is pulled, roof lifts up showing small monkey; coin placed on table overbalances and closes roof; monkey turns head. Variant has small man instead of monkey. Oldest cast-iron patent-marked mechanical bank; there are undoubtedly older unpatented ones. Many minor variations occur. There is still controversy as to whether the bank with a man's head is authentic. Curiously, this is one of the most frequently found of all mechanical banks. The earliest banks show the patent date stenciled on the roof. Immediately thereafter, the patent date was stamped in the iron on top of the roof and is clearly visible through the paint. Later specimens do not show this; doubtless after the patent expired, the date was omitted from the banks. Certainly they were made long after the patent had expired

FIG. 2 — BOY, FROG, AND DOG BANK. Patented January 4, 1870, by W. P. X. Smith, New York City, inventor. Constructed of cast-iron parts. Operation: press dog, boy turns, tossing coin into frog's mouth, which has just opened. Springs reset parts. Coin is placed on cap or dish in boy's hand. We believe this bank has not yet been discovered by any collector

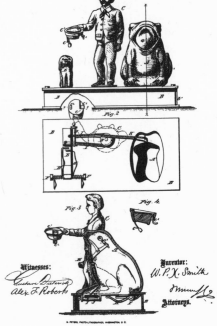

B ETWEEN 1869 and 1910, well over three hundred different mechanical banks, including varieties now important to collectors, were manufactured and merchandised, and nearly all of these were patented. A careful study of early patents has therefore afforded a great quantity of interesting and perhaps new material pertaining to old banks.

One of the most interesting results of this study is discovery of a number of patents for banks of which examples are not yet included in any of the large collections. The 1870 *boy, frog, and dog,* the 1870 *slogan* bank described in this article (*Figs. 2 and 3*), and numerous other banks shown in patents are not represented in the existing ten or twelve large collections of from two to three hundred different mechanical banks. These patents give the collector something new to look for, though it is, of course, possible that the hitherto undiscovered banks were not manufactured in quantity.

The patent papers are frequently of considerable help where a missing part is needed and the owner does not have access to a duplicate bank. In many cases, the patent shows the exact form and mechanical structure as used in manufacture. This is the case, for example, with the *race course* bank, usually called the *horse race* bank (*Fig. 4*).

It was one of the rules of the Patent Office, made effective in 1870, that when a bank

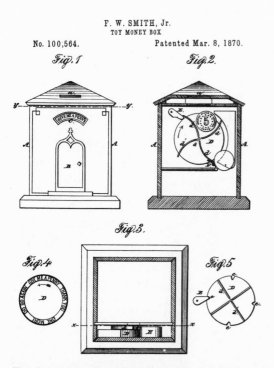

F. W. SMITH, Jr.
TOY MONEY BOX

No. 100,564.   Patented Mar. 8, 1870.

Fig. 1   *Fig. 2.*

Fig. 3.

Fig. 4   *Fig. 5*

FIG. 3 — SLOGAN BANK. Patented March 8, 1870, by F. W. Smith, Bridgeport, Connecticut, inventor. Constructed of cast-iron parts. Operation: coin is dropped in slot in roof of four-sided house; one of four mottoes appears: *Give Me a Penny; Thank You; One More; Do So Again.* In variant photograph swings back of round window. It is probable that no surviving example has been discovered by any collector

was placed on the market the patent application must be filed within a period of two years in order to secure protection. This regulation gives reasonable assurance that the bank was not made earlier than two years before the patent date. Many of the banks marked *Patent Pending* or *Patent Applied For* were made during this two-year period.

Usually comparison of the patent papers with the actual bank will indicate which came first, the patent or the manufactured bank. For example, the *Hall's excelsior* bank patent was probably filed before the banks were actually manufactured (*Fig. 1*). The patent paper of 1869 shows an outside string that could be easily broken by the first boy or girl to play with such a bank, and a cashier's desk as a cubical box made of several pieces of wood — rather expensive and impractical from a manufacturing basis. A later patent of 1875 shows the string on the inside and the cashier's desk exactly as made on banks found in almost all present collections. It is, therefore, quite probable that this bank was first actually made and sold between 1869 and 1875. It is also of interest to note that the patent shows a man as cashier, while most of the banks found have a monkey performing this task. Another difference is that the monkey's head is sidewise when the top of the bank is closed and not in the position shown in the patent. While this bank is very frequently found, it is almost impossible to secure a really perfect and complete specimen, because of their age and frailty. Thus, notwithstanding the modest value of ordinary specimens, perfect examples with all original parts command good prices.

The *home* bank as produced was quite similar to

the patent drawing (*Fig. 5*). Examples occur with and without the eight dormer windows but design patents cover the two varieties. The word *Cashier*, not shown in the drawing, appears on manufactured banks. Otherwise, the design shown in the patent was closely followed.

The *frog on lattice* bank is almost identical with the patent design in regard to form and mechanism (*Fig. 6*). The base is similar to that on the *race course* bank, and both banks are shown in an old trade catalogue of Oscar Strasburger & Company, 443–445 Broadway, New York City.

The *national* bank was somewhat improved in appearance over the patent design (*Fig. 7*). The name *National Bank* was added, as well as the word *Cashier* on the door. The slight curve of the roof line adds another flourish. This is a very rare and desirable bank.

The *novelty* bank is very similar to the patent drawing, except for the detail design of the upper part of the door (*Fig. 8*). The wide brim on the cashier's hat would have presented some foundry problems, so this was eliminated. The door has the knob on the left side and swings open on hinges at the right. Curiously the bank has a bronze or pattern figure of the "tall thin teller" which was evidently made before the bank was patented, as the patent design shows the conventional type of teller holding the tray toward the right, so that the knob of the

FIG. 4 — RACE COURSE BANK. Patented August 15, 1871, by John Hall, Watertown, Massachusetts, inventor. Constructed of cast-iron parts, tin horses. Operation: a spring is set by pulling cord; depositing a coin releases spring and the two horses speed around circular track. Horses start from point marked with a star. This bank is fairly rare. Usually called the *horse race* bank. Some advertisements in old catalogues show sulkeys instead of jockeys

D A. STILES.

Improvement in Toy-Banks.

No. 129,615.   Patented July 16, 1872

fig 1   *fig 2*

fig 3

J. HALL.
RACE COURSE TOY BANK.

No. 118,011.   Patented Aug. 15, 1871

Fig 1

Fig 2

Fig 5

Fig 4

Fig 3

FIG. 5 — HOME BANK. Patented June 25, 1872, July 16, 1872, and July 30, 1872, by D. A. Stiles, Middletown, Connecticut, inventor. Marked *Home Bank* on front. Constructed of cast-iron parts. Operation: when lever is pulled door opens on turntable principle, disclosing cashier at counter. Tip lever to reset. This bank is fairly rare; it occurs in several variants. It was also manufactured as a still bank. The June 25 and July 30 patents are design patents

R FRISBIE

Improvement in Toy Savings-Banks

No 130,575:   Patented Aug 20, 1872

FIG. 6 (*left*) — FROG ON LATTICE BANK. Patented August 20, 1872, by Russell Frisbie, Cromwell, Connecticut, inventor. Constructed of cast-iron parts. Operation: when frog's foot is pressed the eyes blink and the mouth opens to receive the coin. This bank is found rather frequently. The lattice base is similar to that of the *race course* bank. There are several minor variations in the bases

FIG. 7 (*right*) — NATIONAL BANK. Patented August 5, 1873, by H. W. Prouty, Boston, Massachusetts, inventor. Marked *National Bank* on front. Constructed of cast-iron parts. Cashier is a printed paper figure pasted on the iron casting. Operation: bank building with cashier at small window in turntable door. When door is rotated cashier appears at window. Closing door deposits coin and slides cashier to a concealed position

H. W PROUTY.
Toy Money-Boxes.

No 141,516.   Patented August 5, 1873.

FIG. 8 (*below*) — NOVELTY BANK. Patented June 25, 1872 and October 28, 1873, by C. C. Johnson, Somerville, Massachusetts, inventor. Marked *Novelty Bank* on door. Constructed of cast-iron parts. Operation: when front door is opened, teller advances and receives the coin which he deposits in the back; the door swings from one side

C. C. JOHNSON.
Toy Money-Boxes.

No. 144.106.   Patented Oct. 28, 1873.

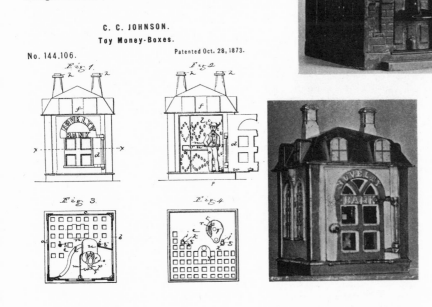

FIG. 9 (*below and right*) —TAMMANY BANK. Patented December 23, 1873, by John Hall, Watertown, Massachusetts, inventor. Marked *Tammany Bank* on side of chair. Constructed of cast-iron parts. Operation: weight of coin placed in the right hand of the effigy of Boss Tweed overbalances arm and deposits coin in his pocket. This is one of the most frequently found banks. One variant has plain circles on side of chair and omits the name *Tammany Bank*

J. HALL.
Toy Money-Boxes.

No. 145,734.   Patented Dec. 23, 1873.

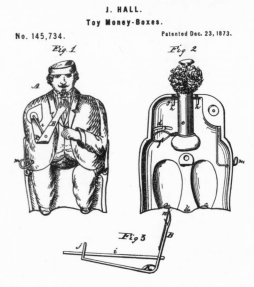

door would have had to be on the right side and the hinges on the left. Moreover, the inside partition in the bank would have had to be in exactly opposite position. Apparently the inventor had considered making the bank in reverse of the conventional type either before he made his patent sketches or before he produced the finished banks. The June 25, 1872, patent was on one of the *home* banks, and evidently had little relation to the *novelty* bank.

The *Tammany* bank patent drawing shows a much more complicated mechanism than the actual manufactured bank (*Fig. 9*). The arm is held up by a spring. The coin is placed in the hand of the seated figure which is held in the upward position by a trigger wire. The trigger wire is then released and the weight of the coin overbalances the spring, dropping the coin in a pocket hole. The bank as found does not include the spring or trigger wire. Part of the arm is used as a counter-weight, greatly simplifying the construction. An effigy of Boss Tweed is used on these *Tammany* banks. Boss Tweed died in 1878, but the toy banks which poked fun at his habit of putting coins in his own pocket have indeed lived after him. Literally thousands of these banks have survived, indicating that tens of thousands must have been made.

IV Hardware: Architectural and Furniture

The articles in this section concern the types of hardware used in the home from the seventeenth through the nineteenth centuries. Three articles illustrated by Dorothy Miller Thorin from the 1920s place emphasis on what one should use in a properly restored interior, while the other seven articles concern door locks, knockers, keys, and furniture hardware.

The two articles depicting pages from eighteenth-century English hardware catalogues whet one's appetite for more material. Donald Streeter, one of America's leading makers of restoration hardware, has written two useful articles on spring latches and stock locks. Martha Mertz's article on keys, Roger Warner's on latch and door knockers, and Wallace Nutting's on house hardware serve as good introductions to each separate subject.

The collecting of antique hardware of all sorts is a popular pastime. The extent of our information concerning European prototypes and types used in North America is still limited. This is a field which can provide diligent collectors and researchers with many hours of worthwhile digging.

KEYS FOR COLLECTORS

By MARTHA MERTZ

Martha Mertz, who lives in San Diego, California, has always been interested in wrought ironwork. She has limited her collecting to unusual old keys from many countries — Palestine, France, Scotland, Spain, England, Mexico.

ENGLISH latch keys for the O'dell lock, patented in 1792 and sometimes called "spade keys."

Illustrations from the author's collection.

BROADLY SPEAKING, locks are bolts guarded by obstacles and controlled by keys — and the variety of keys is almost endless. Since locksmithing, as an industry, is more than four thousand years old and is one of the few surviving crafts today, early examples of the craftsman's skill frequently show such painstaking workmanship, beauty of proportion, and sense of balance that they are a joy to the collector.

In medieval times, the keys of fortresses, castles, towns, and cities were considered significant of ownership, power, and wealth. As a result keys possess a symbolism attached to no other item.

Stephan Doyle was America's first locksmith of record. He came from England and lived in Massachusetts between 1630 and 1650. Most of the early locks used in the Colonies, however, were imported from abroad and it was many years before the smiths of the day were able to supply the demand. Since locks were frequently made for specific buildings or pieces of furniture, many of them were one-of-a-kind items, as ideas of mass production, interchangeable parts, and assembly lines did not begin to develop until the early 1800's. It is said that ironwork, including hinges, latches, angles, and nails, was so scarce that settlers sometimes burned their cabins, gathered the iron pieces from the ashes, and took them along for use in new locations.

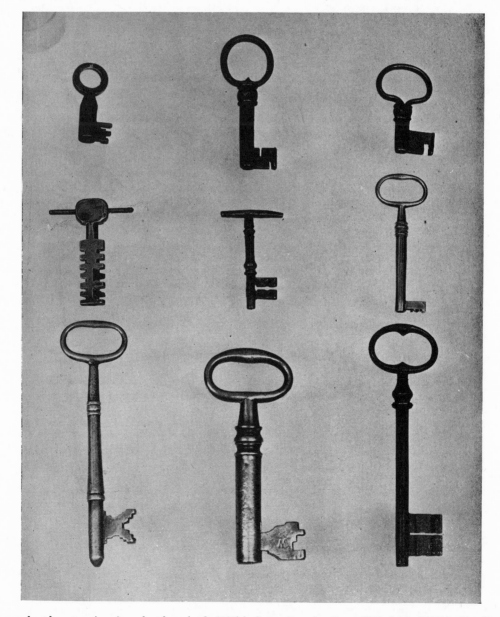

KEYS. *Top,* Black Forest chest key; two American chest keys (early 1800's). *Center,* brass key for padlock (early 1800's); New England door key; brass four-pin key — a principle used by early Egyptians — probably made for the Davis lock, patented in 1799 and used on royal English dispatch boxes. *Bottom,* brass New England door key (probably about 1790); heavy brass sea-chest key (perhaps 1850); key to the New Orleans mint — built in 1835.

Early locks were sometimes nothing more than simple, exposed bolts or latches, and as these became well understood, they were encased in boxes so that their workings were not easily accessible to anyone except with the right key. Part of the effectiveness of some early locks lay in their mere size, rather than in any intricate construction, and naturally keys of equally generous proportions were required to open them. The keyhole frequently appeared only on the outside of the door and a bolt on the inside was thrown by hand. As locks were attached to either the inside or the outside of the door and keys had to be long enough to pass through a thick door and the lock beyond, the shank was very long indeed. As a result, we find keys hinged in the center of the shank, some in which half the shank slid into the other half for greater ease in carrying, and various other size-reducing devices. The mortised lock, set into the door as in common use today, is said to be the rather recent invention of a clever Philadelphian. After this improvement, door keys became appreciably shorter and much of their decorative quality was lost. Over the years, endless variations were introduced, but even the simplest innovation required real inventive skill when used for the first time.

Peculiarly shaped and accurately cut keyholes to fit the right key snugly were among the security devices used. We find them extra thin, abnormally thick, in the shapes of numbers, letters, irregular curves and angles, and sometimes almost complete circles. Keyholes were sometimes covered or masked by cap-escutcheons which were at times part of an elaborate design. Sometimes these covers were unlocked with an individual key, occasionally they merely required touching an unseen spring.

One very substantial and complicated type of lock used pressure to attain security. The hollow key, being shaped like the letter S, was inserted and turned in one direction, then pressed deeper into the lock and turned in the opposite direction.

NEW ORLEANS gate key (1800 or a little earlier).

FRENCH pressure-type key (said to have been in use at the time of the French Revolution).

EARLY SPANISH door key (probably about 1750).

VERY OLD warded key (probably 17th century or earlier).

elaborate cuts in the keys to match the intricate barriers in the locks were handmade with saw, file, or chisel and required much time and skill to fashion. Separate rings or segments were bent and filed from sheet metal, after which they were joined to the inside of the lock by brazing. These formed the obstructions which were intended to impede all but the right key.

Since no patents were granted abroad prior to 1617 and our own patent office was not established until 1790, great secrecy was employed to protect any inventor's ingenuity. The first latch or lock patent was granted to George Black in England in 1774 and seems to have covered a device for "admitting air into the room without opening the door."

Viewing ancient locks from present-day standards of security and finding them wanting is highly unjust, since knowledge and skill have always been correlated to the times. In their day old locks provided as much security, relatively, as modern locks do today. Tools and materials which are now taken for granted were naturally not always available, and fashioning locks and keys from heavy iron bars required skill and a strong right arm. It is probable that sheet iron and the file were both introduced in about the fourteenth century, making new techniques in the locksmith's art possible.

From the earliest times, man wished to secure his own possessions, so we find locked chests for vestments and church properties, for archives, for treasure, for arms, for clothing and household goods, bridal chests, and chests for burial or entombment. Depending on their size and height, these chests could also be used to sleep on, sit on, eat on, or write on, and thanks to their substantial handles could be moved comparatively easily. In the early days of this country, even the various governmental agencies or departments kept their moneys in chests. It is reported that the Marines, for example, had a carefully guarded Military Chest, containing perhaps $50,000 or $60,000 to cover pay, food, clothing, medicines, and so forth.

Most authorities agree that very little definite information is available concerning old locks and keys, considering their importance. This was probably for security reasons, but the fact that locks and keys rarely bore the smith's name or mark makes identification doubly difficult. It is generally conceded, however, that the beauty of old locks and keys usually makes up for the lack of definite knowledge as to their exact age, source, and frequently colorful history.

SCOTCH estate key (probably the early 18th century).

MANY-WARDED door key (probably middle 18th century).

These locks were very secure, since the obstructions guarding them were on varying planes and therefore difficult to tamper with. Such locks were in use at the time of the French Revolution.

The many-warded keys are undoubtedly the most decorative and impressive-looking and were the chief security device known to locksmiths prior to about 1778. The

BY DONALD STREETER

Early wrought-iron hardware:
spring latches

THAT MOST OF THE SPRING LATCHES in early American use were made in England there seems little reason to doubt. Scarcity of recorded American smiths who made such hardware, contemporary advertisements, and British restrictions on American manufactures, all point to the English origin of most of the hardware used here through the colonial period and well into the second half of the nineteenth century. This seems to be particularly true of hardware which appeared in identical form in all the Colonies.

The towns of Wolverhampton, Willenhall, and Bilston, in the county of Stafford, were the center of the ironworking trades in England during this period. Several hundred workers were engaged there in the various metal trades, turning out all sorts of small ironwork. These men were specialists, not general blacksmiths. The smiths who emigrated here were often called upon to do all kinds of work, but those in England produced only one, or at most a few specific related items. It was highly professional work, as the excellent present condition of many of their wares shows.

As examples of the specialized way the trades were organized, consider these listings from among the hundreds carried in the Willenhall directory of 1770: Bratt, William, *Toy maker and Hardware-man;* rBatt, Jonathan, *Latch-maker;* Bratt, John, *Brass nob Lock maker;* Bratt, Isaac, *Pad Lock maker;* Brumall, Richard, *Spring Latch maker.* Evidence that spring-latch making was a separate trade is also contained in the wording of an indenture of apprenticeship dated 1836, in which one John Harper, Jr., ". . . of his own free will being of the age of fifteen years and upwards, doth put himself Apprentice to his father John Harper the Elder of Willenhall, . . . Spring-latchmaker, . . . to learn his Art. . . ." (The apprentice system and child labor were everywhere employed; a visitor to Willenhall wrote that children commonly did

forge work, but that the piercing of keys was seldom done by children under eleven because it required great skill.)

Because spring latches were in use here over such a long period, the few existing signed examples are valuable in restoration research. However, it should be noted that identification of marked latches with the men listed above can only be tentative. Son often followed father, so that the same name may appear on the work of different men over a considerable period of time; for instance, the latch by William Bratt shown here seems earlier than 1770—the earliest listing of the name we have.

Spring latches are found here in two main styles, contemporary with each other, in forms varying throughout the period of their use. One is the latch which is today called the wishbone latch, from the shape of its iron spring, or the keyhole latch, from the shape of the back plate; the other is the square spring latch. Use of both styles can be traced from the early years of the eighteenth century to the latter half of the nineteenth. Similarity in general form persists throughout the period, and it is hoped that these notes may aid the layman to distinguish the early from the late.

Fine eighteenth-century spring latch by William Bratt. Plate is of hammered sheet. Design is early in form, holes are hand punched, plate edges are bevel-filed. All parts are delicately and carefully finished. Compare the daintiness of the wishbone spring with the heaviness of those on later examples. *Courtesy of Ball & Ball.*

Maker's mark incised on above latch, *Wᵐ BRATT.*

Eighteenth-century wishbone spring latch. Plate is of hammered sheet, hand cut, with filed bevels. All parts are hand forged, and well finished with the file. A good example of the simple form of wishbone latch. *Except as noted, illustrations are from the author's collection.*

Small eighteenth-century wishbone spring latch. Plate is too far corroded to identify as rolled or hammered, but delicacy and finish of parts, general craftsmanship, and oval knobs, place it as eighteenth century.

Eighteenth-century square spring latch by Isaac Bratt. Plate is of hammered sheet which has been ground on a grindstone to remove roughness left by the tilt hammer. Almost identical in form with a latch of the same type signed by William Bratt.

Isaac Bratt's mark, Ic BRAT[T?].

The advance of technology in the early nineteenth century, and the decline in hand craftsmanship accompanying it, have left their marks on the products of that time. Chief of these, as applied to the dating of spring latches, was the general use of rolled sheet iron for their plates. Although a definite date is difficult to establish, present evidence indicates that the rolling of such sheets was a nineteenth-century development. In attempting to date original spring latches, then, we should ascribe those with a back plate of rolled sheet iron to the nineteenth century, and not earlier. It is not true, however, that latches with the back plates of hammered sheet iron are necessarily eighteenth-century. As with all new processes, change was gradual, and a transition period existed during which both rolled and hammered sheet were in use. Dating of such transition pieces will be made easier by comparing details and craftsmanship with those of latches falling well within one period or the other.

The decline in craftsmanship which was part and parcel of the nineteenth-century phase of the industrial revolution is shown in the latches themselves. Fine detail and handwork became increasingly scarce; filed decoration and bevels were less frequent; parts became heavier, less delicate; hand-finished oval brass knobs gave way to lathe-finished round ones; use of cast-brass and malleable cast-iron parts did away with the need for much of the earlier hand forging. By the end of the nineteenth century, spring latches had become mere assemblies of ready-made and mass-produced parts.

Bibliography

Zimmerman, Dr. R. E., *Then and Now.* An address delivered at the annual meeting of the First Iron Works Association, Saugus, Massachusetts, 1952; p. 8. American Iron and Steel Institute.

Knight's *American Mechanical Dictionary,* Boston, 1876; p. 1966.

Great Industries of the United States, Hartford, 1873; p. 354.

Mushet, David, *Papers on Iron and Steel,* 1840; pp. 7-8.

Percy, *Metallurgy: Iron and Steel;* pp. 627-639.

John Harper & Co., Ltd., Willenhall, Staffs., England. Reproductions of illustrated advertising dated 1856-1865.

John Harper & Co., Ltd., Willenhall, Staffs., England, *The Story of the Old Works,* 1950; p. 15.

Sketchley's and Adams's *Universal Directory for the Towns of Birmingham, Wolverhampton, . . . 1770.* Photostatic prints of pages listing Bratts and others. Reference Library, Birmingham, England, 1953.

Eighteenth-century square spring latch with brass stirrup drop handles. Both oval knobs and stirrup drops were used on eighteenth-century spring latches, but the oval form is more usual. *Courtesy of Ball & Ball.*

Spring latch of the transition period, circa 1800-1820. Plate is of hammered sheet in this example, but this style occurs also with plate made of rolled sheet.

Early nineteenth-century wishbone spring latch. Plate is of hammered sheet, but machine-punched holes, increased weight of parts, and lack of careful hand finishing, indicate the transition period from 1800 to 1820.

Spring latch, first half of the nineteenth century. The compound spring action has here been made separate from the latch bar guard. Spring action is identical with that used in iron rim locks of the same period. Both parts of the spring are iron, not steel.

Nineteenth-century wishbone spring latch with compound spring. Plate is of rolled sheet iron. Parts are still hand forged, but their greatly increased weight, and introduction of the added spring member, point to a date between 1820 and 1840. Knobs, here removed to show the latch parts, are round brass.

Typical mid-nineteenth-century square spring latch, marked *A & F·W·H*. Compare this latch with eighteenth-century latches of the same shape. Here the plate is of rolled sheet, machine cut, and holes are machine punched. Spring action is compound, with cast-brass relay bar. Latch bar is of malleable cast iron, with the pivot a separate brass bushing. The only hand-forged part of the latch is the simple iron part of the spring. All other pieces are either bar stock, cast iron, or cast brass. Latches of this construction were advertised for sale as late as 1865.

Maker's mark *A & F-W-H*, not yet identified

Early American stock locks

BY DONALD STREETER

THE STOCK LOCK is an iron lock set into a block of wood, attached to the face of a door, and fitted with a key. In its most usual form it is a dead-bolt lock, without a spring mechanism to provide a self-latching device, and therefore requiring a key to lock and unlock it. Very rarely it has a spring lock or drawback, which has a self-latching effect from the room side. The history of the stock lock is as long and continuous as that of any other lock form, yet it has received little attention.

A stock lock was less costly than an iron-cased one, yet economy was not its only recommendation. Because its case was wood instead of iron, it could be used in locations where exposure to dampness might injure an all-iron lock. Thus Joseph Moxon in 1703 refers to "Street door locks,

Fig. 1. Plate stock lock, oak case with decorative iron banding; English, eighteenth century. The sheet iron, originally painted black, appears to be pack hammered, not rolled: Over-all length, 10 inches. *Except as noted, all illustrations are from the author's collection.*

Fig. 2. Interior view of Fig. 1, with backplate removed, revealing bolt, the two lower notches of which indicate that a double revolution of the key was needed to throw the bolt completely. This enabled the use of a smaller key, yet afforded the desired bolt travel. The sharp upper right corner of the backplate forms a tension spring for the bolt.

Fig. 3. Oak case of a Bambury, or plain, stock lock; English, late eighteenth century. The block was rived from the log in such a way that the grain was straight and regular, to avoid splitting or warping because of the mortise. Height 6¼, length 12, depth tapering from 1½ to 1⅛ inches.

Fig. 4. Back view of the Bambury lock in Fig. 3, showing cover plates in place.
The talon of the tumbler is engaged in the right-hand notch at the top edge of the bolt.

called Stock Locks." As late as 1876, Charles Knight's *American Mechanical Dictionary* defines it as a "wooden outside door lock for stables, gates, etc." Its weather resistance may have accounted for its frequent use on exterior doors of early meetinghouses and churches, which were often unheated during much of the damp weather. Stock locks are still manufactured by English lockmakers.

Louis Francis Salzman in *Building in England down to 1540* (Oxford, 1952) includes several references to stock locks in medieval England. In Corfe "4 stok-lokkes with keys for setting on doors" were bought in 1357. In 1376, locks called "platelok" and "stocklok" are recorded in Havering. In 1490, work at St. Paul's called for "a new stock lock with an iron called a stonstaple" (a staple, or keeper, for setting in a stone doorframe). There is a record that at Westminster in 1532 "a stock lock and shutting plate were set upon a dore belonging to one of the logies wherein certain of the masons worke," and "a doble howpid stoclokis" is also mentioned. There is reference at Windsor, in 1534, to "a doble hopped Stock-lock sett upon the Garden dore to save the Kynges platt lock oon to the begynnyng of somere." This last item suggests that the King's iron lock was too fine to be exposed to the dampness of the season.

Throughout American architectural history, reference to the stock lock persists. In *The Boston News-Letter* for February 11-18, 1711/1712, Andrew and Jonathan Belcher offer for sale, from England, "all of the best make . . . spring and StockLocks, Chest ditto, and Padlocks of various sorts." Many other advertisements in newspapers of the colonial period indicate that the stock lock was a staple item among the imports of house hardware. Surviving letters also mention them. Several orders are included in letters from Virginia planters to their agents in London during the eighteenth century. An account of the goods at Pennsbury, William Penn's estate in Pennsylvania, taken in 1687, lists "8 stock locks" among the hardware. Most satisfying to architectural historians is the ample evidence of American use of such locks afforded by numerous parts excavated at

Fig. 5. Back view of the Bambury lock in Fig. 3, with cover plates and bolt removed to show the arrangement of metal working parts as set in the wood. Top piece is the spring, with the taper forged of iron, not steel, which bears upon the tumbler below it. At the bottom is the main, or center ward, at the keyhole. As the key is turned it raises the tumbler, releasing the talon from the bolt notch just before the key engages in the bolt to move it. Usually no assembly marks appear on these plain stock locks, perhaps because once assembled they could not be taken apart.

Fig. 6. American plate stock lock,
nineteenth century.
Rift-sawed pine case,
height 4, length 7, depth 1 inch.

Fig. 7. End view of lock in Fig. 6,
showing maker's mark and catalogue number
incised in the wood case:
NORTH & STANLEY CONN./NEW-BRITAIN/352.

Fig. 8. Works and key of lock in Fig. 6. The main plate and backplate are made from rolled
sheet iron, a nineteenth-century development. Use of cast brass parts is typical of early to mid-
nineteenth century. The heavy section of the bolt is cast iron, with the thin tongue made of
rolled sheet iron and inserted in the mold before casting. This eliminated the need for forging
the bolt in one piece, or for welding, yet provided the toughness of wrought iron where needed.
The locking action is simplified by the use of fewer parts, but the greatest economy was provided by the use of cast brass for the key and wards. This made it necessary, however, to
redesign both these elements since the strength of iron was now missing. The key was no
longer split for a main ward but had a solid bit. The wards of the lock were of cast brass,
with ridges concentric with the keyhole, riveted to main and backplates. Normally the key was
filed to pass the wards. The key shown here has been altered to skeleton form.

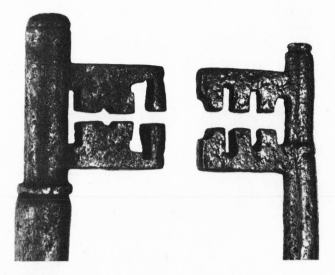

Fig. 9. *Left,* key bit for plate stock lock. Point of bearing is the collar behind the entire bit, which bore upon either front or backplate (see Fig. 10). *Right,* key for Bambury stock lock. Note that the collar, or point of bearing, is at the cleft for the center ward.

building sites in many sections of the country (see Fig. 14 for some Virginia examples).

Humble and inexpensive though stock locks were, it would be wrong to assume that less skill was required to make them than their finer counterparts, or that they were the products of local smiths on the American frontier. The making of a keyed lock, whether cased in wood, iron, or brass, was no job for the typical village smith, who had neither the tools nor the training for such work. It is fairer to say that their lower cost resulted from the fact that they required less time to make.

Even for this simple form of lock there is indication that medieval guilds had maintained some sort of quality control over their members. It is recorded that in London during that period locksmiths were required "to work no stock locks except for seasoned wood."

Most English stock locks were cased in oak, which was sturdy and could be split easily into blocks, although examples survive which are cased in other woods. These may be of American manufacture (Figs. 6-8).

The stock lock occurs in two main forms: the plate, or fine, stock lock, and the Bambury, or plain, stock lock. In the plate stock lock the entire mechanism is mounted on an iron backplate and set into the wood as a unit. In this respect it differs from an iron-cased lock only in the material of the case. The Bambury lock consists of a block of wood into which each part of the lock is embedded individually.

In addition to the difference in cost, there is one basic difference in the form of the key for each of the two types of stock lock discussed here (see Fig. 9). This difference was dictated by the construction of the lock. The plate stock lock, constructed as a unit, always maintained the same spatial relationship among its component parts (see Fig. 10). The principle of the use of rigid front and backplates, in constant position, was the same as that in iron-cased locks, so the keys were similar. In the Bambury lock, however, no such constant relationship could be counted on. The wood might shrink or swell and thus alter the relationships. There was no backplate which gave a bearing to the key. The only constant point was the position of the center ward, set into the wood. It was against this that the key bore as it operated the bolt (see Fig. 11). Both types of lock, and their keys, are illustrated here.

Fig. 10. Key operating in a plate stock lock. Point of bearing in this view is the backplate, which determines that the key is in the right position to pass the wards. Since the main ward is centered, the key will work from either side.

Fig. 11. Key operating in a Bambury, or plain, stock lock. The cover plate has been removed. Here the bearing is upon the center ward. Even if the wood should shrink or swell, this bearing point would assure the correct position of the key. It should be noted that some nineteenth-century Bambury stock locks incorporated a secondary plate, usually of cast brass, which enabled the use of the same form of key as for the plate lock.

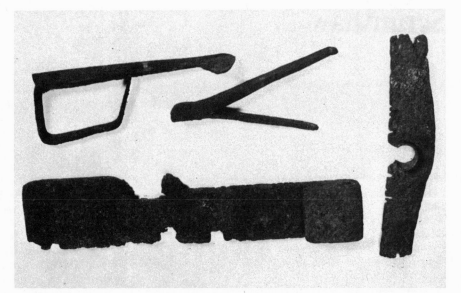

Fig. 12. Staples, or keepers, for stock locks, driven into the doorframe to receive the lock bolt. The shank is offset so that the spike might be driven somewhat back from the edge of the doorframe, to avoid splitting.

Fig. 13. Parts of Bambury stock locks, from a cargo of hardware in a ship bound for Philadelphia, sunk in the Delaware River sometime in the eighteenth century, and recovered in 1949. *Top left,* tumbler. Note the knife-edged tongue at right end, which was driven into the wood. *Top center,* taper. *Right,* main center ward, with knife ends. *Bottom left,* lock bolt. The presence of any of these artifacts in the excavation of a historic site would indicate the use of a Bambury stock lock. None of these forms occurs in any other type of lock.

Fig. 14. Stock lock artifacts from Virginia. *Top left,* tumbler from the Challis Pottery Kiln site, James City County, c. 1725-1730. *Top right,* tumbler from the Hay Cabinet Shop site, Williamsburg, unstratified. *Center left and bottom left,* center wards from Mathews Manor, Denbigh, mid-seventeenth century. *Center right,* key from the John Coster well, Williamsburg, c. 1759. Pin at lower right is one inch long. *Photograph by courtesy of Colonial Williamsburg.*

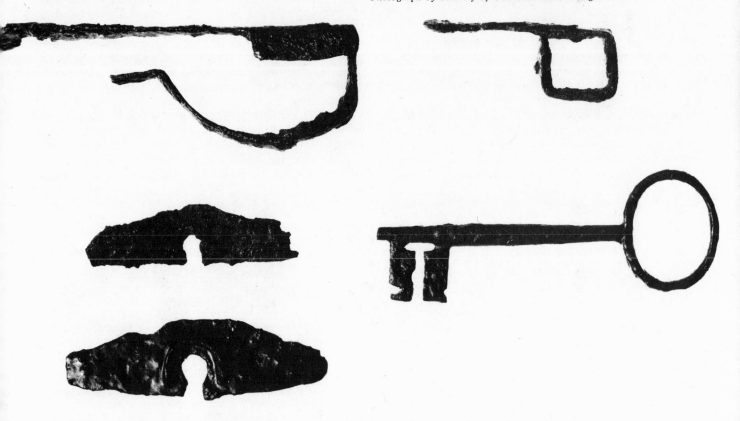

Latch and Door Knocker

By ROGER WARNER

[INTRODUCTORY NOTE:—This brief appreciation, which makes no pretense of being more than an outline sketch, will serve, perhaps, to direct attention to a large subject on which detailed information is lacking. If promises hold, ANTIQUES hopes to be of use, ere long, in helping to make up the deficiency.—ED.]

EARLY American latches and knockers were admirably suitable. They belonged to their doors, and played a most important part in the harmonious entrance units which we admire so much today. Their study is full of interest for those who take pride in America's artistic past. Their selection, too, for use on the homes of today gives unusual chances for personal expression, for the securing of that rare—though much discussed—quality, individuality.

Consider, first of all, America's "iron age" in hardware, which we are just beginning to appreciate. The early buildings—Gothic in stylistic affiliations—erected by the English colonists of the seventeenth century, furnished most interesting latches and knockers of wrought iron.

Such hardware was supplied by the village blacksmith, who was a craftsman indeed; for he wrought on his anvil not only nails and hardware for each new house, but a variety of farm tools, as well as andirons, fire sets, and shoes for the horses of a whole country side. And he toiled with much care and considerable originality, as his handiwork shows. Naturally enough, he followed training received in Old England. He instructed his apprentices to fashion the forms which he knew so well, and they, in turn, their apprentices, so that the early English styles persisted for many years.

The pear-shaped ring (*Fig. 1*), which served as knocker on the first of our Colonial dwellings, was door-handle and latch as well, for at its pivot it released the catch on the inside of the door. Its counterpart may be seen today on the doors of the quaint half-timbered cottages of Essex and Surrey.

Fortunately, a complete first-period Colonial door has been preserved in the museum at Deerfield, Massachusetts.* This, the oaken door of the old Indian House, scarred in the attack of 1704 by savage tomahawks, which

*Discussed at length in *Old-Time New England*, for January, 1922, p. 167.

Fig. 1—LATCH AND KNOCKER
From the "Old Indian House" at Deerfield, Mass.

in one place hacked clear through the thick battens, is adorned with just the kind of wrought-iron latch and knocker described. The ring was placed slightly off centre, and at a height convenient for the hand. Taken in conjunction with the wrought-iron nail heads which stud the door in diagonal lines, it imparts a delightfully simple charm to the doorway. The few but vigorous elements of decoration lift such a structure entirely out of the barn-door class, though it is almost as lacking in embellishment.

In the first quarter of the eighteenth century—and possibly earlier—there was used upon the Colonial door the separate iron door-handle in conjunction with a latch (*Fig. 5*). It was finely wrought, altogether graceful, and nicely tapered to fit the hand. It terminated at either end in a triangular piece of thin hammered iron, which was often given an extra twist or fanciful curve in keeping with the blacksmith-craftsman's humour of the moment. Sometimes a decoration occurred in the centre of the handle—a series of ridges, or the initials of the owner impressed with a chisel.

This style of door-handle was used all through the eighteenth century and even into the nineteenth, until the passion for the modern door-knob took full hold. In rural communities, it continued to be made of iron—sometimes of steel. After braziers became established in the Colonies, the latch handle was cast in solid brass to match the new styles in knockers.

For knockers during the eighteenth century, brass was the popular material—good white brass with a gleam and lustre all its own. It was not the only material used, however, for even the most refined knockers sometimes appeared in bronze or in iron. Instead of being wrought by hand, knockers were now cast in sand moulds from woodcarver's models. As a consequence, the touch of the craftsman persists, for the carvings were not absolutely symmetrical. Their little variations in design add to the interest and charm of the finished product. Brass knockers were often hand-chased in fanciful scrolls, or were engraved with the owner's name. The bolts that attached them to the door were still wrought in iron, as were the crudely threaded nuts.

Fig. 2—DOOR-KNOCKERS OF THE "S" TYPE
An early Georgian form which combines grace of curve with simple massiveness of general effect. Nothing much better has been devised. *From the Metropolitan Museum.*

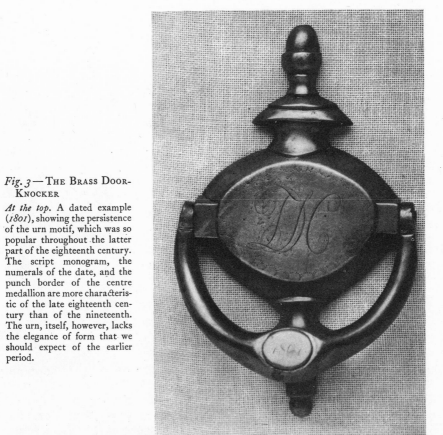

Fig. 3 — The Brass Door-Knocker

At the top. A dated example (*1801*), showing the persistence of the urn motif, which was so popular throughout the latter part of the eighteenth century. The script monogram, the numerals of the date, and the punch border of the centre medallion are more characteristic of the late eighteenth century than of the nineteenth. The urn, itself, however, lacks the elegance of form that we should expect of the earlier period.

Lower left. A patriotic type, with the name of the householder engraved and enamelled. Difficult to date with certainty. Lettering suggests first quarter of nineteenth century.

Lower right. A late Georgian type in which the favorite Sphynx and urn are brought into conjunction. Interesting and vigorous design, though lacking in finesse.

All three examples in the Frishmuth Collection, Pennsylvania Museum.

With the dominance of classical architecture, more elaborate knockers became popular. They were used all through the Georgian period and for some years after the Revolution, in connection with the type of architecture now popularly called Colonial. Through these epoch-making years, knockers were so varied in design and hence in cost that they frequently revealed much of the social, political, and economic circumstances of the people on whose houses they appeared.

The "s" type of knocker seems to have been the first to be used on Georgian dwellings in America (*Fig. 2*). It was a powerful thing, easy to grasp, and protruding with a fine assurance from the middle of the panelled door. Its knock was deep, sharp, resounding: just the kind of sonorous summons for the homes of a people now realizing economic power and social importance! This type of knocker was usually placed on the centre stile of the door; but, where the door had more than three stiles, on the one nearest the door handle. Often it was placed lower on the door than the "urn"-shaped knocker which followed it in popularity.

The "urn" knocker (*Fig. 3*) signalized the full tide of Georgian architecture. It appeared in numerous variations and underwent changes as the years passed, and changing public taste in England was reflected somewhat belatedly in America. The urn-shape appeared in connection with shells, garlands, sphinxes or sphinxes' heads, lions, lyres, and other items of classical ornament which the brothers Adam had done so much to popularize. It varied in size, refinement, and proportions. Toward the end of the eighteenth century, as American doorway treatment became less robust, urn knockers grew almost spindling in shape—their ornament almost super-refined and delicate. They were in harmonious accord with the graceful urns on the gateposts and with the slender flutings of columns and pilasters.

One of the best of these "urn" knockers is one of which I am myself the proud possessor. I procured it from the door of an old house in Long Island. The piece is of cast iron, (see cover) but well executed. The design appears to be Georgian, very nearly at its best for this sort of thing. The first illustration in Figure 3 shows the subsequent debasement of the type.

After the Revolutionary War a newly awakened national consciousness found expression in the "eagle" knocker, a type which promptly ousted the British lion that had been popular in earlier years. It was a fine thing indeed to have the national bird perched upon the door, to be seen and touched by all who entered!

Fig. 5 — Latches

Some fine examples of blacksmith production. Exact dates for this kind of work are difficult to set. These pieces may be of the eighteenth century or of the early nineteenth. Center example probably early eighteenth.

Today, of course, the awakened affection for all things early American has not failed to include old-time knockers and latches. In consequence, ancient Colonial doorways, with their original hardware, are becoming annually more rare. Yet this does not preclude the necessity for selecting for suitability in procuring old hardware for modern use. The satisfaction of depriving an ancient door of its pristine glory of iron or brass offers insufficient compensation for unsuitability. Choice should always be determined by appropriateness to the general design of the home, and it may well be undertaken with deliberation and arrived at only after careful searching. Latch and knocker, more than other detail, will decide the first effect of the dwelling upon those who approach it. Modern knob and doorbell are usually efficient enough, but they are bound to be much like those on the house across the way, and similar to all on the next street. And they possess—do what you may—an atmosphere definitely impersonal and frigid. There's something about them that seems to hold you off. "Punch the door-bell and wait for somebody to let you in," is the warning they seem to sound. But latch and knocker are cordial, hearty, familiar. "Raise the knocker, lift the latch—walk in," runs their invitation. By all means—the latch and knocker!

Fig. 4 — Door-Knocker — Old and New Types

From left to right: "S" type; Adam; early Empire; Pseudo-Classic; Jenny Lind (*1850*); Adam; Nondescript. Actual date of making is not necessarily that which the style suggests. *From the Metropolitan Museum.*

Early American House Hardware. I

By Wallace Nutting

IT seems probable that the simplicity of American house hardware has given the impression to architects and students that it is not worth attention. But this very simplicity is one of its greatest merits. A few quiet lines of beauty are more consonant with the spirit of Colonial architecture than are the intricate, and even flamboyant, designs of European hardware.

The exceedingly rich and elaborate work of the German, Spanish, old French and Italian masters was, no doubt, inspired largely by their great skill as armorers, since in that work they brought the genius and enthusiasm of artists to their task. They naturally carried into the decorative features of house hardware no little of their cunning as artificers. But in the belief that Americans of this generation are ready to observe and admire the work of early American smiths, I have prepared these articles and illustrated them altogether with original examples.

The first call on the house smith was undoubtedly for locks for chests. While these were not strictly house hardware, they had to do with the furnishings of the home. We do not find here anything like the beautiful locks which have been imported from old European chests. The chest lock, in this country at least, was often concealed. Hence it is left outside the scope of present observations.

In the earliest settlement, and for a considerable period after, in certain localities wood was substituted for iron to such an extent that some houses used practically no iron except for nails; and these were confined to the attachment of boards, clapboards, shingles and finish, not being employed at all in the frame.

Latches

A door latch consists of five pieces, besides the great nail which serves as a pivot for the latch. These parts are the *handle*, or pull, the *thumb piece*, the *latch bar*, its *guard*, and the *striker*.

The handle consists of an arched, or bowed, central section connected at each end to a base plate, more or less decorated. In this plate, at the top, a hole is mortised for the insertion of the thumb piece.

The thumb piece in the earlier latches is sometimes remarkably attractive in its construction. The section on the inside of the door is split, or barbed, horizontally for one or two inches back from the plate. After the thumb piece is inserted, the barb is bent outward so as to secure this section of the latch in place. Later on, the latch plate was thickened at the mortise hole and a hole was drilled through this part of the thickened plate and thumb piece for the insertion of a small iron dowel. This was considered a refinement; but the earlier latches were far more quaint.

The thumb piece, in rare instances, was decorated on the outer edge to correspond with some motive on the plate. At the inside and curved end, where the thumb piece tapered to a pig tail, various curlicues were used. In some instances, a very simple curve produced a strong effect of quaintness.

In the latches of the early nineteenth century, the tail piece was generally cut short, leaving an unsightly straight stub which gave no hold for the hand. As a compensation, a small cast or hammered knob was riveted to the latch bar, or the bar itself was curled back at the end to form a handle.

The latch bar proper, of course, was of a size proportioned to the door. The least artistic form terminated on the inside end with a circular or oval flattening, pierced for the pivot nail. In the artistic forms advantage was taken of this necessary broadening of the latch bar to apply various motives.

The catch, or striker, terminated with a long, square taper, sometimes ragged to prevent the likelihood of its becoming loose. In some instances, but rarely, the end was clinched. In a good example, the head of the catch terminated in a long scrolled brace returned to the door and pierced with a nail. In a few instances, as in one shown in this article, two such braces at right angles to one another were employed.

Locks were not used in connection with early latches. If employed, they were entirely separate. The latch was sometimes secured on the inside by the insertion of a wooden or metallic wedge between the latch and the upper part of the guard. But the doors, for the most part, were secured by solid bars of wood running across the inside and fitting into great iron staples, although one *iron* door bar was recently discovered in Pennsylvania. It is stamped with a hammered design and, of course,—like all such things—belonged to General Washington!

The latches of wood were generally of oak, but sometimes of maple. There is no question that these latches, especially when large, are very picturesque; but architects have hesitated, no doubt with good reason, about employing them on new houses; and even when restoring old houses, they have used them very sparingly. Such a huge latch is still in use in the Maria Mitchell House on Nantucket.

Since the iron latch was first made of bog ore, which is the best and purest sort, the claim is made that it resisted rust more than modern iron. Those familiar with the subject inform us that the oxidation of iron is encouraged by impurities. We find, however, that many old latches are badly rusted, while others are still smooth and show the beautiful gray which is the normal color of iron. We must conclude that then, as now, there were variations in the quality of iron and differences in the degree of its exposure to the weather according to its placement in the dwelling.

The bog ore was tough and permitted of a nice manipulation. For the same purpose, Scandinavian iron is now used.

The dates of surviving hardware are difficult to fix, as we have rather meagre information. Even in the case of a very ancient house, and perhaps all the more if the house is sufficiently ancient, the hardware is likely to have been renewed. Nor can we say that the very earliest types were necessarily the best. In fact, the handsomest

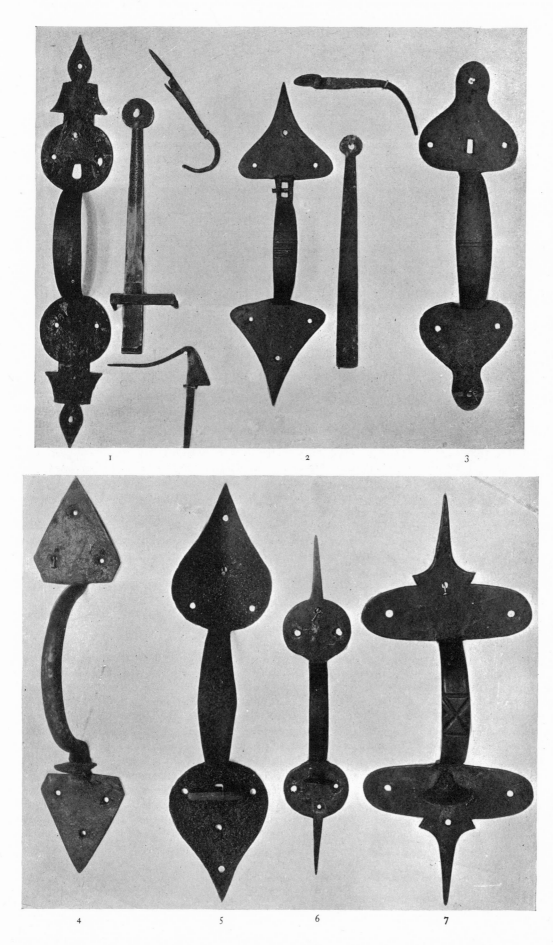

1   2   3

4   5   6   7

latches we have found date very much nearer 1800 than 1700. After 1800, however, there was a distinct and rapid decline; and by 1830 cast handles riveted to plates were in common use; and from that time on nothing was produced at all worthy. The finest examples of latches are often found on church doors. There a latch large enough to allow very bold design and to be visible at some distance was permissible.

In the following notes on the illustrations shown, if no date is mentioned, it may be assumed that it is so close to the nineteenth century as to require no closer approximation:

NUMBER 1, *Size: 16½ by 2⅞ inches*. Found in New York. The thumb piece is particularly good. The striker is restored.

NUMBER 2, *Size: 13 by 4 inches*. A type often found on the North Shore.

NUMBER 3, *Size: 14 by 4⅛ inches*.

NUMBER 4, *Size: 13 by 3 inches*. A triangular latch, with round corners. The handle is of a round section.

NUMBER 5. *Size: 14 by 3⅜ inches*. A pointed heart design.

NUMBER 6, *Size: 12 by 2¼ inches*. The ball and spear design.

NUMBER 7, *Size: 14 by 5¾ inches*. A most quaint fashion, called the flat ball and spear.

NUMBER 8, *Size: 11¾ by 2½ inches*. A rounded triangle design. It might possibly be called a heart.

NUMBER 9, *Size: 12 by 2¼ inches*. A scroll design, which we must otherwise leave unnamed.

NUMBER 10, *Size: 12½ by 3 inches*. This is peculiar in having a keyhole mortise as well as a thumb-piece mortise. We await the suggestion of a name.

NUMBER 11, *Size: 9⅞ by 3½ inches*. A somewhat crude pattern of the ball and spear.

NUMBER 12, *Size: 12½ by 3⅝ inches*. The round triangle pattern.

126

NUMBER 13, *Size: 13 by 3 inches.* A somewhat elongated variant of Number 8.

NUMBER 14, *Size: 11⅜ by 3⅜ inches.* A triangle with two rounded corners. It seems to have no appropriate name and no special merit.

NUMBER 15, *Size: 11¾ by 3 inches.* The most perfect of the strongly shaped heart design.

NUMBER 16, *Size: 11⅞ by 3⅛ inches.* The only tulip pattern we have noticed.

NUMBER 17, *Size: 13⅜ by 5 inches.* It might be called a disc pattern. The edges of the circular plates are finely serrated.

NUMBER 18, *Size: 13½ by 2¼ inches.* An attenuated design not as easy to attach rigidly to a door as that which has a wider plate. It was probably made for some door which had a very narrow stile.

NUMBER 19, *Size: 16 by 2 inches.* An extremely lean brother. One sees how the narrowness of the plate was sought to be overcome by no less than five nails; whereas, three is the rule.

NUMBER 20, *Size: 13¼ by 3¼ inches.* Might, perhaps, be called a ball and arrow pattern.

NUMBER 21, *Size: 24 inches long (the largest shown in this article).* We digress here to show the beautiful latch of Dr. Irving P. Lyon of Buffalo, New York, the son and worthy successor, in his spirit of exact scholarship, of Dr. Lyon of furniture fame. It is a latch of very remarkable characteristics. The plate is scrolled with a sword-fish end. Indeed, we think we shall give it this name.

For so simple a plate it is most striking. But in spite of the attractiveness of this plate, the palm for merit in an artistic way is carried off by the latch bar. This is 17 inches in length. The spike at the inside end is 5½ inches long. The enlargement for the nail is heart shaped and the bar is nicely ornamented at both the top and bottom of the heart; and the spike ends in a ball. At the large end, this latch has a curious, short square turn. The thumb piece shows a little Colonial pig-tail scroll.

Another distinguished feature of this latch is the striker, the only one I show with two braces, which are scrolled in such a way as to diverge from the striker head at right angles. Comparing this latch with NUMBER 25 I find that each has features of merit not found on the other; but I am of the impression that the remarkable latch bar, together with the striker, place NUMBER 21 in a class above the others shown.

NUMBER 22, *Size: 8½ by 3 inches.* A triangular style. This latch and all of its size, or smaller, were appropriate for inside doors.

NUMBER 23, *Size: 9 by 2¼ inches.* It has a very shallow bow for a handle and is also,

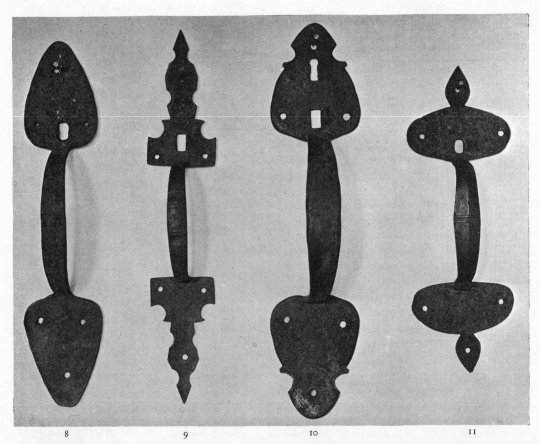

8   9   10   11

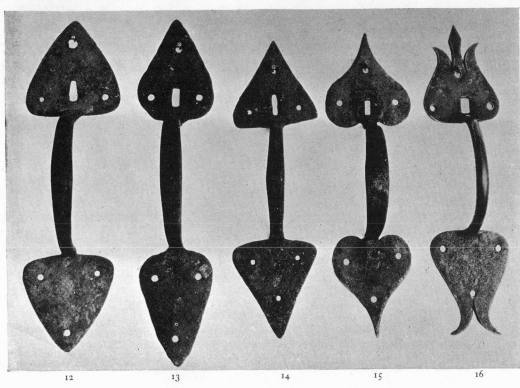

12   13   14   15   16

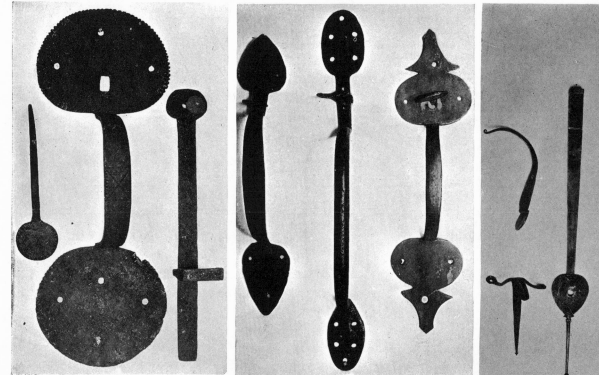

17

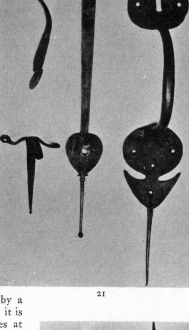

18   19   20

21

probably, therefore, an inside latch.

NUMBER 24, *Size: 8 by 2⅜ inches.* Another heart-shaped latch.

NUMBER 25, *Size: 22¾ by 4 ⅛ inches.* A very elaborate latch probably taken from a church. It was found in Lenox. It is simply a variant of the ball and arrow style. The handle at the centre of the bow is decorated with a raised medallion, undoubtedly a simple imitation of the elaborate decorations on foreign latches. This raised work could scarcely be done with a

hammer, and, apparently, was not done with a file. It is fair to presume that a die was made on which this section of the handle was placed when hot, and the raised design was embossed upon it by vigorous hammering. Probably a stamp carrying a grooved molding was also used. This handsome complex groove appears on the handle of the medallion just described, on two places on the latch bar, and even on the guard. Completely carried out on the various

elements of the latch, this molding gives a finish to the style.

The latch bar is scrolled by a a curl at the inside end and it is ornamented by finger grooves at the other end. These suggest somewhat the knuckle carving on the later Windsor chair arms. The bar is also bevelled, as well as the guard. The striker of this latch, while not original with the latch, is contemporary. All other parts are original.

22   23   24   25

Ready Reference for Furniture Hardware, III

Drawings by Dorothy Miller Thormin

Photographs from original specimens in the private collection of Israel Sack

THE variety of patterns of brasses, from which choice may be made, greatly increases when we come to deal with furniture of the period 1780-

1800. The fundamental forms, however, during this late period, remain very nearly constant either as circles or as ellipses. Occasionally, too, we encounter rectangles

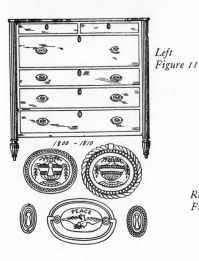

Left Figure 11

1800 - 1810

PEACE

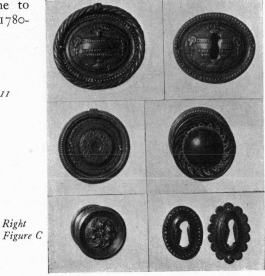

Right Figure C

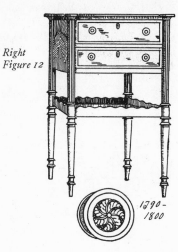

Right Figure 12

1790-1800

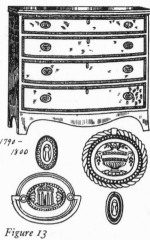

1790 – 1800

Figure 13

whose corners have been clipped. In this period, back plates are no longer cast and engraved, or ornamented with a pierced pattern; they are made of thin metal stamped in relief. On fine and delicate furniture, handles of this type may be of silver or silver plate. We occasionally find the bail or ring handle giving way to the flat circular knob, particularly on smaller pieces. The face of this knob is sometimes decorated with a small rosette, sometimes with concentric circles. Ivory knobs occur on dainty sewing tables, and keyholes are framed in ivory or light colored wood.

It is virtually impossible to lay down rules as to choice of patterns among the innumerable designs which the stamping die has made available. In general, however, the circular or nearly circular back plates bearing a heavy urn design, of Roman or Pompeian suggestion, should be avoided in connection with the lighter scale specimens of American furniture. They are really appropriate only on pieces of rather dark, rich mahogany in which the classic influence of the Brothers Adam is more or less apparent. Such pieces are more frequently encountered among English than among American examples. Ring handles with a circular rosette back plate, however, have a wide measure of suitability.

In the case of old furniture of the late eighteenth century, however, the shape of the handles required is usually determined by the hole marks of original applications. Sometimes the original holes have been plugged and a knob set between them. Examination of the

inner side of the drawer front will usually reveal the nature and style of the early handles.

In the case of sideboards, it will frequently be found that cupboard doors and bottle drawers show no indication of ever having been equipped with handles or knobs. Since drawers and cupboards of such pieces harbored articles whose preciousness required protection with a lock, a key frequently served all the requirements of a knob or handle. Where original knobs or the marks of them do not occur on sideboards, it may be the part of wisdom not to supply the deficiency. Victorian knobs or handles will sometimes be found as disfiguring late additions on the doors and deep drawers of old sideboards. In such cases, it is not always easy to decide whether completely to remove the excrescences and heal the resultant scars as well as may be, or to supply the most nearly correct substitute obtainable.

* * *

Toward the close of the eighteenth century and during early years of the nineteenth, as furniture grew heavier, the apparent weight of hardware increased proportionately. The lion head carrying a ring handle belongs in the transition period between Sheraton and Empire, and serves as effectively on pieces that are classifiable as Empire as on those which must properly be known as Sheraton. On Empire pieces, such as the chest of drawers in Figure 15, a large form of knob, shown at the right in the second row of Figure C, frequently appears.

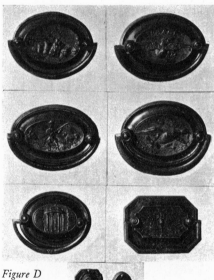

Figure 15

1810   1820

Figure D

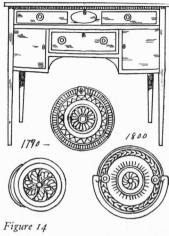

1790 –   1800

Figure 14

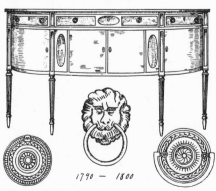

1790 – 1800

Figure 16

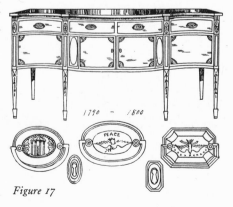

1790 – 1800

Figure 17

Types of Wrought Iron Hardware Applicable to Early American Architectural Treatment, II

Drawings by Dorothy Miller Thormin

EXAMINATION of the doors *A*, *B*, *C*, and *D* in Groups III and IV of this number of ANTIQUES and the doors pictured in the October number should suffice to give a fair idea of the progression of door types from the early and simple sheathed form to the elaborate six-paneled door. The sheathed door is not necessarily earlier than the one with two panels; it is merely cruder. Both suggest the late seventeenth and early eighteenth centuries and both are, perhaps, best hung with long strap hinges, such as were used mainly between 1700 and 1780; though any citations of date in such matters should be accepted with reservations.

Group III

Two types of such hinges are shown in Figures 6 and 7 of Group III. The possible variants are, however, almost innumerable. Such hinges are still procurable in the original. If reproductions are used, care should be exercised to make sure that the whole piece is hand forged and is not merely made of strap iron with the edges slightly refined on a grindstone and the surface given a few hammer marks either with a machine or with a few careless blows of a hammer. Hammer marks on silver, pewter, iron, and copper, it should be remembered, are properly incidental to the workman's process of shaping his material. On silver every effort of the good craftsman was exerted to eliminate these marks

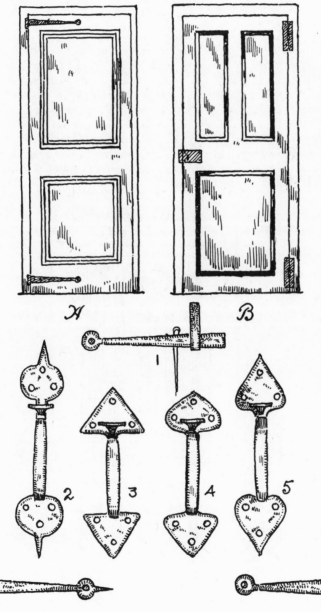

in so far as possible. The only reminder of their existence which is permissible is that slight, almost imperceptible, irregularity of surface which differentiates handwrought articles in the precious metals from the slick forms pounded out with metal dies.

On more intractable metals, such as pewter, copper, and iron — metals, further, whose wrought value does not justify exacting care in final finish — the marks of the hammer are likely to be more in evidence. Their simulation, however, in a network of overemphasized wounds, depressions, and gouges, constitutes a form of vulgarity which any person truly sensitive to the quality of the antique will not long tolerate.

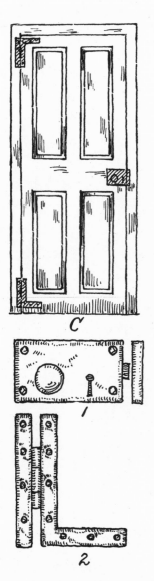

C

1

2

H hinges and *H L* hinges (*Group IV, 4 and 2*) were used contemporaneously with strap hinges, and until a later date — until the nineteenth century, in fact. They are likely to occur on doors of lighter weight than those which call for strap hinges. On doors with many panels, the *H* or *H L* (*Group IV, 4 and 2*) hinges are probably to be preferred to the strap type. But on heavy outside doors, strap hinges, while not invariable, are the general rule.

Foliated hinges — that is, hinges of the *H* type — with a kind of trefoil finial at top and bottom (*Group IV, 6*) seldom occur in large sizes. They are, therefore, more appropriately used on cupboard doors and on interior shutters. The *H* and *H L* hinges, likewise, occur on cupboards, whether built in or free standing, and light strap hinges are likewise appropriate on wide lower doors of heavy cupboards, where their use may serve to prevent sagging of the door itself.

Various types of latches are shown in Groups III and IV. But there are as many variants as there were early blacksmiths. If one wishes names for latches the following designations seem acceptable: Group III, 2. *ball and spear;* 3. *triangle;* 4. *rounded triangle;* 5. *pointed heart.* Group IV, 5. *tulip bud.*

In Group IV, 1 is shown a box-lock latch with brass handle suggestive of the late eighteenth century or early nineteenth. The latch shown in Group IV, 3 stands as an adequate intermediate between the thumb latch and the box latch.

D

3

4

5

Group IV

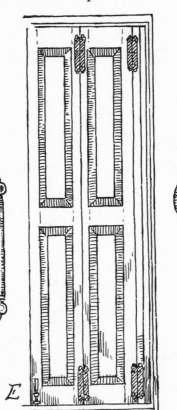

6

7

E

In houses of late eighteenth-century type it will be found both secure and decorative. The handle is usually of brass. Thumb latches of cast metal with the handle riveted to the plate came into use about 1830.

If one wishes the most primitive type of latch, he will have to carve it out of wood. Such latches are known to have been used in 1690, and they probably were called into requisition at later dates in communities where hardware was scarce or the expense of securing it beyond the means of the humble homesteader.

Types of Wrought Iron Hardware Applicable to Early American Architectural Treatment, III

Drawings by Dorothy Miller Thormin

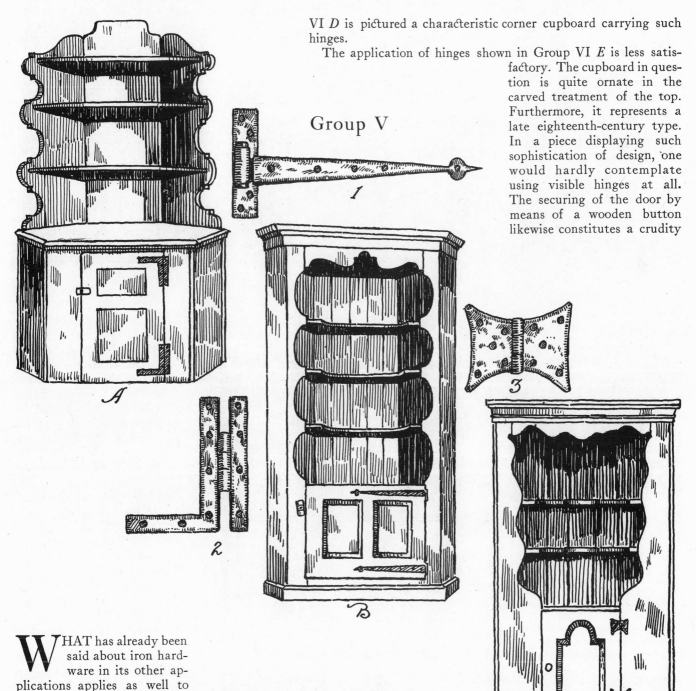

VI *D* is pictured a characteristic corner cupboard carrying such hinges.

The application of hinges shown in Group VI *E* is less satisfactory. The cupboard in question is quite ornate in the carved treatment of the top. Furthermore, it represents a late eighteenth-century type. In a piece displaying such sophistication of design, one would hardly contemplate using visible hinges at all. The securing of the door by means of a wooden button likewise constitutes a crudity

WHAT has already been said about iron hardware in its other applications applies as well to its use on built-in furniture. The same kinds of hinges were used on small doors as upon large; they were merely modified in size to satisfy the dictates of harmonious proportion. It is on cupboards particularly that the hinges with foliate ends are appropriate, though they may be used with equal propriety on narrow inside shutters and on light casement windows. In Group

of treatment hardly justified in so elaborate an example. In late and delicate pieces of this kind, concealed brass hinges and a brass door catch would be preferable to the hardware shown, unless the pine has been stripped and finished in the natural wood. Even then brass would seem to afford the more satisfactory trim.

Strap, *H L*, and butterfly hinges and

Group VI

their correct application are shown in Group V. The choice among these types will be regulated primarily by considerations of proportion. The light, rather narrow, door of cupboard *C* in this Group, and the wide unbroken surface of the supporting sides are pleasingly patterned by the spreading wings of the butterfly hinges — perhaps more correctly known as "dovetail" hinges.

The wide door of *B*, with its horizontal emphasis, quite obviously calls for long strap hinges; whereas the solid rectangularity of *A* is well supplemented by the *H L* form.

Peculiar to the furniture of German Pennsylvania is the so-called rat-tail hinge, shown in Group VI, *2*. The characteristic cupboard or dresser door of the Penn-

sylvania Germans is applied *over* the opening which it covers, instead of being *inserted* between stiles and rails. This method obscures hasty cabinet work and, by the provision of a lip which overlaps the edges of the opening, serves in some measure to prevent the intrusion of dust.

Such a door could hardly be hung with the usual type of hinge. Hence a kind of bracket was devised, whose lower end was fastened to the case and whose upper end protruded sufficiently to serve as pivot for a hinge plate fastened to the inside of the door. Rat-tail hinges are among the most picturesque items of early hardware; but their use must be confined to those Continental types of furniture which carry an applied rather than an inserted door (Group VI *F*).

Fig. 1 — Candle Brackets, Drawer Handles, and Escutcheons

An Eighteenth-Century English Brassfounder's Catalogue

By R. W. Symonds

A RECENTLY published book entitled *Knowing, Collecting, and Restoring Early American Furniture* by Henry H. Taylor includes an extremely interesting chapter dealing with furniture handles and mounts. The author writes:

It is probable that nearly all those [brasses] on the furniture in the American Colonies before the Revolution were produced in England, where the manufacture of such goods had obtained a considerable magnitude and a great degree of perfection. At any rate, we find record of a steady flow of furniture brasses from England to the Colonies prior to this time.

In support of this author's contention, I am able, through the courtesy of Messrs. Batsford of London, to reproduce the accompanying series of engraved plates of furniture hardware from what is presumably an eighteenth-century brassfounder's catalogue. This volume has no title piece, nor does it bear any name or date on any of the pages of engraved designs depicting handles, escutcheons, hinges, bolts, catches, clock mounts, and candle branches.

That this book was originally a manufacturer's catalogue would appear to be proved by the fact that not only does it contain no letterpress whatsoever, but each illustrated item is numbered. Such a book could be shown by a cabinetmaker to his customer without disclosing the name and address of the actual maker.

One particularly interesting feature of this catalogue is the de-

sign of a mount showing a wreathed bust of John Wilkes, with his name beneath (*Fig. 1; Item 1445*). The presence of such a design in this catalogue suggests that it was intended for the American as well as the English market, since John Wilkes' violent espousal of the cause of American independence would naturally make him a very popular figure in America.

The inclusion of this portrait of John Wilkes among the designs is also of material assistance in dating the catalogue. By 1760 Wilkes had achieved considerable public notoriety, and, as the American Revolution had really started on its course by 1770, it may be surmised that the catalogue was published during the intervening decade. This is also borne out by the designs of the handles, none of which exhibits the full Adam style that came into vogue after 1770. A handle (*Item 528*) shown on the plate illustrated in Figure 14 displays the first influence of this new style; it has lost the rococo scroll, and is designed instead with circular rosettes to the bolts, while the drop of the handle is of a simple curve formation.

Another interesting feature of the catalogue is the inclusion of designs that, at the date of publication, must have been already out of fashion for a number of years. The most striking example is the design of a single pear-drop handle (*Fig. 3; Items 348–350*). This type of drop handle is associated with late seventeenth-

1931

135

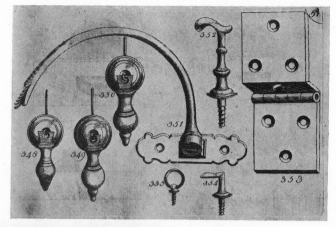

Fig. 2 — METAL DECORATIONS TO BE USED AS APPLIQUÉS ON FURNITURE
The catalogue is generously illustrated with such items

Fig. 3 — HINGES, HOOKS, AND HANDLES
Items 348–350 are associated with an earlier period than that of the catalogue

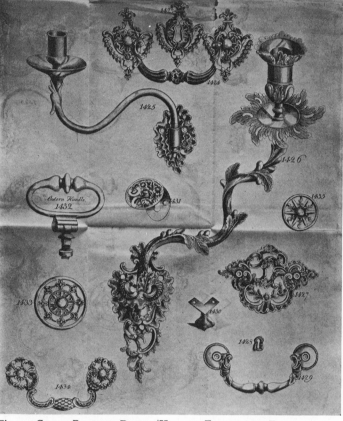

Fig. 5 — HEAVY HARDWARE
Suggestive of the period 1720–1750. Contrast with pierced work of Figure 7, which was used until about 1770

Fig. 4 — CANDLE BRACKETS, DRAWER HANDLES, ESCUTCHEONS, ETC.
Item 1430 may be a tea caddy foot. Items 1433 and 1435 seem to be merely decorative bosses

Fig. 6 — HARDWARE WITH SOLID PLATES
The delicately engraved cabinet hinges of Item 341 are of an early pattern

Fig. 7 — TYPICAL PIERCED-WORK
HANDLES OF THE PERIOD
In vogue until 1765 or 1770.
Compare Figures 5 and 6

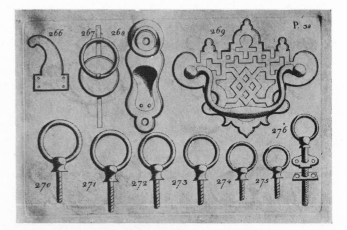

Fig. 8 — VARIOUS HARDWARE
Item 268 is the catch for ad-
justing the panel of a pole
screen

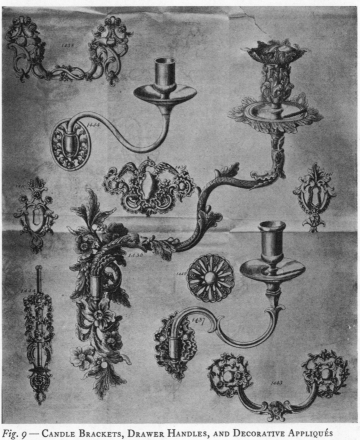

Fig. 10 — CATCHES FOR THE TOPS
OF TIP TABLES

Fig. 9 — CANDLE BRACKETS, DRAWER HANDLES, AND DECORATIVE APPLIQUÉS

Fig. 11 — KEYHOLE ESCUTCH-
EONS FOR CABINET DOORS

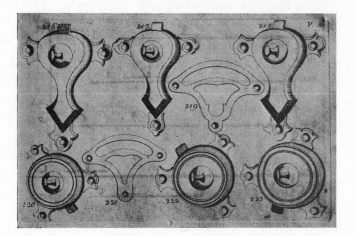

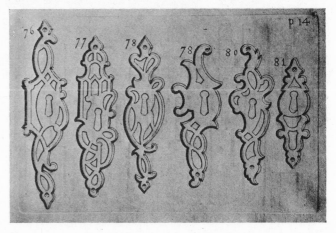

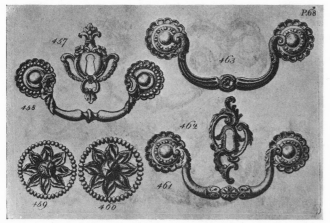

Fig. 12 — Various Items of Furniture Hardware

Fig. 13 — Decorative Door Bolts, Brackets, Screws, and Plates

century furniture, and it would seem extremely unlikely that any English cabinetmaker would make use of it in the third quarter of the eighteenth century.

The handles with the shaped solid back plates (*Figs. 5 and 6*) were in vogue in England between the years 1720 and 1750. Those with pierced back plates (*Fig. 7*) were, however, used until 1765 or 1770. Both types were much favored by the American cabinetmakers, who employed them long after they had been discarded by their English confreres. The inclusion of these old-fashioned designs in the elaborate and profusely illustrated catalogue is contributory evidence that it was produced primarily for the American market, where the taste in furniture hardware was more conservative than in England. Other designs shown, which were no longer fashionable in England in 1760 to 1770, are the engraved H hinge (*Fig. 6; Item 341*), and the drop-ring handle (*Fig. 8; Item 267*). Both of these had gone out of fashion by 1750, the ring handle being much used on walnut and early mahogany furniture between the years 1720 and 1740.

The candle branches, which were intended for mirrors or small mirror sconces, also show a wide variation as regards their date. The swan-necked design (*Fig. 4; Item 1425*) and the two plain examples (*Fig. 9; Items 1434 and 1437*) belong to the period of 1725 to 1750, whereas the more elaborate specimens illustrated all date after 1750. The design of candle branches, however, was not subject to the same fluctuations of taste as that of handles, and the inclusion of the earlier types, therefore, is much less remarkable.

One plate (*Fig. 15*) shows a set of mounts for a clock case. The quarter cap and base are for the

quarter reeded column often found decorating the front corners of long case mahogany clocks dating from the last half of the eighteenth century. The smaller Corinthian cap and base are for the columns supporting the cornice to the hood. The finial is of a well-known pattern often found on walnut and mahogany clocks dating from 1740 to 1780. Item 268 (*Fig. 8*) is a catch to hold in position the panel of a tripod pole screen, while two designs of catches for fixing the hinged tops of tripod tables are also pictured (*Fig. 10; Items 219 and 221*).

As further evidence that the firm that issued this catalogue had an eye to American export as well as home trade, it would be interesting to find on pieces of American Colonial furniture possessing their original mounts, any hardware of which the design is identical to an example illustrated. One may reasonably infer that the firm in question, judging from the importance of the catalogue with its eighty-seven pages of finely engraved plates, was of some standing and that, in consequence, its trade in hardware with the American Colonies was equal to that of other contemporary English firms. As the firms engaged in this particular type of export trade cannot have been numerous, it is not unreasonable to hope that examples of this firm's handiwork may be identified in the manner suggested.

Perhaps the readers of ANTIQUES will be able to throw some light on the subject of this very interesting brassfounder's trade catalogue. To this end the hardware on early American pieces should be carefully noted for designs identical with patterns here illustrated. Furthermore, it would be advisable to keep a lookout for any additional copies of the catalogue.

Fig. 14 — Drawer Handles
Item 528 shows circular rosettes about the bolts, and a simple curved bail, both perhaps suggestive of Adam influence

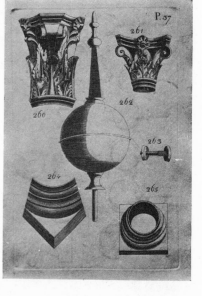

Fig. 15 — Clock Case Hardware
Finial of a well-known pattern often found on walnut and mahogany clocks dating from 1740 to 1780

English Hardware for American Cabinetmakers

By Samuel W. Woodhouse, Jr.

IN Antiques for February, 1931, were published some notes by R. W. Symonds on an eighteenth-century English brassfounder's catalogue. Chiefly through the courtesy of the Essex Institute of Salem, Massachusetts, I am now able to supplement these notes and their accompanying illustrations with a number of engravings taken from English catalogues, evidently compiled with some special reference to the American trade. The books in question were, it appears, discovered by Colonel Henry A. Hale in the warehouse of a forebear who had long been a hardware merchant in Salem. Very generously the Colonel presented his find to the Essex Institute. None of these

volumes bears any printed indication of the firm by whom it was issued or any notation of date. One, however, carries the written inscription *J. Belcher & Sons, High Street, Birmingham,* with a water mark of 1818.

It is, in fact, a moot question whether all such beautifully engraved trade catalogues were not composites representing the work of several associated manufacturers. The metal trades of Birmingham were highly organized, and were controlled by price-fixing agreements and other devices intended to strengthen the group against individual competition.

Those manufacturers who made furniture hardware were known as "stampers," and their catalogues are highly prized. Besides the collection of these volumes in the Essex Institute, which is perhaps the finest in the world, I recall a small group in

the Victoria and Albert Museum in London. Its ably arranged descriptive catalogue, by W. A. Young, is prefaced with a brief but informing discussion of the metal manufactures of Birmingham and Sheffield and their methods of maintaining contact with their customers. According to this authority, manufacturers began, about 1770, to send out engravings of new patterns. At first these were forwarded in loose sheet form. Later the sheets were bound together. Thus developed the catalogue. The actual production of such volumes is uncertain, although the accuracy of detail suggests that the drawings were made by the craftsmen themselves.

The trade catalogue cited by Mr. Symonds doubtless antedates any in the Essex Institute group. In the main it pictures cast ornaments, the product of brassfounders, whereas the Institute specimens, with few exceptions, show the stampers' work, made according to a process first utilized for certain purposes in Birmingham in 1769, and later, in 1777, adapted to the manufacture of cabinet goods. It is interesting to observe that this date, marking the first production of light-weight hardware, closely corresponds to the shift in furniture styles toward slender and delicate forms.

Most of the catalogue designs that I have selected for reproduction are so familiar as to call for no special comment. It may be noted that the enamel knobs generally known to collectors as mirror knobs are designated as "cloak pins." Other illustrations, on this and the two following pages, are self-explanatory.

Figs. 1, 2, 3 — Mainly Cast Ornaments (*c. 1780*)
All of these patterns are from the same book, probably the earliest of the lot, and closely following in date the catalogue discussed in Antiques for February, 1931. Though Adam designs occur, the rococo dominates

Figs. 4 and 5 — FROM A BOOK PUBLISHED *c. 1790*
Designs to please royalist and republican tastes, and to
appeal to sympathy for France as well as love for England

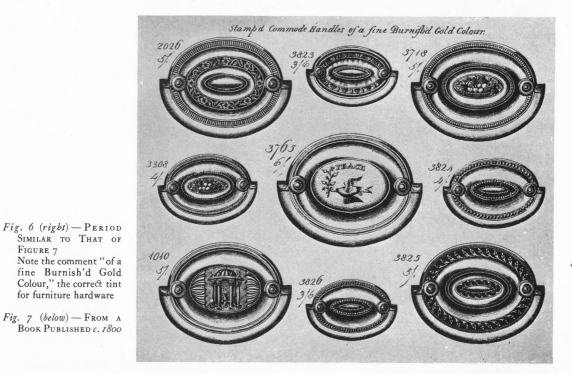

Fig. 6 (right) — PERIOD
SIMILAR TO THAT OF
FIGURE 7
Note the comment "of a
fine Burnish'd Gold
Colour," the correct tint
for furniture hardware

Fig. 7 (below) — FROM A
BOOK PUBLISHED *c. 1800*

Fig. 8 (below) — VERGING
ON THE "EMPIRE" *(after
1800)*
Anthemion ornamenta-
tion and excessive size
differentiate the centre
handle from its fellows

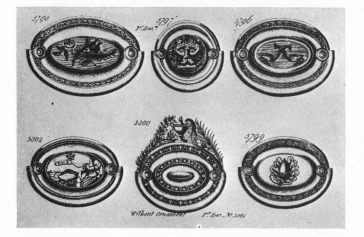

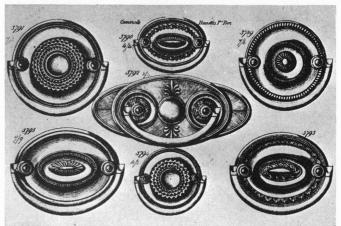

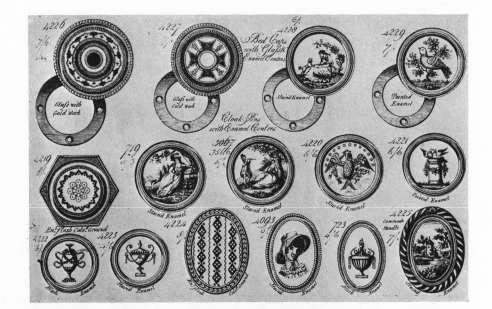

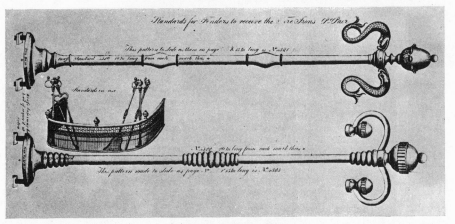

Figs. 9 and 10 (at top and bottom of page) — ENAMELED AND GLASS ORNAMENTS (c. 1800) So-called "Battersea" knobs, handles, and appliqués. Glass

work also appears in the drawings. It will be remembered that Seymour of Boston used such enameled handles on certain of his daintier pieces of furniture

Fig. 11 — FIREPLACE IMPLEMENTS

V Instruments, Tools, Nails, etc

Assembled here are seven articles on instruments, tools, nails, and weights. Both Peter Welsh's and Marshall Davidson's contributions are photo essays which focus on the aesthetic aspects of their subject matter. William Guthman's, J. Paul Hudson's, and Roger Gerry's articles concentrate on special objects and the men who made them. The article by Gertrude Whiting, a general essay on scissors, is typical of those useful studies found in ANTIQUES over the years. That on nails is a description of their manufacture, with assistance in dating offered. It serves as a prologue to a more lengthy chronology of nails published as a technical leaflet by the American Association for State and Local History.

One of the noticeable gaps in this anthology concerns clocks. While clock cases are certainly pieces of furniture, their works are made from common metals, including brass, iron, and steel. They are not included here because of their special mechanisms and manufacture and properly deserve separate treatment in another volume.

Surveyors' equipment and the western frontier

BY WILLIAM H. GUTHMAN

SURVEYING INSTRUMENTS have played a significant role in the history of the United States, perhaps more so than in any other country in the world. Partly because of their historical interest, and partly because of their appeal as precise mechanical tools, they have been desirable as collectibles for a long time. The few books and articles about American surveying instruments, however, deal primarily with their scientific aspect, not with their historical associations. One of the few isolated exceptions refers to the surveying compass that belonged to George Washington, who was a surveyor in his youth.

Beginning with the Land Ordinance of 1785, the entire western expansion of the United States relied on the surveyor and his instruments. That ordinance specified that Congress was to appoint one surveyor from each of the thirteen states, all to work under the direction of one man, whose title was geographer of the United States. Each of the thirteen surveyors was to be sent out in a separate party consisting of himself, chain carriers, markers, Indian guides, and soldiers. Except for a handful of explorers, the surveyors, in conjunction with the Federal army, were the first to penetrate the Northwest Territory, dividing and marking the land upon which the frontiersmen later settled. Those men who entered the untamed wilderness to measure out townships on the hunting grounds of hostile Indians were as colorful and brave as any of the legendary heroes of the frontier. In 1790 and 1791 surveyors charted the course through unexplored regions for the first major United States military campaigns against the warring Indians near present-day Fort Wayne, Indiana. These expeditions produced the first accurate maps of that part of the Northwest Territory.

Surveying in America before the Revolution, however, was motivated by a completely different set of political conditions from those that existed after the war. The United States emerged from the struggle as a bankrupt victor. Hopelessly in debt to her European supporters, unable to pay her disillusioned soldiers for their services during the war, and torn by jealousy among the states, the new nation quickly turned toward her one asset that could possibly solve many of her problems: land.

According to the terms of the peace treaty signed in Paris in 1783, Great Britain had ceded to the United States lands bounded on the north by the Great Lakes as far west as Lake of the Woods, on the west by the Mississippi River, on the south by the Florida-Georgia border and the St. Mary's River, and on the east by the Atlantic. Before land could be granted to Revolutionary veterans or sold to prospective settlers, however, a protective force was needed to guard the surveyors and settlers from marauding Indians and to evict squatters from government land that was to be sold. On June 3, 1784, Congress, apprehensive of a large standing army, established a small force of seven

hundred noncommissioned officers and privates. Next, to establish a set of rules for the disposition of the land, Congress passed a land ordinance on May 20, 1785. This ordinance called for surveys dividing the territory into townships six miles square. The townships were to be offered at public auction in units of no less than one square mile, or six hundred and forty acres. The government considered well-regulated order more important than rapid settlement or immediate profit. Therefore, land could go on sale only after the surveyor had finished his work. Settlers could not move out into the wilderness and stake out their own plots. Moreover, lots could be sold only in proportions of entire townships, half townships, or sections of townships. The average citizen was unable to afford pieces of land this large, so speculators formed land companies to

Fig. 1. Surveyor's compass made by Joseph Halsy, Boston, Massachusetts (d. 1762). Frame of apple wood with cherry cover inscribed, *Richard Baxter his compass/bought Marche ye 2d anno 1747.* The engraved compass card has a medallion with a two-masted ship in the center surrounded by the inscription, *Made & Sold by Joseph Halsy in Fish-Street Boston New Eng.* Diameter 5¼ inches. *All illustrations are from the collection of Pamela and Scott Guthman.*

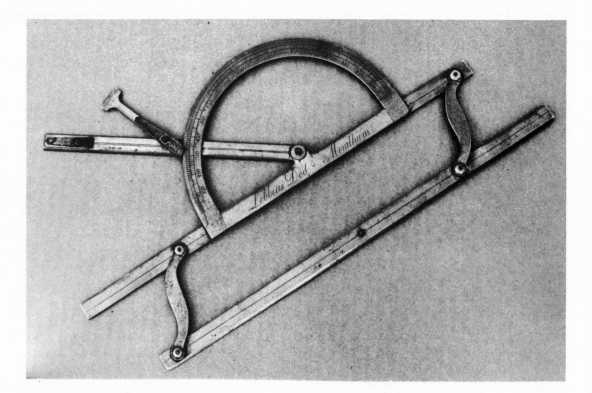

Fig. 2. Surveyor's combination brass parallel rule and protractor, engraved by the maker, *Lebbeus Dod Mendham;* New Jersey, c. 1780. Dod operated an armory for the Continental Army during the Revolution. Length when closed, 12 inches.

Fig. 3. Brass surveyor's compass by Frederick A. Heisely, Fredericktown, Maryland, c. 1783. Inscribed *F. Heisely Fredk. Town.* Diameter 6 inches.

Fig. 4. Brass surveyor's compass made by John Avery, Preston, Connecticut. The cover is inscribed *M D F/4th Jany 1787.* Diameter of compass, 5½ inches.

Fig. 5. Surveyor's compass with walnut frame and ebony sights, made by William Guyse Hagger. The compass card bears the engraved inscription, *Hagger, / Maker/ near the Draw Bridge/ Boston*. The date 1754 was added years ago but does not correctly identify the year the instrument was made. The card is signed by the engraver, *Callender scp*. Hagger is listed, on Ann Street, in Boston directories for 1789 and 1796. Both Benjamin and Joseph Callender were engravers also working in Boston during that period. Diameter 6¼ inches.

Fig. 6. Printed trade card of Isaac Greenwood, who worked in Providence, Rhode Island, from 1787 to 1810. Among the items he advertised are surveyor's compasses and chains as well as other surveying instruments. 9 by 7 inches.

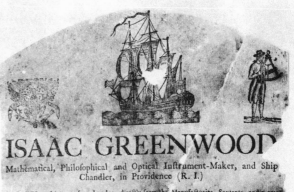

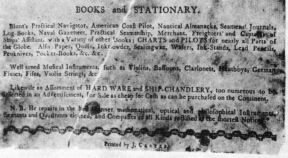

Fig. 7. Brass vernier compass, on wooden tripod, made by Thomas Whitney who worked in Philadelphia from 1798 to 1821. A vernier compass is one with an attachment that shows compensating adjustments for magnetic variations. Diameter 6⅛ inches.

buy huge tracts from the government and then sell smaller plots to individual settlers at a profit.

The geometrically precise method of rectangular land division has remained as a lasting monument to the ordinance of 1785 and to the surveyors who carried out its terms. This method of surveying was followed through the nineteenth century, and the entire midwestern and far western portions of the United States were surveyed exactly as the first tracts had been in 1785. The result is plainly visible in the rectangular patterns of farms, ranches, and parallel roads that form a continuous grid from the Alleghenies to the Pacific, as well as in the design of towns laid out on a basis of right-angle intersections. Monotonous but efficient, this unimaginative system of town planning and rural development is the trade mark of the West.

This article is adapted from a chapter in Mr. Guthman's forthcoming book, *March to Massacre,* a history of the first seven years of the United States Army, from 1784 to 1791.

Fig. 8. Brass surveyor's compass mounted on gimbals; shown here in original pine carrying box with cover removed; c. 1780-1815, maker unknown. The compass is of primitive construction, and bears the initials *G F* stamped on one limb of the main plate. Length over all, 15¾ inches.

Fig. 9. Tomahawk owned by Daniel Smith while surveying the Tennessee-North Carolina boundary in 1779. Haft of curly maple with silver inlays. On the obverse of the steel blade, an inset piece of silver in the shape of a scalping knife is engraved, *Dan. Smith Opost*. Opost was the eighteenth-century English corruption of the French designation *Au Poste* for Poste Vincennes, Indiana, an early French trading post and fort. According to his diary, Smith lost the weapon on the 1779 expedition. The reverse side of the blade bears the crudely scratched inscription *James Stephenson,* the name of one of the Kentucky riflemen guarding this group of surveyors. Tomahawks of this type, usually thought of as exclusively Indian, were frequently used by frontiersmen as weapons, as axes, and as pipes. The bowl is at one end of the head and the hollow handle serves as the pipe-stem. Present length 11 inches: the handle has been shortened and originally was probably 20 inches long.

Fig. 10. Brass surveyor's compass, made by Richard Patten of New York City, c. 1815 (see Antiques, July 1959, p. 56). The compass card is inscribed, *R. Patten, New York*. Diameter 5¾ inches.

Fig. 11. Brass vernier compass, elaborately made and engraved by Goldsmith Chandlee, Winchester, Virginia (d. 1821), probably near the end of his life. The compass card is inscribed, *G * Chandlee Winchester*. The name *A. Stowell Jr.* is engraved on the brass cover. Diameter 7⅛ inches.

Fig. 12. *Top,* surveyor's compass, in cherry frame, made by Thomas Salter Bowles of Portsmouth, New Hampshire. The engraved compass card is inscribed *Callender scp.* The instrument is stained red, like country furniture of the period, and was probably made before 1820. *Bottom,* semicircumferentor. The maple frame is inscribed *T. Lincoln 1803,* for either the maker (unrecorded) or the owner; 5¼ by 9⅜ inches.

Richard Patten:

mathematical instrument maker

BY ROGER G. GERRY, Captain, DC, USN.

Fig. 1. Brass surveyor's compass made by Richard Patten; probably an early example as it has no spirit levels and the compass needle cannot be locked, but must be removed and placed in the case when not in use; length 15⅝ inches. *Except as noted, illustrations are from the author's collection and photographs are by Morton Russin.*

Fig. 2. Accessories of the compass shown in Fig. 1 which were kept in the case under the compass. The case itself is crudely made of yellow pine, perhaps by the purchaser of the instrument.

AMONG EARLY AMERICAN METALWORKERS and engravers, Richard Patten is virtually unknown today, although he was undoubtedly an important craftsman in New York during the great period of commercial expansion of the early nineteenth century. His surveyor's compasses illustrated here exhibit a standard of workmanship and decoration remarkable for such utilitarian instruments.

No record of Patten's birth or training has been found. He was first listed in Longworth's *Directory* in 1813 as working at 350 Water Street. He moved to 184 Water Street in 1815 and was at 180 Water Street (perhaps just a change in house numbering) in 1820, where he stayed for most of the remainder of his working career. He was last listed in 1842 with a business on Washington Street and a residence at 119 Mercer Street.

Many other men are listed in connection with mathematical instruments in New York during this period, but most of them were merely dealers who sold used or imported instruments. Patten, in fact, described himself as the "only Manufacturer of Sextants and Quadrants in New York," and there is no good reason to question his claim. He also stated in his label that all his instruments were "warranted, being divided on an Engine after the Plan of Ramsdens," which establishes the soundness of his training and the accuracy of his work. Jesse Ramsden (1735-1800) was an English astronomical instrument maker who, according to Thomas Dobson's *Encyclopedia* (Philadelphia, 1798), invented an extremely complex apparatus for the calibration of instruments in London in 1775 and was awarded the sum of £615 by the Commissioners of Longitude for training not more than ten persons in the use of his device. While each of these quite obviously must have trained others, and Patten worked a full generation after Ramsden, it is not likely that there were many similarly trained workmen in the United States, and Patten's "Engine after the Plan of Ramsdens" may well have been the only one in this country.

In spite of Patten's ability and apparent industry, few of his instruments seem to have survived. Since early nineteenth-century American instruments of this type do not bring the same high prices as some other American artifacts of the period, they have not found their way into the antiques market. Correspondence with museums which might be likely to own examples of the work of a New York maker of navigation and surveying instruments, such as the New-York Historical Society, the Museum of the City of New York, the Peabody Museum

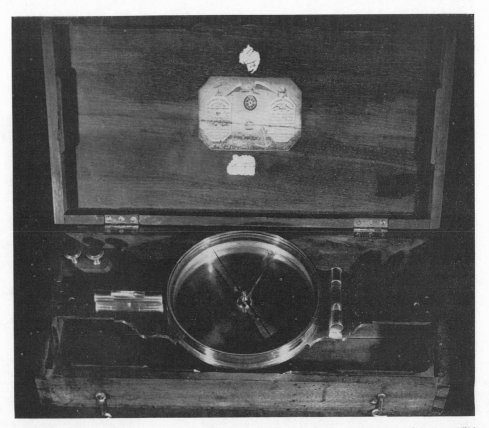

Fig. 3. Brass surveyor's compass made by Patten between 1820 and 1833, with two spirit levels and a locking device to prevent needle rotation when the instrument is not in use. The mahogany case was obviously made by a professional. Length of compass, 16 inches.

Fig. 4. Dial of compass shown in Fig. 3. Letters and numbers are engraved, but decorative detail is etched.

Fig. 5. Paper label in case lid of compass shown in Fig. 3; the only example of Patten's trade card known to the author. The plate used in printing this label was probably engraved by Patten, who describes himself as the "only Manufacturer of Sextants and Quadrants in New York."

Fig. 6. Brass surveyor's compass made by Patten and sold by a Boston dealer; probably the latest of the three instruments illustrated, as the spirit level is of a more recent type and the dial is less vigorously decorated than either of the others. Instrument and case are similar to those shown in Fig. 3, but less attention has been paid to details of finishing. *Mariners' Museum, Newport News, Virginia.*

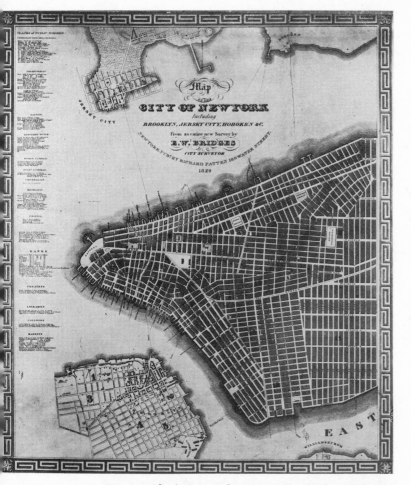

Fig. 7. *Bridges' Map of the City of New York* published by Patten in 1829. Patten probably also made the plate. Most of the map is etched, with the details finished in engraving. *New-York Historical Society.*

of Salem, and the museums at West Point and Annapolis, have produced no specimens. There are no examples of his trade card in the Bella C. Landauer Business and Professional Collection at the New-York Historical Society or in the collection of American trade cards at the Metropolitan Museum of Art. A surveyor's compass by him was located at the Mariners' Museum at Newport News and this instrument, as well as two similar instruments in my collection, is illustrated. Others must certainly have survived, and it is to be hoped that some, especially a few sextants and quadrants, will be brought to light.

While Patten has been almost completely forgotten as a mathematical instrument maker, there is even less evidence of his work as an engraver, though it seems fair to assume that he himself did the decoration as well as the calibration on his dials. A. Hyatt Mayor, curator of prints of the Metropolitan Museum of Art, has expressed the opinion that the engraving on these and on his trade card is "very well designed and executed in a highly competent manner," but Patten is not listed in either Fielding's or Stauffer's check lists of American engravers. E. W. Bridges' *Map of New York*, which was published by Patten, is superior to much contemporary work; I. N. Phelps Stokes, in *The Iconography of Manhatten Island,* lists its publication among events which took place in the year 1829. The quality of the engraving and etching of the Patten compass dials suggests that he also etched and engraved the plate used in printing this map. It would be interesting to know whether signed or documented examples of engraving by Patten exist.

The opinions and assertions expressed herein are those of the writer alone, and do not necessarily reflect the official attitude of the United States Navy Department.

Bits of brass

BY MARSHALL B. DAVIDSON

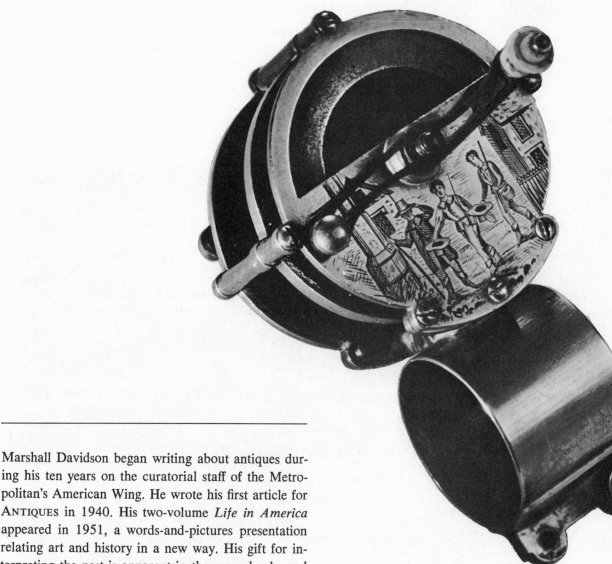

Marshall Davidson began writing about antiques during his ten years on the curatorial staff of the Metropolitan's American Wing. He wrote his first article for ANTIQUES in 1940. His two-volume *Life in America* appeared in 1951, a words-and-pictures presentation relating art and history in a new way. His gift for interpreting the past is apparent in the many books and other publications he has written and edited since, among them the recent American Heritage histories of antiques and architecture. He is the husband of Ruth Davidson, who has been a member of our editorial staff for over thirty years. We take pleasure in presenting him in a new role: as a collector.

An early nineteenth-century English fishing reel, engraved on the side illustrated above with a scene showing three fishermen, rods in hand, passing through a village street. Why two of the anglers hold their hats upturned in their outstretched hands may have been clear to contemporaries, but the meaning of their gesture remains obscure for the present. The reverse side of the reel, reproduced here about twice its actual size, is marked: W. DANN. MAKER. NOTT^M (Nottingham) in a decorative cartouche.

Except as noted, photographs are by Lee Boltin.

PROFESSING AN UNACQUISITIVE NATURE, a few years ago I was surprised to note that somehow I had formed a modest but growing collection of old brass objects. I had not meant to do this, really, but every once in a while—here or in Europe—some such thing would gleam at me from a dealer's shelf or a secondhand-shop window, and demand my appreciation of its design and craftsmanship. That aroused an unwonted covetousness that was often irresistible—so long as my purse was not outraged by the price tag. I found myself enjoying the heft of these solid substances as I handled them, and admiring the skill of some usually unknown metalworker, as I studied them. Thus it came about that a highly miscellaneous assortment of nutcrackers, snuffboxes, portable sundials, candlesticks, and other pleasant shapes and tools started to spill off the table tops at home and take up shelf room sorely needed for books. By then it was too late.

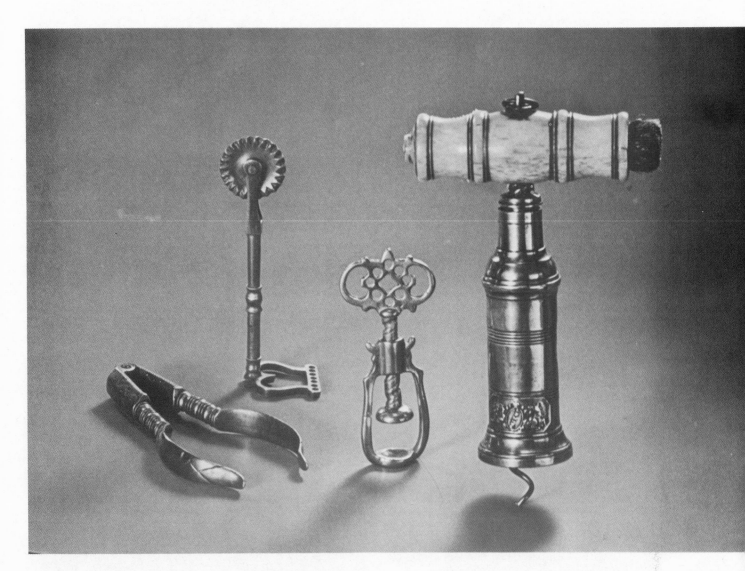

Above. *Left to right*: A nineteenth-century nutcracker; an early eighteenth-century pastry or pie crimper with crown-shape ornamental stamp; a mid-eighteenth-century hazelnut cracker; a nineteenth-century "patent" corkscrew with bone handle and an inset brush for removing dust and cobwebs from wine bottles.

Opposite, above. A combination ruler, level, and square, c. 1800, marked LEREBOURS À PARIS (Noël Jean Lerebours, 1761-1840); a protractor (for measuring and constructing angles); calipers. The last two are probably early nineteenth century.

Opposite, below. An assortment of candlesticks, *left to right*: Mid-seventeenth-century Dutch; one of a pair, English, 1725-1750; mid-eighteenth-century English; early eighteenth-century collapsible pricket candleholder (the piece folds into a flat, compact form when not in use); early eighteenth-century English(?). A small nineteenth-century whale-oil lamp.

Right. A snuffbox with monogrammed silver insert and engraved Masonic symbols. The opposite side is inscribed: *May an honest heart never know distress.* *Photograph by Century Photographers.*

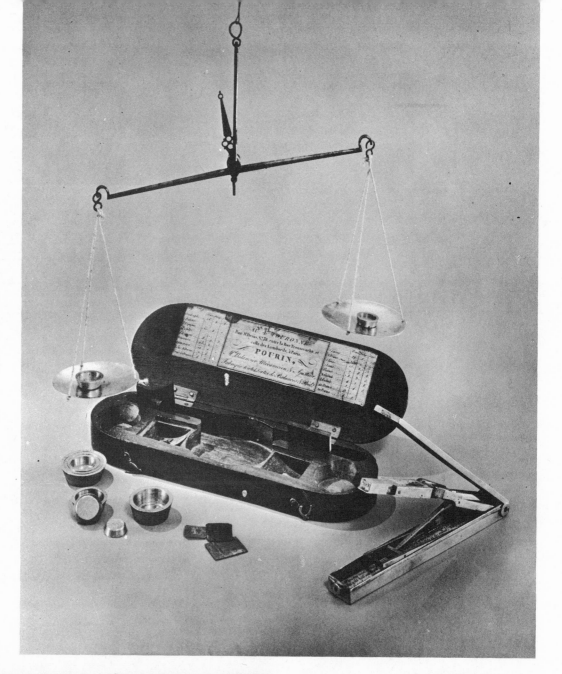

Goldsmith's scales. Eighteenth century, in a mahogany case with graduated weights and a balance, labeled "Au P Couronne, Rue S.ᵗ Denis, N.º 38, entre la Rue Trousevache et celle des Lombards, à Paris, Pourin . . . Balancier Mécanicien & Ajusteur . . ." and listing relative weights of French and foreign coins. Engraved late eighteenth-century folding scales with label of A. Wilkinson, Ormskirk, Lancashire, asserting that they "may be tried with sealed weights at any time, for the satisfaction of such as refuse to take money by them: If they vary, they are soon brought to by the slide . . . [they are] portable, almost not possible to be out of order."

Left to right: A small eighteenth-century writing stand, including a quill holder, a sander, and an ink container; a handled sander for drying ink; a quill holder; a portable inkstand (the lower element is the ink container; a penknife for sharpening quills screws into the tapered upright).

An eighteenth-century trivet, pierced with heart shapes and a Masonic symbol. As may be seen in the mirror image of its reverse side, it was made from a considerably larger sheet of brass that had earlier—possibly in the late seventeenth century, to judge from the engraved characters and ornament—served as a quadrant, an instrument for measuring altitudes in astronomy, surveying, and other scientific pursuits.

A portable brazier (about 5½ inches long). Like so many of these pieces, unmarked and of unusual designs not approximated in other mediums, this example can hardly be dated with any accuracy. A fair guess would place it in the late eighteenth or early nineteenth century, probably of English or American manufacture—which is of less importance to this "collection" than the fact that it is handsomely designed and skillfully constructed.

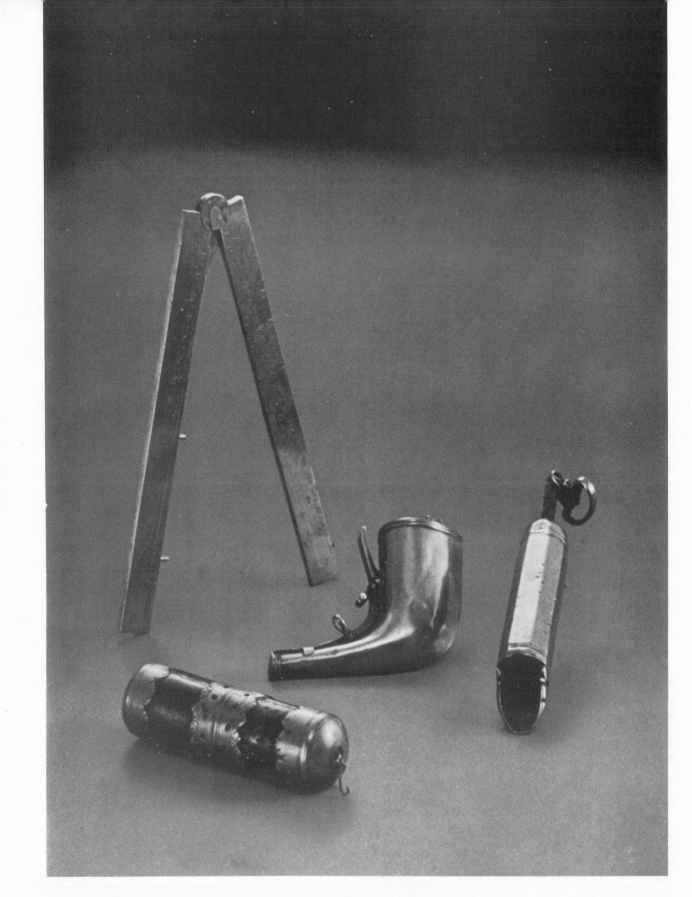

An assortment of objects related to guns and gunpowder. The jointed rule is a
seventeenth-century French artillerist's gauge and angle finder, as the inscriptions
attest, designed to measure the caliber of firing weapons, the weight of the balls
(*boulets*) to be propelled, and other data important to a cannoneer of the time.
At the lower left is what may be a tinderbox, made of copper mounted in brass
late in the seventeenth century. The two objects at the right are powder charges,
both of Near-Eastern origin and probably made in the eighteenth century.

A small, early eighteenth-century Dutch teakettle (it is less than 7½ inches tall with handle extended) with a duck's-head spout and boldly turned wooden grip. In the Western world, distinct from traditional Oriental ritual, tea was brewed in a teapot rather than in the individual cup, and kettles were required for adding water to the pot. The first reference to a teakettle in the English language appeared in 1687. This example was made sometime in the next twenty or thirty years. In the background is an eighteenth-century brazier with claw-and-ball feet.

A variety of portable sundials. *Clockwise, starting upper left*: A dial of the Butterfield type, so called after the well-known English mathematician and instrument maker, Michael Butterfield (c. 1635-1724), who worked in Paris; marked BUTERFIELD PARIS, the misspelling suggesting that a contemporary maker may have been trying to cash in on Butterfield's reputation; the latitudes of eighteen European cities are engraved on the reverse side. Unidentified dial, eighteenth century. Mid-eighteenth-century dial by Andreas Vogler, Augsburg, inscribed on the reverse and listing the latitudes of eight cities. Late seventeenth-century dial, marked on the reverse JOHÁN SCHROTTEGGER IN AUGSBURG.

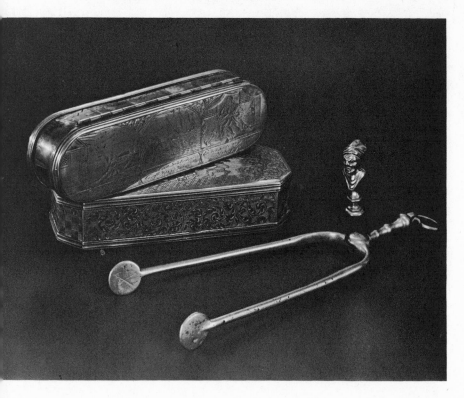

Smoking equipment. Two eighteenth-century Dutch tobacco boxes, a pipe tamper in the form of a human head, and tongs for handling a hot coal. The upper of the two boxes is engraved, top and bottom, with a series of ribald and earthy scenes illustrating the accompanying coarsely humorous aphorisms; a comic hunting scene enlivens the sides. The other box is more decorously engraved with the arms of Amsterdam, ornamental motifs, and illustrated pious admonitions.

Notes on Scissors

By Gertrude Whiting

THE old forms—cysowres, sisoures, cisors, cissers, sizars—show that our present term is of French origin, from the former *cisoires*—shears—later modified to *ciseaux* or in the singular *ciseau*, an earlier spelling of which was *cisel*, a chisel, derived from the Latin *caedere*, to cut; *cisorium*, a cutting instrument; or *scindere*, to cleave. The Latin *scissor* was a carver, butcher or gladiator's knife.

Shells and sharp-edged stones were probably the first implements used for this purpose.

But in Roman days came iron, bronze and steel shears of a single piece of bent metal sharpened at the ends. In Pompeii occurs a decoration of cupids cutting flowers, and there is, at the Museum of Sens, a Roman painting of a man cutting cloth. A Greek earthenware group portrays a barber cutting the hair of an old man. These single strip shears continued up to mediaeval times. In the Cathedral of Chartres is treasured an instrument of torture, an object resembling scissors, but probably used for tongue-slitting.

The modern implement, as we know it, appeared in the sixteenth century and is attributed to the Venetians, though some crossed blades belonging to the fourteenth century have been found. The Persians originated the bird-form scissor with the elongated beak serving as a blade. The Renaissance brought wick cutters or candle-snuffers and coal scissors—those fascinating extension, twisted brass affairs like magnified, jointed sugar tongs—and also the idea of ornamenting the instruments with a device, such as entwined hearts on scissors intended as wedding gifts.

Tortoise-shell and ivory girdle cases were introduced that small

"What are little boys made of?
Scissors and snails
And puppy dogs' tails,
And that's what little boys are made of."
—*Mother Goose.*

(Some versions say *snaps* [metal-workers' shears] and some *snips* [glass-blowers' nippers] for scissors.)

"Without rasour or sisoures."
—*House of Fame*, by Chaucer.

"Wanting the Scissors, with these hands I'll tear
(If that obstructs my Flight) this load of Hair."
—*Henry and Emma*, by Prior.

"Knives to grind, good masters,
Sweet mistresses, scissors to grind."

"We lawyers, like shears so keen,
Ne'er cut ourselves, but what's between."

An old seal depicting a pair of open scissors, has for motto, "We part to meet again."

Fig. 1 — Metal Horse Clippers
Found at La Cañada Honda, Spain, and very much rusted.
Courtesy of the Hispanic Society of America.

scissors might be conveniently carried about. Some instruments were inlaid with gold and gems. The damascened variety from Toledo, Spain, is always decorated with golden arabesques. Folding pocket scissors also were invented during the Renaissance. France, in the eighteenth century, had a fad for the so-called *jambes princesses*—princess's legs with fancy boot-tops!

Nowadays we have graduated sets of three or four pairs of different size scissors in one leather case: but now, as formerly, since sharp edges might cut friendship, one is supposed to accompany the gift of a knife or a pair of scissors with a penny to avert ill luck. In mythological days, it was not only Friendship, but Life itself that might be severed, for though one of the Fates spun the Thread of Life, another—Atropos—cut it off. The painting of these three Parcae, which has been attributed to Michelangelo, distinctly shows the one-piece, bent shears of earlier days.

Coming down to the present day, one might remark that the finest scissors are hand-forged of the very best steel only, this being necessary to insure a keen cutting edge, hardness and uniformity, so that a high, smooth polish may be given the metal, together with tenacity to withstand the heat incident to forging, and later to hold their correct and exact form after the blades are tempered and chilled.

Sometimes only the cutting edges are of steel, welded to iron shanks and bows, or handles: but these must be burnished, for irregularity of surface interferes with polishing. These are called *shot* scissors. Tailors' shears sometimes have brass or bronze bows riveted or dovetailed to steel blades. First a strip of metal the length of the whole tool is cut and one end

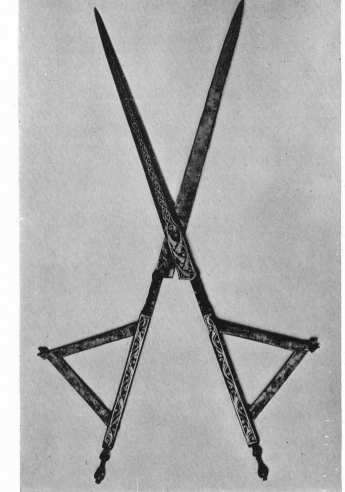

Figs. 2 and 3 — Persian Steel Scissors
Inlaid with gold. Note the collapsible, triangular handles. *From the collection of Mrs. DeWitt Clinton Cohen.*

Fig. 2

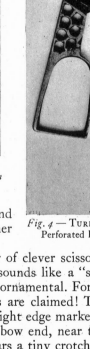

Fig. 4 — Turkish Steel Scissors
Perforated handles of uneven length.

curved into the shape of the finger hole or bow. The opposite end is then hammered into a blade. This is done by eye guidance, and is called *forging*. The two halves of the scissor are then *fitted:* that is, filed to match precisely and drilled in the centre of their shanks, preparatory to being screwed together.

Next they pass through the process of *grinding*. Following this they are bound together with wire and heated to a purple color, which indicates their proper *tempering*. *Polishing* ensues. Great care is required in order to obtain a proper cutting adjustment: so the surfaces of the blades are slightly bossed and each has a small triangular prominence to make

the blades cant more and more towards each other as they close.

Not long ago a pair of clever scissors was invented in France. The product sounds like a "stunt" and is probably more useful than ornamental. For this all-round pair eighteen different uses are claimed! The flat side of the under blade has a straight edge marked off as a ruler and measure. Toward the bow end, near the joint, when the blades are open, appears a tiny crotch which catches and cuts wire. Next to it a larger, circular one clips cigars. A screw between the handles adjusts a button-holer, which, in addition, is toothed so that it can hold and sever a small tube. One edge of the upper blade serves as a nail file. The

Fig. 5 — French Steel Scissors (*eighteenth century*)
Made of hand-wrought steel with inlaid gold handles. The centre of the scissors and the ridge of the blades are inlaid with silver wire. *From the collection of Mrs. DeWitt Clinton Cohen.*

160

square flattened end or butt of the upper blade forms a screwdriver, which can also be used to pry up a box lid. A tiny notch near the lip of the under blade enables one to withdraw cartridges from firearms.

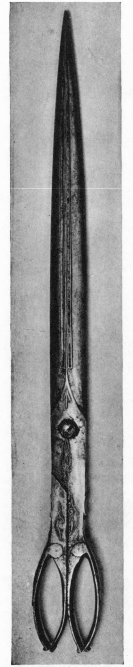

Fig. 6 — Turkish Scissors *(sixteenth century)* Hand-wrought steel scissors inlaid with gold. *From the collection of Mrs. DeWitt Clinton Cohen.*

A spread portion (like the plate or die of a seal ring), flattened out upon the outer rim of one handle-bow, may be used as a tack hammer. The lower blade has, at its centre, a projecting cylindrical pivot: but this is ellipsoidal to the upper blade. The latter has an elliptic opening for the pivot to slip into, becoming cylindrical, so that the blade can rotate on the pivot. With this little arrangement (similar to some of the

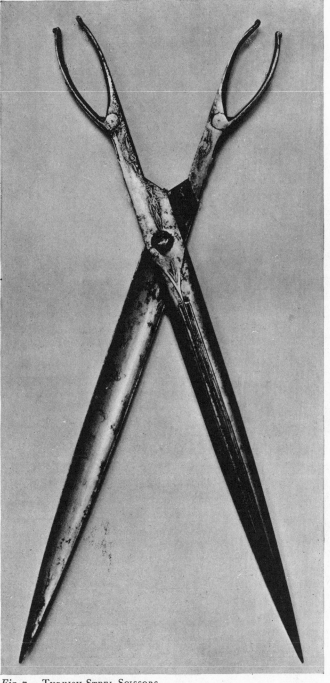

Fig. 7 — Turkish Steel Scissors
This is *Figure 6* opened. Note the spring handles that cling to the fingers and thus assure a firm grip.

removable handles on convertible Sheffield vegetable dishes, whose covers may be turned and used for additional bases) one may disjoint the scissors at will. When apart, one blade may be used as a penknife to sharpen pencils, or for other purposes. The base of one bow contains a tiny revolving steel wheel for cutting glass. Glass may also be cracked or split apart by means of a small notch right next the wheel. The other handle extremity has a diminutive toothed wheel (like a pastry jagger) for marking paper or perforating dress patterns. The tip of one blade can be used as an ink scratcher or eraser. The last or eighteenth use of this omnipotent scissor as a stereoscope seems rather doubtful!

The romantic appeal of the scissors grinder is indicated in the following lines, en-

Fig. 8 — Scissors and Sheath
Made of mother of pearl with gold sides and edges. *From the collection of Mrs. DeWitt Clinton Cohen.*

Fig. 9 — VARIOUS SCISSORS OF STEEL

    a. Old Dijon scissors. *From the collection of Mrs. Cohen.*
    b. Italian scissors with Majolica rondelle inscribed "long life."
    c. Chinese scissors and embroidered silk case.

titled the *Lay of the Scissors Grinder*, by Augusta de Bubuna:

    Out in the summer sunshine fair,
    The scissor-grinder with silvery hair
    Goes on his way, the hand bell rings
    As he trudges along, and softly sings
    While he stops to sharpen the cold dull steel
    On the roughened stone of the whirling wheel,
    And the people who loiter along their way
    Smile at the scissor-grinder's lay.
    "Oh life," he sings, "is a tangled thread,
    It's being born, and it's lying dead;
    It's loving much, and it's being wed;
    Then it's smiling—or shedding tears instead;
    And there's knots, and there's twisted, crooked ends
    In the work Dame Nature to some of us sends,
    And we oft times wish for sharp scissors to clip
    The uneven edges of our workmanship;

    But the world it goes round, and round, and round;
      And it's morning and noon, and then follows the night
    And the earth's but a wheel in immeasurable space,
      Revolving through darkness and blinding light,
    And it's down and up, and up and down,
      And it's sunshine and shadow, all through and through,
    And the wheel ne'er stops turning, but ever rolls on
      With a rhythm exquisitely, perfectly true;
    But the power that guides and directs, and attends
      This wonderful wheel in our human life,
    With its tangled threads and twisted ends,
      Its pleasures and joys, its war and strife,
    Ah, that is the hand that sharpens to smite,
      Only when *needed* it so must be.
    For us it is meet but to see the *Right*
      In all that is ordered by such decree!"
    And the old man ceases his work and song.
      "His task is done," then the people say:
    "Oh wise are the words, and true and strong,
      Of the scissor-grinder, old and gray!"

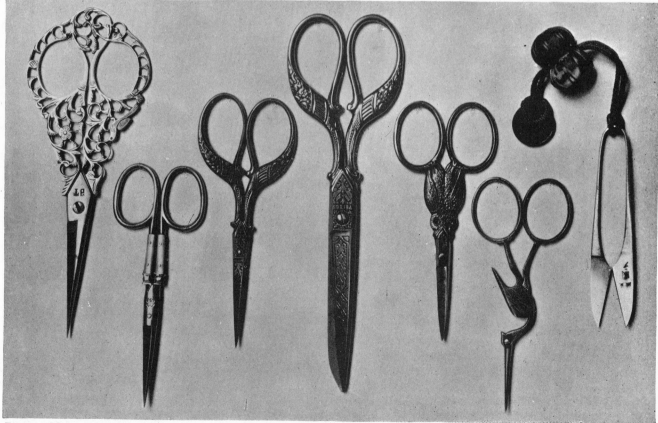

Fig. *10* — MODERN SCISSORS

    a. Italian. *Courtesy of Mrs. Henry E. Coe.*   *b.* German, with ivory insets. *Courtesy of Mrs. William Adams McFadden.* *c* and *d.* Spanish, with Toledo steel blades. *Courtesy of Mrs. McFadden.*   *e.* Owl, with emerald glass eyes. *From the author's collection.* *f.* A familiar pattern. *Courtesy of Brooklyn Museum.* *g.* Japanese, signed on blade; emery tassel.

The decorative appeal of hand tools

BY PETER C. WELSH, *Curator, department of civil history, Smithsonian Institution*

HAND TOOLS MADE before the days of factory standardization often have considerable appeal, quite aside from their evocation of a bygone day; and it is a pity that the mellow patina of a wood plane or the delicately tapered legs of a pair of dividers should so often go unnoticed in our search for pleasing objects of the past. In the examples on these pages clean lines, good proportions, harmony of related parts, and even an occasional simple embellishment combine to produce artifacts well worth consideration as objects of art in their own right.

Fashionable taste affected the form of the most functional objects, and hand tools were no exception. However, they preserved their integrity of shape far longer than most artifacts, despite technical changes that improved the performance of almost every tool in the carpenter's chest.

Above. Screwdriver; American, nineteenth century. Elaborately scalloped, purely for decoration. *Photographs by courtesy of the Smithsonian Institution; except as noted, examples are from the Institution's collections.*

Left, above. Auger, patented by Ezra L'Hommedieu in 1809; from water-color drawing in United States Patent Office records. In spite of the change to a spiral bit, from a blunt to a gimlet point, and from hand to factory manufacture, neither the purpose nor the appearance of the auger has altered greatly through two centuries. *National Archives.*

Left, below. Metallic plow plane, cast iron, patented by Charles Miller in 1870; American. Shell-and-vine motif reflects classic revival styles. *Privately owned.*

Early dividers and calipers often achieve great decorative interest through graceful lines and nice proportions.

Far right. House carpenter's dividers; English or American, early nineteenth century. By this time dividers had become more slender, precise in design, and constant in form.

Right. Wood turner's double calipers; American, early nineteenth century. Completely functional, these are a delight to the eye, suggesting in their very shape the precision they were designed to govern.

Below. Cabinetmaker's dividers; English, eighteenth century. Decorative legs and heart-shape stop at top of slide arm lend this tool distinction. *Privately owned.*

Far right, below. Builder's or shipwright's dividers; French. An attractive example of early eighteenth-century metalwork.

The most prosaic of woodworking tools may be admirable decorative objects, as witness this group of planes. The Northern European examples, with their carved embellishments, are typical of the tools used here by Swedish and German colonists in the seventeenth and eighteenth centuries; the simpler Anglo-American specimens appeal by relation of design to function.

Above. Bench plane; German, dated 1809. Note heart-shape mouth of both Continental planes. *Privately owned.*

Left, above. Bench plane; Dutch, dated 1756. Incised rosette is suggestive of those found on English and American furniture of the 1750's and 1760's.

Left. Rabbet plane (for notching the edge of boards) made by E. W. Carpenter, Lancaster, Pennsylvania; c. 1830-1840. The decorative curve of the throat was intended simply to permit easy discharge of shavings. *Privately owned.*

Left, below. Jack plane (for rough surfacing); American, marked A. KLOCK and dated 1818. A pleasing juxtaposition of straight lines and curves.

Delicacy, balance, patina, and variety in shape or material, qualities with little or no relation to technical efficiency, add to the desirability of many early hand tools.

Left. Compass saw; Dutch, eighteenth century. The custom-fitted grip suggests a feeling of identity between craftsman and tool that transcends the anonymity of its maker.

Right. Bitstock; Flemish, eighteenth century. Bitstocks are never identical from one early example to another, and the slow curve of the handle appears in endless surprising variations.

Far right. Upholsterer's hammer; American, nineteenth century. Well-weighted head combined with an extremely delicate handle to produce a tool admirably engineered for its purpose.

Below. Bevel; English, eighteenth century. The combination of wood (walnut) and brass used here, though less accurate in use than steel versions, is infinitely more attractive to the collector. *Privately owned.*

166

The HORNBOOK
FOR COLLECTORS

The ABC'S

of Nails and Screws

"ALL HELD TOGETHER WITH OLD WOODEN PEGS—not a nail in it" is a cliché often used to suggest the great age of a piece of furniture. Actually the absence of nails is no proof of antiquity. But it is true that the nails found in old furniture frequently confirm its date.

Until late in the 1700's, the ancient handmade or wrought nail of malleable iron was the only nail the woodworker had. The marks of its making are upon it; its hammered head and rectangular shank drawn to a point by hammer blows are easily recognized. The forging of a nail is clearly described by Doctor Henry C. Mercer in *Old-Time New England*, the bulletin of the Society for the Preservation of New England Antiquities (April 1924): "It was made from rectangular strips of malleable iron, several feet long, and about a quarter of an inch thick, called nail rods, which were furnished to the blacksmith or nailer, who, holding one of them in one hand, heated its end in his forge, and then, on the anvil, pointed it with the hammer on all four sides. Next, he partly cut it, above the point, on the 'hardy' with a hammer blow, and then, inserting the hot point into the swage hole, he broke off the rod and hammered the projecting end so as to spread it around the top of the hole; after which, the cooling, shrunken nail was easily knocked out of the orifice."

These strong, tough nails which could be bent back and clinched without breaking were made in many sizes and shapes. H. H. Taylor in *Knowing, Collecting, and Restoring Early American Furniture* speaks of the variety produced, from large spikes for shipbuilding to small brads for cabinet-making, and he sets down some of the names of shapes: rose, clasp, deck, clout, clench, cooper, dog, and horseshoe. According to Taylor, two sorts of wrought nails were mainly used in our old furniture. Both were long, sharp-pointed, and square-shanked, but one sort had a rounded head, the other a flattened or folded head. Tacks, brads, or small nails were made to secure moldings and brasses on furniture, and small nails with large circular heads were shaped to fasten hinges.

The first nails used in this country were undoubtedly imported, but the manufacture of such an important commodity must have been undertaken here as soon as possible. Iron was produced in the Colonies in the 1600's, and slitting and rolling mills were supplying nail rods made of native iron or imported bar iron during most of the colonial period. But the slow hand-forging of nails could never keep up with the demand. This was the bottleneck of more than one early industry; even the railroads had to wait upon it, and there is probably some truth behind the legend that westward-moving pioneers burned down their houses to take the nails with them.

Yankee ingenuity is illustrated in a number of patents, of the late eighteenth century, for nail-cutting machines to obviate this slow hand process. But it was not until 1825 that cut nails were produced in one operation or even by one

machine. The first step in this important development, reached about 1800, is explained by Doctor Mercer in the article cited above. "The smith was here furnished, not with a nail rod, but with a strip of plate iron, several feet long, about two and a quarter inches wide, and often about one-eighth of an inch thick. This strip he slid into a cutter, worked at first by hand-power, resembling those used by book-binders to trim books. . . . This cutter, rising and falling rapidly, clipped off the end of the iron plate crosswise into narrow, tapering, rectangular slices or nails, whose length was established by the width, and thickness, by the depth of the nail plate. The taper of the cut alone, produced the point, but not the head. This was made at first by dropping the freshly cut piece, point downward, into a slotted clamp or vise, and then spreading the larger projecting end with a hammer, as in the case of the wrought nail." This account should make it quite easy to tell the cut nail from the forged. The cut nail will be found to show the parallel striations of the cutter rather than the marks of the hammer; its shank will taper on only two sides, rather than on all four sides.

Cut nails made in the manner described, from 1800 to 1825, roughly, would have, then, irregularly shaped, hammered heads. After 1825 cut nails were made in one operation by a water-powered machine that cut the nail, clamped it, and stamped the head. The earliest of these nails had thin, lop-sided heads, but by 1830 the heads were thick and regular.

By the end of the century the cheaper and more rapidly produced cut nail—or "cold nail" as it was called—had nearly everywhere displaced the wrought nail. If, therefore, we find these machine-made, cut nails in a piece of furniture we cannot put its date much before 1800. Wrought-iron nails may be taken as evidence that a piece dates from the eighteenth century and possibly before 1790, according to Taylor; but he reminds us that wrought nails may also have been made for some time after that date in isolated communities, or used by furniture makers anywhere who had stocks on hand. Easy dates to remember are those given by Doctor Mercer: cut nails after 1800, hammer-headed cut nails from about 1800 to about 1825, and stamp-headed nails after 1825. Wire nails of the type we know began to be produced in New York about 1851.

Wood screws (the proper name for metal screws made to hold together pieces of wood) were also used much earlier than is generally realized. Macquoid and Edwards' *Dictionary of English Furniture* says that the use of tapering metal (brass) screws with slotted heads dates from the 1600's. Taylor, however, writes that he never saw, in a piece of seventeenth-century American furniture, a wood screw that was indubitably used in its original construction. According to his observations, wood screws came in here about 1725, when they began to be used in the hinges of drop-leaf tables with rule joints because they did not "come through" to spoil the appearance of the table top. After the middle of the 1700's they became more common and are found fastening table tops to their frames or holding the cross cleats to the under sides of the tops of candlestands.

These earliest, handmade screws had irregular threads and uneven, off-center slots. They did not have penetrating points like modern screws but were cut off square, so that a hole had to be drilled to receive them. Wood screws began to be produced mechanically in the early 1800's, but there was no change in shape until the middle of the century. Then the "gimlet-point" screw in use today was brought out, and it rendered the old square-end wood screw unsalable.

Wood screws, thus, give us less help than nails in dating early furniture. But if you find old, square-end screws in a piece of eighteenth-century furniture—as one of our correspondents did lately—you will have a welcome corroboration of its date.

—RUTH BRADBURY DAVIDSON

The Blacksmith at work making wrought nails in the old-time manner.
Except as noted, illustrations and captions by L. M. A. Roy.

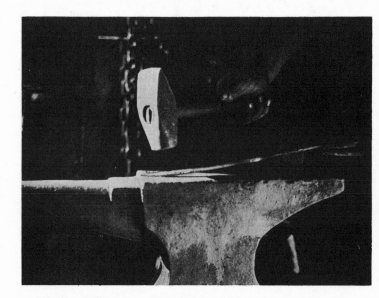

Several nail rods were put into the forge at once to heat to the right temperature. When one was soft enough, the nailer hammered the end to a long tapering point.

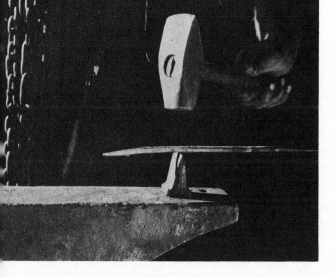

On the "hardy" of the anvil the nailer cuts off the nail rod to the desired length, ready for heading.

The Blacksmith heads the nail, clamped in the vise, by blows of the hammer. Two blows make a "clasp" nail, four make a "rose" head. Here the nail is raised in the vise to show the head.

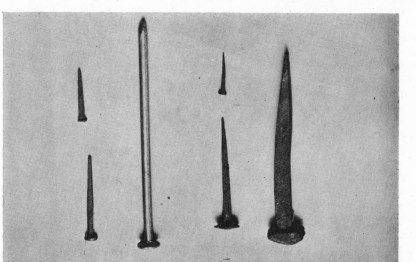

Nails. Left to right, two early nineteenth-century nails, cut from a plate and headed by hammer blows; a modern wire spike, drawn and headed by machine; a wrought-iron nail above a wrought tack; a wrought-iron spike. *Photograph by Louis H. Dreyer.*

168

English bronze wool weights

BY J. PAUL HUDSON, *Curator, Colonial National Historical Park, Jamestown*

A LITTLE-KNOWN but rather attractive metal object which was used in England for many years is the bronze wool weight—the only English weight to bear the royal arms. This was used exclusively in connection with the wool trade.

From medieval days until well into the nineteenth century wool was one of England's most important staples. Sheep were raised throughout the country, particularly in the eastern counties and the Cotswolds, and for long periods of time wool was exported to the Continent in sufficient quantity to bring in customs fees amounting to over half the revenue of the kingdom. The importance of wool to England as a tax-raising commodity during the sixteenth, seventeenth, and eighteenth centuries cannot be overemphasized. Just as cotton was king in our southern states for many generations, for almost three hundred years wool was the chief staple in England.

Wool weights were cast in two sizes, seven pounds and fourteen, of which the lighter was the more popular; today fourteen-pound weights are exceedingly rare. As a tod of English wool weighed twenty-eight pounds, the itinerant official known as a tronator would usually carry two seven-pound weights for weighing half- or quarter-tod lots. For short trips he may have carried a fourteen-pound weight, especially for use in the wool centers. Each weight was pierced with a hole through which a leather strap or thong was inserted.

For many centuries the tronators traveled throughout the kingdom, weighed wool, and collected taxes for the crown. Each had charge of a designated district which he traveled through several times a year, weighing the newly clipped wool on balance scales, receiving the customs due the crown, and stamping an official seal on each tod of wool weighed.

Almost all the English wool weights were made of bronze. A seven-and-a-half-pound lead weight owned by the British Museum—made during the reign of Edward IV—is believed to have been merely a trial specimen, as all legal weights were cast of bronze.

Most wool weights were shield-shape and decorated on one side with the royal arms in relief. Around the flat border were incised various identification marks, including the avoirdupois A, a city mark (a dagger for the city of London), and the royal cipher. The Founders' Company stamped all weights cast in London with a

1 English bronze wool weight of the Tudor period (sixteenth century), used later during the reign of James I; the escutcheon bears the Tudor royal arms. Weight 7 pounds; dimensions, 7⅛ inches high by 5¼ wide by 1½ thick. On the margin: one avoirdupois A, two Guildhall daggers, one flagon or ewer (mark of the Founders' Company), unidentified initials *MT*, and the royal cipher of James I. *Victoria and Albert Museum; crown copyright.*

2 English bronze wool weight, Charles I period (1625-1649), with the Stuart royal arms. Weight 7 pounds. The initial *C* appears above the lion, the initial *R* over the unicorn. On the margin: one avoirdupois *A*, three Guildhall daggers, two Founders' Company ewers, three royal ciphers, and initials *AG. Avery Historical Museum, Birmingham, England.*

1

2

ewer. Occasionally other marks, such as a county identification mark or the initials of a founder, were impressed on the border.

In 1956 the upper half of a bronze wool weight bearing the lions passant of the royal arms of England was excavated at Jamestown, Virginia—site of the first permanent English settlement in the New World. To my knowledge this is the only wool weight which has been found in America. An official in the department of metalwork of the Victoria and Albert Museum reports that the Jamestown weight "has every appearance of being late medieval, though this may be nothing more than the result of the continued use of an early form. As you know, the arms of England [lions passant] were last used alone by Edward III. The weight can hardly be as early as the 14th century, which makes me think that the arms are probably not directly the English royal ones. It seems far more likely that they are those of some town or institution, like the Channel Isles or the Duchy of Lancaster, that went on using the early version of the English arms."

The incomplete wool weight found at Jamestown is an intriguing object, but its history and use in Virginia's first "Capital Cittie" may never be known. Contemporary Virginia records do not reveal whether it was used by a colonial tronator. It could have been, for it is estimated that by 1649 there were three thousand sheep in Virginia.

Five bronze wool weights used in England from Tudor times until the end of the seventeenth century are illustrated. All were official weights and, with the exception of the one used during the period of Oliver Cromwell, all bear the royal arms. They were used during the following reigns: Tudor (probably Henry VIII), James I, Charles I, Oliver Cromwell and the Commonwealth, and William and Mary. The weight used during the time of James I is of particular interest to us, as Jamestown was established in 1607, the fourth year of James' reign. This weight, a seven-pound one, has a rectangular hole pierced through the top and bears the Stuart royal arms. These are made up of the arms of (first quarter) England, three lions passant; (second quarter) Scotland, lion rampant; (third quarter) Ireland, harp; (fourth quarter) France, three fleurs-de-lis.

Because of the scarcity of bronze wool weights their importance during a long span of English history has almost been forgotten. Today only a few are found in English museums and private collections, reminders of a time when tronators traveled on horseback to every part of the realm where sheep grazed to collect revenue for the king's coffers.

3 English bronze wool weight, period of Oliver Cromwell (1649-1660). The armorial consists of the cross of St. George and the Irish harp. On lower part of shield is a trophy of flowers and fruit surmounted by an acorn, with leaves as supporters. A crown and *Suffolk* on upper part of shield. Initials *OC*, for Oliver Cromwell, may have appeared at the upper corners of the shield and have been subsequently gouged out. Weight 14 pounds; dimensions: 8 1/10 inches high by 5 1/2 wide by 1 1/2 thick. On the margin: one avoirdupois A, two Guildhall daggers, three ewers (marks of the Founders' Company), unidentified initials *AG*, two unknown marks, and *Suffolk* surmounted by a crown. The two impressions of the crown and *Suffolk* were evidently stamped on the weight at a much later date, probably during the reign of George III. They no doubt indicate that the weight is certified as standard by the crown authorities for use in the county of Suffolk. *Victoria and Albert Museum; crown copyright.*

4

5

6

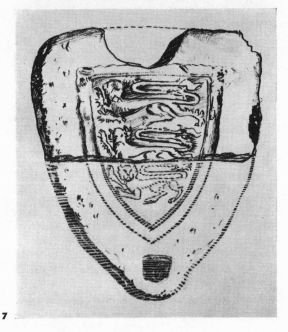

7

4 English bronze wool weight, James I period (1603-1625). This weight was in use in England when Jamestown was settled in 1607. Stuart royal arms; weight 7 pounds. It is 7 inches high by 4 wide and 1¼ thick. The royal initials *IR* (for Jacobus Rex) appear above the arms. On the margin: avoirdupois *A*, 3 times; London Guildhall dagger, 3 times; Founders' Company ewer, twice; and royal cipher, twice. *Victoria and Albert Museum; crown copyright.*

5 English bronze wool weight, period of William and Mary (1689-1702). The escutcheon bears the royal arms. Weight 7 pounds. The initials *WM* intertwined in monogram form appear over the lion, the initial *R* over the unicorn. On the margin: two royal ciphers, three Guildhall daggers, three avoirdupois *A*'s, and three Founders' Company ewers. *Avery Historical Museum.*

6 Bronze wool weight excavated at Jamestown, Virginia. Only the upper portion of the weight was found. It measures 4½ inches from side to side and is 1¼ inches thick. The complete object weighed 7 pounds, and was about 7 inches long. The escutcheon bears the lions passant of the English royal arms. The history and use of this weight are not known. *Colonial National Historical Park, Jamestown; photograph by Thomas L. Williams.*

7 The bronze wool weight excavated at Jamestown may have looked like this when it was complete; the hole may have been pierced at either top or bottom. A wool weight of Henry VII period at the Cambridge Ethnological Museum, which resembles the Jamestown weight in shape and size, is pierced at the bottom.

VI Architectural Appointments: Weathervanes, Firemarks

There are four articles in this section, all of which are concerned with common metals used in objects attached to the exterior of buildings but not forming part of the architectural design. Weathervanes are discussed in three articles and fire insurance marks in the fourth. Those on weathervanes form a progressive discussion from Mabel M. Swan's fine prose essay about English and American forms (1933) through Erwin O. Christensen's general article about vanes documented in the *Index of American Design* (1951) to Myrna Kaye's monograph on the firm of Cushing and White (1976). "The Fascinating Fire-Mark" by Harrold E. Gillingham contains factual information as well as the subjective reminiscences of a dedicated collector. Another article is certainly needed to carry forward Gillingham's 1923 study.

On Weather Vanes

By Mabel M. Swan

Fig. 1 — Italian Weathercock
Cut from sheet metal, and evidently the object of occasional bombardment, this valiant old bird lords it over Florence from the Observatory Tower

Fig. 2 — French Weathercock
Slightly bleary of eye and *distrait* of comb, and stepping warily, but every inch rooster and wrought iron.
From the Victoria and Albert Museum

CLOUDS drifting across the sky, wind-filled sails flashing white in the sunlight, a kite bucking a high wind, tree-tops bowing before a gale — all of them were nature's weather vanes, long before the spirit of progress, demanding something practical, suggested more convenient indicators of the wind's direction. The mythical Mother Shipton materially impaired her reputation as an oracle when she predicted that London would be drenched with blood should the gilded dragon vane on the church of St. Mary le Bow and the huge grasshopper vane on the Corn Exchange ever meet. In 1820 the resplendent copper dragon, Sir Christopher Wren's *chef-d'œuvre*, and the eleven-foot-long grasshopper lay side by side, waiting repairs in a stone mason's yard in London, and all the world walked by in secure peace.

Had the dragon been a weather *cock*, trouble might have been expected because of the natural propensities of cocks in general. There was the cock on the Cathedral of St. Paul in London, which, after being renewed in 1273, 1314, 1420, 1455, and 1461, was regarded with great suspicion when, blown down by a heavy wind in 1505, it crashed against the black eagle sign in the churchyard. This was in the very year when the Archduke Philip of Austria landed on the southern coast of England.

Just why poets and historians should imply the superiority of the weathercock over the weather vane it is hard to say, for both claim relationship with rather prosaic gable finials; both exist at the mercy of exacting winds and changeable weather. Religious significance had some weight, for the cock was used during many centuries almost exclusively on ecclesiastical buildings as a symbol of watchfulness — reminder of the immortal chanticleer whose shrill, admonitory crowing woke Peter's guilty conscience the night he thrice denied his Lord.

In the tenth century Wulstan (*Life of St. Swithin*) wrote of the cock on Winchester Cathedral: "Like the all-vigilant eye of the Ruler it turns in every way."

A mediæval Roman hymn writer, throughout the length of fifteen stanzas, emphasizes the fact that the cock typifies not only watchfulness but the priestly office:

Cock he is a marvelous
Bird of God's creating,
Faithfully the priestly life
In his ways relating,
Such a life as he must lead
Who a parish tendeth
And his flock from jeopardy
Evermore defendeth.

Originally weathercocks and weather vanes were not identical, although of late years the terms have been used almost interchangeably. That there was a difference between the two is shown in the Bayeux Tapestry, where, over the two eastern turrets of Canterbury Cathedral, flutter two pennants indented in three points, indicating the Trinity, while two sturdy cocks surmount the western turrets.

It is not certain just when the word *vane* first appeared. Originally it was written *fane*, meaning a pennant or flag. Later this became assimilated with the Dutch *vaan*, the ensign which, when flown above a building, signified the rank of the owner. The small flags, called *pensels*, which followed later were made from metal for the sake of greater durability. They were mounted on the turrets of chapels or prominent buildings, and their gilded sides were often resplendent with the coats of arms of their owners. The earliest specimen of this kind in existence is the nearly square, banner-shaped flag of gilt copper over the tower of Etchingham Church in Sussex, England. It is pierced with the coat of arms of the De Echynghams.

So far as we know, all these early metal vanes were fixed in position, and, when their broadside caught the force of tempestuous gusts, were often broken down and carried away. The original purpose of the revolving vane, therefore, was to contrive that it should always head into the wind. Later, in the middle of the seventeenth century, compass pointers were added to show the wind's direction. Close on the heels of this device, the cunning mechanics of the time hooked up the vane to a dial or map set in a panel of the chimney breast or in the ceiling of the castle hall. With every shift of wind that moved the vane on the tower, the pointer on the dial would tell Sir Modred and his household of the movements of the circumambient air. This machine enjoyed great popularity for a time following its invention, and there was hardly a ruffian duke in all Italy whose stronghold did not boast one. A vane of this type, mounted on Kensington Palace in London, operates a pointer moving on a gilded map in the King's Gallery below.

The seventeenth-century German vane pictured in Figure 4 shows a very decorative form of the metal flag with cut-out design. Dragons, banners, mermaids, and mermen were other devices made use of by German designers of the earlier, stationary vanes. Until 1650 most of these were supported by single rods, at first plain. Later, under the hands of skilled architects and designers, the balustered, swelled, and heavily scrolled standards appeared.

The stencil vane dated *1711*, from the North Church, Danvers (*Fig. 6*), represents the type of English vane in general

Fig. 3 — Cock of the Court
A wrought-iron device in the yard of the Castle of Gourdon

Fig. 4 — A GERMAN SILHOUETTE VANE (*seventeenth century*)
Man and dragon, cut from sheet iron. Imaginative, as is usual with German design. The most ingenious American vanes come from districts dominated by Pennsylvania German spirit. (See Volume III of Sonn's *Early American Wrought Iron*.)
From the Victoria and Albert Museum

Fig. 5 — ENGLISH VANE (*eighteenth century*)
A fine example of wrought-iron work.
From the Victoria and Albert Museum

use during the first century after the Puritans rose to power.

The Restoration in England was the signal for a departure from the severely plain in vanes. Royal palaces and certain privileged churches had the right to surmount the vane with the royal crown. But the wind, never a respecter of persons or things, resented the additional weight that offered further resistance to its blast, and many of the crowns were blown from their lofty stations, providing omens a-plenty for the superstitious. At the death of Charles II idle gossip recalled how two sparrow hawks had lately dashed themselves against the crown on the White Tower, and how, long before that, when the crown fell from Dover Castle just before the battle of Northampton, the battle was lost even before it had begun.

The ornamental treatment of the shaft supporting vane and pointers received a decided impetus in England after the appearance, in 1759, of a book of designs by Inigo Jones, and again, in 1765, when the Weldons, two master metalworkers of London, brought out a volume of their own. Their vanes were ornamented with elaborately scrolled stems, fanciful openwork pointers, and flags of varied shapes, similar to the vane in Figure 5. The compass points of the latter are both useful and decorative.

An advertisement in the *Gentleman's Magazine* of 1762 mentions a vane of still different form:

A Vane of a new construction has been erected on the spire of Salisbury Cathedral. It is made of copper, gilt with gold, measures near seven feet in length, runs on four wheels, and will turn with the gentlest breeze that blows.

Was this contrivance possibly the forerunner of ball bearings?

Belgium and Holland bristle with interesting vanes. It was the famous dragon of Ghent, made from plates of metal riveted together boiler-fashion, and said to have been brought from Constantinople in the thirteenth century, that gave Christopher

Wren inspiration for the dragon on St. Mary le Bow's. Again, the grasshopper vane on the London Corn Exchange served as pattern for the famous vane — made by Shem Drowne, the clever colonial coppersmith — that still surmounts the cupola of Faneuil Hall in Boston. It was Deacon Drowne, also, who made the Indian that served as a vane over Province House in Boston, the residence of the colonial governors.

It is rather curious, however, that another of his vanes, and traditionally the first weathercock to roost on a Boston steeple, owed its exaltation to a church schism. The installation, in 1720, of the Rev. Mr. Thacher as minister of the North Church was bitterly opposed by a faction in the congregation. Being overborne, the malcontents withdrew and proceeded to build the New Brick Church, called by some in derision "The First Revenge Church of Christ." At the steeple's top "they placed the figure of a cock as a vane out of contempt for Mr. Thacher, whose Christian name was Peter." This weathercock was made by Shem Drowne, who hammered it out of a number of old brass kettles in his shop. The day the cock was hoisted into position, a favoring gale turned the head of the bird in the direction of Mr. Thacher's church, and for jest a young fellow climbed the steeple, straddled the cock and crowed lustily three times, as a sort of ceremony of christening.

From this weather vane, which kept watch over the New Brick Church in the north end of Boston for more than a hundred years, and now surmounts the Shepard Memorial Church in Cambridge, the New Brick Church acquired the alternative name of The Cockerel Church.

American weather vanes seem to present more originality of design than English specimens, and often bear a particular significance, sometimes referring to an industry of the locality. An outstanding example is the well-known whale on the spire of Marblehead Church.

Modern vanes are outside the field here surveyed, and in any case rarely arrest attention by any outstanding originality in design or excellence in workmanship.

Fig. 6 — EARLY AMERICAN VANES IN ENGLISH STYLE
Vanes now in the Essex Institute at Salem. It is probable that originally a crown topped the rod supporting these vanes

Fig. 7 — COCKEREL VANE (*1715*)
Very primitive. Once surmounting Sandy Hill Church at Amesbury, Massachusetts.
From the collection of Miss E. F. Morrill

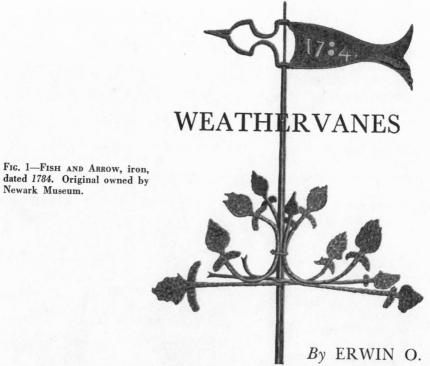

WEATHERVANES

FIG. 1—FISH AND ARROW, iron, dated *1784*. Original owned by Newark Museum.

By ERWIN O. CHRISTENSEN

The famous Index of American Design is an inexhaustible mine, from which material on almost any aspect of American arts and crafts can be quarried. Mr. Christensen, its Curator, turns his attention to weathervanes, and finds them interesting not only for their design but for their significance in American life.

OLD WEATHERVANES interest us chiefly for two reasons. Individually they are often fine examples of American folk art; collectively they represent America. Aside from their practical use, weathervanes illustrate castle, church, Indians, occupations, and patriotism. The first two link us to

FIG. 2 — WOODEN ARROW, about 1880. Original in the South County Museum, North Kingston, Rhode Island.

FIG. 3—COPPER ARROW AND SCROLL, factory-made about 1881. Owned by the New York Historical Society.

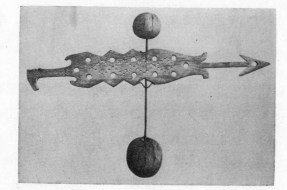

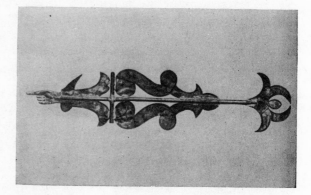

FIG. 4—COCK, sheet brass on wood, 1642. Original owned by the St. Nicholas Society, on exhibition at the New York Historical Society.

FIG. 5—WOODEN GAMECOCK TYPE, probably the work of an individual craftsman.

FIG. 6—CROWING COCK, copper on zinc ball, 1800's. Original owned by Edison Institute, Dearborn, Michigan.

Europe; the other three types belong to this country.

The banner type of weathervane, with its family arms or monograms, derives from an aristocratic European background. One of these, dated 1699, in the Pennsylvania Historical Society, includes the monograms of William Penn. The banner motif is sometimes combined with other forms, as in Figure 1, where the shape suggests the combination of fish and arrow. Judging from old illustrations of eighteenth-century houses, the horizontal banner-arrow type of weathervane was common.

Arrow weathervanes were widely used in Europe, and in America too, where they took on an added significance because of an association with the Indians. Especially appropriate was the arrow vane, dated 1833, made for the Seneca Indian mission church in Buffalo. The arrow design in Figure 2 is embellished with the zigzag lines and circles which are common to folk art the world over. The lack of perfect symmetry and the irregularity of the outline point to a rural carver, who was not necessarily a professional weathervane maker. Arrow designs were later carried over into machine-made products. Figure 3, made about 1881, combines arrow and scroll motifs. The line of development was presumably from home-made vane to artisan-made vane, to commercial product.

Weathervanes made for churches were traditionally in the form of a cock, a reminder of Peter's denial of Christ and a warning not to follow his example. The word "weathercock," in fact, came to be synonymous with "weathervane." The cock in Figure 4 was made for New York's first City Hall, which was demolished in 1700. Realism has been abandoned in favor of almost geometric contours. Unlike most of the other weathervanes illustrated, probably this design was already traditional before this vane was made. The maker has followed the old pattern with little variation.

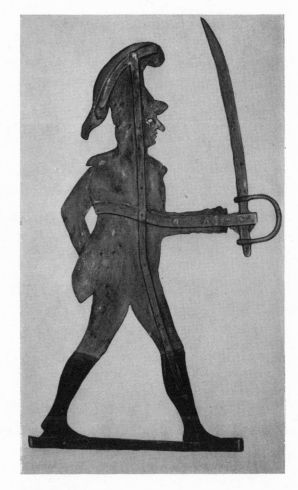

FIG. 8—COUNT PULASKI, wrought iron, late eighteenth century.

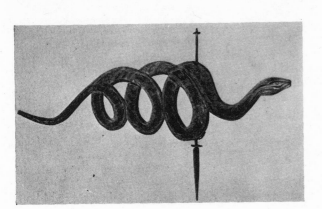

FIG. 7—WOOD SERPENT. Original owned by Concord Antiquarian Society.

Renderings as follows: (1) E. J. Gilsleider, (2) Robert Pohle, (3) and (4) Helen Hobart, (5) Lucille Chabot, (6) Beverly Chichester, (7) Lloyd Broome, (8) Elmer R. Kottcamp, (10) Nicholas Amantea, (11) Hazel Hyde, (12) Salvatore Borrazzo, (13) Robert Barton.

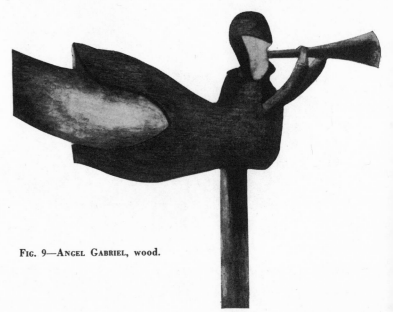

FIG. 9—ANGEL GABRIEL, wood.

FIG. 11—MAN BOWLING, iron, from Boscawen, New Hampshire, about 1840.

FIG. 12—"LIBERTY," sheet copper, found in Penobscot Valley, Maine, after 1886.

FIG. 13—FLYING EAGLE, metal.

All photographs courtesy National Gallery of Art, Index of American Design.

FIG. 10—HORSE, sheet iron, nineteenth century.

A more lively and individual rendering is seen in Figure 5. This wooden rooster, with his smooth curves and unusual tail, apparently follows no known type, and may therefore have been designed by the artisan who made it. The lack of balance, with the pole at an angle to the legs, is a peculiar detail which one would hardly expect in a commercial vane.

In Figure 6 the drawing of the silhouette consists of a series of straight lines, and that gives the vane a professional touch. This is a realistic bird, craning his neck and actually crowing.

The Angel Gabriel, according to Christian belief, blows his horn for the resurrection. This complicated pose would be difficult for the amateur artist. He therefore, in Figure 9, compromises and draws the figure down to the waist in the usual upright position. At this point he breaks the vertical and attaches a horizontal portion in the flying garments. It shows how a folk artist gives the idea of flight without depending on realism. There are some amusing interpretations of this theme: one weathervane I saw in the Catskills showed Gabriel wearing a stovepipe hat!

The occupations, particularly agriculture, provided other motifs for weathervanes. Various farm animals, especially horses, are numerous in the commercial catalogues of weathervane manufacturers. Each horse has a name which is associated with a special pose; *Ethan Allen*, *Dexter*, and *Smuggler* are shown in movement; *Luke*, *Blackburn*, and *Arabian* in standing position. Before they were made commercially, horse weathervanes were sawed out of thick boards by local artisans. The same designs, worked out in metal, are thinner and more elegant *(Fig. 10)*. In commercial products, less attention was paid to design and more to realism, with a consequent decline in artistic quality.

The vane in Figure 11 was probably made for a local bowling alley. One made for a butcher shows a long knife, along which a man is driving a pig to market. Seafaring communities favored the sperm whale.

The serpent in Figure 7 probably has a specific meaning. A coiled serpent, with the words *Don't tread on me*, was used on a naval flag, and serpents were used in cartoons and political writings. The Revolutionary figure of Count Pulaski is seen in Figure 8, wearing a feathered helmet and holding a tremendous sword. The features in profile show a large nose which may have been characteristic of the man, because his portrait, taken from front view, also shows a long nose.

Liberty, a personification of the new republic with flag and liberty cap, is an example of a type created presumably by our folk art. After Bartholdi's Statue of Liberty was unveiled in New York harbor in 1886, the motif with a torch served as a model *(Fig. 12)*. By this time the crown of rays had displaced the earlier liberty cap. Another popular patriotic motif was the eagle *(Fig. 13)*, which was used especially on federal buildings such as post offices, courts, and custom houses.

Cushing and White's copper weather vanes

BY MYRNA KAYE

Pl. I. Weather vane depicting the trotter Dexter, first manufactured by Cushing and White in 1868. Hollow copper with cast white-metal head; length 42 inches. Recently regilded. Widely circulated lithographs of Dexter, who was known as "King of the Turf," almost always depicted him in this head-down pose. Cushing's 1883 catalogue depicted Dexter on the title page. *Private collection; photograph by Richard Cheek.*

IN SEPTEMBER 1867 Leonard Wareham Cushing and Stillman White acquired a small copper weather-vane business in Waltham, Massachusetts, and set out to redecorate America's rooftops with gilded sculptures. During the next two decades, the firm and a handful of copper weather-vane manufacturers in New York and Boston dominated such a booming nationwide trade that their copper weather vanes quickly outnumbered the hand-wrought ones that had adorned rooftops for generations. By the 1880's a barn without a weather vane was an exception and a carriage house without one looked unfinished (see Fig. 1).

Fig. 1. Engraved letterhead on the stationery of L. W. Cushing and Sons, successors in 1872 to Cushing and White. The copperplate was cut in 1885. *Waltham Historical Society.*

Cushing's journals record the daily activities of the shop that produced much of America's nineteenth-century non-academic sculpture.[1] In the fourth, and last known, volume Cushing documents the genesis of some of the weather-vane models that Cushing and White (L. W. Cushing and Sons after 1872) continued to produce until 1933. He names the carvers of the wooden patterns, and records the steps used in transferring the designs from paper to wood, to cast-brass or cast-iron molds, and finally to beaten copper. The journal is a valuable addition to the 1883 catalogue of L. W. Cushing and Sons in documenting the many surviving vanes made by the company.

The copper weather-vane business that Cushing and White bought in 1867 had belonged to Alvin L. Jewell, who had been a pioneer in the industry. Jewell began in 1852 selling mostly cast-iron and brass products such as umbrella stands, dentists' spittoons, shelf brackets and the like, as well as lightning rods and weather vanes made of sheet copper hammered into shape in cast-iron molds. By 1865 Jewell's weather-vane trade was of prime importance, but on June 20, 1867, as he and a workman were erecting a sign, the staging collapsed and Jewell was killed. The business then was sold at auction.

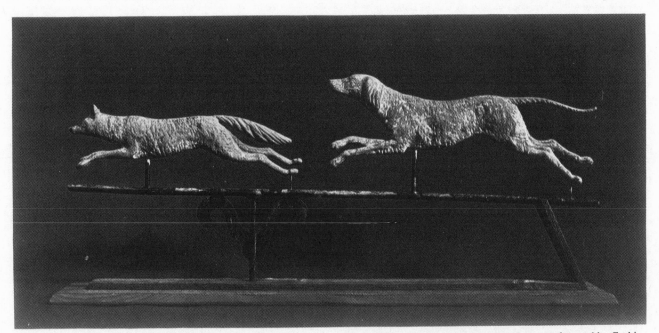

At the time Leonard Cushing, a civil engineer, was managing the machine shop of a watch factory in Providence, Rhode Island, and Stillman White was working for him as a machinist. Both were from Waltham, and in fact Cushing returned there weekly to see his wife and children. Although neither man knew anything about making weather vanes, acquiring Jewell's business appeared to them a good way to return to Waltham permanently. At the auction Cushing and White were outbid by Josephus Harris of Brattleboro, Vermont, who offered $7,975. Harris failed to meet the security, however, and Cushing and White bought the firm for $7,950.[2]

The new owners immediately began to add weather vanes to the existing line. Jewell had offered a vane depicting the champion trotter Dexter, two depicting the Morgan horse Ethan Allen, and two showing Ethan Allen drawing a sulky (see Fig. 2). Cushing and White added new models of the Ethan Allen and Dexter vanes (see Pl. I). To make the new models they needed concave molds of iron, brass, or bronze into which sheets of copper were hammered to shape. These molds, which assured virtually identical products each time, were cast from wooden sculptures of the weather vanes.

On December 12, 1867, Cushing went to Boston and "saw Mr. Leach a carver" and arranged to have Leach "carve some horses for us."[3] Henry (or Harry) Leach had had a varied career,[4] but in 1867 he was a pen dealer and fancy carver living at 2 Indiana Street, a neighborhood of many woodworkers and cabinetmakers.

On December 14, 1867, White bought pictures of the trotters Ethan Allen and Dexter. These were no doubt lithographs, as photographs at the time could not capture trotters in motion sufficiently clearly to make them useful to weather-vane makers.[5] The Ethan Allen lithograph was probably similar to that shown in Figure 3. Early the next month, according to his journal, Cushing made a drawing of Ethan Allen two-and-a-half-times larger than the lithograph to be used for the forty-five-inch vane, and he began another drawing twice the size of the print, to be used for the twenty-nine-inch version. The partners also worked up scale drawings from the lithographs for their twenty-eight-inch and forty-two-inch Dexter weather vanes.

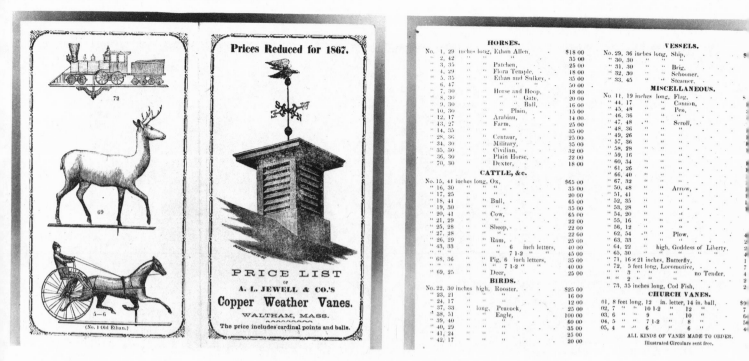

Fig. 2. Four-page price list of A. L. Jewell and Company, Waltham, Massachusetts, 1867. Many of the models that Jewell manufactured continued to be produced by Cushing and White and L. W. Cushing and Sons. *Waltham Historical Society; photograph by Mike O'Neil.*

The lithographs provided an outline and a detailed image of one side of the horses, but for a three-dimensional vane the other side had to be drawn as well. On January 13 Cushing went to Cambridge to see a Mr. Clark, "found him at his shop and he drew me an Ethan Allen as well as he could." This is the only time Cushing mentions Clark or any artist aiding in the drawings. Since most lithographs of Ethan Allen and other horses represented the side of the horse with his legs extended, Clark presumably sketched the other side.

Cushing's ability to draw a horse, as seen from the title page of his journals (Fig. 4), was certainly limited in 1858, when the first volume was begun. However, after starting work on weather-vane designs, he carefully observed and sketched horses so that his drawing improved. The day after he saw Clark, Cushing drew and painted a final version of the side of the twenty-nine-inch Ethan Allen "that Mr. Clark sketched for me yesterday."

The next day Cushing started on the pattern, or wooden statue the size and shape of the finished copper vane. He cut out each half of the body separately with a jig saw, then glued the halves together. On January 22, Cushing took the pattern and pictures for the twenty-nine-inch Ethan Allen to Leach to carve, and on January 30 he picked up "the carving of Ethan Allen a splendid thing." Cushing then cut the model up, as head, body, tail, and each leg

Fig. 3. *Ethan Allen*, lithograph by C. H. Crosby, 1868. *Smithsonian Institution.*

A RETROSPECTIVE REVIEW.

"Sweet Memory, wafted by thy gentle gale,
Oft up the stream of time I turn my sail."

Fig. 4. Title page from the first volume of Leonard Wareham Cushing's four-volume manuscript journal recording his activities from December 13, 1858, to March 26, 1871. *Waltham Historical Society.*

Fig. 5. L. W. Cushing and Sons catalogue number 9, 1883, p. 8. The twenty-page (each page is 8⅝ by 12¼ inches) catalogue has sixty-nine illustrations of weather vanes and two of mortar-and-pestle emblems. The illustrations are accurate depictions of the vanes, although the trotter Ethan Allen is shown as a mirror image of both the actual vane and its lithographic source (see Fig. 3). *Author's collection.*

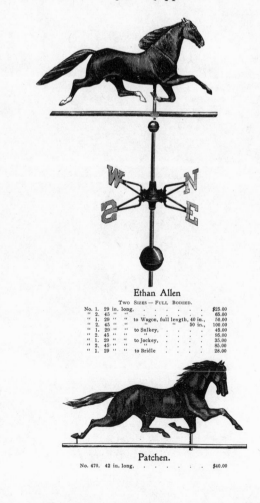

Illustrated Catalogue of Copper Weather Vanes,

Ethan Allen

TWO SIZES — FULL BODIED.

No. 1.	29 in. long,										$25.00
" 2.	45 " "										65.00
" 1.	29 " "	to Wagon, full length, 40 in.,							50.00
" 2.	45 " "	" " " " 50 in.,							100.00
" 1.	29 " "	to Sulkey,								45.00
" 2.	45 " "	" "								95.00
" 1.	29 " "	to Jockey,								35.00
" 2.	45 " "	"								85.00
" 1.	29 " "	to Bridle								28.00

Patchen.

No. 470. 42 in. long, ... $40.00

had to be cast separately and each part required a left and a right mold. On March 3 Cushing picked up the castings for the twenty-nine-inch Ethan Allen at Hooper's Brass Foundry in Boston.[6] By the end of March Cushing and White had the molds for their small and large Ethan Allen (see Fig. 5) and their small and large Dexter weather vanes.

The drawing for the large Goddess of Liberty vane (see Fig. 9, Pl. IV) was begun at the end of February 1868, but the wooden pattern was not worked on until April. On May 9, a painted wooden pattern was placed "in the Window of H. C. Sawyer[7] where in the evening it attracted a thousand people." In September 1868 White himself carved the head and face of the small, thirty-inch, Goddess weather vane. At the end of March 1869 Cushing's journal records that he went "to see Mr. Leach and had the large Goddess carved in" (Fig. 10).

Henry Leach carved many animal patterns for Cushing and White, and no other animal carver is mentioned in Cushing's journals. During 1869 and 1870 Leach carved eagles, roosters, a fox and hound (Pl. II), a squirrel, a forty-two-inch cow, and a deer (Pl. III, Fig. 6). He probably also carved the pattern for the English setter vane (Figs. 7, 8), because the carving on the setter's coat resembles the carving on manes and tails of horses Leach carved. The carving of the setter's eyes is also similar to that of the eyes of the Dexter and Ethan Allen patterns that Leach is known to have carved. Leach presumably made the carving of the setter after March 1871, since it is not mentioned in Cushing's journals (which end in that month), but before 1872, when he is no longer listed in the Boston directory.

Leach did not, however, carve the pattern for the Angel Gabriel vane (Pl. V). In June 1869 when Cushing needed both the Angel Gabriel pattern and a seven-and-a-half-foot statue of Justice for a courthouse in Delaware, Ohio, he went to E. Warren Hastings on Commercial Street, Boston. Hastings had been doing ornamental carving for ships since at least 1865 and was well known for his figure carving.

In the next-to-last entry in the journals, Cushing noted that he went "to see about setting the Steam Fire Engine," a vane ordered by a firehouse in Somerville, Massachusetts, on February 13, 1871. The vane, which was probably similar to the one shown in Figure 11, was apparently the first fire-engine vane Cushing and White made. It was drawn, cast, formed, assembled, and painted between February 23 and March 21, 1871. To make the engine shown in Figure 11 was a complicated job, for it is an accurate copy of a real Amoskeag steamer. Some of the more intricate parts of vanes such as these were cast in zinc or lead rather than made of hammered copper. Most human figures and many animal heads were also castings.

Cushing notes that he painted the steam fire engine, but almost all the firm's vanes were gilded with twenty-three-carat gold leaf. Until May 1868, Cushing and White employed a gilder; thereafter Cushing did much of that work himself. The partners also employed Cushing's brother-in-law, Freeman Hodgdon, and several men who had worked for Jewell, including a Mr. Tweed, a Mr. Jackson, and Arch McKeller.

In 1872 White sold his share of the business to Cushing, who soon took in his sons Charles and Harry and formed L. W. Cushing and Sons. The weather vanes which L.

Pl. V.   Angel Gabriel weather vane, first manufactured by Cushing and White in 1869. Hollow copper; length 32 inches. *Smithsonian Institution, Eleanor and Mabel Van Alstyne collection.*

W. Cushing and Sons produced until 1933 included some from the A. L. Jewell days, and a few models added in much later years, but most were designed during the five-year partnership of Cushing and White, and were carved by Henry Leach.

Fig. 6.   Cushing and White's impressed mark on the weather vane shown in Pl. III. *Cheek photograph.*

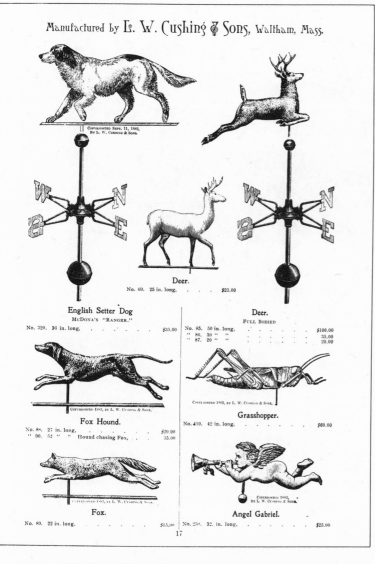

Fig. 7. L. W. Cushing and Sons catalogue number 9, p. 17. The leaping deer, the fox, and the hound were carved by Henry Leach in 1869 and 1870; the setter was probably carved by him in 1871. The Angel Gabriel was carved by E. Warren Hastings in 1869. The copyright dates do not date the origins of the models, but rather when the illustrations were first published. *Author's collection.*

Fig. 8. Wooden pattern for Cushing and White's English setter weather vane (see Fig. 7), probably carved by Leach in 1871. Length 35⅝ inches. *Collection of Herbert W. Hemphill Jr.; photograph by Helga Photo Studio.*

Fig. 9. L. W. Cushing and Sons catalogue number 9, p. 19. According to a brochure of c. 1868, Cushing and White sold the same three sizes of Goddess of Liberty vanes at the same prices. The model for the squirrel weather vane was carved by Leach. *Author's collection.*

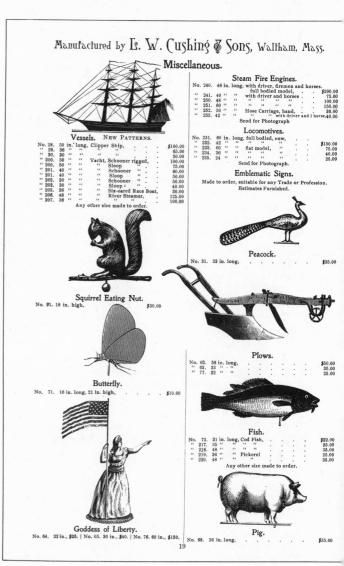

[1] The four extant volumes of the journals extend from December 13, 1858, to March 26, 1871. They are in the Waltham Historical Society. See also Myrna Kaye, *Yankee Weathervanes* (New York, 1975).

[2] Harris and his son Ansel J. Harris went on to make and sell weather vanes and ornamental ironwork in Boston as J. Harris and Son.

[3] This and the other quotations in this article are taken from the Cushing journals cited in n. 1.

[4] Henry Leach sold maps at 21 Cornhill, Boston, in 1847 and 1848. By 1850 he was selling books at 1 Mercantile Wharf, and from 1855 to 1860 he sold clothing at the same address. He became a pen dealer in 1861, and in 1867 he also called himself an ornamental carver. After 1868 he was solely a carver. In 1872 Sarah A. Leach was still listed at 2 Indiana Street, but Henry was not, indicating that he may have died by this time.

[5] In November 1867 Cushing did acquire photographs of cattle and horses standing still.

[6] Many of Cushing and White's molds were brass, although most weather-vane molds were cast iron.

[7] Henry C. Sawyer had a shop on Main Street in Waltham, where he sold books, fans, paint, and the like.

Fig. 10. Wooden pattern for Cushing and White's sixty-inch Goddess of Liberty weather vane carved by Leach in 1869. The feet are missing. The figure was once thought to be a ship's figurehead and was called "Columbia." *Shelburne Museum.*

Fig. 11. Steam-fire-engine weather vane marked CUSHING & WHITE WALTHAM MASS on the smokestack. Copper and brass; length 49½ inches. *Greenfield Village and Henry Ford Museum.*

The Fascinating Fire-Mark

By Harrold E. Gillingham

Illustrations from the author's collection

HOW many readers of ANTIQUES, or who, among the ever-increasing army of collectors, know the meaning of *fire-marks*; or, as they are sometimes incorrectly called, house-plates or insurance-signs? Yet these emblems for the identification of certain insured buildings, have been in use in England since the latter part of the seventeenth century; though they were not adopted in the United States until 1752.

The acquisition of these interesting relics of the past offers a pleasurable field of collecting, and is certain to afford many interesting experiences. One collector told me that, after locating several desired specimens high on building fronts, he arranged with a builder to employ a workman to fetch them down. In a week or so a rough specimen of humanity appeared at the collector's office. With him he carried a bag well filled with choice marks, some of great rarity. His report was that only once had he been molested in his work of removal; and that he had met the situation by threatening the objecting tenant with violence, if he prevented the removal of an "old bit of lead."

Another collector secured some of his examples by adopting the method of substituting newer and less rare signs for the desired ones. Tenants and owners alike are now well aware of the interest in fire-marks and refuse to allow their removal unless paid much

Fig. 1 — A FIRE-MARK IN USE
On a Philadelphia house built in 1786. *Photograph by Philip B. Wallace.*

more than the pieces are worth. But this was not always so. In walking through one of the older streets of Philadelphia, sometime since, I chanced to see a specimen on a dilapidated building. The offer of fifty cents to the Jewish barber tenant soon secured for me the prize. To obtain a certain variant of the "Green Tree" for my collection, I was forced to lean far out the the third story window of an old house, while the occupant clung to my legs to prevent my pitching headlong to the street, as I pried out ancient hand-wrought nails, which secured the mark to the 1805-built wall. It may be well to add that a permit from the owner of the property had first been obtained.

While motoring through England, ten years ago, I was accused by my family of looking more for fire-marks than at the picturesque houses. As our car stopped before the charming St. Mary's Church, Redcliff, in Bristol, I chanced to see a rare "Westminster" mark under the third story window of a "pub," as the English saloon is familiarly called. Five shillings were handed to the chauffeur, with instructions to secure it, while I did my duty and inspected that church with my family. Naturally, I have no recollection whatever of its interior, so keen was I to possess that emblem. As we emerged from the church, our driver left the "pub," carrying a small newspaper bundle.

Fig. 2 — HAND-IN-HAND OF LONDON. (*1715*)

(All dates given are those of the emblem, not of its company's founding.)

Fig. 3 — WESTMINSTER OF LONDON. (*1720*)

Fig. 4 — HIBERNIAN OF IRELAND. (*1775*)

Handing it to me with two shillings change, he apologized with the remark that he had to "treat the house" three times to secure my much desired piece from the owner.

When in London, we have always stayed at an old and well-known hotel on Jermyn

Street, that little thoroughfare so loved by Thackeray and Dickens, where so many of their characters had their lodgings. The porter of our hostelry, like others of his ilk, was a self-important individual and particularly haughty toward us Americans. But as we returned to the hotel one day, from a visit to a rag market, each of us laden with plunder (I believe I carried a large framed sampler, tied up in a piece of gaudy wall-paper) we were met most graciously by the porter, with the impressive announcement:

"Lord G——, the son of the Duke of R——, 'as called twice to see you, hand telephoned. Will you kindly, sir, call 'is lordship hup himmejeet." Needless to say, I took my time about responding to this extraordinary summons. As the event turned out, it developed that "'is Lordship," a well-known resident of the St. James district, desired to see me regarding a collection of fire-marks which he held for sale, as my inquiries in various quarters had apparently given the impression that I was one of those "wealthy American collectors." I soon disabused his mind of that notion, and we came to no terms. The next morning—as I was leaving the hotel on another hunt, I casually remarked to Simpson: "If Lord G—— calls again, he will have to wait to see me—I've no time to go to his house."

From that time, we were all treated with the greatest deference by that porter, who, when we left for home, informed us that he "'oped we would soon return."

It is uncertain who first suggested the use of fire-marks; though it has been stated that Dr. Nicholas Barbon's Com-

pany, *The Fire Office*, used them in 1667. Some English insurance historians are inclined to give credit to *The Friendly Society for Insuring Houses*, established in London in 1683. Their Proposals for Insurance conditioned that, "*To prevent fraud in getting any policy after a house is burnt, no house is to be esteemed a secure house, till the mark hath been actually fixed thereon.*"

That statement offers one reason for the use of these curious emblems. It is to be remembered that, in the seventeenth and eighteenth centuries, there were no municipal fire departments, such as we have today, not even the volunteer brigades. The earliest insurance companies or societies employed their own firemen, whose duty it was to save, as far as possible, only the property which the company had insured. Each office had its own brigade, consisting usually of men, who, according to law, were distinguished by the coats and badges of their offices, and were free from being impressed to go to sea, or serve as marines or as soldiers on land. When not occupied in extinguishing fires, many of these men worked at the wharves or acted as boatmen to ferry people across the Thames: hence their title "water-men."

It was to indicate to these "water-men," which property to save, in the event of fire, that the insurance society required that its fire-mark should be attached to the building before the policy might take effect. The work

Fig. 8 — Philadelphia Contributionship. (*about 1823*)
Size of shield, 11 x 15 inches.

was done by the company's own employee, and a fee was charged the owner,—sufficiently large to cover the cost of the emblem. This operation possessed another advantage, since at the time of it the company's representative made an inspection of the building to determine whether it was properly de-scribed and sufficiently insured.

It has been frequently stated that these company firemen had a habit of returning immediately to their several occupations, when they found that they had been called to a fire in a building *not* insured in their particular "office." It has further been suggested "that, in times of political excitement, the official indication that a house was insured might protect it from incendiarism, since it would be manifest in such cases that the loss by fire would fall not upon the owner of the building — on whom the mob might wish to be revenged —but on the innocent necessary insurance office, with which they had no bone to pick."

In America quite a different custom prevailed. There were volunteer firemen's associations in many of the larger eastern cities. Different insurance offices had their favorites among these, and contributed to their support. Such beneficiaries were naturally keen to protect the property insured by their patrons. The fire-mark thus became an indicator of the favorite office.

The first American company to adopt a fire-mark was *The Philadelphia Contributionship for the Insurance of Houses from Loss by Fire*, established April 13, 1752. This is the oldest fire insurance company in the United States to remain in continuous business. The many-sided Benjamin Franklin was one of the first private citizens to sign its "Articles of Association and Agreements" creating the Society. Their insignia reminds one of the childhood game, *Carry a Lady to London*. It is a lead casting of four hands clasped at the wrists, fastened to a shield shaped board. Owing to this device, the company is usually called the *Hand-in-Hand*.

At a meeting of the Society April 9, 1781, it was "*Re-solved*, That no houses having a tree or trees planted before them, shall be insured or reinsured." This ruling was due to the fact that trees interfered with the proper handling of ladders and accurate directing of streams of water. The action of the *Contributionship* in declining to insure tree-protected houses, so incensed some of the citizens of the Quaker City, that, on October 21, 1784, a new company was formed, which *would* insure houses having trees close by. This concern was called *The Mutual Assurance Company for Insuring Houses from Loss by Fire Within the City of Philadelphia*. It adopted as its fire-mark a lead casting of a tree, painted green and attached to a shield-shaped board. It is not surprising that this organization has long been styled "The Green Tree." It later adopted a cast-iron plate with a similar tree thereon.

Other Philadelphia insurance companies used fire-marks — *The Insurance Company of North America* (*1792*) adopted an eagle; *The Fire Association* (*1817*), a fire-plug, hose, and the letters F.A.; *The Philadelphia Insurance Company* (*1804*) a dove holding an olive branch and standing on a hand; the *Hope Mutual*; the *United Firemen's and Lumbermen's*, both had their individual emblems.

In New York the *Mutual Assurance Company* (established 1787 and long since retired) used a painted oval of tin, with its name painted thereon. The *Baltimore Equitable Society* and the *Firemen's Insurance Company* were the only organizations of the Monumental City to adopt such insignia. Four companies in Pittsburg, three in Cincinnati, one in Hartford, and three in Charleston, were the only other American insurance companies known to have used the

Fig. 9 — Fire Association of
Philadelphia. (*about 1832*)
Size, 8 x 11 inches.

Fig. 10 — Pittsburgh Insurance Company. (*1832*)
Size, 9 x 11 inches.

fire-mark. While Boston had an insurance society, one of the founders of which is said to have been the famous Paul Revere, yet there is no known record of its ever having used these emblems.

So rapid in our cities is the destruction of the older houses, owing to the advance of so-called modern improvements, that these signs of the earlier insurances are fast disappearing. Meanwhile, the companies have long since discontinued the practice of requiring their being attached to an insured property. One sees occasionally, on a modern, so-called Colonial, house a *Hand-in-Hand* or a *Green Tree* fire-mark; and often it has been placed in a position absolutely contrary to the old traditions.

The earliest English fire-marks were of lead, with the policy number stamped on the lower portion, as iron would rust and mar the walls. The first American marks were likewise of lead, fastened to a wooden shield, the policy numbers being painted on the board. About 1800 some marks were made of cast iron, with the number similarly painted on the flat surface of the emblem. About 1825 tinned iron and, in some cases, impressed copper plates were adopted. These were gaudily painted or gilded and were quite elaborate. This style was never popular in this country, except for advertising purposes. It was no uncommon sight, thirty years ago, to see, in country districts, these painted "signs" tacked on barns and outbuildings, for many ignorant farmers thought such decoration was necessary to guarantee them proper insurance. I heard of one enterprising—if unscrupu-

Fig. 11 — Lumbermen's of Philadelphia. (*1873*)
Size, 9 x 9 inches.

lous—agent in western New York, who, each year, nailed a new sign on a man's barn and collected the premium, but delivered no policy contract. When the fire occurred and the fraud was discovered, the agent had left for parts unknown.

No complete collection of fire-marks is known;—a friend of mine in Surrey has well over four hundred in his interesting hoard. Another friend, a keen student of the subject, in Edinburgh, has over three hundred; yet both these men are continually on the hunt for some hard-to-find specimen. Philadelphia has four modest collections, including my own, which numbers about one hundred and twenty-five. New York has a couple of small ones; and the Insurance Library of Boston possesses a number of specimens of marks.

When one compares the American with the English fire-marks, a sharp contrast is observable between the plainness of one, and the artistic beauty of the other. Note the *Hand-in-Hand of London* (*1696*), with its clearly-defined crown and clasped hands, denoting mutuality; *The Westminster* (*1717*) with the portcullis and the Prince of Wales feathers; *The Dublin*, with the Arms of the City of Dublin, surrounded by a graceful ribbon and floral border; and *The Hibernian* (*1771*) with the crown and harp, the latter so dear to the Irishman's heart.

It may not be out of place to recall how the poets have mentioned fire-marks. William Cowper, George A. Fothergill, James and Horace Smith, and others have enriched their metaphors with the aid of these picturesque devices.

Fig. 12 — United Firemen's of Philadelphia. (*1860*)
Size, 8 x 10 inches.

Fig. 13—Associated Firemen's of Pittsburgh. (*1850*)
Size, 8 x 8 inches.

VII Household Objects

The articles in this section discuss objects found in the home. Most of them are small, small enough to be held and used with one's hands. Some of the objects are simply decorative, but many, such as teakettles and kettles, were used in the kitchen for the preparation, cooking, and serving of food. They are among the most popular of antique objects collected today. For this reason, such items are rapidly increasing in value and rarity.

The majority of the articles are concerned with objects of American manufacture, although the metal used may have been imported. Among the exceptions are tobacco boxes, Pontypool and Usk Japanned ware, French tole, and French antique steel furniture. Esther Stevens Brazer's two articles on the tinsmiths of Stevens Plains are especially valuable and provide a wealth of detailed information on this early center of metal working in Maine.

French antique steel furniture

BY MICHAEL GREER

Louis XVI console, all steel, with onyx top; made to be attached to the wall. The fluted legs, with flat coin feet and leaf capitals, are detachable. The openwork apron consists of classic motifs from which the rosettes and leaf ornaments can be unscrewed. Above, two of a set of four Empire steel sconces with *bronze doré* medallions for back plates, and *bronze doré* bobêches and ornaments attached to the flat bands of steel which form the curved arms. *Illustrations from the author's collection; except as noted, photographs by Taylor and Dull.*

Directoire settee, 65 inches long, made of steel bars with gilded cast-iron connecting members. The cast rosettes at the center of the X's are finely chiseled. All parts of the settee are welded together.

THOUGH ARMOR, WEAPONS, AND MECHANICAL instruments of the past are known to have been made of wrought or forged iron and steel, it is not well known that furniture was made of steel in the middle of the eighteenth century, and that wrought-iron furniture appeared long before that time. An iron chair, for example, appears in the inventory of the Dukes of Burgundy as early as the sixteenth century.

There are almost no references to eighteenth- and nineteenth-century steel furniture in the great museums and reference libraries in France, where it was most popular, or in this country; and few authentic pieces are known to exist. The Musée des Arts Décoratifs in Paris has only one, a steel and *bronze doré* bed, in its vast collection of antique furniture. The Musée Nissim de Camondo in Paris also has only one piece, an eighteenth-century bed of the same materials, "*garanti d'époque*." Because of its scarcity, so little is known about steel furniture that it has been virtually overlooked. The connoisseur, however, appreciates the precision, delicacy, and strength of these exceptional pieces.

Authentic Louis XVI examples have been found, but the majority of the items illustrated here, and others extant, are of the Directoire (1795) and Empire (early nineteenth century) periods. During the Directorate, and especially during the Napoleonic campaigns, gunsmiths and ironworkers executed steel furniture, designed by the *ébénistes*, which could be easily folded or disassembled and moved without fear of serious damage. Steel furniture is solid enough not to break in transit (Napoleon's warriors must surely have found that an advantage), and collapsible campaign desks, beds, tables, and folding chairs occupy a minimum of space when packed for transport. The polished, blue-silver appearance of steel is aristocratic and luxurious. Thus steel furniture combines solidity and compactness with esthetic appeal.

It is unlikely that any type of room, or campaign tent, for that matter, was ever furnished entirely in steel. Indeed, few pieces of furniture were made solely of steel. The most frequent combinations were steel with ornaments of *bronze doré*, or steel with applied gilded details. Tables, desks, and consoles had wood or marble tops.

The most elegant pieces, such as the Louis XVI console with marble top shown here, illustrate the advantage of steel over wood. Steel can be more finely chiseled and chased, with details more delicately accentuated. The strength of steel permits it to be forged in elements of such extreme lightness that they appear at times virtually to defy the laws of gravity, even under a marble top. Moreover, steel resists parasites.

Most steel furniture consists of quite simple parts: tubular shapes of different circumferences; tapered legs with contrasting terminals; flat bands of varying widths and thicknesses; and classical motifs and ornaments. Because of the unadorned simplicity of many examples they may be mistaken for modern, and they are appropriate either in traditional settings or in rooms in the present-day eclectic style.

Steel furniture, by its very nature, is the product of a highly sophisticated taste. It is regrettable that the steel itself was required to make guns and weapons, for many pieces were melted down to supply weapons for Napoleon's armies and those of subsequent wars. Surviving examples, however, illustrate in an unusual medium the artistic achievement of the designers and artisans of the eighteenth and nineteenth centuries.

Steel tables. *Left*: Directoire, with X stretcher and steel casters. Cast-brass rosette on stretcher. Gilding on rings joining the arc legs and on top and bottom terminals of legs. Marble top not original. *Right*: Louis XVI style *guéridon* with red tôle top. Tapered steel shaft is attached to steel tripod base which is sheathed in a thin layer of *bronze doré*. *Bronze doré* rim, lion's-paw feet, and pomegranate finials.

Directoire steel chairs. The campaign chair *(left)* can be folded to fit into a case approximately the size of an umbrella case. Original sling seat and back were probably of thin leather. The chair is a complicated though successful combination of precision parts. The "X" legs, triangular in section, are connected from front to back by solid round members at seat and base. The parts connecting back to seat, the top crosspiece, and the front and rear stretchers are flat and hinged to fold. The Directoire folding chair with lyre back originally had a faïence bidet, covered by a wood panel upholstered like the present seat. An upholstered panel finished the top of the back. Frame and seat are made of thin flat steel; stretchers and elements of the lyre are round in section. Applied rosettes on rolled crest and lyre and applied lion's-paw feet are *bronze doré*.

Empire writing table with amboina wood top. The steel base has highly polished tapered legs in a familiar Empire shape, with finely chiseled stretcher terminating at each end in a *bronze doré* rosette. The small ball feet and the capitals are also in *bronze doré*.

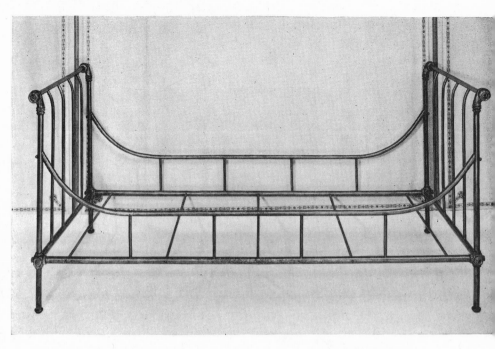

Directoire bed, 74 inches long. Steel side rails and stretchers can be detached from the ends. Cast-iron connecting sections, decorations on bed ends, and coin feet are gilded.

Bedroom with Directoire steel bed and Empire table with steel frame (both illustrated also in detail). Other antiques here are a Louis XVI mahogany *bureau plat* or flat-top desk, a pair of Empire painted armchairs, tôle lamps and chandeliers, and an Aubusson rug of the Empire period. Walls and ceiling are hung with beige silk to suggest the interior of a tent; on the walls the silk panels, edged with braid, are suspended from *trompe l'oeil* steel poles connected by upright stanchions. *Photograph by Ernest Silva.*

French tole

BY MICHAEL GREER

AMONG THE FURNISHINGS of the palace of Versailles sold at auction during the Terror was a Sèvres porcelain *cabaret* or coffee set "on a painted tole tray imitating lacquer." This indicates, for one thing, that articles in *tôle peinte*, or painted sheet metal, were in the height of fashion at the end of the eighteenth century. It also recalls the origin of this craft, which originally sought to achieve the effect of costly Oriental lacquer.

Tole, to use the English name for it, appeared in France in the 1760's. Parisian newspapers of 1770 carried the announcements of a Sieur Clément, master painter and varnisher, who claimed that his "latest efforts to attain perfection" in this manufacture enabled him to supply "carriages, baths, commodes, and other pieces of furniture." Presumably decorative panels for furni-

ture were meant, as Clément also proposed to replace with the products of his industry the panels of Oriental lacquer used in the decoration of fashionable interiors. A few years later, another factory on the outskirts of Paris was offering such wares as *garnitures de cheminée* (mantel ornaments) and writing stands in tole.

But France was lagging behind England, where the commercial production of decorated metalwares had been established by the Allgood family at Pontypool, near the Welsh border, as early as 1720. Since the late seventeenth century, both amateurs and professional decorators had painted metal objects, as well as furniture and decorations made of various materials, in imitation of Oriental lacquer. "Japan ware" was the earliest name given to the craft. Manuals, of which Stalker and Parker's *Treatise* is the best known today, gave instructions as well as designs for working in this medium. But the composition of Oriental lacquer remained a mystery until the publication in 1760 of the Jesuit Father d'Incarville's *Mémoire sur le Vernis de la Chine*, and the early European japanners had to experiment with many substances in their efforts to reproduce its durable surface. The four Martin brothers, who developed around 1740 the *vernis* so well known by their name, were the most successful of many who worked on this problem in France. The Allgoods, however, were the first to develop a varnish or lacquer for metal that could be rendered permanent by baking at controlled temperatures.

In addition, they discovered the perfect base for such decoration in the thinly rolled, smoothly finished tinplate (iron coated with tin) being produced in quantity at Pontypool by the Hanburys. This is perhaps the place to remind ourselves that the French word *tôle*, which comes from the Old French *taule*, from the Latin *tabula*, a tablet, actually means sheet metal. France had her own tinplate industry, founded by Colbert in the late 1600's and revived by the researches of Réaumur in the

Oval tray with dark red background and transfer-printed decoration in black and gold; the pierced gallery is brass. Larger tray with turned-up border, dark blue with gold and black decorations. Pair of candlesticks and coaster with ivory-color background and painted classical figures in deep blue green. In contrast to these pieces in the classical style, the octagonal pintray is painted with a military scene.

Pierced *corbeilles*, or baskets, decorated in red, gold, and black. They may have belonged to a set of three intended for use on a dining table.

Pair of jardinieres with heavy pewter bases in the form of classical figures, painted to simulate bronze, surrounding a tripod. The upper parts, with lyre-shape perforations, are painted blue with gold and black decorations.

One of a pair of jardinieres with pastoral scenes in reserve on black grounds and narrow gold borders. In the foreground, a realistic *rex begonia* in natural colors in a gold-banded red pot. A pair of plates with classical scenes in the style of Angelica Kaufmann within red and gold borders.

early 1700's; works at Mansvaux in Alsace, Bains in Lorraine, and Imphy near Nevers were in operation before 1750. Tinplate and pewter were the bodies most often used for French tole. Copper was also employed, but the black iron favored at Pontypool for large pieces like trays is rare. Fine gilt-bronze mounts are found on many French pieces; this is another feature that distinguishes them from the English-made wares, which usually have brass, pewter, or lead mounts.

French tole is noted for its fine color and for the striking effects obtained by the use of transparent over-varnishes. These usually incorporate gum copal, which was not used at Pontypool; and this ingredient may account for the tendency of the French varnishes to crack. In some examples, particles of metal suspended in the transparent varnish give an almost gemlike appearance to the surface, and recall the name *vernis diabolique* given to these lacquers in Jaubert's *Dictionnaire des Arts et Métiers* of 1793. Relief decorations in a material that shows up with a mat luster under the varnish vary the surface in other cases. Pieces with fruit and flower paintings on light grounds were intended, we know from old advertisements, to imitate porcelain. Green, black, blue, red, mustard-yellow, and ivory were favorite ground colors; and imitations of marble or wood were also popular.

During the last quarter of the eighteenth century and the first decades of the nineteenth tole served innumerable household needs. Jaubert lists as the objects most commonly made in this material wine coolers, *cabarets* (tea and coffee services on matching trays), shaving bowls, bulb pots, toilet articles, *corbeilles* (baskets for bread or fruit), centerpieces, trays, plates, dessert services, vases of many shapes, and *verrières*. The last are flat-bottomed vessels, usually oval, with deeply notched edges from which wine glasses were suspended by their feet (such pieces have been erroneously called jardinieres). Artificial large candles for churches are also mentioned by Jaubert. Among the other tole articles that have survived in some quantity are coffeepots, teapots, bottle coasters, *cachepots* to hold flowerpots, cruet stands, and lamps, chandeliers, and candlesticks of every kind.

Both the decoration and the shapes of tole wares followed current fashion. The swelling contours and naturalistic flower painting of the *Régence* and Louis XV styles gave way to classical forms and decorative motifs before the end of the century. Chinoiseries in the style

Typical early nineteenth-century oil lamps. The marbleized column at left still has its original glass globe. The urn-shape base with simulated tortoise-shell ground has painted gold and black decorations. Like the tall column at the right, it has been adapted to electricity and equipped with a shade decorated to harmonize. The *quinquet*, or student lamp, in the foreground has its original tole shade in deep red with gold decorations.

of Pillement, never quite out of favor, had to compete with Napoleonic subjects and the whole repertory of classical ornament, from representations of mythological episodes to the familiar stylized laurel and oak leaves. Paintings by recognized masters were reproduced or adapted, probably from engravings, on large trays from about 1785 to 1810. Landscapes with or without architecture, frequently in the style of Hubert Robert, found favor in the early 1800's. Transfer-printed decoration was introduced in the 1820's.

While some makers of tole are said to have marked their wares, we know little enough about the early industry. A factory named *Au Petit Dunkerque* flourished in Paris in the late eighteenth century. In 1799 the Citizen Deharme put tole wares of his own manufacture on view in the first exhibition of industrial art in Paris. Tavernier, 12 rue de Paradis, and Pierre Lessard, 302 rue Saint-Denis, were represented in the exhibitions of 1819 and 1823. The first had supplied large vases for the Louvre; the latter specialized in lighting devices. There

must have been many others. The great popularity of tole wares in the late 1700's and early 1800's may have owed something to the hard times that followed the Revolutionary and Napoleonic Wars. At any rate, the success of papier mâché, an even less expensive material that imitated tole as tole had at first imitated lacquer, was one cause of their fall from favor. The industry died out around 1850, to be revived only in the late 1800's.

The Cooper Union Museum in New York has the most extensive collection of French tole accessible to students in the United States; in France, the largest collections on public display are in the Decorative Arts Museum in Paris and the Le Secq des Tournelles Museum in Rouen.

At top, red tole eggwarmer with gilt bronze handles in the form of swans and a cylindrical case for spectacles. Tole boxes were made in every shape, and decorated in every style. The one shown here at upper left, in the form of a shell, is lined with vermeil or gold plate. The three in the center row are decorated in gold on cream-color grounds. At lower left is an amusing snuffbox with a scene of dancing figures and musicians, and at right, a red tole desk box containing receptacles for ink, sand, and other writing equipment.

From the top, clockwise, a wine cooler with pierced gallery, yellow with transfer-printed decorations in black; a *verrière* decorated in red, black, and gold; a pierced, footed, red basket; a green and gold bread tray with pierced sides; and a teakettle and stand in red with gold decoration. In the center, a blue funnel with gold decoration.

Fig. 1 — EARLY BASKET WITH PIERCED RIM: PONTYPOOL (*c. 1760*)
In one piece. Rim elements bent upward from the flat sheet; overlapping edges riveted together. For this awkward process was substituted a method of pressing the sheet to the desired form. Decoration entirely worn away

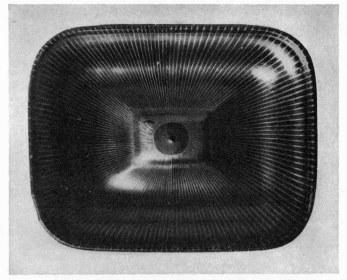

Fig. 2 — OBLONG TRAY: USK (*1800–1810*)
Decorated with stripes radiating from a black central disc. One half of the tray is crimson; the other half is covered with golden varnish. This was probably a trial piece

Fig. 3 (*left*) — CIRCULAR TRAY WITH PIERCED RIM: PONTYPOOL (*1770–1790*)
Tortoise-shell japan, with small bouquets and ribbon in silver. Tortoise-shell japan was favored at Pontypool

Fig. 4 (*right*) — WAITER: USK (*early 1800's*)
Black ground with wriggle pattern (known as Stormont) in crimson; sprigs and scroll border in silver

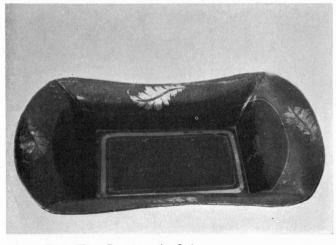

Fig. 5 — BREAD TRAY: PONTYPOOL (*c. 1800*)
Black centre with gold bands. Border in deep blue with oak leaves in gold

Fig. 6 — FRUIT TRAY, PAPIER-MÂCHÉ: USK (*early 1800*)
Chocolate brown. Decoration in silver

The Japanned Wares of Pontypool and Usk

An Editorial Note

Photographs from the National Museum of Wales

ON ITS westward side the English county of Monmouth jabs an elbow into the rocky ribs of Wales. Its southern border is hemmed by the waters of the River Severn, where the stream begins to expand in anticipation of its union with Bristol Channel. Not far from the centre of this diminutive scrap of British soil are the two villages of Pontypool and Usk, which enjoy the distinction of having produced the first and perhaps the best of England's japanned metal wares.

So-called japan differs from oriental lacquer in very important respects. Lacquer is a gum procured from a particular species of tree. Reduced to soluble form, it is patiently applied in successive coats to objects usually of wood or of *papier-mâché*. The process is quite completely described in ANTIQUES for November 1932 (*p. 183*). Japan is opaque paint carried in a varnish medium, which is applied with a brush. This varnish may be a vegetable derivative or it may be a mineral product. Apparently the first mineral varnish to be employed was a coal product discovered by one Thomas Allgood, who, in 1660, settled in Pontypool, already an iron-manufacturing town, and began experiments in extracting oils from soft coal. Precisely what was the nature of Allgood's varnish we are not told. But apparently it could be used either as a transparent finishing coat or, mixed with pigments, as a kind of enamel paint.

The Pontypool iron mills were equipped to turn out thin plates of iron and to give them a protective coating of tin. From such plates, trays, boxes, cans, and innumerable other articles could be made. Allgood's varnish permitted the glorification of such tinware with colors and traceried designs which could be rendered enduring by a process of baking, and which, when thus treated, shone with a lustre similar to that of oriental lacquer.

The commercial exploitation of Thomas Allgood's discoveries is credited to his sons Edward and John, who protected their method as a family secret, and apparently worked together in complete harmony. When, however, their respective children inherited the business, friction promptly arose. In 1761 three of this third generation of Allgood japanners left Pontypool, and, armed with the family secret, hied themselves to the neighboring town of Usk. Here they set up a rival manufacturing establishment.

Meanwhile, the large and favorably located industrial cities of Bilston, Birmingham, and Wolverhampton had developed their own modes of japanning metal and were trying hard but unsuccessfully to wrest the market from the squabbling Allgoods. "Billy" Allgood of Pontypool, who flourished between 1779 and 1790, maintained the quality of his wares, assembled competent decorators, and succeeded not only in holding his position in England but in finding French and Dutch importers who were glad to purchase his merchandise. His death, which occurred about the year 1800, was followed by a decline in the fortunes of his enterprise. The works closed in 1822.

The factory at Usk lasted somewhat longer. When, early in the 1800's, the light-weight *papier-mâché* began to supplant the more unwieldy iron for trays, the Usk concern dabbled with the new substance, managed to survive the first competition of electroplate, in the 1840's, and in 1860 succumbed.

Fig. 7 (above) — COFFEEPOT WITH WICKER-COVERED HANDLE: PONTYPOOL (*1760-1770*)
A fine example; mottled brown and gilt ground. Shepherdess in gold and brown. Rococo ornament in gilt

Fig. 8 (left and right) — COFFEE URNS: PONTYPOOL
If, as assumed, the ovoidal example at the left was decorated by Thomas Barker (*1769-1847*), it would date prior to 1790, when the artist, who later became famous, visited Rome to pursue his studies. The shape and decoration accord with the 1785-1790 period. The urn at the right, with decoration in the Chinese taste, is evidently somewhat later: about *1800-1810*

Fig. 9 — TEAPOT: USK *(c. 1790)*
Silver border decoration emulating bright-cut engraving of silverware. Chocolate japan ground with picture of Raglan Castle in colors

Today the National Museum of Wales harbors a collection of more than a hundred well-authenticated examples of the output of the Pontypool and Usk factories. By permission of Cyril Fox, Director of the Museum, ANTIQUES is permitted to picture some of the more significant items. Persons who wish a more detailed account of the factories may ob-

Fig. 11 (right)—TEAPOT: USK *(c. 1800)*
Gorgeously painted in crimson japan with black handle and gilt ornamental bands. The design of these bands is typical of Usk

Fig. 10 — TEA CADDY: PONTYPOOL *(c. 1790)*
Tortoise-shell japan, considerably worn. Pointed oval shape, with hinged lid and lock. The interior is divided into two compartments

tain a small brochure on the subject by sending twenty cents to the National Museum at Cardiff, Wales. Apparently nearly all of the surviving pieces of Pontypool and Usk japan are of the late 1700's and early 1800's. Those here illustrated are accompanied by brief descriptive comment. The approximate dates indicated are in each instance based on the style of the article. This is more easily determined in the case of urns, boxes, coffeepots, and the like, than it is of trays.

Fig. 12 (above) — CHAMBER CANDLESTICK: USK *(c. 1805)*
Removable cup and extinguisher. Black ground dotted with silver stars, another favorite motive at Usk

Fig. 13 (left and right) — CHESTNUT URNS: PONTYPOOL *(c. 1790)*
Black ground with decorations in gold, silver, and colors

BY MARGARET MATTISON COFFIN

Decorated tinware

Photographs by Charles Coffin

THE FIRST AMERICAN TINSMITHS, Edward and William Pattison, settled in Berlin, Connecticut, in 1738. Until this time, the few pieces of tinware used in the Colonies were expensive imports. In 1749 the English parliament passed a law prohibiting rolling and plating mills in the Colonies. There was no production of tinplate here until after 1829, when Amherst's Professor Hitchock discovered tin near Goshen, Connecticut. (Tinplate is sheet iron rolled very thin and coated with layers of molten tin.)

The Pattison brothers imported sheets of tinplate from Wales, then the sole producer of tinplate for export. They worked up an assortment of household utensils in their home, and sold it door-to-door. The demand soon grew so great that the Pattisons had to hire peddlers.

In 1750, roads in rural areas were non-existent, and the tinmen walked, carrying baskets. Later they traveled on horseback, with packs hanging on either side. By 1800, peddlers started using brightly painted carts, usually red, but sometimes yellow or green. Doors of the carts swung down, revealing compartments filled with tinware.

Routes of peddlers were extended as turnpikes were built. When Shubael Pattison inherited his father's tinware business in 1787, his peddlers had routes in Canada. He himself did some peddling there and traded for furs, which he hired girls to make into muffs. When he died in 1828, he was wealthy, and was said to have had the largest funeral ever held in town.

In Maine, peddlers started out from Stevens Plains, where Zachariah Stevens opened one of the first tin shops in 1789, and "Old Briscoe" first peddled tinware. An old-time peddler, writing for the Portland *Argus* reported that most peddlers were "green young men from the farm who wanted to see the world and earn enough money to buy some land."

The South was a profitable field for peddlers. Northern roads were passable only from May through the middle of November. In autumn, peddlers loaded their carts and started southward. When supplies were sold, they headed north again, sometimes selling horses and carts to return by boat.

Distances covered by the tin peddlers are amazing. Timothy Dwight wrote, "I have seen them in 1797 on Cape Cod and in the neighborhood of Lake Erie—distant from each other more than 600 miles. They make their way to Detroit 400 miles further—to Canada and to Kentucky, and if I mistake not, to New Orleans and St. Louis."

New York State had many tinmen. Augustus Filley, manager of the tin shop in Lansingburg, New York,

Fig. 1. Document box with typical Connecticut design, probably from the Filley shops. *John J. Vrooman.*

Fig. 2. One typical kind of Pennsylvania pattern, with orange acorns, the paint smudged when wet into the "saucer" of the acorn. *Author's collection.*

Fig. 3. Document box which looks like the work of Ann Butler. *Ruby M. Rounds.*

Fig. 4. Large domed-top box, with one kind of decoration found in New York State. *Mr. and Mrs. A. P. Robertson.*

Fig. 5. Typical pattern found on canisters and boxes along the Vermont-New York border. *Mr. and Mrs. George Pierce.*

wrote to his cousin Oliver in Connecticut on July 17, 1815: "The Canady peddlers wanted more tin than I could let them have . . . Albany City tinmen was here Thursday & wanted $200 jap. tin." "Honest" Wilson peddled tin along the eastern state line, coming down from Barre, Vermont. Hiram Lahue, a cripple, lived near Granville, in Washington County, and always carried striped stick candy and spruce gum to encourage youngsters to care for his horse. Erma Shepherd Griffith of Binghamton, New York, reports that Paul Phelps, born in Mansfield, Connecticut, in 1786, settled in Palmyra, New York, and drove a tin peddler's cart throughout that section for years. Peddlers were so much a part of rural New York life that Danforth Brayton and his wife added an extra room to their house at East Lake George just for peddlers.

The tin peddlers served their countrymen well. They offered a means of delivering goods, and took the place of present-day radios and telephones. By about 1900 the era of the tin peddler had passed. Tin kitchen utensils became impractical, as hundreds of new industrial uses for tin were found. The romance of the tin peddler passed away, and now only the few remaining pieces of the tinware they sold remind us of the peddler's cart clattering up a country lane, as dogs barked, children shouted with excitement, and mother set another place for dinner.

The tinware carried by the first peddlers was plain, but very soon japanned and decorated wares became popular. These first American-decorated pieces were done with brushes and oil paints, not stencils. Backgrounds were most often "japanned"—painted with asphaltum, a transparent substance with a tar base, which required heat to dry. The names Mygatt, Hubbard, Francis, and North were prominent among the early Connecticut decorators, who were also in demand in the Filley branch shops in other states. Their designs were stylized, and they favored a white band surmounted with a design over a japanned surface (Fig. 1). Variations of brush strokes and swags were used as borders. Almost transparent green leaves showed fine black veins, stems, and tendrils. Some of the yellow used was ochre, brownish and transparent. Pastel shades were occasionally used. Striping was plentiful.

The Stevens Plains decorators—Zachariah Stevens, the Francis girls, Oliver and Mary Ann Buckley—produced more realistic designs. Background colors used in Maine were often bright, and of solid colors, without banding. Much of "Uncle Zach's" work which has been preserved was done on a cream-colored or a mustard-yellow background. Sally Francis was a prolific rose painter, and her roses have been found on trays and caddies, coffeepots and table tops. Leaves in the Stevens Plains decoration are often chubby, with straight veins, sometimes resembling the leaves of the strawberry plant. Zachariah Stevens produced some scenic decorations, but flowers and fruit were preferred—peaches, strawberries, clusters of cherries, whitish flowers with gay accents. Designs of yellow and vermilion alone are found. Stevens Plains borders are unusual—a distinguishing characteristic; one looks like a string of pearls and another combines berries and leaves with symmetric artistry.

Pennsylvania tinware designs resemble peasant decorations from the central countries of Europe (Fig. 2). They are often symbolic, and at times appear to be an impression rather than an accurate representation. Pennsylvania craftsmen sometimes used asphaltum and sometimes bright background paints which did not adhere properly. Red was a favorite background, while blue, yellow, and brown were used in designs. (Brown was rarely used elsewhere.) An orange-vermilion appears sometimes in stems, and many designs are placed on white circles. The popular tulips, pomegranates, and star-shaped flowers are often outlined in black. Some Pennsylvania decorators used their fingertips to blend wet paint of different colors, at times leaving distinct fingerprints.

In New York State, unique decorating was done by Ann and Minerva Butler, daughters of Aaron Butler of Greene County, who ran a peddling and decorating business from 1824 to 1859 (Fig. 3). Their flowers and leaves are formed by brush strokes neatly laid together. Many patterns include delicate cross-hatching in flower centers. White bands, dotted lines, and "zig-zags" are characteristic. Stems are hair-like, of green, yellow, or vermilion, and tiny dots form forget-me-nots. Some greens are olive, others emerald; the vermilions are bright but not orange and the yellows and blues bright and clear. Backgrounds are either of dark asphaltum or black

paint. Borders vary, but the "rickrack" and "rope" types were the most favored.

Another type of decoration found in New York State is characterized by large vermilion flowers, with alizarin crimson and white over-strokes (Fig. 4). Dark green leaves with yellow veins resemble either elongated elm leaves or willow leaves. Yellow brush-stroke tassels abound.

A group of pieces found in western Vermont and eastern New York State has simple designs on an asphaltum base (Fig. 5). A spray of dark green stems runs diagonally from the lower left-hand corner to the upper right, and flowers are formed of elongated brush strokes of vermilion, with accents of dark blue, sometimes blended into white.

The various decorating formulas which may thus be distinguished teach us a little more about a truly American folk art. The best of these designs reveal expert craftsmanship. The Stevens, Butlers, Filleys, and others have left us an artistic heritage of which we may be proud.

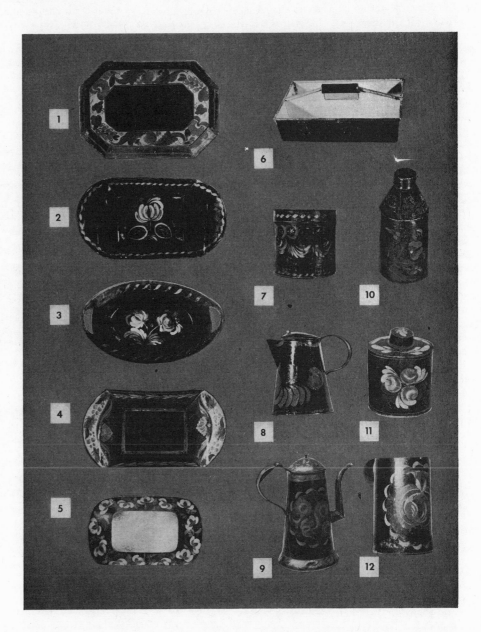

Fig. 6. Chart of tinware shapes. (1) Octagonal tray, Pennsylvania. *Metropolitan Museum of Art.* (2) Bread tray, Butler. *Mr. James C. Stevens.* (3) Oval bun tray, Butler. *Author's collection.* (4) Bread tray, Connecticut. *Mrs. Robert Wilbur.* (5) Rectangular bun tray, Maine. *Mrs. Clyde Holmes.* (6) Knife and fork tray with marbleized finish, found in New York State. *Author's collection.* (7) Round, flat-topped canister, New York. *Author's collection.* (8) Syrup pitcher. *Mrs. Robert Wilbur.* (9) Crooked-spout coffeepot, Pennsylvania. *Metropolitan Museum of Art.* (10) Tea caddy, found near Vermont-New York border. *Farmers' Museum, Cooperstown, New York.* (11) Squat, oval caddy. *Miss Florence Wright.* (12) Measure, Pennsylvania. *Miss Florence Wright.*

THE TINSMITHS OF STEVENS PLAINS

By ESTHER STEVENS BRAZER

PART I

STEVENS PLAINS is the old name of a community situated three or four miles from Portland, Maine, in the direction of Westbrook, of which it was formerly a part. The present residential appearance of the Plains does not even remotely suggest the swarming beehive of industry and trade that the town truly was in the first half of the nineteenth century. Now that railroads have made Portland the "gate city of Maine," it is difficult to realize that the direct stage route from Boston to Augusta and central parts of Maine once ran northwest of the city along Stevens Plains Road, and that Isaac Sawyer Stevens' tavern in the Plains was the chief ordinary for Portland.

Early history of Stevens Plains has already been outlined in the story of how Zachariah Stevens, the tavernkeeper's son, started working sheet tin there in 1798 (ANTIQUES, March 1936, *p. 98*). At that time the community consisted of little more than the tavern and two or three other Stevens homes. But after Zachariah came other tinsmiths, tin peddlers, horn-comb makers, and pewterers in rapidly increasing numbers. It is hard to understand *why* such a community of craftsmen should gather here — unless Zachariah Stevens consciously encouraged it. Yet whatever the cause, we know that the tin industry grew by leaps and bounds until, in the year 1832, there were eleven tinshops on the Plains manufacturing $27,300 worth of tinware annually (*Cf. Documents Relative to the Manufactures in the U. S., collected and transmitted to the House of Representatives in compliance with Resolution of Jan. 19, 1832*).

With such an aggregation of tinsmiths all making similar wares, and with several local young ladies decorating the tin, it becomes well-nigh impossible to single out the product of an individual craftsman. None of the tinsmiths signed their wares. I have therefore classed together in one big category of Stevens Plains tin the ware that seems indigenous to this section of Maine. When all the decorations are studied as a whole, however, two separate groups may be differentiated. First, there are the Zachariah Stevens designs — largely *floral* in character, though simply painted in country-tinsmith manner. A large number of Zachariah's pieces have previously been illustrated; others are here shown (*Figs. 1, 2, 3*). Many of his patterns contain the single- or double-cherry motive, in combination with flowers revealing infinite inventiveness. Some of these "Zachariah" designs may have been executed by Hattie and Maria Francis after 1822, but no doubt the pattern was "set" for them to copy. Secondly, we find a large group of Stevens Plains tin decorated in "Connecticut" fashion — chiefly *conventional or geometrical* in design,

with simple brush strokes for both flower and leaf forms. Examples of this treatment will be illustrated with Part II of this article. The white-band border, with gay patterns painted on it, is also of Connecticut derivation, pointing to the possible authorship of Buckleys, Norths, or Goodrich. These Stevens Plains smiths, all of whom are known to have received their apprenticeship in Connecticut, will be further discussed in the succeeding installment. No white-band border has yet been found on a Zachariah Stevens pattern.

In 1888 the Portland *Argus* printed the three letters here quoted. They were written by two old peddlers who, though slightly inaccurate about early Stevens history, still presented a more vivid description of Stevens Plains than I might compose:

A few now living can remember when nearly all the tin ware and horn combs used in Maine were manufactured in what is now Deering, between Morrills Corner and Woodfords, on the road over "Stevens Plains," and when hundreds of active young men were employed in peddling these all over the state. This one place was headquarters for all. But who was the first tin peddler in Maine? We think "Old Brisco" was that man. He had no children but adopted daughters who married tin men and have raised good families. We think Mr. Brisco might have been tinman, peddler and tinker, — it was said he loved "twitch-eye" too well, consequently he left no mark on "the Plains" to show that he ever lived there. Then came from Connecticut Elisha and Elijah North, and Oliver Buckley, who were tinmen, set up "tin shops," peddled some, took apprentices to learn the trade, but soon sold their wares by others whom they hired as peddlers. Then came from Connecticut the brothers Isaiah, Chauncey and Ebenezer D. Woodford, comb makers, and went to work at their trade. They manufactured more combs than enough to supply Maine; selling largely to Boston, New York and Philadelphia. Then the Stevens went in to the tin and comb business more or less. It was all Westbrook then. About 1830 the "hive" began to be too close. Campbell and Mills and apprentice

FIG. 1 — SPICE, TRINKET, OR MONEY BOX OF DECORATED TINWARE (*1815–1835*)

Made and painted by Zachariah Stevens, master tinsmith of Stevens Plains. Characteristic decoration.
From the collection of Mrs. J. W. Silley

FIG. 2 — BREAD TRAY
By Zachariah Stevens.
From the author's collection

FIG. 3 — PAINTED TRAY (*1815–1835*)
By Zachariah Stevens. Note the ingenious arrangement of decoration, so that tray is right side up whichever way it is turned. The floral motives are typical of Zachariah's work.
From the author's collection

FIG. 4 (right) — STEVENS PLAINS TINWARE
Ornamented with designs similar to those painted by Zachariah Stevens but less expertly executed. Possibly the work of Hattie and Maria Francis, done while they were painting "for the trade."
From the collection of Mrs. Evelyn Holmes

FIG. 5 — PAINTED TRAY
Apparently painted by someone familiar with Zachariah Stevens' designs, probably Maria Francis, who married Walter B. Goodrich in 1829. Border is well executed, but center decoration reveals inadequate proficiency on the part of the painter.
From the collection of Mrs. John H. Allen

FIG. 6 (left) — PAINTED TRAY
Known to have been decorated by Sally Briscoe Francis, who married Samuel Butler Stevens in 1821.
From the collection of Miss Caroline Stevens, granddaughter of the decorator

and peddler swarmed out, went to Bangor and set up tin shops for custom work and peddling, soon occupying all that part of the state as their field. Soon others did the same more or less extensively in towns along the coast and on the Kennebec and Penobscot Rivers. Consequently business began to fall off at Westbrook.

In my last communication concerning tinmen, comb makers and peddlers in old Westbrook in old times, "Jack Brackett" should have been named. He was a peddler, farmer, tinman and brick maker. His farm and residence where he did business was on the Windham Road, about one mile north from Pride's Bridge over the Presumpscot River. He had "too many irons in the fire" which we think went out and left him in the cold. A few others on "the Plains" were more or less engaged in the business. But now for the peddler — He was generally a green young man from the farm in the country who wanted to see the world and earn some money to buy some land or to start in with something else. But few followed the business long, if they possessed skill, they would soon get all the money they needed, or if they failed in skill and industry, they would drop out in the start. . . . The outfit was a horse, a "tin cart" and a pair of steelyards. The tin cart was four wheels, axle trees, arms and whiffle-tree like a light truck wagon, a large box for a body with an L in front to sit on. The body rested solid on the axle tree, a rack was fitted on the off side to fasten (truck) to, and a rod some three feet long, sharp at the upper end, was secured uprightly to the center of the back end of the box to string sheep skins on. Paint the cart red, fill up with tinware and "trinkets," hitch "Dobbin" in his place, mount the cart, boy, and be off on trading ground for a few weeks! Soon the horse and man returned, drawing the cart under a load of truck as large as a load of hay, consisting of paper rags, wool, wool skins, slats (sheep skins with the wool off), hog's bristles, old copper, brass and block tin (pewter), and all sorts of peltry, etc. etc., generally worth double what they started off with. Paper rags were then worth from four to ten cents a pound. Sometimes the "truck" or "plunder" would come by water carriage from "downeast" to Portland. Those who traded with the peddler in those days paid him no money, but let him have at his own price such as they did not know what to do with. The horses and carts, the "tin team" — improved from year to year until the business stopped. A few are now living who started life on one of those tin carts and multitudes of families in good circumstances in life are now

scattered from San Francisco to Eastport whose fathers or grandfathers were once tin peddlers from "Stevens Plains" or "Woodfords Corner."

From 1800 to 1835 more young men, natives of Maine, graduated from "tin carts" than graduated from Bowdoin College in the same time, and it is believed and judged a far less proportion of all the peddlers have been failures in life than of the college graduates.

These two letters, appearing in the *Argus* for April 10 and 16, 1888, are signed *Will*. A few days later they were followed by the reminiscences of one who signed himself *Stevens Plains*:

In the Argus of April 10 was a very entertaining letter, at least to one resident of the Plains, an old man now, weighted tremblingly down with the burden of more than four score years. It was a pleasant reminiscence to have so forcibly brought to mind names of familiar friends and companions, bearing the business cognomen of "tin plate workers." Uncle Briscoe passed in retrospection before me, and his novel conveyance, which was very like the dump carts of to-day, having but two wheels, whereby his horse could feed along by the roadside, waiting patiently his master's pleasure. His unique method of trading, too, would stagger some of the avaricious tradesmen of to-day. Money was not plenty, and when he found it was impossible to make a bargain he would banter them for their old dippers receiving with them a few pennies in exchange for new, go on his way rejoicing, presumably repairing some for future use, while others would be tossed to the roadside as rubbish, leaving his patrons delighted in the possession of a new drinking cup.

The Stevenses, if not the first, were among the first settlers of the Plains, and there are still twenty male descendants ranging from the age of five to eighty-two, residents here. The home or place from which the first Stevenses scattered could never be ascertained with any degree of accuracy, but it is known that in the year 1769 Isaac S. Stevens built the house since so generally known as "Uncle Billy's" Tavern (a part of which is still well preserved) and is the first Stevens of whom there is any record. He was Lieutenant in the Revolutionary War, and reared a family of four girls and five boys, all of whom married and settled in this immediate neighborhood. The ones to whom you probably have reference as carrying on the tin business, Mr. Samuel B. and Alfred Stevens, were born on the Plains in 1799 and 1801, being grandsons of Isaac, and sons of Zachariah B. Stevens. [It is obvious that these reminiscing tin peddlers did not arrive at the Plains while Zachariah was an active tinsmith. They probably knew him in the days when he was general storekeeper and postmaster.] Before Campbell & Mills went to Bangor, Hilton and Bartlett commenced business there, but were not successful. In your second communication you speak of Jack Brackett, a slight mistake in name only. He was usually called "Black Zack." He graduated from the community of "Shakers."

By correlating the facts gleaned from these letters, from Portland real-estate records, and from genealogical notes in the Stevens family, we may derive a chronological sequence of tinsmithing events at Stevens Plains.

In the beginning, of course, there was Zachariah Stevens, who established himself as a tinsmith in the Plains in 1789, and became one of the leading citizens of the town. His attractively decorated ware, which met with immediate popularity, has already been described in detail (ANTIQUES, March 1936, *p. 98*). At some time prior to 1804, Thomas Briscoe must have taken up residence here, for in that year Isaac Sawyer Stevens sold to "Thomas Brisco, tinsmith of Falmouth" a lot of land "adjoining said Brisco's house." (Falmouth was one of the early names of Portland.) Briscoe is said to have been an Englishman who learned his trade in his native country. By his marriage to Sarah (Sally) Rose, Paul Revere's niece, he was related to the patriot-silversmith's family. I have previously suggested the possibility that Revere was interested in a tinshop which may have been under Briscoe's management, with Phillip Rose (Briscoe's brother-in-law) as decorator, and Zachariah Stevens as apprentice. There should be some good reason why Briscoe was the first tinsmith to follow Zachariah after the latter's apprenticeship was completed and he returned to Stevens Plains to marry and settle down. In 1815 it is recorded that Paul Revere named Thomas Briscoe as mediator in settling a dispute over payment for a church bell at Cambridgeport. Revere must have had a real respect for Briscoe's business judgment to send all the way to Maine for his services in this capacity.

About 1806, "Aunt Sally" Briscoe adopted her five orphaned nieces, daughters of her sister Mary (Rose) Francis who died at Sterling, Massachusetts. There is a family tradition that Aunt Sally painted tinware, or that Uncle Briscoe taught all five girls to decorate. Careful sifting of actual evidence reveals the fact that three, at least — Hattie, Sally, and Maria — *did* paint tin, and that the latter two became wives of Stevens Plains tinsmiths. Several bread trays known to have been painted by Sally are still in the family (*Fig. 6*). It is possible that Hattie and Maria may have become professional decorators for the trade. As luck will have it, the journal kept from 1818 to 1825 by Zachariah Stevens at his general store shows that late in 1822 (shortly after Aunt Sally Briscoe's death) "H. & M. Francis" opened their account at the store. If I interpret the entries correctly, Hattie and Maria were being paid by Zachariah to decorate tinware, though charged for the paints and varnishes they were using. We find such entries as:

FIG. 7 — PAINTED BOXES
Possibly made by Thomas Briscoe. The ball feet are very unusual, apparently an English characteristic. The boxes may have been painted by Sally Briscoe Francis, grandniece of Paul Revere. *Top*, yellow box and lid; the original decoration here shown in top and side views was covered with two subsequent coats of paint that have been carefully removed. An almost identical box is in the author's collection. *From the collection of Miss Frances Stevens. Bottom*, yellow box said to have been given in 1834 as a Christmas gift to Susan Morrill of Stevens Plains. *Still owned in Stevens Plains, by Miss Sarah Morrill*

Dr. to H. & M. Francis

Dec.	1822 To cash....	$9.42	Feb. 12, 1823 to turpentine	1.16
Jan. 15, 1823 to Rose pink.		.19	Ap. 2, 1823 to varnish...	.70
	to Prussian		June 21, 1824 to paints....	6.13
	blue.....	.25	July..., 1824 to paints....	6.13
Feb. 7, 1823 to varnish...		.70	to cash.....	1.00
	to Orange		*(Dates obliter-* to 1 lb. crome	
	lead......	.37	*ated)* yellow....	....

to 1 lb white lead		to 1 pt oil...	.14
to 1 lb ver-		to cash	1.50
million...	1.25	to cash	24.00

The journal ends in 1824, but the tin industry at Stevens Plains was still rapidly expanding, so we have every reason to believe that Hattie and Maria continued their artistic efforts. Certain small items exhibiting motives similar to Zachariah's, but not so fluently painted as his products, may be examples of their work (*Fig. 4*).

In October 1821 Sally Briscoe married Zachariah's son, Samuel Stevens, like his father a tinsmith. In 1829, her younger sister Maria Francis married Walter B. Goodrich, a local tinsmith who had come from Berlin, Connecticut. In the Goodrich home some years ago was found a large, rectangular tray, not definitely known to be of Stevens Plains manufacture, but apparently painted by someone who had known Zachariah's work (*Fig. 5*). The border is expertly done with unfaltering brush strokes, though the center pattern is just a little too ambitious for the decorator's capabilities. The complex shading of the central fruit is not professionally executed. We might safely attribute this painting to the hand of Maria Francis.

All attempts to locate tinware made by Uncle Briscoe have failed to produce definite results, though it is possible that he made the ball-footed boxes which seem to have been painted by Sally Francis (*Fig. 7*). The only other ball-footed tinware I have observed is in the Pontypool collection in Wales. This circumstance may afford confirmation of the family tradition that Uncle Briscoe learned his trade in England. By the time he reached Stevens Plains, his best days were over, and his fondness for an easy-going existence led him into the roving life of tin peddler. He seems eventually to have vanished without a trace; not even a tombstone indicates his final resting place. The old peddler called Will, quoted above, spoke truly when he said that "Brisco left no mark upon the Plains" to show that he had ever lived there.

Members of the Stevens and Briscoe families were the pioneers of the tinsmithing industry in the little Maine community of Stevens Plains. But, as the recording peddlers have written, they were followed by a number of other craftsmen, many of whom were attracted to the location from great distances. Though some may hardly be classed as notable in their achievements, yet for the sake of presenting a complete record I have compiled a chronological history of all those concerning whom I have been able to glean information. The present installment brings the story up to the early years of the 1800's. In the concluding part, which will appear in a later issue of ANTIQUES, I shall proceed chronologically to the 1860's, covering a generous half-century of productive craftsmanship.

THE TINSMITHS OF STEVENS PLAINS

By ESTHER STEVENS BRAZER

PART II

In Part I of this article, published in ANTIQUES for June 1939, I sketched the background of the tinware industry of the Maine community of Stevens Plains, and traced its early history. We now proceed with a chronological consideration of its later development, which continued until well past the middle of the nineteenth century, and with identification of individual smiths.

IN THE YEAR 1804, Isaac Sawyer Stevens sold a lot of land adjoining Uncle Briscoe's property to Samuel Clary of Falmouth, a tinman related by marriage to the Stevenses. What kind of tinware Clary made it is difficult to say, since his stay in Stevens Plains was brief. For, three years later, Isaac Sawyer Stevens sold to Elisha and Elijah North, tinmen of Falmouth, a lot of land adjoining the property they had already purchased of the above-mentioned Samuel Clary. Elisha and Elijah North were doubtless members of that well-known North family of Berlin, Connecticut, the town where sheet tin was first worked into tinware in this country. (William Patterson established the tin industry in Berlin as early as 1740.)

Likewise in 1807, land was purchased of the innkeeper by Oliver Buckley, tinman from Connecticut. Buckley's signature as witness appears on Clary's deed of purchase, so Buckley must have been at the Plains for at least three years. Buckley was undoubtedly that Oliver Buckley, a "minor 14 years of age, son of Solomon Buckley, late of Wethersfield, Conn." over whom Selah Buckley of Berlin, Connecticut, was appointed legal guardian in the year 1795. It is easy to surmise how Oliver learned his trade. He must have taken his widowed mother to Stevens Plains, for "Martha, wife of Solomon Buckley," died there September 15, 1839.

I had been wondering whether Oliver Buckley made any *japanned* tinware when a box bearing the scratched initials *M.A.B.* was brought to my attention (*Fig. 1*). It had an unusually blocked cover of a type that occasionally comes to light in Maine antique shops. Now, Buckley had a daughter named Mary Ann, born about 1805. The decorative painting on this box was of a type associated with Connecticut japanners. Would it not be quite logical, then, to attribute this box, and others like it, to Oliver Buckley? Incidentally, Mary Ann Buckley became the wife of Freeman Porter, well-known pewterer of Stevens Plains.

By 1815, Buckley was advertising in the Portland papers that he carried on the "Tin Plate working and Plumbing business in its various branches." Thus he may have made many of Portland's tin roofs and gutters, or some of those shiny tin bathtubs we can still remember — who knows? Buckley lived until 1872, long enough to see the Plains rise to its height of prosperity about 1835, then decline to a quiet little suburb whose chief attraction was Westbrook Seminary for the polite education of young ladies and young gentlemen.

In the same year that Buckley established his home at Stevens Plains, Isaac Sawyer Stevens sold land he had recently purchased of Samuel Butts, to Zachariah Brackett, tinman. As Isaac had owned all the Plains property after the death of his father-in-law, his purchase from Butts probably means that the land in this deal was somewhat removed from the Stevens holdings. This consideration would certainly point to the Zack Brackett mentioned by the early tin peddler, quoted in Part I, as having lived over by the Windham Road. As the name would imply, Brackett was a cousin of Zachariah Brackett Stevens, the first tinsmith of our story. Jack-of-all-trades and master of none, Brackett probably made very little tinware, and left none that can be identified.

In 1818, Benjamin Campbell, tin-plate worker of Westbrook (as Stevens Plains had now come to be called) purchased land of Elisha North, tinman. How long Campbell had been at Stevens Plains is a question. By 1830, he speaks of himself as a resident of Bangor, disposing then of his Westbrook property to Gerry Cook, a "trader" and tinman. At Bangor, Campbell became associated with another tinsmith named Mills, whose venture seems to have met with success.

Zachariah Stevens in 1822 began turning over his tinware manufacture to his two sons. The elder, Samuel Butler Stevens, was educated as a surveyor, but since he was not constantly employed in his profession he spent much of the time at the tin shop. Samuel seems to have continued the business faithfully, making tea caddies, teapots, bread trays, and rectangular boxes in the manner of his father. From 1825 to 1835, he was associated with his brother Alfred, who claims to have turned out tinware worth $1,500 a year. Alfred then went into the manufacture of cook stoves with Walter B. Goodrich. Alfred had married the latter's cousin, Nancy Goodrich Buckley, second daughter of Oliver Buckley, the tinsmith. A tin box painted by Mrs. Alfred Stevens is said to have been exhibited in 1896. Its present whereabouts are unknown, but if its owner reads this article, I hope he will communicate with me. In later years, Alfred became senior member of Stevens, Smart, and Dunham, britannia makers. The third partner was the well-known pewterer who came to Stevens Plains in 1831 as apprentice to Allen Porter and later married Alfred Stevens' sister, Emmeline.

In 1821, the elder brother, Samuel Butler Stevens, married Sally (Sarah), one of the five Francis sisters who painted tin (*Figs. 3, 4*). She continued her painting as long as she lived, and left behind her a large album of floral bouquets painstakingly and lovingly painted in bright colors. On a small table in her front room, her paints were kept in readiness, with a small bottle of turpentine and her many brushes. She painted roses on everything — on panels of doors, on tables, on chairs, and trays.

Mr. and Mrs. Samuel Butler Stevens went to live in an old Stevens home which Oliver Buckley had purchased in 1818, now unhappily destroyed in the expansion of Evergreen Cemetery. They enlarged the dining room, built a second kitchen, and a long two-story ell, whose upper floor was often occupied by tin peddlers when they stopped in town to load. There were barns and sheds where rags taken in barter for tinware were sorted for sale to the paper mill, and where the tinware was finished and packed in the peddlers' carts. Samuel had four sons, Samuel Henry Stevens, Grenville, Frank, and Augustus Ervin. The last became an iron and steel merchant, and was mayor of Portland when the disastrous fire of July 4 swept one third of its buildings to destruction. April 11, 1842, Samuel Butler Stevens' tin shop was burned, with a loss of his books, ware, and tin plate amounting to $1,500. As the tinware business had been running downhill since the introduction of cook stoves and the banishment of tin kitchens, it is highly probable that Samuel B. Stevens never reëstablished his business with any degree of success. He died six years later, in July 1848, survived for many years by his widow.

Among the Samuel Butler Stevens papers is a tiny notebook in which are recorded the names of his tin peddlers, the dates when they loaded their carts with tinware, and the value of their loads, as well as the date when they returned and the value of the products they brought back. It is interesting to note that occasionally the value at return is greater than at the start, suggesting that they had on previous trips allowed credit somewhere, or had placed tinware on consignment at some country store. They

FIG. 1 (*below, left*) — PAINTED TIN BOX (*c. 1815–1820*)
Bearing scratched initials M.A.B. It was probably owned by Mary Ann Buckley. It is here attributed to her father, Oliver Buckley, tinman from Connecticut. This box has a cover of unusual shape. The decoration is typical of "Connecticut" technique. *From the author's collection*

appear to have been paid a dollar a day for peddling.

Among the peddlers listed we find Elijah Deshon, who worked in 1831 and 1832, Thomas Deshon, and J. M. Deshon, both of whom worked in 1832. These names caught my eye because on the bottom of a box in my collection is scratched what appears to be *E. Deshon 6/* (*Fig. 5*). One might jump to the conclusion that the 6-shilling price mark indicates English origin, but the fact is that many of these old-time countrymen clung to the English monetary system long after dollars and cents had been officially adopted. In filling out an inquiry of the American Business Index in that very year, 1832, Samuel Butler Stevens himself said that he paid his men 7/6 a day. So this box was probably made by him about 1832, decorated by his father, Zachariah Stevens, or by one of the Francis sisters painting in his manner, and peddled by Elijah Deshon. Probably the name and price were scratched on the bottom by a country storekeeper who took the box on consignment for sale at six shillings.

Walter B. Goodrich, tinsmith, arrived at Stevens Plains in January, 1824. He kept a journal in which we read the following:

Born May 19, 1802, at Wethersfield Connecticut. Went to learn tinman's trade, at the age of sixteen at Berlin, Connecticut. Left Berlin May 1823. Arrived at Lynn, Massachusetts, and worked eight months for E. A. Yale. Left Lynn for Westbrook, Maine, January 1824, commenced work for Oliver Buckley in February and worked for said Buckley until 1825. Commenced tin business with Oliver Buckley and dissolved in 1827. I purchased stock in trade. Built tin shop and barn in 1827. Married Maria Francis June 11. 1829. Commenced tin business with James A. Thompson, February 23, 1830.

From this point on the record became the journal of Goodrich and Thompson. Strange to relate, one of the very first items was charged to the account of Zachariah B. Stevens, July 10, 1830, "To Working 1 Box plate......$8.00." There can be but one reason why Zachariah Stevens should have other tinsmiths do his work, particularly when he had two able-bodied sons already established with tin shops. The answer is that Zachariah, now become too busy with his general store, was unwilling to lose his hold upon what he knew was a profitable business, and therefore farmed out part of the labor to this newly established firm of Goodrich and Thompson. At any cost, the japanned ware had to be made ready for the peddlers to take out while the summer season allowed them to travel with ease.

Goodrich and Thompson made, among other things, "Large

Kichins at $4.00 apiece, large bakers, coffee pots at $2.00 apiece and Dowli Reflecting Bakers." Just how much, if any, of their product was japanned, I cannot say, but in the journal, among other bits of useful information, are written directions for making various brightly-colored varnishes — asphaltum, rose, gold, blue, and so forth — and for applying bronze stenciling in powder form. Was this information a part of Walter Goodrich's training before he finished his apprenticeship at Berlin, Connecticut, or did he acquire these recipes after coming in contact with Zachariah at the Plains? I believe that Goodrich brought the knowledge with him, since stenciling was introduced into Connecticut about 1817, and since there is no evidence of Zachariah's knowledge of the use of stencils. Only one Zachariah piece, the large document box made for Alfred Stevens, appears to show a use of bronzes, and the work is done in an experimental, *freehand* fashion. If any Stevens Plains tinware was stenciled in bronze, I am inclined to attribute

FIG. 2 (*left and below*) — THREE BOXES PROBABLY BY FRANCIS BUCKLEY
The decorative design is largely of "brush-stroke" type — strokes perfectly graduated from the tiny leaf forms to larger and larger forms. The design is probably of Connecticut derivation, tending toward the conventional and geometrical.
From the collections of the author and of Mrs. John Oldham

The decoration in the oval, *above, left,* is from a tray painted by Zachariah Stevens

FIG. 3 (*right*) — PAINTED BREAD TRAY
Decorated by Sally Briscoe Francis, an indefatigable tin-painter of considerable skill and fine taste.
From the collection of Miss Elizabeth Stevens, granddaughter of the decorator

FIG. 4 — CIRCULAR TRAY
Decorated by Sally Briscoe Francis for a friend. Unusual treatment of a lace-edge tray, which would normally have been adorned by a large central design of flowers.
From the collection of Miss Elizabeth Stevens

it to the short-lived firm of Goodrich and Thompson (*Fig. 6*).

This firm moved to Augusta in 1833; and in 1835, Goodrich sold out his interest there to Charles S. Buckley (son of Oliver), tinsmith of Stevens Plains. Goodrich then engaged in the manufacture of cook stoves with Alfred Stevens, as before noted, at Stevens Plains. In 1837, Goodrich returned to the working of tin plate with Oliver Buckley, continuing until 1842, when the partnership was terminated. In 1850 Goodrich recorded, "I commenced Business with Freeman Porter to manufacture Brittania and tinware." Under the date November 17, 1852, he wrote, "I dissolve partnership with F. Porter."

A couple of years later an amusingly informal entry was made in the journal:

August 23, 1854. "Romance and Reality." Scene: Tin Shop. Hopeful, ardently engaged on ten quart pails, in a melting mood, performing Hymn to the Virgin in subdued melancholy whistle, and taking huge strides into the poetical and sentimental. Sire — soldering teapots, "I should think that was the tune the old cow died on by the sound of it." Hopeful, rudely awakened from his dream, — "You haven't much poetry in your composition, have you? I suppose you would prefer Rory O'More, or Saint Patrick's Day in the Morning?" Sire, steadily gazing at the bottom of a revolving teapot through his specs, — "I suppose I should."

The "hopeful" was undoubtedly young Goodrich Junior, referred to in this 1855 quotation from Goodrich's journal:

Buckley is out of stock, so also Goodrich, and consequently Goodrich Jr. is thrown upon his oars.

A few more brief cullings from the journal are worth citing here:

R. Dunham started for the west, Sept. 14, 1857, left business with me June 12, 1859. F. Porter repaired house, moved shop etc.
Nov. 7, 1861. Rufus Dunham's Brittania shop burnt. Loss $6000.00. Insurance $4000.00.

And finally, entered in the handwriting of Walter Goodrich's son:

August 4, 1869. Father died this morning at ¼ before 9 o'clock.

It is said that James A. Thompson, second member of the original firm of Goodrich and Thompson, went to California in the gold rush, and later was manufacturing jewelry of a very high order in New York City. John Jacob Astor and other notables were among his patrons.

I find mention of three other tinsmiths on the Plains, but have been unable to identify their work: one Proctor, Ebenezer Holton Sawyer, and George Mead Stevens. The last named belonged to a younger generation, and his handiwork was not produced in the period with which we are concerned.

Until recently, we collectors of early American japanned ware have found it well-nigh impossible to identify the source or

maker of most of the pieces that gaily ornament our shelves. Due to the fact that no tinsmith signed his wares, as the pewterer and silversmith took pride in doing, we have had little data to guide us. As I have attempted to indicate, however, the maker's cryptic but nevertheless personal signature lies in the decorative design itself — its motives and their treatment. To be sure, it may take a design analyst to interpret this signature. But now that the large group of Stevens Plains tinware is shown to be recognizable, collectors may derive added pleasure in their ownership of these cheerful pieces from a small Maine town.

FIG. 9 (*left*)—PAINTED BREAD TRAY
Probably decorated by Sally Eriscoe Stevens.
From the collection of her granddaughters, the Misses Merrill

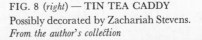

FIG. 8 (*right*) — TIN TEA CADDY
Possibly decorated by Zachariah Stevens.
From the author's collection

FIG. 5 (*above, left*) — PAINTED BOX
Scratched inscription on base: *E. Deshon 6/* Probably made and decorated by Zachariah Stevens, for whom Elijah Deshon was peddling tinware in 1832.
From the author's collection

FIG. 6 (*above, right*) — TRAY STENCILED IN BRONZE
Possibly manufactured by Walter B. Goodrich, who is believed to have learned bronze-stenciling in Connecticut before his removal to Stevens Plains about 1804.
From the collection of Mrs. Mary Mountfort

FIG. 7 (*left*) — STEVENS PLAINS TINWARE BY UNKNOWN MAKERS
Decoration is all in yellow and red.
From the collection of Mrs. O. H. Perry

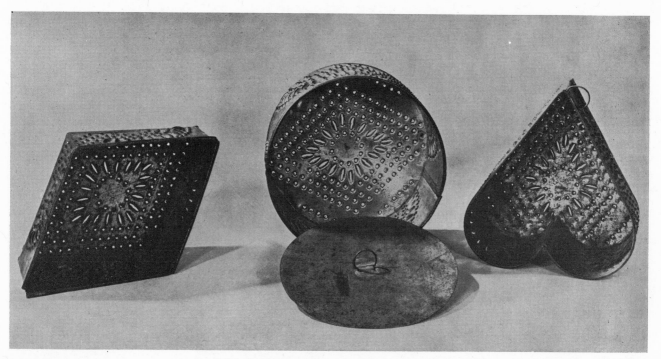

Quart-size cottage cheese colanders in conventional shapes, round, diamond, and—by far the most popular—heart. Solidified cheese retained the shape and pierced design of the mold.

Decorated tinware east and west

In Pennsylvania   BY EARL F. ROBACKER

THE FONDNESS OF THE Pennsylvania Germans for ornamenting even the simplest of their handicrafts is proverbial, and the piercing or punching of the sheet tin used for household objects as a means of enhancing their beauty seems to have been particularly popular. True, pierced tin performed both a utilitarian and a decorative function in the familiar "Paul Revere" lantern, and in the more or less ubiquitous footwarmers, both of which are of eastern seaboard rather than purely local provenance; but it remained for the Pennsylvania German craftsman to turn a merely convenient practice into something of an art.

Tinware, pierced or punched, seems to be almost entirely a nineteenth-century product. Such few dates as are found range from the 1830's to the 1860's, with more falling in the 1840's than at any other time. In a few instances the piercing of tin for ornamental purposes seems to have continued up to contemporary times.

"Piercing" and "punching" are, of course, two different things. As the name implies, piercing denotes a complete perforation—a chisel making a slit, a nail a round hole. The rough surface created by the process is always on the outside of the object decorated. Punching, done with a hammer and nail or a hammer and a fine die, dents the surface of the tin but does not cut it. Punched objects were usually intended to hold liquids.

At once the most important and the most distinctive pierced tin object is the pie cupboard, or pie safe, the primary function of which was to provide storage space after the weekly or semi-weekly orgy of baking. It is curious to note that museums seem to have neglected this most characteristic—in function, design, and meticulous execution—of Pennsylvania German products. The cupboard is a simple, sturdy framework of pine, either pegged or nailed, with a hinged door or pair of doors constituting the entire front. Over this framework are tacked the perforated sheets of tin which provided circulation of air while the pies cooled, at the same time protecting them from insects or mice. The decoration may be an over-all one, as in the hanging cupboards, or may be executed in small identical panels in the stationary type. The rare eagle motif is particularly sought by collectors; also desirable are the six-pointed geometric design sometimes erroneously referred to as a "hex" sign, and the five-pointed star. The free design of scrolls or arabesques is more usual. Large six-pointed figures were evidently laid out with a compass; smaller designs were probably done by following a pattern superimposed on the tin.

Similar to the tin panels of the pie cupboard in details of fashioning are the colanders for shaping cottage cheese, into which was poured the scalded milk for draining and eventual solidifying. Heart-shaped strainers of

Perforations on the door of this foot-warmer—which held a hot brick wrapped in flannel—show representative heart motif.

Three hearts at center back form the sole embellishment of this simple punchwork candle sconce.

Important pierced tin pie cupboard with unusual rooster and four-pointed star motifs. Typical projecting corner posts at top are bored so cupboard can be strung with rope and suspended from the ceiling. Taller cupboards, with two vertical doors, were stationary.

Already a rare item because of its limited vogue in the early days of the parlor store, the "ash protector" was placed on the iron hearth before the grate to check draft and keep hearth neat.

All illustrations from author's collection; photographs by Alden Haswell.

The punched tin coffeepot on the left is a prize specimen complete with maker's name, initials of recipient, and date: *J. Ketterer, H.G., 1843;* central decoration, an urn filled with tulips and other flowers, is this maker's favorite. Heart motif on pot at right occurs infrequently in coffeepots. An interesting variant is the miniature, dated 1860, with its single elaborate tulip.

this type—some of them obviously of recent manufacture —are still in use in the Pennsylvania German country. Some strainers have lids, others do not. Early examples are likely to be footed; both early and late ones may have convenient tabs or wire handles for ease in manipulation and for hanging.

As is the case with pie cupboards, the actual perforation is done before the pieces are assembled and soldered. Designs are usually elementary, with stars and rayed concentric circles predominating. Nail punching makes a neater, more compact, and more attractive design here than chisel perforation because of the limited area for decoration.

Other objects decorated by the Pennsylvania Germans in pierced tin were nutmeg graters, foot warmers, and "ash protectors"—the last in use for only a very brief time, since space heaters improved and changed so rapidly.

Compartmented bureau box with six-pointed punchwork geometric figure.

It is in punched tinware that the student will find the most finely detailed work, with coffeepots the best specimens. The punching was done with great care—a single too-vigorous indentation would have ruined the entire undertaking. At the same time, it is doubtful that these capacious and attractive pots ever saw active duty; they belonged then, as they do now, to the category of things kept "just for fancy."

Modest craftsmen that they usually were, the Pennsylvania Germans refrained from putting their mark on any but pieces that were obviously a matter of pride; it is significant, therefore, that of all punched tin objects, coffeepots alone are commonly identifiable by maker. Three names occur: J. Ketterer, M. Uebele, and W. Shade; but even these artisans did not, apparently, mark all their pieces. When the name does occur, it is die-stamped on the handle.

Exterior evidence indicates that punched tin coffeepots, like the best sgraffito or slipware pottery, were made as special presentation pieces, possibly for brides. Frequently the initials of the recipient—or of the owner—appear, one on either side of the central motif. When the date is added, the *18* appears at one side on the reverse and the two remaining numerals on the other. Designs frequently use the profile tulip of fractur, of dower chests, and of ironware. The heart occurs infrequently, as do comet-shaped figures (the Chinese *yin* and *yang* symbols), conventionalized floral patterns, and stars —usually four-pointed.

Other than in coffeepots, punchwork occurs only incidentally. One instance is the candle sconce shown. Occasional cooky cutters have elementary punchwork designs, presumably for identification, and one specimen has an elaborately outlined *F* for the same purpose.

Decorated tinware east and west
In New Mexico

BY E. BOYD

WHAT IS POPULARLY KNOWN as "old Spanish tin" did not exist in our Southwest. The first tin articles came, ready made, over the Santa Fe Trail during the second quarter of the nineteenth century. These, from records, seem to have been tin candle molds and tin-framed looking glasses. As in other Spanish countries, candles had been made by dipping; but the molds must have found buyers—we find copies of them, country-made from tin scraps pieced together. The looking glasses are mentioned in several contemporary accounts; they hung in churches as well as in private homes. In 1846, Lieutenant Colonel W. H. Emory spoke of "Yankee looking glasses without number"—all hanging so high that they could not be looked into!

After the military occupation of New Mexico by the United States in 1846 and the steady influx of emigrants from our eastern states, various staples in tin containers were freighted over the plains. When the tins were empty, they were salvaged for reworking by ingenious native artisans. To understand how desirable tin, as a material, was in the eyes of New Mexicans at that time, we must remember their perennial lack of metals. For more than two hundred years small tools, hardware, nails, and bolts were brought by caravan from Central Mexico by a long and dangerous route, and there were never enough to supply even the rudimentary needs of the northern frontier province. As a result, every scrap of worn-out metal was made to serve again and again. Local folk artists supplied secular and religious decorative pieces, ingeniously contrived from local materials, but they had nothing to satisfy the human fondness for sparkle and brilliance. Tin had this property, it was easily worked with blacksmithing tools, and it could be had for the taking from gringo trash heaps.

Early New Mexico tin pieces have several distinguishing characteristics: very heavy tinning of soft pewter color, the presence of brand names and other commercial marks on the reverse, and the fact that each object was pieced together from assorted snips of tin cut without relation to the structure—the result of their having been made from cut-down containers instead of from new sheet tin.

Candle sconce made of 13 scraps of tin joined with pine rosin. *Except as noted, illustrations are from the Museum of New Mexico.*

Glazed tin *nicho* with panels of painted paper, predominantly blue, and candle sockets at lower right and left. Note piecing of both tin and glass.

With the exception of candleholders and molds, tin was used in New Mexico purely as an ornament. The lack of commonplace implements made of tin is the more surprising when we learn that iron or copper vessels were itemized as valuable properties in last wills and testaments, while dippers, mugs, bowls, and other kitchen trifles were made at home, whittled from wood, cow horns, or gourds. The profound religious devotion of the province offers an explanation: the silvery tin was reserved for the little pantheons of saints and holy persons then seen in every home as well as in the churches. A tin frame, or a *nicho* (small glazed tin shrine), was made for an old family image, which might be a locally-made *santo* or an engraving brought by a pilgrim from some Mexican shrine. In record time for those days, the enterprising N. Currier sent out a series of colored lithographs of religious subjects for the new Spanish Catholic market. Later on European clergymen who came after Archbishop Lamy to the diocese of Santa Fe, created in 1851, distributed inferior prints from France, Germany, and Benziger Brothers' Cincinnati press.

Candleholders, the functional form in which tin was used in New Mexico, were obviously a vast improvement over wooden ones. Shapes ranged from a single sconce of a tin scrap bent at a right angle and fitted to a socket, to ceiling chandeliers with a central lantern form and perhaps twelve candle sockets on curved straps. Like most of the tin pieces, these were not only much pieced but made from several different tins, as the original stamping and factory grooving of different parts of the same piece show. Later in the nineteenth century cut-out fins, floral and bird forms were soldered among the tiers of candelabra.

Among other useful and attractive innovations brought by the Anglos to New Mexico, such as fashions in dress and the distilling of spirits, were two items taken for granted by most of the population east of the Mississippi—window glass and wall paper. It is a matter of record that in 1846 the only building in the Territory with glazed windows was the Palace of the Governors. Yankee families who came to stay sent to St. Louis for

window panes and rolls of wallpaper, to recreate in strange adobes the mid-Victorian parlors they had left behind. The earliest tin pieces contain heavy plate glass with air bubbles in it like the surviving original panes in the old Palace itself. The oldest wallpapers, which have been preserved in tin pieces but not on walls, are in William Morris neo-classic patterns. After these we find a sequence familiar to anyone who has seen old sample books, or our grandmothers' homes. Since tin was so often combined with glass and wallpaper by New Mexicans, we must give due consideration to all three materials in dating any example, as well as to the image which forms the central motif.

In recent years it has become a custom to paint gay designs on windows in New Mexico style interiors and to call the result "Spanish colonial painted glass," but if there was almost no glass before 1846 how can painting on glass be a "Spanish colonial" craft? In the course of twenty-five years of keeping notes on indigenous Spanish artifacts, I have noted only three examples of small wooden panels in which irregularly cut ovals of hand-blown glass were painstakingly inlaid, with a small tempera painting on paper of a religious image, more or less in the manner of the folk artists who made *santos,* under the glass. It is the glass in these three pieces which is remarkable, and the labor which went into its inlay indicates its rarity at that time. When scraps of window or picture glass did become available to tinsmiths, they adapted the process described above to tin pieces. A pattern of wavy lines and floral scrolls was painted on common paper, laid under a small clear glass panel, backed with tin or makeshift cardboard, and the whole

Multiple-windowed frame of the type used for family portraits in the East, with N. Currier print dated 1848 of Our Lady of Guadalupe of Mexico. Each section was separately made, the whole soldered together and braced by ornamental bosses.

Tin chandelier, circa 1850, made in vicinity of Santa Fe and used in church at Cañoncito, New Mexico. *Wash drawing by the author, Index of American Design, National Gallery of Art.*

Frames in "Federal" style, with motifs copied from cabinetwork brought west by emigrants. Surface decoration was done with the point of a nail or small dies already in use for stamping leather.

Cross of mid-nineteenth-century wallpaper, in terra cotta, black, and yellow, mounted in tin.

was soldered together with a narrow tin rim. (Since tinsmithing as a profession did not exist prior to Yankee influence, solder did not arrive in New Mexico as quickly as tin containers, so some of the first locally re-fashioned tin pieces were put together with pine rosin which is still visible.) Multiple panels, each carefully sealed, were joined to make larger pieces. The painted inlays, which are usually more attractive to today's collectors, were not used as frequently as wallpaper.

One of the first designs for frames, which seems to have been copied from furniture in the Federal style, was a vertical rectangle with corner bosses and a pediment of the spread eagle or other motif. Later versions had small rosettes of tin, or curlicues, soldered around the rim. The repetition of simple geometric figures gave added sparkle to the tin, and was used with pleasing restraint. After the Civil War an amusing adaptation of the family portrait gallery frames, common in the East in the form of a heavy oval or polygonal wooden molding with multiple openings to show small photographs of many members of the family, was made of the same tin, glass, and wallpaper scraps, with a religious subject at the center.

After the railroad reached the Rio Grande in 1880, there were more commercial items and more variety in materials. Storekeepers offered oil paints for woodwork and wagons, and tin pieces were pointed up with gaudy colors rather thickly daubed on. Objects grew larger, and flying superstructures in flamboyant shapes were attached. Neither functional nor well made, these gaudy pieces have seldom survived intact. The earlier reserva-

tion of tin to the greater honor of religious images seems to have been forgotten, and an increasing supply of colored prints, magazine and catalogue covers, advertising and greeting cards, found its way into tin frames. When cheap copies of gilded plaster or dark wooden frames reached local stores, tin itself became démodé, except in distant villages where the old crafts persisted well into the present century.

The many artists who moved to New Mexico in the past two generations encouraged native artisans to revive tincraft as a means of livelihood, and the WPA Federal Art Project gave further impetus. Now, under the direction of various regional craft shops using traditional and recent designs, it has gone into a more mass-produced phase to supply the new demand for this type of ornament so appropriate to southwestern adobe homes.

Tin and glass trinket box with commercial colored cards inset. Reverse shows cards for Peter's Cornstarch and Ayer's Cherry Pectoral—"For the Cure of Coughs, Colds, Asthma, Croup, Bronchitis, Whooping Cough and Consumption." 1885-1890.

PENNSYLVANIA COOKY CUTTERS

By EARL F. ROBACKER

Illustrations from the author's collection

WHILE collectors have for years been on the trail of the tulip, the peacock, and the pomegranate in Pennsylvania *fraĉtur* and on spatterware, it is only recently that a byroad in the same general direĉtion has led explorers in search of the lowly tin cooky cutter. Without doubt, tin cooky cutters have been used in every part of the country, and probably from earliest times. New England has yielded a few, and many more might have been rescued from ashheap and oblivion had anyone taken them seriously. Some turn up in Maryland and Virginia and farther south. But it is not surprising that the finest examples come to light in the Pennsylvania-German country, where delight in color, love of ornamentation, and appreciation of good food have been manifest in a variety of household gear.

Just who the first cooky-cutter makers were will never be known, and does not really matter. It is not improbable that each early family could boast some member who could turn out a recognizable, if not anatomically accurate, tin pattern for horse, mule, star, heart, or tobacco pipe. By the beginning of the 1800's, however, itinerant craftsmen, including tinsmiths, were making their way over the countryside, and from then on if the "Dutchman" himself still made the cooky cutters for his wife before she began her Christmas baking, it was by choice and not from necessity.

The tinsmith was a welcome visitor in many a rural home, where he might spend a day or a week according to the number of odd jobs he could persuade his host were desirable. Somewhere along the line of his endeavors, after the cake tins, dippers, funnels, pans, and pails had been fashioned, came the cooky cutters. These were constructed for the most part from left-over scraps of tin, and even from the flattened remains of tin canisters or cooking utensils. A stately deer, for instance, bears an unmistakable baking-powder-can ridge across his back, and a dog proudly displays the letters —FRAM. So far as is known, not a single early craftsman thought highly enough of his cutters to mark them with his name.

It has commonly been assumed that early cooky cutters were made by fitting a strip of tin (the cutting edge) around a wooden mold of the desired shape, then soldering it to a strong backing. After removal of the mold, the backing would be trimmed down, roughly following the outlines of the design, and sharp edges cut off or bent under slightly. While some credence may be given to this theory, so few molds exist which might conceivably have been used for the purpose that there

FIG. 1 — HEARTS AND TULIPS, WITH VARIATIONS
Both motives were popular in Pennsylvania

FIG. 2 — HUMAN FIGURES AND FACES
Showing more or less stylization

216

may be more than reasonable doubt about this method. A few comparatively heavy steel-plate patterns have been found that may possibly have served in such a capacity; but, again, little more than speculation may be offered in their behalf. A more telling indication that the mold method was not generally used is the almost complete lack of duplication among surviving cooky cutters. Had a tinsmith taken the time and trouble to fashion a pattern, he would hardly have used it only once; yet it is virtually impossible to find one cutter that appears to be a replica of another. A large elephant cutter in my collection seems to have been constructed by first placing the cutting edge about a flat pattern, and then soldering the whole to its backing. It is equally possible, however, that the "pattern" was merely a reënforcement, since the cutter is a very large one.

The probability is that from the earliest specimens, which are perhaps too crude to have been made by a self-styled tinsmith who must look to his reputation, to those whose design indicates a date well after the Civil War, cooky cutters were constructed "freehand," by the use of such simple tools as would form the necessary curves and angles.

The pattern, crude though it may be, is one of the best indications of the cutter's age. A Continental soldier on horseback, closely resembling figures seen on Pennsylvania sgraffito plates, may reasonably be ascribed to the period between the Revolution and the end of the century. Many cutter patterns are clearly related to the hearts on Ephrata fractur, cut-paper work, and furniture; to the conventional designs on painted chests and bride's boxes; to the bird figures on enameled glass; and to the peacocks on samplers and door towels, many of which are dated. The artisan in tin may usually have complied with the artistic demands of his patrons; but it is probable that, more widely traveled and familiar with the "outlands" than they, he may likewise have contributed patterns of his own suggestion, such as the eagle, the Forty-Niner, the preacher, the plain-clothes sectarian, the broad-hatted "Dutchman," and the lady in a puffed-sleeve gown. In search of new ideas after executing the universally popular tulip, star, heart, and peacock, the tin worker frequently drew his inspiration from whatever domestic objects happened to be visible. This would account for the rough approximations of

bottle, clothespin, broom, basket, gun, hatchet, shoe and boot, pitcher, and coffeepot. Flowers, curiously enough, are rare, except for the tulip and the thistle- or carnation-like blossoms. Patterns that recur so often as to indicate a perennial popularity are variations of the tulip and the characteristically shaped Pennsylvania-German heart — more squat than the modern valentine heart — as well as birds whose close counterparts appear on fractur dating from the late 1700's to 1840 or even later.

Pattern is of course not the only criterion of age. Equally important considerations are the character and condition of the material, and the method of soldering. Early cutters are as a rule very heavy, made of a strong, thin steel plate generously coated with tin. In many instances, the plating has worn away or rusted heavily. The method of soldering is an indication not only of the age of the cutter, but also of the degree of the artisan's skill. Containing a large quantity of lead, probably about fifty per cent, and with a flux that was undoubtedly rosin, the heavy

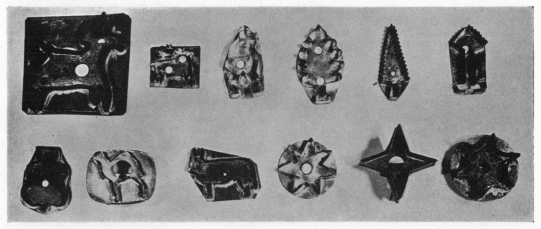

FIG. 3 — CHRISTMAS PATTERNS
Reindeer, Kris Kringle, Christmas trees, bell, camel, sheep, stars

FIG. 4 — ANIMALS AND FISH
Rabbits, dogs, cat, pigs, calf, donkey, goat, squirrel, skunk, bear, fish

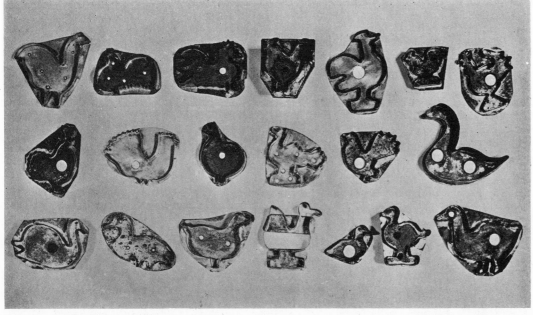

FIG. 5 — DOMESTIC FOWL
Hen, setting hens, roosters, turkey, peacock, guinea hen, bantam, fan-tail pigeon, swans, ducks, ducklings, goose

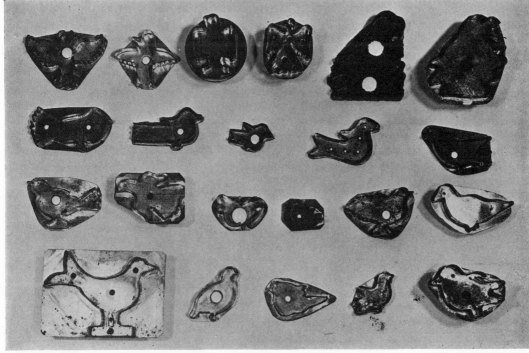

FIG. 6 — BIRDS
Note resemblance of certain forms to birds depicted in *fraktur*

soldering usually goes a much lighter, cheaper quality of tin, and, toward the end of the 1800's, a less elaborate design — a concession to the busy housewife who, in her cookymaking, had little time to bother with hard-to-handle beaks, legs, or wings.

In early examples, made for hard service, the backing was seldom a geometrically cut piece of tin, but was sheared close to the outline of the pattern. A circular, oval, or octagonal backing may safely be considered indicative of late origin, and customarily displays, by way of corroborative evidence, an over-shininess, a thin solder, a design lacking in detail, and few signs of wear. As far as wear is concerned, however, only the most popular of the real Pennsylvania-German cutters are greatly worn, for they were seldom used except at Christmas; and similarly, those which show signs of hardest wear are generally found to be the oldest. Plain circular forms and those with fluted edges served for ordinary occasions, and the "fancy" designs were kept carefully packed away.

Cherished figures must sometimes have been claimed by certain children of the family for their own, for once in a while a scrawled name appears, scratched in an unformed hand. Occasional words in more mature writing indicate, perhaps, a means of identification for other purposes. Still other tokens of ownership are a lightly punched initial, tin-lantern style, an asterisk, or a comparable symbol.

amalgamating ingredient was originally applied by hand, according to what is still known as the soft-solder method. In earlier forms the cutting edge was laid on its backing and the solder was applied in several places along the outer edge. Enough was used to make sure that it would last for time and eternity: a whole cutter will often rust away before a single piece of solder lets go, even though the soldering iron had been used in only a few spots. Later a shinier solder, indicating a higher percentage of tin, was employed, and a smoother, more even coat applied, revealing fewer tool marks. If the entire cutting edge has been secured by a thin, almost invisible line, the chances are that the article is not much more than forty years old. Along with more modern

Variety is likewise to be found in the handles applied to the backing, though they offer relatively little help either in identifying or in authenticating patterns. For the most part, handles were formed by flat strips of tin, the edges more or less neatly turned under for reënforcement, and the whole then curved and fitted to the backing. Some of the earliest examples never had handles. Often handles have been bent out of shape by hard use, and a great many of the oldest ones are missing, though the solder still remains.

An evidence of quality in workmanship is the hole occasionally punched or stamped in the backing. Its purpose was to allow the air to escape when the cutter was applied to the dough.

The perforations range from about an eighth to three quarters of an inch in diameter, and were strategically placed where they would be most useful. Some cutters are carefully supplied with as many as six, while others have only one. Sometimes a supplementary nail hole has been punched by the housewife to facilitate her work. This helps to explain why certain older cutters are found in good condition. Hard-to-handle patterns, such as horses with their four slender legs, ears, long neck, and tail, often exhibit but one perforation, usually in the middle of the back. Obviously making cookies with such cutters took a good deal of time and patience, and punching nail holes was dangerous since the necessary pounding might weaken the solder or bend the cutting edge. Resoldered cutters are probably evidence of an attempt to right this sad condition. The owner's simplest solution to the difficulty, of course, was to use the complicated cutter seldom or never.

Cutting edges range in depth from less than a quarter of an inch to as much as an inch and three quarters. With a few notable exceptions, one finds that the older the cutter, the deeper the cutting edge. Three quarters of an inch seems to have been a satisfactory working dimension. However, the oldest heart form known has a cutting edge less than a quarter of an inch deep, and that of a strange, horselike creature measures just under two inches. In very late forms the cutting depth decreases to three eighths of an inch.

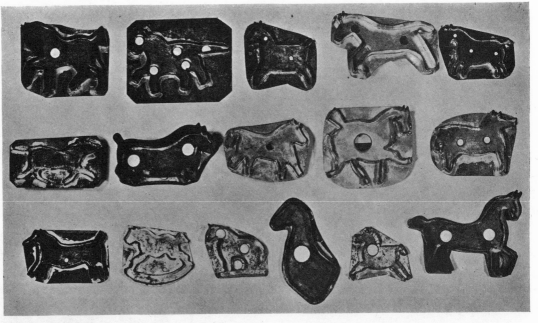

FIG. 7 — HORSES
Galloping, standing still — and rocking

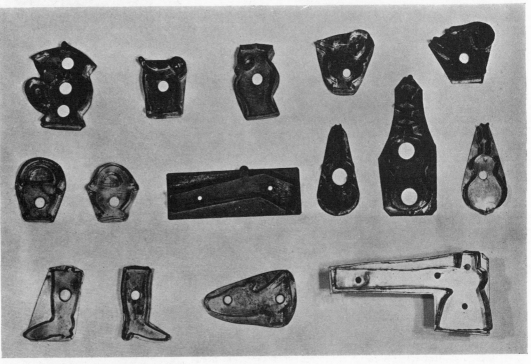

FIG. 8 — DOMESTIC IMPEDIMENTA
Pitchers, coffeepot, baskets, gun, fiddles, boots, shoe, hatchet

Subsidiary cutting edges, set within the pattern outline, were occasionally used. In some cutters the exterior cutting edge and the inset were of exactly the same depth, so that holes could be made through the dough. In others, a shallower inset simply impressed a design upon the cooky's surface. Cut-out and impressed line were sometimes combined, with effective results.

Overall measurements of cooky cutters vary. Some miniatures could be covered by a quarter-dollar; on the other hand, an astounding gingerbread man in the Bucks County Museum stands more than fifteen inches tall, and is, moreover, outfitted with hat, coat, buttons, shoes, pipe, and all the other trimmings. Apparently the smaller sizes were popular, since they show greater signs of wear. Tiny figures seem not to have been used a great deal, perhaps because the housewife could not make rapid progress with them in her baking, perhaps also because nobody wanted to see too small an allotment of cooky fall to his share. The delicate problem of just how many little ducklings equaled a large horse may help to explain why cooky cutters of extreme sizes are in such flourishing condition today.

Naïve in design, humble in origin, inextricably associated with memories of bygone Christmases, a few tin cooky cutters are even today passed about among the great-great-grandchildren of their original owners. Others, retired from active service, are taking their place among informal but appealing collectibles.

Cast-iron cooking vessels

Technological features as a guide to date and source

BY JOHN D. TYLER, *Curator of science, industry, and technology, Pennsylvania Historical and Museum Commission*

Fig. 1.   Bronze pot, seventeenth century or earlier.
Height 6 inches; diameter at lip, 6 inches.
This and Figs. 6 and 7 are in the William Penn Memorial Museum; photographs except Fig. 8 by courtesy of the Pennsylvania Historical and Museum Commission.

LOWLIEST OF household furnishings, the cast-iron cooking pot has been neglected in the many volumes of exhaustive research devoted to more elegant antiques, though information about it is needed by every museum that installs a period fireplace and every collector who wishes to furnish his hearth correctly. A study of basic forms and of certain technological features can provide a means of dating iron vessels, which are rarely marked, and may eventually provide clues to provenance.

Cast iron, that is, iron smelted from the raw ore in a blast furnace and cast in molten form into usable shapes by means of a mold, was first introduced to England shortly before 1500. Prior to that time, and even after, cooking pots and kettles were made of sheet copper beaten to the desired form and soldered together, or cast in bell metal or bronze (Fig. 1). The forms of the earliest cast-iron hollow ware were similar to those of the earlier nonferrous vessels. The development of iron-casting techniques was stimulated by the need for cannon, the result of an increasing use of gunpowder at the end of the Middle Ages. By the late fifteenth century large quantities of shot were being cast in the Ashdown Forest of England, and by the mid-sixteenth century British iron founders were producing cast-iron guns.

Firebacks and a few pots are mentioned from 1547 onward, although the cast-iron pot was not in general use at this early date. The simple flat castings of the time included firebacks, firedogs, branding irons, anvils, hammers, and grave slabs; but the special technique of core casting, necessary for making hollow ware, was not sufficiently perfected to be practical for most of the rather primitive foundries of the day.

By the mid-seventeenth century the cast-iron industry was firmly established in Britain. New items requiring core-molding techniques, notably rollers for crushing sugar cane, were now in production. Nevertheless, British founders had not yet achieved success in the casting of pots that were light and smooth enough for use in the home. Importation of many such vessels from the Low Countries, where foundry technology appears to have been more advanced, continued for some time.

The average iron pot of the seventeenth century, whether from England or the Continent, was very heavy and thick-walled for its size compared to the products of the eighteenth and nineteenth centuries. One characteristic that should be especially noted is the continual decrease in the thickness of the sides of pots from the seventeenth century through the nineteenth. The pot walls also became smoother as casting techniques improved.

René Antoine Ferchault de Réaumur (1683-1757), a Frenchman intensely interested in the science of iron and steel, wrote in 1722 a celebrated treatise, *The Art of Converting Iron into Steel,* in which he explained why the cast-iron pot was not used in the better homes of France. It is a revealing statement:

There are three reasons why cast-iron utensils of this sort have not been adopted for more general use. (1) They always look dirty. Because they are rough both inside and out, it is not easy to clean them. (2) They are thicker than vessels made of forged copper and for that reason more difficult to heat. (3) Finally, they break easily. It would not be easy for the cook to handle them. They must be treated with care; it is risky to rap upon them sharply.

Such was the status of the iron pot in France at the beginning of the eighteenth century, and we may assume that the same objections were voiced elsewhere as well. Nevertheless, the poor householder was forced to use the relatively cheap iron pot, regardless of its drawbacks. Changes in pot-founding technology which would solve most of these problems, however, were already under way in England.

The increasing demand for cooking vessels prompted Abraham Darby of Shropshire to go to Holland in 1704. His original intention was to learn the secrets of brass founding and he planned to set up a foundry on his return. The iron pot usurped his attention, and after a number of failures he finally succeeded in casting iron pots in sand after the fashion of the Dutch. On April 18, 1707, he was granted patent number 380 for:

A new way of casting iron bellied pots, and other iron bellied ware in sand only, without loam or clay, by which iron pots, and other ware may be cast fine [that is, thin, smooth, and lightweight] and with more ease and expedition, and may be afforded cheaper than they can be by the way comonly used, and in regard to their cheapnesse may be of great advantage to the poore of this our kingdome, who for the most part use such ware, and in all probability will prevent the merchants of England going to foreign markets for such ware, from whence great quantities are imported . . .

There are several key phrases in this preamble to Darby's patent. "Their cheapnesse may be of great advantage to the poore . . . who for the most part use such ware" supports Réaumur's statement and indicates that

Fig. 2.   Cast-iron pot, early eighteenth century. Height 6¾ inches; diameter at lip, 7½ inches. *Author's collection.*

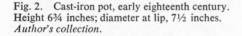

Fig. 3.   Bottom of pot shown in Fig. 2.

221

in England, as well as on the Continent, the well-to-do family used copper or bronze cooking pots. "In all probability will prevent the merchants of England going to foreign markets" proves the source of most vessels in use in Britain at that time to have been Continental. Consequently, we should not expect to find today many seventeenth-century British iron pots, though they were produced in limited numbers.

The mention of "iron bellied pots" in the patent indicates the shape, which remained standard with minor variations throughout the eighteenth century. This was a full-bodied, three-legged, cordon-bound form distinctly different from that of the pot of the preceding century (*cf.* Figs. 1, 2). A distinction should be made between the terms pot and kettle. The *Oxford English Dictionary,* quoting the mid-eighteenth-century edition of Samuel Johnson's *Dictionary,* says: "In the kitchen the name of pot is given to the boiler that grows narrower towards the top, and of kettle to that which grows wider." Both forms had been made from the earliest times, and continued into the nineteenth century (*cf.* Figs. 2, 4). Pots tended to be no larger than twelve gallons; kettles frequently reached sizes of thirty gallons or more, especially in the early nineteenth century. These massive butchering or potash kettles are most commonly found today filled with growing petunias.

The most important phrase in Darby's patent was "in sand only." He made a significant contribution with the introduction of molds of dry sand encompassed by three-part wooden molding boxes, or flasks, for the casting of pots. Previously all pots had been molded in damp loam, a technique that required the total destruction of the mold to remove the finished product. In loam molding the basic shape of the core, or pot interior, was built up of rope wound around a central tapered rod, or spindle, then covered with loam and shaved with a wooden

pattern to the exact form desired. This was baked, dusted with a layer of charcoal or lampblack, and given a second layer of loam. This layer of loam determined the wall thickness of the vessel. After a further dusting of charcoal, a third layer of loam was applied to form the outer shell of the mold. The mold was then baked again to fix its shape and hardness. For a bellied pot the outer layer of loam was slit vertically down one side, under the bottom, and up the opposite side to the rim. The mold could then be removed in two halves. The middle layer of loam was scraped away, the two halves were reunited, and, after being trussed together, the mold was ready to receive the molten iron. When the central spindle was removed, it left a hole through which the iron could be poured into the mold. The hole and the residue left at the hole once the iron solidified were both known as the sprue. The loam mold had to be broken in order to remove the finished pot, so that the making of another pot involved the same tedious process all over again.

Pots made by this method have a vertical seam where the two halves of the mold met, and they retain a small projection on the bottom where the sprue was broken off (Fig. 3). Since the loam molding technique was the usual way of making pots until Darby's time, most, if not all, produced prior to 1707 have a vertical seam and usually a round sprue.

Darby's method consisted of using a wooden flask filled with fine, dry sand of a certain cohesive type in which the form of the pot was impressed by a wooden pattern in three sections (bottom and two sides), so that the pot could be removed without disrupting as much of the molding equipment. The process was more precise and produced smoother and lighter pots.

Early Darby pots had a round sprue, indicating that cores were still being formed of loam over rope in the older manner. The Darby accounts reveal that sand and

Fig. 4. Cast-iron kettle, early nineteenth century.
Height 5⅝₁₆ inches; diameter at lip, 6¾ inches.
Author's collection.

Fig. 5. Bottom of kettle shown in Fig. 4.

Fig. 6.   Cast-iron pot, c. 1830.
Height 9¾ inches; diameter at lip, 11½ inches.

Fig. 7.   Cast-iron pot, 1850-1860.
Height 10 inches; diameter at lip, 12½ inches.

loam were sometimes used together for castings, and that some molds and cores were baked.

Pots that have a round sprue, yet also bear marks indicating the use of a three-part mold, must be among the earliest made by Darby's method, and in general can be said to date from the first half of the eighteenth century. There is a pot in the collection of the William Penn Memorial Museum which has a round sprue, covered by an elongated protruding strip of metal called a gate, which exemplifies loam molding of the core in combination with pattern molding of the exterior. The gate was essentially a better form of sprue (Fig. 5), and the name applies similarly to both the hole and the residue left at it. The round sprue was difficult to break off after casting without cracking the pot. By utilizing a narrow, elongated slit, or gate, through which to pour in the molten metal the founder was able to insure proper breakage when the iron cooled. Increasing use of patterns and flasks made the loam-molded core with its round spindle obsolete by the mid-eighteenth century, and the round sprue soon disappeared. The gate will be found on the majority of pots and kettles available today. Small vessels have a single gate, while larger kettles and caldrons often have two.

Some exceptions should be noted. Large potash kettles of the early nineteenth century, cast in a loam mold in the "lip up" position, will have a round spruelike projection at bottom center. This is not a true sprue, but merely the mark left by the rotation of the molding board during the making of the mold.

Other large kettles and pots of the same period are frequently found with three smaller sprues located, not in the center, but as far from it as the legs, each sprue halfway between two legs. These are invariably pattern-molded in sand, and have either the three-part-mold marks, if a pot; or a two-piece, horizontal mark, if a kettle.

Since most pots made before 1800 are not marked, it is often impossible to determine their provenance. It may be possible, however, to determine whether a pot is of European or American origin by an analysis of the physical properties of the metal.

A fuel is needed to fire the blast furnace where cast iron is produced, and until 1709 in England, and up to about 1855 in the United States, charcoal was the fuel generally used. Timber, which was required for making charcoal, was at a premium from the sixteenth century onwards in England, and by the beginning of the eighteenth century a substitute fuel was desperately needed. Darby solved the problem in 1709 by developing the use of coke, a product obtained by distilling coal. By the 1750's coke-fueled ironworks were the rule in Britain.

In America all ironworks used charcoal until the late 1830's, but by 1855 more were using coke than charcoal. Those continuing to use charcoal had ceased to produce the smaller items that had been their mainstay in the eighteenth century, and were instead turning out pig iron for railroad-car wheels or for rolls used in rolling mills, where metal plates and bars were manufactured. The making of stoves, pots, and the like was left to individual foundries which purchased pig iron from coke furnaces to remelt and cast into useful objects.

A sample taken from the gate of a pot or kettle, when subjected to spectrographic analysis, will reveal whether charcoal or coke iron was used. If the pot has an eighteenth- or early nineteenth-century form and is made of charcoal iron, we may safely assume it to be American. If, however, its form is of that period and its material is coke iron, it is probably English.

The usual way to date pots has been to examine and compare forms. Seventeenth-century pots were bellied and often had three faceted legs. Those made in the next century were also bellied but had three simpler triangular legs tapering almost to a point. Small pots, such as sauce pots, often had longer legs so that they could be set above coals on the hearth; larger caldrons had short, stubby legs only long enough to keep them from tipping over when set down, for they were made to hang on hooks from a crane or lug pole. In general the legs became more stubby as time went on, until by the early nineteenth century they were no more than half-inch projections on the bottom of the pot (Fig. 6). By 1850 hollow-ware cooking vessels were being made to fit into the tops of the new cookstoves and the legs disappeared entirely, replaced by an inset bottom (Fig. 7).

The shape of the body of pots also changed, from the bulbous to the cylindrical. By about 1830 the bulbous pot was on its way to becoming the cylinder of the 1850's (cf. Figs. 6, 7).

Another point for comparison is the shape of the ear, or handle attachment. Pots of the seventeenth century and earlier have large, angular ears, cast in two pieces and joined at the bend. Later examples retain the angularity, but the size is diminished (cf. Figs. 1, 2). By the early nineteenth century the ear had become a rounded, thickened projection resembling a cow's horn (Figs. 6, 7).

Two types of pot frequently found today should be recognized as of later production. One is the so-called gypsy pot, a bulbous form cast in sand in a three-part mold but with one difference from the normal pattern-molded pot: the mold joints run completely around its perimeter and are all therefore horizontal rather than vertical. A close look is required to see these marks, since they usually occur at a cordon or at the beginning of the flare of the lip. Such pots were made in the South and in England during the mid-nineteenth century, and generally have a capacity number cast on them. They are being sold in large numbers today.

The other type is, in form, exactly like the pots of the seventeenth century and earlier, and comes from Spain, Portugal, or Italy (Fig. 8). This sort often has faceted legs, a round sprue, and vertical mold marks and was apparently made by the old method of loam casting. On many, however, the ears have been cast in halves vertically rather than horizontally and are located exactly at the vertical seam on the pot. Examples of this type are often stamped with a maker's trade mark that appears to be of nineteenth-century date, and usually their weight betrays their recent origin, for they are lighter than genuine early pots.

With the advent of the cookstove in the 1850's the classic iron pot became outmoded and soon disappeared, except in remote hunting or mining camps, where more primitive conditions prevailed. Farmers continued to use the larger varieties in hog butchering or in making apple butter, but the day of the cast-iron cooking pot was past.

Fig. 8. Cast-iron pot, apparently nineteenth century, Iberian. Height 7⅝ inches; diameter at lip, 4⅞ inches. Both pot and lid are stamped 30. *Collection of Edward F. LaFond.*

The American copper teakettle

BY HENRY J. KAUFFMAN

THE CONTEMPORARY ANTIQUE market place is being flooded with recent imports from Europe. Such importation focuses attention on the obvious fact that American antiques are increasingly scarce, and yet to many collectors they are of more interest, if not more importance, than those of European origin. This abundance from abroad and scarcity of indigenous antiques points up the need for reliable criteria by which to differentiate between the native and the imported.

The problem of distinguishing between metal objects is particularly acute, because there is so little difference in their inherent color and texture. Many antique metals, moreover, from both domestic and foreign sources lack makers' touch marks to indicate their place of origin. Even when they are present these identifying symbols or impressions are not always conclusive, and one must rely on stylistic differences in making an attribution.

Large quantities of early copper teakettles of English and Continental origin have been imported of late. Since the domestic production was never large, the identification and classification of the characteristics of the American copper teakettle take on particular importance today. Sometimes the differences between the native and the foreign are extremely subtle. A close scrutiny of some outstanding examples of early American craftsmanship in this metal may help to isolate the distinguishing features that should be watched for, particularly by the young collector.

The surest means of determining the origin of a teakettle, of course, is the maker's name on the strap handle. This touch mark is on occasion difficult to decipher; both the natural oxidation of the copper and the abrasion of harsh cleaning compounds have worked through time to decrease legibility. Sometimes the strike of the maker's die was uneven or defective to begin with.

But not all kettles are marked. So far as I have been able to estimate, there are three or four times as many unmarked examples. When the maker's name does appear, it is without exception on the handle, and almost always on the topside. (In the one exception I know of, where the name appears on the underside of the handle, one could surmise that the coppersmith inadvertently attached the handle upside down.)

In the eighteenth century most of these makers' impressions were made with intaglio dies. The dies themselves were made of tool steel, with the lettering of the name cut in reverse. The dies were held against the handle and given a hard blow with a hammer while the metal was cold. Sometimes the strike was uneven, particularly if the maker's name was long, such as Schlosser or Morrison. To improve an imperfect impression, a maker would sometimes give the die a second blow which frequently resulted in a double or blurred impression. Most marked teakettles carry only a name, but there are examples of dies that also include a town or city.

During the late eighteenth century and into the early nineteenth, craftsmen bought and assembled individual dies of block letters; this added a certain versatility to the touch marks on later teakettles. Some coppersmiths added to their names and towns their street addresses, while others included the year and the capacity of the

Copper teakettle made by G. Reed of Winchester, Virginia. From a variety of sources it is known that Reed was born in Ireland in 1766, settled in Winchester in 1788, and died in 1849. In addition to being a coppersmith he was a Methodist preacher, mayor of Winchester, and magistrate and high sheriff of Frederick County, Maryland. His name is imprinted on the handle of the kettle (see detail). The kettle is rather more bulbous than most of those made on the eastern seaboard. Note its attractive tapering spout and its handle in a clover-leaf design. *Colonial Williamsburg.*

A very large kettle made by John Getz (early 1800's) of Lancaster, Pennsylvania, and a very small one which is unmarked. The small one has a diameter of five and one-half inches and the large one, twelve inches. Detail shows the intaglio mark of John Getz in plain cartouche; some marks are in cartouches with scalloped edges. The pleasing hand-wrought texture of the surface of the handle is evident. *Collection of Mrs. Robert McMurtrie.*

kettle. The impression made by the individual letters is usually deeper than that made by a single intaglio die. One example is known on which a maker stamped his name in block letters over the earlier touch, worn down by years of polishing, of a previous coppersmith. In a few cases names were engraved on the handles; one craftsman of Reading, Pennsylvania, named Kidd is well known for marking his kettles by this method.

Another means of distinguishing between American and European teakettles is through a comparison of their stylistic differences. Most imported ones have come from either England or one of the Scandinavian countries. Teakettles from the latter have flat handles and only on rare occasions are found with the makers' names stamped on them; and when marked, they have generally been stamped with individual letter dies rather than with an intaglio die. English examples usually have cast-brass handles and are therefore without flat surfaces on which the makers' names could have been struck.

Identifications made on the basis of style are, to be sure, less reliable than those from makers' marks. Yet it is an established fact that a distinctive type of teakettle

did develop in America. Even the numerous Pennsylvania coppersmiths of German birth failed to imitate faithfully the styles of their native country. Rather, the craftsman working in America, no matter what his origins, produced a kettle with pronounced differences from European examples, particularly in the critical areas of the lid, spout, and profile of the body. When one compares the American and Scandinavian types, for example, one perceives a noticeable flare in the body of the American kettle; and the Scandinavian spout is usually hinged, a feature rarely, if ever, found on those of domestic manufacture. The gooseneck spout found in America seems to derive its form from English sources. The American kettle shows a closer relationship with the Dutch than with any other European product, yet even these are so different that there is little chance of confusing the two. Many Dutch kettles were of brass rather than copper, and I have never heard of an American one of brass.

Another outstanding feature of American copper kettles is the range of sizes in which they were made: while they are all of more or less the same shape, some have a capacity as large as two gallons, while others hold about a pint. All are distinguished by workmanship of the highest quality. Hasty finishing and poor joining can generally be blamed on a later repairman; the early craftsman took obvious pride in the neatness of his seam when joining metals. It should be pointed out, however, that the basic pattern of construction in a kettle is not unique to any one area or time period. Joining by dovetails (similar in appearance to those used in cabinetmaking, though lacking the flared shape of the tenon) is a traditional device used by coppersmiths not only in eighteenth-century America but also in twentieth-century Scandinavia.

Most extant teakettles of early American origin seem to have been made in the East in the region between Boston and North Carolina, and as far west as Ohio.

Copper teakettle by J. Dunn of New York City. John Dunn and Sons are listed as coppersmiths in the New York City directory of 1831-1832. Without the name this kettle would be regarded as a typical product of a Pennsylvania coppersmith. *Collection of John P. Remensnyder.*

The kettle by Geddes and Stewart of Baltimore, Maryland, also closely resembles the typical product of Pennsylvania craftsmen. The manner of imprinting the name on the handle suggests late production—certainly not in the eighteenth century. *Remensnyder collection.*

Typical Scandinavian copper teakettle, nineteenth century. The flat handle stamped with the single letter O, the straight-sided body, and the hinged spout proclaim its Scandinavian origin. *Collection of Richard S. Machmer.*

Pennsylvania was particularly prolific. The famous Boston coppersmith William C. Hunneman made a typical product, as did a number of Virginia coppersmiths, including G. Reed of Winchester. The inspiration of construction and design features used by Reed could have come down the Shenandoah Valley from the larger and more practiced Pennsylvania school.

A survey of coppersmithing in early America focuses attention on both the products and the men who made them. There is little doubt that the teakettle that evolved in this country is unique in the profile of its shape, its construction details, and its decorative features. Once established, the style became traditional and underwent little change for a century, from 1750 to 1850. Even perceptible regional differences, common in so many antiques, seem to be missing. The humble American copper teakettle can easily elicit our admiration for its beauty of line and richness of color and texture.

Latten Spoons of the Pilgrims

BY PERCY E. RAYMOND

AMONG the actual possessions of the original Pilgrim settlers which have been unearthed by the restoration work now being carried on at Plymouth are latten spoons. Examination of the specimens discovered sheds new light on some rare early utensils.

Latten, also written in old records as lattin, lattyn, laton, or laiton, is sheet brass. Brass as a compound of copper and zinc was not made in England until the latter part of the sixteenth century. Before that time it had been imported in sheets from Germany and from the Netherlands, chiefly for use in the monumental brasses of churches and cathedrals.

Spoons made from it on the Continent were imported to England as early as the fourteenth century. So far as is known, John God was the first to make them in that country, in 1578, thereby bringing upon himself the wrath of the Court of the Worshipful Company of Pewterers, who ordered that there "should Be no spones made of Bras or latten or any yelow metall." Nevertheless, God seems to have continued to make them, and during the next century many other spoonmakers joined in the nefarious occupation.

"Alkemie" spoons, as they were also called, were highly prized by the American colonists, and are rated in many inventories as of greater value than pewter ones. Henry Shrimpton of Boston, "Brayser" and pewterer, had them on sale before his death in 1666. It would be interesting to know whether he made any.

Nearly all spoons, whether of silver or base metal, made between the mid-fourteenth and the mid-seven-

Fig. 2—*Left to right:* (*a*) The stalk of a Puritan spoon, showing the typical nicks at the end. (*b*) The upper end of a primitive trifid spoon. (*c*) A slip-top spoon with flattened handle. (*d*) An implement made from a broken stalk. All from the Josiah Winslow site.

Fig. 1—Two tinned seal-tops from the Josiah Winslow site, with an older, untinned one between them.

teenth centuries had fig-shaped bowls, shallow, rather flat, wide at the front, and narrow where they joined the stalk. During their evolution, the bowl tended to become more and more oblong, till an oval shape was reached which had the greatest width in the middle rather than near the front. The stalk was slender, hexagonal in section and, in most cases, had a knop of some sort at the upper end. Spoons with a flat, circular knop are called seal-top.

Seal-top spoons show numerous variations, identified by technical terms. At the top of the stalk is the flat seal, in most cases circular. Below it is a knop, which may be definitely lobate, melon-shaped, incised by vertical grooves; or be a smooth sphere. Below this is the upper annulus, a narrow button-like ring. Below this some specimens have a four-faced ornamental knop, with a stemmed rose on each side. This may be called the flowered support. Beneath it is the lower annulus, or, more rarely, two lower annuli. The specimens without the flowered support have slenderer stalks than those with it, and seem not to have been made after about 1650. These are called the short type by F. G. Hilton Price in his *Old Base Metal Spoons* (London, 1908), the best source of information on the subject. Spoons with the flowered support he calls the long type.

The seal-top was popular from the mid-1500's till the reign of Charles II. The early seal-tops, mostly pewter, had hexagonal stalks, but a tendency toward flattening developed rapidly during the seventeenth century, and those made after about 1650 have flat handles. Some are six-sided, some almost rectangular, and a few oval in section *(see Fig. 1)*.

The only early spoon without a knop is the "slipped-in-the-stalk," or "slip-top," which first appeared early in the sixteenth century. The upper end of the stalk is obliquely truncated—slipped in the horticultural sense *(Fig. 3, left)*. This produced a handle difficult to grip, yet the type was popular for two hundred years. Those happen to have been years before forks came into common table use; is it possible that the owners of slip-tops brought both ends into service?

A probable derivative of this type was the Puritan spoon, made in silver as early as 1651. This was the first in which the greatest width was in the middle of the bowl, and the first to have a wide, strong handle.

It was succeeded by the trifid or *pied-de-biche* spoon, whose handle end was notched to form three lobes. The trifid came from France with Charles II, and was not of British descent. Records of 1663 mention the "new-fashioned" spoons. They were stronger than the older ones, for the handle was broader, and the back of the bowl was stiffened by a rat-tail.

Two sorts of spoons, the seal-top and the slip-top, seem to have been favored by the Pilgrims and their descendants. Since both were made over a long period of years, it is difficult to date individual specimens. The worn condition of the bowls of most of the seal-tops found on the Winslow site at Marshfield gives evidence of hard usage: the Pilgrims scraped the iron pot as well as the wooden trencher. These specimens show too that the slender stalks were easily broken. One long fragment *(Fig. 2, right)* had been converted into another implement, possibly a fork or skewer, by filing the sides and end.

It will be noted that this latten handle has two

annuli beneath the flowered support, an unusual feature. At Pilgrim Hall in Plymouth there is a complete specimen of this sort *(Fig. 3, right)*. It now shows no tin, but the touch says *"Double Whited."*

Plating latten spoons with tin, presumably to make them more like silver, became customary some time during the seventeenth century. The words *Double Whited* or *Double Tinned* were included in many touches. Probably the spoons so marked were plated by dipping twice into molten tin. We need more definite information as to when the tinning of latten spoons was adopted. Price says "about the middle of the seventeenth century." Only one tinned fragment was found at the Pilgrim Eel River site, which, so far as other evidence goes, was abandoned before 1660. This is part of a seal-top, with flattened handle *(Fig. 5)*. It bears a touch, RT below a rose, previously noted by Price on pewter slip-tops which he assigned to the sixteenth century.

Fig. 3—*Left*, the only known "engine-made" latten spoon, with the unrecorded mark of Daniel Barton. Both in Pilgrim Hall, Plymouth. *Right*, a seal-top with two lower annuli.

Fig. 4—*Left*, the bowl of a Puritan spoon, from the Winslow site. *Center*, terminal of a "short" seal-top from Eel River. *Right*, the bowl of a seal-top from the Indian burial ground at Kingston, Massachusetts (Peabody Museum, Harvard University). Note the typical "three-spoon" touches.

The Eel River site yielded a fragment of the upper end of one of the "short" seal-tops *(Fig. 4)*. Beneath the seal there are a plain ball and single annulus. Since the stalk is very slender, rounded-hexagonal, and not tinned, this fragment is definitely older than any of the "long" specimens. It was probably extant in 1620, although there is no indication that it came on the *Mayflower*.

An entire spoon of this type is in Pilgrim Hall. It is 5¾ inches long, and has an unusually narrow fig-shaped bowl. The Worcester Historical Society has a splendid bright yellow example, marked with a fleur-de-lis, the Paris touch. It is exactly like one with the same touch figured by Price, which he considered to be late sixteenth or early seventeenth century.

A complete, little-worn, tinned specimen of a slipped-in-the-stalk spoon was found at the Winslow site *(Fig. 2c)*. It has a rounded fig-shaped bowl, and a flattened, but six-sided stalk. It shows one of the transition stages from slip-top to Puritan type, but had not yet acquired the oval bowl of the latter.

At Pilgrim Hall there is a yellow slip-top which was found in the subcellar of an old house in Kingston *(Fig. 3, left)*. The bowl is typically fig-shaped, 2¾ by 2 inches, and the 4¼-inch stalk is six-sided, flattened, with a uniform width of ¼ inch. The touch is shield-shaped, with the date *1687* above the initials DB.

This spoon is of particular interest, because of both its shape and its maker. It proves conclusively that slip-tops with fig-shaped bowls were made almost up to the end of the 1600's, whereas Mr. Price tells us that at about the middle of that century the bowl became oval. This statement has lured us into supposing that any slip-top with a fig-shaped bowl was made before 1650. The DB of this hitherto unknown touch was doubtless Daniel Barton, pewterer and spoonmaker in London from 1670 to 1699 at least. He made silver and latten spoons, along with the usual run of pewter utensils. In 1687 he began making spoons with an "engine" (press ?), and Welch tells us in his *History* that his fellow spoonmakers complained of him for the new practice. However, he convinced the Company's Court that his spoons were well finished, and he undertook not to sell them in the country for less than six shillings a gross, nor in London for less than four. Apparently he was allowed to continue on condition that he adopt a new touch for the engine-made product. This is the only specimen of the "engine-made" spoon so far recorded, and the only example known with this touch.

Puritan spoons are represented at the Winslow site only by fragments, and at the Eel River site not at all. A typical Puritan stalk, 4½ inches long, ⅜ inch wide at the top and 5/16 inch wide where broken from the bowl, is rectangular in section, and bears the characteristic three grooves at the top *(Fig. 2a)*. There is also an elliptical bowl with a part of the handle *(Fig. 4, left)*. Both are tinned, and the touch in the bowl, three spoons between the initials GP, is listed by Price as occurring on latten Puritan spoons, but also on trifids.

The one fragment of a trifid spoon is the upper part of a handle, rounded at the end, with two shallow notches. The present length is 3½ inches, and it is ¾ inch across at the top *(Fig. 2b)*. It is unusually thin and flat, the stalk rectangular in section, and is one of the most primitive types of trifid known.

For permission to study the latten spoons so far found at Plymouth, I am grateful to Henry Hornblower II, President of the Plimoth Plantation, Inc., who excavated the site of the Governor Josiah Winslow House at Green Harbor, and that of an earlier Pilgrim at Eel River; Sidney Strickland, architect of the project, who excavated the foundations of the John Howland house at Rocky Nook; and Warren Strong, Keeper of the Cabinet at Pilgrim Hall.

Fig. 5—A fragmentary seal-top, with the RT touch. From the Eel River site.

Specimens from the Winslow and Eel River sites are in the collection of Henry Hornblower II. Photographs, except Figure 3, by Frederick P. Orchard.

BRASS

TOBACCO

BOXES

By KATHARINE MORRISON McCLINTON

THE BRASS AND COPPER TOBACCO BOXES of Holland and Germany are both decorative and useful, and they offer historical sidelights to the collector. While the German boxes relate largely to the glory of war, the Dutch boxes give the story of the quiet peaceful life and the interests of the Dutch sailor, small merchant, or housewife.

The Dutch boxes are made of copper or brass or a combination of the two. They are from four to six inches in length and two to three inches wide, according to shape, and are about one and one half inches in depth. They are oval, circular, rectangular, octagonal, or of book shape. Some few date from the seventeenth century, but most of them were made in the eighteenth. They were also copied later for the tourist trade.

The Dutch boxes were usually engraved. Most oval boxes have borders of floral scrolls or raised rope-like borders, and the scenes or inscriptions are placed within ovals, circles, or cartouches. Sometimes the workmanship is very crude and the inscriptions are in colloquial Dutch.

Some of the engraved scenes depict religious subjects, such as the Crucifixion, the Resurrection, Adam and Eve, Queen Esther, or the saints of the Catholic church (*Fig. 1*). Mythological subjects are also seen — Venus and Amor, Neptune, and others. Sometimes both religious and secular scenes appear on a single box, while boxes with secular scenes only offer wide variety. Depictions of the bear pit show one of the interests of the people, while tavern scenes and street scenes, hunting scenes, ships and landscapes, historic events, and local customs are the simple subject matter of other boxes. Drinking or tavern scenes and pictures of the sailor and his sweetheart were among the most popular.

The inscriptions are as varied as the scenes, and often though not always related to them. One box is inscribed *Oh my beautiful mistress*; another, showing a man and woman and servant in a cart, reads *Is it not fine to have a cart and horses in this world*. A scene of a departing traveler and a ship has the inscription, *I am sailing like a hero to faraway lands, / Were it not for money I should prefer to remain quietly here*. This is probably a sailor's box, as is another engraved on one side with a countryside and on the reverse with ships, and the inscription *I kiss my beloved on the land and by the sea*. A finely wrought rectangular box of this type in the Metropolitan Museum of Art, with chased and engraved borders, inlaid brass sides, and inlaid panel in the lid, is inscribed, *A deceptive tongue is vicious. It brings nobody anything*. A brass book-shaped box has incised panels showing a man and woman and the inscription, *Goett Begin — Goett Bekage (Good beginning — good ending)*.

Another type of oval brass box has molded and corded edges, engraved floral borders, and coats of arms or monograms engraved on the tops and bottoms. Oblong brass boxes with a perpetual calendar top and bottom are rare; they were made as early as the sixteenth century in Holland. They were also made in the eighteenth century in Germany.

Most of the Dutch boxes were made at Amsterdam. Occasionally the decoration was the work of accomplished engravers, such as Johannes Bernardus Barckhuyzen, an engraver at the mint in Amsterdam in the eighteenth century. Rarely, however, was the engraving on Dutch boxes signed.

Brass and copper tobacco boxes were made in Germany between about 1750 and 1780, at Iserlohn, an ancient metal manufacturing town in Westphalia, and at Elberfeld, a center of metal manufacture near Düsseldorf. These boxes were of the same materials as the Dutch boxes, and were almost always oblong with curved ends, the sides formed by a twelve-inch strip of copper curved and joined. The tops and bottoms, of brass, usually carried embossed rather than engraved designs. For the most part the decoration consists of portraits and battle scenes with rococo embellishments (*Fig. 3*). The battle scenes are usually drawn from the Silesian or Seven Years' War and show the triumphs of Frederick the Great over the French, Austrians, and Russians, though scenes from the Russo-Turkish wars also occur. Portraits, besides that of Frederick the Great, include those of Ferdinand of Brunswick, George II, and George III, Marshall Daum, the Princess of Orange, Maria Theresa, and Francis of Lorraine.

The battle scenes are similar and without the inscriptions one could not be distinguished from the other. The usual pattern placed a large battle scene in the center space with an inscription below, and round medallion portraits at either end; sometimes the center space was given to the medallion portraits and the battle scenes were put in small spaces at the ends; again, coats of arms replaced the battle scenes and the rest of the surface was covered with rocaille decorations.

The designs of these boxes show an interesting relationship in both subject matter and treatment to the decorations of glassware made in Nüremberg, Silesia, and Bohemia throughout the eighteenth century. Battle scenes, medallion portraits of Frederick the Great inscribed *Vivat Fredericus Borussorum*, hunting scenes, pictures of ladies and gentlemen at a tea or dinner party, and the rococo embellishments are almost the same on both. The inference to be drawn is that the inspiration for the box decoration came from the glass, since many of the old goblets and covered glasses date early in the 1700's while the boxes were not made before the middle of the century.

Another type of subject matter used in the decoration of German tobacco boxes relates to the life of the times, but to court life rather than to that of the sailor or farmer, as on the Dutch boxes. Scenes of boar and deer hunting with dogs and mounted riders and forest backgrounds, set within rocaille decorations, are especially interesting. But perhaps most appropriate of all the decorations are some small cartouches framing smoking-party scenes. Frederick William II of Prussia had a smoking club in 1740, setting the style for such entertainment. As the fashion for smoking spread, the brass tobacco box grew in popularity — and many surviving specimens must have been used at such genial gatherings.

The workmanship of the boxes varies. The same design is often found on different boxes, sometimes well placed, sometimes with its edges overlapping the top cover, and on some the lettering is so near the edge that the tops of the letters are cut off. The embossing is sometimes fine and clear, sometimes not rounded or clear-cut. The majority of the boxes were signed with the artist's or maker's name or initials and often the place of manufacture. Signatures that may be encountered are: *J. H. Hamer, fecit*, listed as working in Iserlohn in 1760. *John. Hen. Giese, Giese, Johan Hendrich Giese, John. Henr. Giese — Iserlohn*, for Johann Heinrich Giese, engraver of Iserlohn in 1756. *J. Henry Becker*, or *J. Henrich Becker f.*, also of Iserlohn. *Keppelman* was Johan Adolph Keppelman of Iserlohn. *JAKM* or *Jadma*, also found on Iserlohn work, may also be Keppelman signatures. *H & W/D & H/ Elberfeld*, usually found with the date 1759, was the signature of workers as yet unidentified.

Undoubtedly some of these boxes were made for Dutch trade since they have inscriptions in Dutch rather than German, and even Dutch scenes, though carrying signatures of the German artists and often also the name of the place of manufacture.

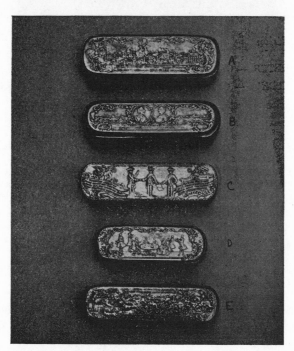

VIII   Surveys, Introductions, Regional Studies

Brought together in this last section are articles which discuss metals in general and are based on the materials from which the objects were made. These articles serve as an appropriate conclusion to the volume. The methods of the tinsmith, coppersmith, and blacksmith are explained along with their wares. Dean A. Fales, Jr., discusses a number of documented pieces of American brass and copper which are in the collection of the Henry Francis du Pont Winterthur Museum. Two other articles explore ironwork made in places which are quite dissimilar in time and location, Jamestown and the state of Ohio. The early Virginia work is unmistakably English in form; that of Ohio evidences its English antecedents but also shows what changes have been wrought by two hundred years of use and manufacture in North America.

THE BLACKSMITH WAS ONE OF THE FIRST and most essential of American craftsmen. James Read, blacksmith, came to Virginia with the Jamestown colonists in May 1607; in the very next year another blacksmith arrived, and four more were among the badly needed "mechanicks" sent out by the Virginia Company of London in 1611. In 1789 a business directory of Boston lists two coppersmiths, three braziers, five founders, two silversmiths, seven tin-plate workers, seven farriers, and four pewterers, but blacksmiths reach the amazing total of twenty-five. Nevertheless, little is known about the personalities or the products of those early artisans.

It has frequently been said that in the center of each early settlement a portion of ground was allotted free to the smith for his shop and residence. That such a practice did exist is indicated by this excerpt from Samuel Orcutt's *History of the Old Town of Derby, Connecticut, 1642-1880:*

"Voted that the town grant John Smith of Milford, blacksmith, four acres of land for a home lot, to build upon, anywhere within one mile of the meeting house where he shall choose, in land not laid out, upon the condition that he build a mansion house and smith's shop, and set up the trade of blacksmith, and follow it for the benefit of the inhabitants of the town for the space of seven years." To this day near the center of many a small town along the eastern seaboard the old blacksmith's shop can still be seen, now converted to the service of horseless buggies.

The blacksmith was trained in much the same way as other early craftsmen. He usually served an apprenticeship of seven to nine years before his twenty-first birthday. If he was apprenticed to his father (as was customary in the eighteenth century), he often continued to work with him and then succeeded him, following the pattern which kept a business in one family through many generations.

The customary apprenticeship training is indicated by an advertisement from the *Pennsylvania Packet and Daily Advertiser* of August 1, 1789:

"WANTED *at* [Delaware] *works,*/APPRENTICES from ten to fourteen years of age, to learn the Nailing and Smith's business. The boys will be placed under the direction of sober, industrious workmen, and will be suitably cloathed and fed during their apprenticeship; and instructed in reading, writing and arithmetic; and when of age will each receive one new suit of cloaths, and fifteen dollars in money, for the purpose of furnishing themselves with a set of tools."

The blacksmith's most frequent medium was charcoal iron, a material famous for its malleability, its resistance to rust, and its adaptability to welding on the forge. It was obtained from a city merchant, a rolling mill, or a

Skimmer, fork, and ladle. Such utensils were usually made in sets of three with matched handles, sometimes entirely of iron, occasionally of copper and iron, frequently of brass and iron. This skimmer has a brass bowl and plain iron handle, stamped on the back *F. B. S. Canton, O. Pat. Jan. 26, 86.* The iron fork has a brass plate applied at top of handle, stamped *L. Bauman;* probably made in Lancaster or Lebanon County, Pennsylvania. The ladle has a brass bowl attached to the iron handle by three rivets. The ridge down the middle of the handle is the mark of a blacksmith who worked in central Pennsylvania, where a number of similar sets have been found. *Author's collection.*

blacksmith

BY HENRY J. KAUFFMAN

forge, in a variety of sizes. On special occasions the smith would use Swedish iron, which was regarded by Moxon, in his treatise called *Mechanick Exercises* (London, 1703), as the finest for forging purposes.

By heating and hammering the blacksmith refined and reshaped the mass of stock into objects of utility and sometimes beauty. His hearth was usually built of brick and covered by a hovel which conducted the smoke to the chimney. His tools were arranged around the hearth within ready reach. The major tools as enumerated by Moxon were bellows, anvil, tongs, sledge or hammer, file, vise, and workbench. There were also chisels, hardies, race wheels, mandrels, hand vises, and the specialized equipment for horses.

What did the early blacksmith make? The answer varies with each community and every period. For example, a smith in a small agricultural community early in the eighteenth century might make and repair farm equipment, while a century later another smith in the same town, even working in the same shop, might be producing grills and railings for houses or shoeing horses for hard city streets.

What we can learn from surviving daybooks and newspaper advertisements indicates that most smiths did primarily repair and replacement work. These were the general blacksmiths, but more interesting to us today are the specialists. Their products fell into such categories as nails, tools, window grills, railings, fences, shipwork, and even guns. The advertisement of William Perkins, blacksmith, in the *Pennsylvania Packet and Daily Advertiser* for July 7, 1789, offers "Wood or Falling Axes, Broad Axes, Adzes, Carpenters Mauls, Hatchets of different kinds, Ditching or Banking Shovels, Weeding or Corn

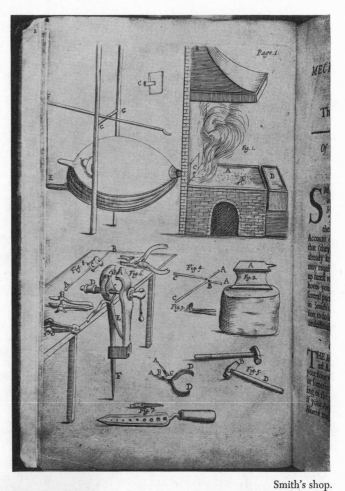

Smith's shop.
From *Mechanick Exercises* by Joseph Moxon,
London, 1703.
Colonial Williamsburg, Inc.

Nineteenth-century blacksmith's shop,
reproduced at the
New Jersey State Museum, Trenton,
as part of the
New Jersey Iron 1674-1850 exhibition
held May 16-October 31, 1954.

Suffolk latch, marked *D. King*, from a house in Massachusetts built by a blacksmith named D. King. The design is a variant of the ball and spear motif used in Massachusetts and Connecticut. All the edges are carefully filed and the latch is of fine quality. Signed latches of this type are extremely rare. *Worcester Historical Society.*

Weathervane from an old mill near Chester, Pennsylvania. The initials are for William Penn, Samuel Carpenter, and Caleb Pusey, co-owners of the mill. Probably the work of a local blacksmith. *Historical Society of Pennsylvania.*

Hinges of modified cockshead form, from a barn door in Maryland near the Pennsylvania line. Their wavering symmetry and unequal size suggest production by a country blacksmith. *Author's collection.*

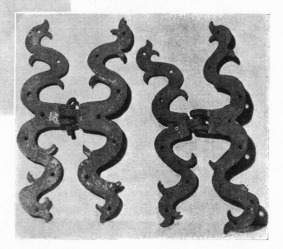

Door hinge with tulip motif, on a meeting-house door at Blooming Grove, Pennsylvania. Probably made by a local smith. *Photograph by courtesy of Russel W. Gilbert.*

Hoes, Grubbing Hoes, Tucking Hoes, Chissels, Plane Irons, 10d and 12d Nails, Hooks and Hinges, and many other Articles too tedious to mention." The most revealing newspaper advertisement I have found is that of George M'Gunnegle, who announced his "Blacksmith & Whitesmith Business" in the *Pittsburgh Gazette*, August 1, 1789:

". . . He has furnished himself with a very good horse shoer and country smith, and likewise makes locks, keys, hinges of all sorts, pipe tomahawks, scalping knives, boxes and pins for vises, grates, polished and unpolished andirons, shovels, tongs, skimmers, flesh forks, scewers, with all kinds of work for kitchens, curry combs, chaffing dishes, bread toasters, plates saddle trees, makes craeping, curling, and pinching tongs, rupture belts, grinds swords, razors, scissors, and pen knives, cleans and polishes pistols . . ."

These versatile craftsmen were often wheelwrights and farriers as well; but usually the farrier, whose specific function was shoeing horses, and sometimes also caring for horses' medical and surgical needs, was a separate entity. For that reason, and also because shoeing was not generally necessary for the few hard roads of the eighteenth century, references to horseshoeing are very infrequent in the blacksmiths' daybooks I have examined.

By the mid-nineteenth century mechanized industry had absorbed many of the early blacksmith's tasks, and the number of horses used on the roads had greatly increased, so the blacksmith turned to forging and fitting horseshoes. Later, industry took over the task of making the shoes, and all that remained for the smith to do was to fit them and nail them on. Finally, the horse itself disappeared from the highways of America, and the blacksmith's shop became a museum exhibit; the spray of sparks and the ring of the anvil vanished from Main Street, U. S. A.

Notes on early American brass and copper

BY DEAN A. FALES, JR., Secretary of the Winterthur Museum

THE STUDY OF THE BRASS AND COPPER industry in this country is as baffling as it is rewarding. While a considerable body of information exists in both old records and documented objects, the field is so vast that the definitive study on the subject has yet to be written. It is hoped that the range of brass and copper pieces illustrated here (many examples have not been previously published) will swell the census of surviving items and, in some degree, stimulate interest and lead to discoveries in this field.

The terms *coppersmith*, *brazier*, and *brassfounder* were frequently as confusing to the colonial artisan as they are to us. Since the men who worked in brass and copper were often also pewterers, silversmiths, tinsmiths, or blacksmiths, it is difficult to separate their productions successfully. Yet it is in this very versatility within a broader field that the peculiar genius of the American craftsman can be found.

The raw material for both copper and brass is copper ore; and, while copper mines existed early in the eighteenth century in New Jersey and Connecticut, the limi-

Brass and ivory "memorandum book" dated 1746, made by Jeffrey Lang (Salem, Massachusetts; w. 1733-1758)—one of the earliest of a small group of silversmiths who occasionally worked in brass. The ivory cards fan out and can be easily written on. The engraved clasp is reminiscent of William and Mary and Queen Anne furniture brasses, while the form is similar to that of some Queen Anne looking glasses.

That pewterers, too, could produce brass and copper is seen in records of the Dolbeare family and of practically all Rhode Island pewterers, in the many ladles and skimmers made by Richard Lee and his son in New England, and in the teapots of Benjamin Harbeson, of Lancaster and Philadelphia. The WK mark on this skimmer is very similar to initial touches used on pewter by William Kirby, who worked in New York from c. 1760 to 1794, when he gave up pewtering and became a merchant.

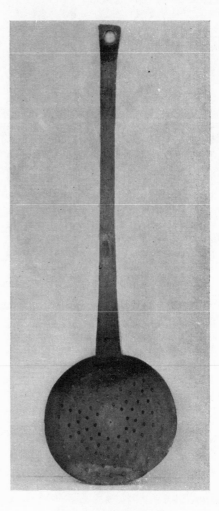

All illustrations from the

Henry Francis du Pont Winterthur Museum.

Photographs by Gilbert Ask.

tations imposed by England were so strong that little of this raw product was available for American consumption; and the coppersmith and brassfounder, like the pewterer, were forced to assay and reuse old vessels. Also since the exports of finished objects to the Colonies were so numerous and so inexpensive, the American metalworker would normally sell imported wares as well as his own. Consequently it is difficult to identify vast amounts of undocumented early copper, brass, and iron used in this country.

A typical advertisement of a colonial metalworker is this one, from the Boston *Gazette* in 1736:

BRAZIERS' WARES.—Mary Jackson, at the Brazen-Head, in Cornhill, makes and sells all sorts of Brass and Founders Ware, as Hearths, Fenders, Shovels and Tongs, Hand-Irons, Candlesticks, Brasses for Chaises and Saddles, of the newest Fashion; all sorts of Mill Brasses; Mortars, Cocks, large and small; all sorts of polish'd Brazier's Ware, at Reasonable Rates. A Quantity of large Brown Paper fit for sheathing ships, to be Sold: Likewise buys old Copper, Brass, Pewter, Lead and Iron.

The range of articles produced in brass and copper was very wide. Besides such household articles as fireplace equipment, pots and pans, lighting fixtures, and furniture hardware, all sorts of tools, construction materials for ships and houses, stills, and commercial equipment were produced by the early metalworkers. During the Revolution they manufactured cannon and firearms.

One of the greatest services of brassfounders was the making of tools for other crafts. As early as 1723, pewterers' spoon molds were being advertised in Philadelphia by Thomas Gregory and James Smith. Thomas Yates, a brassfounder, advertised in New York in 1759 that he made "all sorts of small Steel and Iron Tools for Cabinet-Makers, Carvers, Silver Smiths and Engravers, such as Chizzels, Gouges, Drills, Scorpers, Gravers, Punchers, &c. &c." In Philadelphia, Benjamin Harbeson made silversmiths' boilers in 1766, and in 1819 Hedderly and Riland were advertising all sorts of pewterers' molds "at the shortest notice."

After the Revolution, the metalworkers tended to specialize more and more. The brass-button business flourished, as did the production of fittings for ships and the making of bells. In the 1818 Philadelphia directory Thomas W. Levering, a bell- and brassfounder, wrote glowingly of his product:

Without entering into an elaborate history of the origin and usefulness of Bells, he will merely advert to their utility in Churches, from national rejoicings to national lamentations—from the modest peal of the assiduous lover to the 'lost child restored'—from the tintinnabulary clatter of a dun to the delightful tones of a dinner bell—from the decorations of a

The teakettle is the form most frequently found in marked copper and brass. Since most examples are by Pennsylvania makers, it is no surprise to find that this copper one was made in Philadelphia. The firm of Oat & Cooke at 182 North Third Street advertised in directories from 1794 until 1798, when the partnership was dissolved. This example is typical of those made in the middle states in the late eighteenth and early nineteenth centuries.

cheerful hearth, down to the jingle of a Conestoga team, he is able and willing to supply them.

In the Joseph Downs Manuscript Library at Winterthur there are several interesting documents on this field. One shows the variety of wares carried by James and Aaron Rogers, brassfounders and ironmongers of New York. An inventory of their shop made in 1798 contains no fewer than twenty-three pages of itemized goods. While some of the items are listed as English, it is safe to assume that a great many were made by the Rogerses. Included in the huge stock were two hundred gross of button molds, as well as bells of many different sizes. Twenty dozen furniture brasses and ten dozen escutcheons of five different types were also listed, as were all kinds of tools and household equipment. Among the more interesting entries were dustpans, fishhooks, thirteen dozen padlocks, seven and one-third gross of iron jew's-harps, and twelve gross of brass jew's-harps! Objects of all sorts made of brass, copper, iron, pewter, and steel were listed, showing the variety and quantity of goods successful brassfounders and ironmongers had to carry.

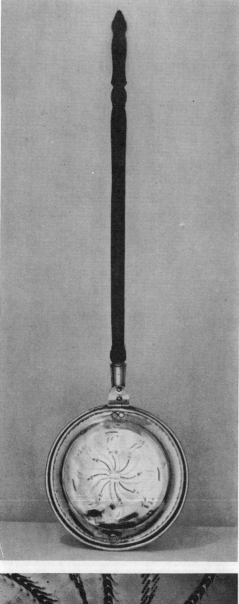

Wrought-iron candlestand, with pewter finial and brass candleholders and drip pans, made for the Covert family of Long Island in the second half of the eighteenth century. While many of the early brassfounders advertised candlesticks, no eighteenth-century examples by known American makers have yet been found. This type of double cross-armed candlestand, however, seems to be peculiarly American; most European examples have only single arms.

Brass warming pan, engraved, with grained maple handle, made by William C. Hunneman (Boston, early 1800's; see ANTIQUES, June 1930, p. 534). Hunneman, who had been apprenticed to Paul Revere, started his own business in 1797. Many of his nineteenth-century andirons survive. The painted graining on this handle is like that on the fancy Sheraton furniture so popular during the second decade of the century.

Another even more lengthy inventory is that of the estate of John Stoutenburgh, a brassfounder and hardware merchant of New York, taken in 1814. Thirty-one of the forty-two pages of the inventory are devoted to shop goods. Besides all sorts of iron and steel cutlery, Norfolk latches are listed, as are many H-hinges. In brass, there are sets of "Clock Case Balls" mentioned, as well as "oval Escutcheons" and brasses, and "Handles & Roses." The last two indicate he carried furniture brasses in both Hepplewhite and Sheraton styles.

A final inventory is one made in 1818 in New York, listing the shop fittings, tools, and raw metals of David Phillips, a brassfounder and metalworker. Witnessed by Richard Wittingham (or Whittingham), a maker whose andirons and fire tools survive today (ANTIQUES, April 1957, p. 350), this document of eight pages lists the equipment of Phillips' shop, as well as vast quantities

Brass triple-armed candlestick with adjustable green tin shade, made by Baker, Arnold & Co., Philadelphia; early nineteenth century. This type of lighting fixture was popular in France toward the end of the eighteenth century; examples have been found in both ormolu and bronze. The firm of Baker, Arnold & Co. is not listed as such in Philadelphia city directories, although metal workers with these names are listed separately.

of unworked brass, steel, iron, lead, and "sodder," all indicating the scope and versatility of the craftsman's work.

The American brassfounder and coppersmith supplied goods for people and their businesses, buildings, horses, carriages, and shops. Success required a varied stock, and the craftsman frequently relied for this on imported goods, whether by choice or by necessity. As Levering said later in his advertisement, "Neither is he selfish—his labours are not confined to any sect or party, nor by geographical bounds—he works for all. Though friends are frequently inimical to his works, he is quite as willing to dispose of his brass as they are."

The author wishes to thank Carolyn Scoon, assistant curator of the New-York Historical Society, for providing some of the information contained in this article.

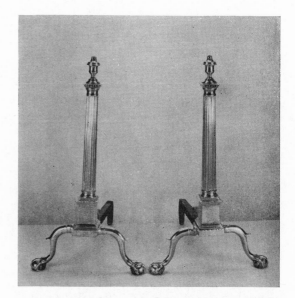

Pair of brass andirons signed by Daniel King (Philadelphia, 1765-1795). King, one of the most successful of the early American brassfounders, was in charge of the float representing his profession in the Grand Federal Procession in Philadelphia on July 4, 1788. The brassfounders' marvelous banner read "In vain the Earth her Treasure hides." (Benjamin Harbeson headed the coppersmiths in the same procession.) A great deal of fireplace furniture was made by the early brassfounders, and some early nineteenth-century andirons and firetools bear their makers' marks At Winterthur there are two King bills. One, to Edward Shippen in 1789, lists a large brass fender; the other, to "Mr. Leaming" in 1798, lists shovel and tongs, a pair of brass dogs, and a pair of chimney hooks.

Besides products for the home, many brassfounders made precision instruments. The weight on the left, marked PS, is attributed to Philip Syng, the brassfounder of Annapolis, Maryland, who advertised in 1759 that he made candlesticks, heads or knobs for shovels and tongs, furniture brasses, door knockers, and bells. The weight on the right is one of a set, including scales, all marked by George Plumly of Philadelphia, who was admitted to the city as a freeman in 1717. A label on the lid of the small wooden box containing them states, "The original standard of penny weights and grains are kept by George Plumly in the Third Street, Philadelphia; who is authorized by law to make and seal weights to weigh silver, and gold &c." The initial marks on both weights are similar to those of early eighteenth-century silversmiths.

Brass protractor made by Isaac Greenwood (New York City, 1783-1787). The son of an instrument maker and grandson of a professor of mathematics at Harvard, Greenwood started his career as a dentist, worked in Providence from 1787 to 1810, and returned to New York. Other instruments at Winterthur include a brass surveyor's compass by Rittenhouse and Potts of Philadelphia, a brass thermometer by Christopher Colles of New York, and marble-and-brass scales by H. Croemer of Philadelphia.

Set of copper measures made by J. W. Cluett (Albany, New York, early 1800's). All are stamped with an eagle mark and N.Y., indicating they were approved by a sealer. Two are inscribed *Dutchess,* the name of the county. While sealers' marks were required by law on all English measures, this practice was followed in America only in certain counties in New York State. Pewter measures with sealers' marks of Westchester County have been found. John Cluett is listed in the 1835 and 1836 Albany directory as a tin-sheet and iron worker in partnership with one Chauncey Whitney.

It is difficult to know whether the copper pieces shown on the elaborate trade cards engraved by John Norman and Henry Dawkins of Philadelphia for David Cummings and Benjamin Harbeson were products of the craftsman's shop or of the engraver's imagination. This simple billhead, however, rings true and serves as a useful document showing typical forms made in the 1790's. It is interesting to note that Bailey worked in brass, copper, and iron.

The Village Tinsmith

By Mabel M. Swan

ONE does not need to be three score and ten to remember the Yankee peddler, who, his cart filled to overflowing with tin utensils of every description, started out each spring to find a market for the products of the village tinsmith.

The praises of the village blacksmith have often been sung, whereas the tinsmith has quite failed of laureate celebration. Perhaps tin making was too simple a craft to touch the romantic imagination, and the composition of the ware itself was too lacking in permanence. Then, too, the rather questionable reputation of the tin peddler for sharp dealing tended to overshadow the real value to the community of the men whose goods he marketed.

Fig. 1 — TIN LAMPS AND CANDLE SCONCE
Owned by the Dedham Historical Society

Up to the year 1700, very little tin was seen in America; and what few pieces there were had been imported from England. Andrew Faneuil, a Huguenot, came to Boston in 1700, and started in business as a merchant. Among the articles he offered for sale were wooden and tin lanthorns, dishes, pans, and kettles — all imported. Their cost was very high, and only the wealthy could afford them. Governor Winthrop possessed a few tin plates, and some Southern planters owned tin pans and "tynned covers." But tin pails were unknown; and, often, pails were made of wood, brass, or latten ware, a kind of brass.

BEGINNINGS OF THE AMERICAN TIN INDUSTRY

The first manufacturing of tinware in America was probably begun at Berlin, Connecticut, in 1740, by William and Edward Patterson, natives of Ireland, who imported from England sheet tin from which they made tin utensils.*

These sheets of tin came packed in oak boxes, and, though marked as "best charcoal tin," were really not tin at all, but sheets of pure iron, which, under the fierce

*Lathrop's *Brass Industry*.

Fig. 2 — TIN COFFEEPOT
Made in the Whiting and Parsons tin shop, about 1803. The pot is lightly japanned, and is decorated in gilt with medallion and monogram. *Owned by Mrs. Joseph Guild of Dedham*

heat of burning charcoal, had gone through a series of changes from a bubbling liquid of melted iron to a thick pasty mass of metal. This, after being beaten and kneaded to free it from impurities, was passed, in the form of a thick bar, through huge rollers, until it was pressed into a sheet about two feet wide and of the thickness of a sheet of paper. Such sheets, after being cut into squares, were sent to the pickling tub of dilute sulphuric acid, which cleansed them of their covering of black oxide. They were then "tinned" or dipped in iron cisterns of melted tin. It was very important that sheets of exactly the same thickness be packed together, a very difficult thing to accomplish. A unique method of selection was, accordingly, employed: a keen-eared man took each sheet by the corner, gave it a quick shake, and judged its thickness by the sound produced.*

It was not a difficult matter to make articles from this sheet tin; and, as the Patterson brothers produced far more than their local market could absorb, they kept the manufacture to themselves until 1760, when they began training a few apprentices.† During the Revolution, it was, of course, impossible to obtain sheet tin, so that it was not until later that the scope of tin manufacturing was extended through the medium of the tin peddler.

At first the tinsmith peddled his own wares in a basket. Then routes were extended to neighboring towns. Later, a particular type of wagon was perfected, the tin peddler's wagon; and the Yankee trader, with his well-known qualities of wit, imagination, and trading ability, came into his own. In fact, the instinct for selling and trading was so strong in

*Chamber's *Magazine*, 1883.
†Lathrop's *Brass Industry*. Further details concerning the affairs of the Pattersons, as well as concerning the diversified activities of itinerant peddlers, will be found in Richardson Wright's entertaining volume, *Hawkers and Walkers in Early America*.

these men that they often sold even their horse and wagon before reaching their original starting place.* When tin manufacturing was at the height of its success, tin trading organizations had supply stations at Montreal, Richmond, Charleston, and Albany, and various other places.†

The peddlers would leave Connecticut in the spring, with their carts well stocked for business, and would gradually work toward the supply stations where they could restock their wagons, turn over the profits — sometimes in cash and sometimes in other articles — and then start back towards Connecticut.

At this time all industries suffered from prohibitive transportation charges; and the tin peddlers, taking advantage of the fact, gradually swelled their stocks with brass kettles, lamps, and "notions," all of which found a ready market back in country districts. After the Connecticut grandfather clock had been abbreviated to shelf dimensions, and had been priced within the means of country folk, it, too, had a place in the wagon. Many a tin peddler thereafter won reputation as a "tinkerer," able to start any balky clock that he found along his route. Often he would take his pay in rags; and many a household was glad to give him a seat by the fire and space in the barn for his horse, in return for the outside news which he was always ready to retail.

Some Eminent Tinsmiths

In the *Columbian Minerva*, a newspaper of Dedham, Massachusetts, for August 1, 1799, there appears the following advertisement:

ELI PARSONS

Takes this method to inform his friends and the public that he has newly set up the

Tinning Business

n the town of Dedham, about three quarters of a mile west of the Court house near Mess Whiting & Newell's store; where he determines

to carry on the Manufacturing of Tin Ware in all its various and particular branches — likewise particular pains taken to do justice to all those who will oblige him with their custom. All kinds of Tin Ware warranted good and on as good terms as can be had in this state.

ELI PARSONS.

Evidently business prospered in this tin shop, for, a month and a half later, occurs the following advertisement in the same paper:

ELI PARSONS

Respectfully informs his friends and the public that he continues to carry on the Tin Ware Making near the usual place in Dedham; also that he makes all kinds of Sheet Iron Stoves and Funnels, and Lead Pipes for Conductors to Houses. Any Gentleman who wishes to furnish himself with any of the above will be faithfully served on the shorteth notice by applying as above.

He likewise wants immediately a LAD about 15 years of age who can be well recommended as an Apprentice.

December 25, 1800.

In an article in the Dedham *Historical Register* for January, 1924, Calvin Guild says:

Calvin Whiting entered into partnership with Eli Parsons, a tin ware worker, supposed to have come from Connecticut, for the manufacture of tin ware. Workmen skilled in that trade came with Mr. Parsons from that state with tools, tin carts, and all else necessary for successfully carrying on the business. This created a necessity for many other kinds of trade. The coming of these men gave the Upper Village its name of Connecticut Corner.

The exact date of this partnership is not known, but, among the papers of Calvin Whiting, occurs the following particularly interesting note, dated 1803, showing that Whiting, part owner of the store of Whiting and Newell, referred to in Parson's first advertisement, had lost little time in associating himself with the tinsmith:

Boston, June 6, 1803.
Major Whiting Sir, I have a distant relative a very clever fellow but as I have no tin here any more than I want myself if you have any tin unsold if you will let him have a load out of your shop I will be answerable for the same in so Doing you will oblige him & me & not disoblige yourself I am yours &c
DIVAN B. YATE *tin Pedlar.*

On the same slip of paper, in the same handwriting, appears the following list:

JAPANN'D WARE
36 Sugar Boxes of Difrent Sizes
60 Bread Baskets
6   Large Coffee pots
6   2nd size Do

Fig. 3 — Two Tin Lanterns and a Foot Stove
Such lanterns are erroneously called *Paul Revere* lanterns, without regard to the fact that their feeble illumination could never have been sufficient to serve signalling purposes.
Owned by the Ohio State Archaeological and Historical Society.

Fig. 4 — Pennsylvania Coffeepot (*early nineteenth century*)
An example of the Pennsylvania-German genius for decorative metal work. The pot is of tin elaborately decorated with punch patterns.

*Johnson's *History of Connecticut*.
†Lathrop's *Brass Industry*.

Fig. 5 — CAN FOR BURNING FLUID (*mid-nineteenth century*)
Found in Ohio.

6 L graters
6 Flour boxes
60 Harts and rounds
12 graters
12 Gill cups

The name of Caleb Downing, evidently the bearer, is written on the back of this note.

Whiting was not only a successful merchant of West India goods, but he was also an inventive genius, who spent much of his time devising machines to save time and labor in the manufacture of tin. An amusing story is told concerning one of his inventions. The law, even as late as 1800, required attendance at church at least twice a year. Whiting was careful not to break this law; but neither did he exceed the required number of services, and, on the fifty free Sundays he continued his experiments in a mill which he owned in Dedham.

After a very busy week which he had spent in trying to perfect a certain motion in one of his machines, Whiting dutifully went to church; but, as the law failed to specify close attention to the service, he took advantage of the opportunity for needed rest, and promptly fell asleep. In the course of this sanctified slumber, he dreamed the solution of his mechanical problem. Thereupon jumping into the aisle, he threw up his arms and

6 small size Do
12 Court Cafes
4 Flower Boxes
13 Pepper Do
36 Tumblers
24 Servers
6 Large Kettles
2 Waterpots
16 Ten Quart pails
36 Large Pans
4 Large Covered pails
48 Milk Pans at 2/4
9 round cannisters
9 half Do
9 Quarter Do
24 Back Candlesticks
43 Cream Pitchers
12 Coffee pots
6 Cullenders
2 Candleboxes
6 Quart Measures
6 Do Funnels
12 Yeast Dishes
6 pint measures
43 flat cups

shouted, "I've got it."

In the *Norfolk Repository,* then the weekly newspaper of Dedham, for May 9, 1806, appears the following advertisement of a machine invented by Whiting and Parsons:

PATENT MACHINE FOR WORKING TIN PLATE

The public are respectfully informed that a machine has lately been invented by Calvin Whiting and Eli Parsons of Dedham (in the county of Norfolk and commonwealth of Massachusetts) for working Tin Plate into the various kinds of ware necessary for use, for which a patent is obtained according to law. The Machine is considered by those who have had an opportunity to examine it to be one of the most useful and important inventions that ever originated in our country and worthy the attention of every Tin Plate worker who considers his time of any value. Although it is simple in its operations above described it will make from ninety to one hundred and twenty revolutions in a minute. Those who incline to purchase patent rights to the above machinery may have opportunity by applying at the Patent Tin Manufactory a little west of the Court House Dedham where shopkeepers and others may be supplied with any quantity of Japanned and Gilt Tin Ware at the most reduced prices of any in the United States.
Dedham, May 9, 1806

Fig. 6 — TIN LAMP (*mid-nineteenth century*)
Found in Ohio.

FOOT STOVES

The foot stove was a regular article of tinsmith manufacture, and in time it was not uncommon for a tinsmith to add the manufacture of sheet iron stoves to his business. Yet, in days when the fervors of piety were deemed sufficient to relieve the chill of meeting houses, neither foot stoves nor the later sheet iron stoves were always viewed with enthusiasm.

The Boston *Evening Post*, in 1783, printed the following verse:

Extinct the sacred fire of love,
Our zeal grown cold and dead,
In the house of God we fix a stove
To warm us in their stead.

An amusing account of the reception of the sacrilegious stove

Fig. 7 — REFLECTOR BAKING OVEN WITH SPIT

Fig. 8 — STENCILLED BREAD OR FRUIT DISH
Probably a late specimen, not particularly desirable.

Fig. 9 — TIN CHANDELIER (*late eighteenth or early nineteenth century*)
Such chandeliers, usually mounted on a turned wooden core, and sometimes, as in this instance, braced with wooden arms, were something of a work of art.

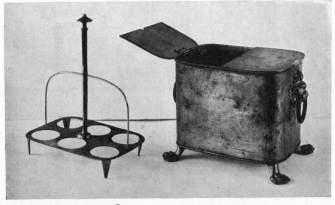

Fig. 10 — TINWARE DE LUXE
An egg cooker attributed to Thomas Clark, the Hingham silversmith. A handsome piece, of superior workmanship.
Owned by W. W. Lunt

has been accredited to the old meeting house in Litchfield, Connecticut. It is told by Samuel Goodrich, "Peter Parley," in his *Recollections*. The wife of one of the deacons, who was strongly opposed to the introduction of the stove, overcame her prejudices to the new acquisition sufficiently to come to church on the first Sunday after it had been set up. She walked into the meeting house and swept haughtily into her pew without even a glance in the direction of the unwelcome addition. There she sat, growing warmer and warmer from the unaccustomed heat, until the minister's words "heaping coals of fire," overwhelmed her, and she fainted. She was carried out, and, upon recovering, blamed the fainting to the heat of the stove. The story ends by relating her most complete "coming to," when she was told that because of the omission of some part of the funnel there had been no fire in the unhallowed contraption.

CONCLUSION

Some interesting comparisons of prices for tin may be made from the old bills.

Wm. Herman Mann
    to C. Whiting, Dr.

1802–Dec. 11 to mending stove funnel $0.17
1803 Apr. 26 to tin kitchen 3.25
    July 17 to a skimmer 17

Three small scraps of paper, all of the same date, tell their own story:

Dedham, Feb. 17, 1803

Madam please to deliver to Calvin Whiting or order the tin ware which I left locked in your stable.
Mrs. Clark   Yours Alpheus Cleveland.

Madam please to deliver to Calvin Whiting or order the tin ware which I left in your care.
Mrs. Sally Curtis.   Yours Alpheus Cleveland

Rec'd of Calvin Whiting Forty Dollars being in full of all demand.
                                             Alpheus Cleveland.

So began the tinware industry in the United States. The venturesome beginnings of the Patterson Brothers in Connecticut were doubtless emulated by other men in other parts of the Colonies. What Eli Parsons and his inventive partner Whiting accomplished in Dedham found its counterpart in other communities. Indeed Whiting's tin working mechanism and his efforts to place it on the market are indicative of the extent to which the humble art of tinsmithing was practised in a small way throughout the country. And tinware is still an essential article of domestic use. For some purposes it has been superseded by enameled iron, by steel, and by aluminum; but still, in remote places, the path of civilization is blazed by the tin can of the explorer.

COPPERSMITHING
IN EARLY AMERICA

By HENRY J. KAUFFMAN

We are glad to be able at last to publish an article on American copperware, a subject too little investigated by students. We hope that others will amplify this contribution. Mr. Kauffman of Lancaster, Pennsylvania, besides being an author and collector, has a practical, working knowledge of metals, and teaches his college students to make copper teakettles and pots in the old manner.

COPPER WEATHER VANE by Shem Drowne (1683-1774), one of the earliest authenticated pieces of American coppersmithing. It once surmounted Province House in Boston, residence of the colonial governors. *Courtesy Historical Society of Massachusetts.*

THE ORIGINS of coppersmithing in America are shrouded in almost complete obscurity. Unlike pewter, silver, and iron, which have received definitive study, our early work in copper seems to have been neglected. This is hard to understand, in view of the important role played by this metal in colonial America, and later. Nevertheless, in spite of the scarcity today of both antique copper objects and documentary materials, sufficient of both are available on which to base a study of the subject. I have now gathered together enough fragments of data from sources like newspaper advertisements, tax records, deeds, and general historical works, so that a preliminary presentation seems justified.

The first known coppersmiths of America were the mound builders of the Mississippi Valley. There is evidence that they knew of the great copper deposits in the Great Lakes region, and worked nuggets that were either broken off by glacial action or by the pounding of their stone hammers. Some remnants of their work are preserved in museums, but they are of course not very numerous. Indian excavations in Pennsylvania have yielded copper arrow heads and other utility pieces that were buried with the warrior so as to be available to him in after life. All of them were made from European trade pieces, apparently.

Despite the fact that Indians had roamed the country for an unknown time, there were still some outcroppings of copper to be found by the first settlers. Erosion kept revealing veins of copper in several regions. Johann David Schoepf, in his *Travels in the Confederation* (1783), makes an observation concerning the occurence of valuable ores in America.

Unfortunately, copper could not simply be picked up off the ground and made into utensils. There were problems first of all in connection with mining. Mine owners were constantly dogged with problems such as water in the mines and the raising and crushing of the ore. Many ran short of money and credit, and the expensive mining and refining facilities often broke them before they actually got started. If an owner was fortunate enough to secure metal previous to 1775, he then had to hammer it into sheets or else send it to England to be rolled, which was found to cost more than the value of the copper. All seemed to be of no avail until rollers were brought to America. In view of the English attitude toward American manufacturing, the securing of rolls and their installation at the Van Horn mine near Newark, described by Schoepf, seems like a most unusual incident:

Then the need of skilled workmen was felt, the raw copper not being saleable in America unless first prepared in sheets under the hammer for the use of the coppersmith. In former years it had been necessary for such establishment to send to England either the ore (of no great value) or the unrefined copper. On this basis the dealer gained very much at the expense of the mine owner. So rolling machines of a nice construction were brought from England, of a sort which could not be cast or fitted in America. Such an apparatus (two smooth iron rollers working horizontally) made it possible to get out the copper with more convenience and expedition than under the hammer. In a short time nearly four tons of sheet copper were got ready for the market, as fine as any ever brought from Europe; and by the use of the roller it was found

KETTLE AND CHAFING DISH by Paul Revere (c. 1780). Best known for his silver, Paul Revere was also a pioneer in American coppersmithing. *Concord Antiquarian Society. Anderson and Wood by photographs.*

KETTLE WITH BRAZIER (eighteenth century), probably American. *Metropolitan Museum of Art.*

KETTLE (*probably eighteenth century*). Stamped on handle *I. Roberts Phila. Author's collection.*

ENGRAVED BILL-HEAD of Benjamin Harbeson, Philadelphia coppersmith. Note the forms illustrated. Harbeson "Makes and Sells all Sorts of Copper Wares, Viz. Stills, and Kettles of all Sizes, Tea Kettles, Coffee Pots, Saucepans, Boilers, Chocolate Pots, Brass Kettles of all Sizes, Pewter, and Copper Worms for Stills, Brass, and Iron Wire, and Sundry other Goods, at Reasonable Rates." The bill is dated 1794. *Pennsylvania Historical Society. Wallace photo.*

possible to prepare 2½ tons a week. The first specimens of this Jersey-made copper were brought to Philadelphia precisely at the time when Congress had passed the non-importation act in 1775; and there was so much pleasure taken in this successful and really fine product of the country that without any hesitation a price was offered 6d in the pound higher than for English sheets, quoted at 3s 8d to 4s Pennsylvania current.

Contemporary with the copper mining and smelting activity in New Jersey there is evidence that similar work was being carried out in the area of Frederick County, Maryland. In the *Maryland Journal* (Baltimore), February 2, 1780, William Hammond inserted the following advertisement, indicating the difficulty of disposing of bar copper as well as the practice of sending it to Europe to be rolled. It is also interesting to note that the people of Maryland had trade connections with the Continent while the Colonies settled by the English usually traded with England:

To Silversmiths, Coppersmiths, Braziers, Buckle Makers, etc.

William Hammond having purchased a quantity of copper from Dr. John Stevenson, is determined (if he meets with encouragement) to have it melted into bars of two and three pounds each, if not, he intends to ship it in two months from the date hereof to France or Holland. It is expected that a deposit will be made by the contractors.

N. B. He has a small quantity of copper bars on hand he will dispose of.

The prospects for the continued mining and smelting of copper must have appeared good in this region, for an advertisement of Dr. John Stevenson's of August 20, 1782, mentions the names of two rolling mills in addition to his own.

Doctor John Stevenson begs leave to inform the Public, and the Gentlemen in particular who have been long waiting for copper, that they may now be supplied, he having brought his works to perfection; it has been rolled and tried by Mr. Hazlet and Mr. Minshall, coppersmiths in this town, who say they never worked better. I must inform the Gentlemen in Frederick County, who wanted their copper to be left at Mr. Wood's rolling mill that I shall not send any there; but if their demands are pressing, I will supply them with plates which I will engage and roll; but at the same time will not be answerable for any misconduct in cracking the plates at the rolling mills.

The purchasers in Pennsylvania take it from the works in plates and get it rolled there. I have a letter from Major William Bailey of York-town, who says that my copper is equal in goodness to any in the world. John Stevenson. N. B. Mr. Richardson Stewart, at Elk Ridge Landing, expects to have his rolling mill in order in two weeks.

These and many other advertisements would seem to indicate a great activity in the mining, refining, and rolling of copper in the Maryland area, but this must have been short-lived, for when the previously mentioned Schoepf

passed through the area about a year after Stevenson's advertisement, he made the following observations:

From Frederick-Town I passed, over the York-Town road, eleven miles north through limestone soil; then turned east over Rocky-hill, to reach the copper mine lying back four miles from this road, owned by Dr. John Stevenson of Baltimore. . . . There had been no work done for some time at the copper mine. However, I obtained several small pieces of ore. It was copper glass-sand ore with feldspar and a talc crust. It is called here "silver-grey ore." . . . Dr. Stevenson had long been offering a half interest for sale, having been at great expense latterly for upkeep.

Schoepf goes on to explain why metals were not more successfully mined and manufactured in America:

Several important reasons may be given why mining has not been generally more successful. In the former times, the English government sought to hinder as much as possible all digging after gold, silver and other metals, so that the working hands of a country still young might not be withdrawn from agriculture, the one true source of the peopling of a country, of its trades, and of its wealth. The export of unwrought as well as of wrought copper from England to America was always a considerable article of trade, and in discouraging American mines, it was a subsidiary purpose of the government to bolster that trade.

In view of the problems involved in the production of copper, one may wonder where enough metal was obtained to keep the coppersmiths at their benches. That there *were* a considerable number of native coppersmiths we know from various records and advertisements. By the time of the Revolution there must have been a hundred coppersmiths working throughout the Colonies.

Lancaster, Pennsylvania, the largest inland town in America, was a beehive of industrial activity in the late eighteenth century. Benjamin and Philip Schaum are recorded as coppersmiths in 1792, and at the turn of the century the great coppersmithing family of Benjamin Harbeson opened a shop in Lancaster at the southwest corner of King and Queen Streets. In York-town, too, many coppersmiths were busy. Major William Bailey operated a large coppersmithing establishment, employing several hands, and there were smaller branches of his business in Hagerstown, Chambersburg, and Frederick. He visited Carlisle at Court time, so that gentlemen there could place their orders for copper without inconvenience. Bailey states in one of his advertisements that despite the scarcity of copper there were good hands at all his shops. Major Bailey himself had served his apprenticeship under Francis Sanderson at Lancaster.

Included in the ranks of American coppersmiths was one of America's greatest craftsmen, Paul Revere, who worked at this along with his many other activities. In 1798 he wrote as follows to Benjamin Stoddard, Secretary of the Navy:

MEASURE, with applied spout and handle. Possibly this piece started as a mug and the spout was applied later. *Author's collection.*

WARMING PAN, with shovel and waffle iron. The warming pan is of copper, engraved, and has an iron handle. *Metropolitan Museum.*

CONTAINER FOR LAMP FLUID *(nineteenth century).* Largely handmade, very possibly American. *Author's collection.*

I understand that you have advised the Committee for the building of the Frigate in Boston not to send abroad for anything they can get manufactured in this country; these sentiments have induced me to trouble you with this letter. I can manufacture old or new copper into Bolts, Spikes, Staples, Nails, etc., or anything that is wanted in shipbuilding. . . . I supplied the Constitution Dove-tails, Staples, Nails, etc. My greatest difficulty is to get copper. Could I get a sufficient supply of copper, I could undertake to roll Sheet Copper for sheathing ships, etc. . . . You will permit me to offer my Services to you in manufacturing Brass Cannon, Bells, Copper Bolts, Spikes, etc.

The problem of getting copper sheets, of which Paul Revere writes so feelingly, was solved partly by the production of sheets here—at first by hammering and later by rolling—and partly by the importation of sheets from England. The quantity of imported sheets must have been very small.

In addition to the sheets, much finished copper ware was of course imported. Merchants advertised such items as copper teakettles, brass and copper warming pans, saucepans, and brass candlesticks. Many of these pieces, after long use and extensive repairing, found their way to local craftsmen, whose advertisements invariably ended, "N. B. Old work repaired in a neat manner, on the shortest notice, and the highest prices given for old copper, brass, pewter and lead." In the *Pennsylvania Gazette* English copper stills were advertised for sale early in the eighteenth century. It must have been a happy day for a coppersmith when he got a discarded one of these, which would have provided ample material to make a good many small kettles and saucepans.

In view of the scarcity of copper, many smiths were forced to carry on some other business on the side. The most frequent combination was that of coppersmith and brazier, doubtless due to the similarity of the metals and their interchange in the making of certain vessels. Pewter making and tinplate working followed. Occasionally one finds others, such as portrait painting (Eichholtz of Lancaster), japanning, dry goods and groceries, and iron mongery or blacksmithing.

Copper vessels were hard soldered or brazed with a substance known as spelter, and the inside was tinned to make them safe from the poisonous oxides that would otherwise form. This tinning often wore thin before the vessel was discarded, and then it was taken to a smith for retinning.

Advertisements like the following were common:
Caleb Allen, Brazier from Boston

Hereby informs the Public, that he has opened a Shop at the North End of Providence near Liberty-Tree; where he makes and mends Brass Kettles, Tea-Kettles, Skillets, Fish-Kettles, Sauce-Pans, Stew and Bake-Pans, Warming and Frying-Pans, Skimmers, Ladles, Wash Basins, etc. He likewise mends old Pewter and Tin, and tins old Brass and Copper Kettles, etc. All who please to favor him with their Custom, may depend on having their Work done in the neatest Manner, with Care and Dispatch. N. B. Old Pewter, Brass, and Copper, will be taken in exchange for any of the above Articles, or in Pay for his work.

Unfortunately, there are very few marked pieces of copper and brass. Why this should be so is a mystery. Laughlin mentions about forty men who combined pewtering with braziery or coppersmithing, but while practically all of them marked their pewter, very few marked specimens of their copper work have been found. True, copper was more difficult to mark than pewter, but that did not keep some from marking their wares. I know of only one smith who used more than one mark on his copper products, and he was John Getz, the son of Peter Getz, the Lancaster silversmith. A few men, such as I. Roberts of Philadelphia, included their city in their mark, but this procedure was not common.

The absence of a mark makes it difficult in many cases to say with certainty whether pieces were imported or made here. There is no hard and fast rule for distinguishing European from American copperware. Most of the eighteenth-century craftsmen in America were trained in Europe, or apprenticed to men trained there, and our early pieces are in the European tradition.

Gradually, however, an American pattern began to be established. I have found my greatest source of information along this line in a study of copper articles that I knew to be imported. When I found a piece of copperware, perhaps in the hinterland of Pennsylvania or New England, of a shape and character I had not seen in foreign pieces, I felt I had some basis for believing it to be American. By persistent observation and research of this kind I hope eventually to build up a body of documentary data about American coppersmithing. Perhaps some day it will come into its proper perspective with the other great crafts of our colonial era.

THE OLD HARDWARE OF JAMES TOWNE

By HENRY CHANDLEE FORMAN

IN THE year 1606 King James divided this country into two parts, named North Virginia and South Virginia. The line of division between these wilderness territories lay in the present State of Maryland. The capital of the northern colony, St. George's Fort, on the Kennebec River, was established in August 1607, but failed miserably after one year, leaving the way open for a Plymouth. Jamestown, first "plantation" of South Virginia, was founded May 14, 1607, by Edward-Maria Wingfield, and survived through frightful hardships as the first permanent English settlement in the Americas.

While old James Towne, or James City, as it was called, is now known as "permanent," virtually everything belonging to the settlement has perished. Of the seventeenth-century town only a massive, ruined church tower remains, its vine-clad head roofless to the sky. Recent excavations under the auspices of the United States Government have revealed that along the shore of Jamestown below the church tower lie the remains of two dozen or more brick and wooden buildings (*Fig. 1*). Fragments of hardware, pottery, and other materials have been unearthed which for the most part indicate a high degree of culture. It is true that most of these artifacts have been damaged by fire, corrosion, or breakage, yet the inherent simplicity and strength of their designs are still visible. The accompanying pen-and-ink illustrations all show the objects as restored from their damaged condition.

Most of the hardware found at Jamestown is made of wrought iron, and iron was early a commodity in Virginia. If you are willing to believe the Spanish spy, Don Maguel, who took down notes in this city in 1610, only three years after the founding, then the Jamestonians possessed in Virginia "many iron mines, to work which, as well as to work other metals, they have already erected there [in Virginia] some machinery" (Report of Francis Maguel, July 1, 1610. Brown's *Genesis of the United States*, p. 398). Later, in 1619, Sir Edwin Sandys, Treasurer of the Virginia Company, declared that his organization had "sent 150 persons, to set up three Iron workes; proof having been made of the extraordinary goodnesse of that Iron." In 1621 he reported that at "great care and Cost of at least 4000£ they [the Company] had heretofore given direction for the setting up of certain Iron worke in Virginia." Although the Indian massacre of 1622 destroyed the iron-works, manufacture of iron was revived afterwards, for by 1627, "Iron, Pitch & tarr e&. &" were mentioned as staple commodities at Jamestown (*Records of the Virginia Company*, I, 472; III, 115, 464; IV, 168). Perhaps a souvenir of two of these articles may be found in the name of the "Pitch and Tar Swamp" in this settlement.

In spite of the manufacture of iron and other metals from the very early days of the colony, the excellent quality of most of the hardware discovered at Jamestown gives rise to the belief that many objects were imported. The historian Bruce believes that the contents of the old Virginia house with few exceptions were

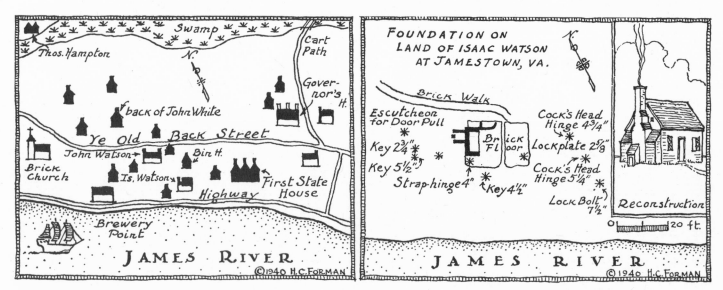

FIG. 1 (*above, left*) — MAP OF THE "NEW TOWNE" AT JAMES CITY. *Illustrating buildings mentioned in the text, and based on a map in the writer's* Jamestown and St. Mary's

FIG. 2 (*above, right*) — PLAN OF A HOUSE-FOUNDATION ON THE LAND OF ISAAC WATSON AT JAMESTOWN. *Showing the distribution of important hardware, and a reconstruction of the house*

FIG. 3 (*right*) — OLD DOOR AND FURNITURE HARDWARE FROM JAMESTOWN. From the foundation on Isaac Watson's land was found *a*, 4 ½″ key; *c*, 2 ½″ square door-pull escutcheon; *e*, part of a strap-hinge; *i*, 4 ¾″ cock's-head hinge. From the First State House foundation came *b*, 6 ⅜″ cock's-head hinge; *d*, 8″ key; *f*, 4 ⅝″ stock-lock main-plate. From the ruin on Thomas Hampton's land, *h*, 1 ¾″ keyhole escutcheon; and from that on land of John Watson, *g*, a small brass hinge, probably from a box. All hardware is drawn restored

Illustrations by the author

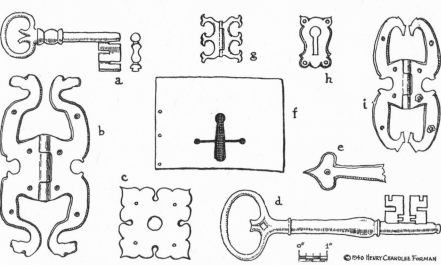

imported from England, and consequently had the same character and quality as those of the mother country (P. A. Bruce, *Economic History of Virginia*, I, 133). Moreover, the records seem to confirm the existence of hardware importations. In 1637 Sir John Harvey, quick-tempered Governor of Virginia, sailing a second time from England for Jamestown, carried with him "iron wares to the value of upwards of £45" (*Colonial Papers*, IX, No. 6). Even as late as 1700, a year after Jamestown had given place to far-famed Williamsburg as the colonial capital, the vestry of a church situated not many miles from the settlement on the James sent to "England this present Shiping for Iron work, Glass for Sash windoes and paint for the aforesaid Church" (*Vestry Book and Register of St. Peter's Parish, New Kent County, 1684–1786*). Therefore, it seems reasonable in the light of the foregoing evidence to assume that the hardware of excellent quality or of elaborate design found in the Jamestown excavations was made in Britain and shipped across the sea.

When the buildings at Jamestown burned or rotted, the fragments of hardware fell upon the foundation or the ground, and were gradually covered by the earth. Figure 2 shows a typical

FIG. 4 (*below, right*) — A CORRODED H-HINGE FROM JAMESTOWN. *This 8 ½″ hinge was found on the mud floor of the foundation "back of John White's land." The pintle or "hook" is very long*

foundation without cellar lying close to the bank of the James River, and the distribution of the important hardware fragments which were excavated in the foundation area. The house, having but one chimney, and made of wood, stood on the land of the old Jamestonian, Isaac Watson, and therefore has been labeled *Is. Watson* on the map (*Fig. 1*). As a matter of fact, no one yet knows anything about this gentleman, except that in 1644 he owned this acre. But the house was no destitute dwelling, even though there was only one downstairs room. From this building alone came two treasured cock's-head hinges (*Fig. 3, i*), as well as other pieces of ornamental hardware.

The cock's-head hinge has a pattern which goes back to Roman times. A rarity in America, the hinge is actually an elaboration of the H-hinge, which is more common at Jamestown. In the inventory of one of the old-time Carters of Virginia there was found this item: "2 pr & half of H hinges" (*Virginia Magazine of*

History, VI, 267). One of the simplest kind of H-hinge is that with the rounded terminations shown in the photograph (*Fig. 4*). Here the pin or pintle, sometimes called the "hook," was made long enough so that there was no danger of the door becoming unhinged. (The Court House at Town Fields, Northampton County, Virginia, in 1664 was specified to have "two doors to be well hinged with hooks and hinges.") Other H-hinges with heart-, lobed-, and spear-shaped terminations are illustrated in Figure 5.

But by far the commonest type of hinge at Jamestown is the strap, and this has many varieties of terminations, one of which is shown in Figure 3, e. From the First State House at Jamestown were discovered as many as thirty-two strap-hinges, averaging in length from one to two feet. No doubt many came from cupboard doors, trunks, and chests. Two corroded hinges in Figure 6 are unusual specimens. The one at the left in the picture has a splayed back plate with fixed pintle, and may have been used on a cupboard; that on the right, possibly from a wagon-box or wooden chest, has been broken off at one end, leaving a jagged edge.

Butterfly hinges are usually beautiful; their design is undoubtedly modeled on the "double-axe" motif of early Cretan palaces. An example picked up in the foundation on the land of Thomas Hampton is shown in Figure 5, d. The delicate brass hinge with foliations (*Fig. 3, g*), only three sixty-fourths of an inch thick, may have been employed on a small box.

The ancient doors of Jamestown had an abundance of locks and keys, if the hardware recovered is any indication. Joseph Moxon in his *Mechanick Exercises* (1694) made note of several kinds of English locks, such as "Street-door Locks, called Stock-Locks; Chamber-door Locks, called Spring-Locks; Cupboard-Locks; Chest-Locks; Trunk-Locks; and Pad-Locks." The principal door of a house carried, as Moxon stated, a stock-lock, which comprised a box, either metal or wooden, with a throw or bolt turned backward and forward by means of a key. The chief door of the Court House at Town Fields, Northampton County, Virginia, was specified to have "one stuck lock & one pair of hinges." In the First State House

ruins on the Jamestown shore was found a great bolt, twelve and a half inches long, a size giving a fair indication of the length of the original stock-lock. Unfortunately, of the Jamestown stock-locks only parts remain, such as the "Main-Plates" or lock escutcheons. The plate with the cross keyhole (*Fig. 3, f*) may possibly have been wrought in this shape for religious reasons. The charming little iron keyhole escutcheon (*Fig. 3, h*) probably embellished a wardrobe or closet door.

Jamestown keys show a tendency toward decoration of the handles. From the little house foundation on Isaac Watson's land there came to light four wrought-iron keys. The smallest of these (*Fig. 3, a*) is four and a half inches long and possesses not only a molded shank, but a bit which is curved in section. Most of the bits are rectangular, like that on the eight-inch key from the State House (*Fig. 3, d*). In this example, part of the bit is missing in actuality, and indications of the brass with which the bit was welded to the shank are visible. The escutcheon of a door-pull, without ring, is a good specimen of door hardware (*Fig. 3, c*).

Not all Jamestown hardware is building ware, however. Various tools and household utensils and weapons have been found. A silver spoon with the initials *WC/E*, from Jamestown, was described in the May 1936 issue of ANTIQUES, and a "Chuckatuck" spoon in the issue of April 1938. One of the most interesting implements is a branding-iron with the owner's initials, *R L N* (*Fig. 7*). Another iron of this kind discovered at Jamestown has the monogram *TR*. These samples may have been employed not only to mark cattle but also to brand hogsheads. Hening's *Statutes* declared that every Virginia tobacco hogshead had to be marked by means of "a marking-iron, or branding-iron," with "the true weight thereof on the bulge and head of the hogshead; together with the first letter of his [the owner's] proper name and sir name."

It was with the discovery of a brass sword handle in three pieces (*Fig. 8*) on the mud floor of a cellar back of John White's land in James City that the romance and flavor of the bygone cavalier days was most clearly brought home to the archæologists. This handle, richly decorated with *putti* and other ornaments in high relief, must have been owned, not by a worthy dirt farmer — of which there were plenty at Jamestown back among the swamps — but rather by a proud cavalier. The old records often mention a Sir George Yeardley, a Sir William Berkeley, a Sir Francis Nicholson, as living in the settlement. This sword brings vividly to mind the knightly age which flourished in old historic James Towne.

FIG. 5 (*left*) — A BUTTERFLY AND H-HINGES FROM JAMESTOWN. From the First State House ruins were discovered *a*, 7 ¾″ H-hinge with heart-shaped terminations, and *b*, (part of) another H-hinge with lobed terminations. From the ruin on Hampton's property came *c*, (part of) an H-hinge with spear-shaped ends, and *d*, a 3″ butterfly hinge

FIG. 6 (*below*) — TWO UNUSUAL JAMESTOWN STRAP-HINGES. *Left*, 4″ hinge with splayed back and fixed pintle, from foundation on Hampton's land; *right*, 5 ½″ hinge (broken), probably from a wagon-box or chest

FIG. 7 (*below*) — A BRANDING IRON FROM JAMESTOWN. This implement for marking cattle or hogsheads with the initials *R L N* came to light in the ruins of the First State House. On the right is shown the side view, with most of the twelve-inch handle excluded

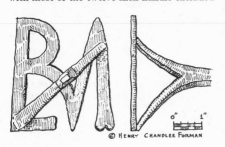

FIG. 8 (*center*) — A BRASS SWORD HANDLE IN THREE PIECES. Artifacts found on the mud floor of the Jamestown foundation "back of John White's land." Ornamented with *putti* and other motives. *Left*, the handle proper; *center*, the weight which balanced the blade; *right*, the shield which protected the hand

FIG. 9 (*below*) — PUNCHED BRASS KEY ESCUTCHEON. 2 ⅝″ long, engraved with whirls, and found in the "Bin" house north of Isaac Watson's at Jamestown

251

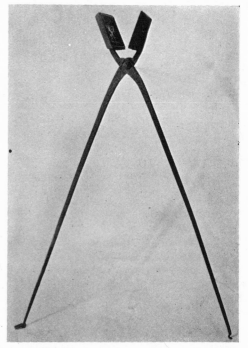

Fig. 1 — One of a Pair of Wrought Firedogs (*1790–1810*)
Found in central Ohio, where they had long served in a log house. Simple, yet graceful; unusual base

Fig. 2 (centre) — Corn Popper
Found in a German community in southwestern Ohio. Handle hollow to accommodate a wooden haft. Pan and cover solid. This piece is very heavy

Fig. 3 — Waffle Iron
Fashioned at the early Zoar community. This waffle iron is a very heavy piece with unusually long handles; it must have been exceedingly difficult to manipulate. The relief pattern inside the boxlike irons impressed a floral design on waffles baked in them. In the detail at the left the pattern is shown more clearly

Early Ohio Ironwork

By Rhea Mansfield Knittle

THE widely heralded fact that iron ore was an abundant natural resource in the Ohio territory attracted hundreds of ironworkers in the early years of the nineteenth century. From nearly every coastal state in the Union and from many European countries they migrated to Ohio, bringing their own traditions of style and workmanship, which they contributed to the region's diverse and plentiful output of ironware. All manner of iron utensils, tools, and fixtures were required in the pioneer settlements, and innumerable ingenious devices were produced to meet the need. The blacksmith's forge became, like the trading post, a popular foregathering place, whither frontiersmen from miles around came to gossip and catch up on the latest political news.

Ohio ironwork embraces a wide variety of types and exhibits skilful workmanship. The accompanying illustrations present typical examples of everyday household wares, designed for utility and incidentally achieving decorative merit.

Fig. 4 — Toaster
Forged in the Miami Valley. Finer toasters than the one here illustrated are seldom discovered in Ohio. This is a good example of an ingenious and decorative type

Fig. 5 — Broiler, with Drippings Saucer
Attributed to Columbus. Another ingenious device. Disk revolves to ensure even cooking. Drippings run down the spiral grooves and along the handle into the saucer, from which they are easily dipped for basting

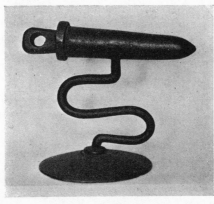

Fig. 6 (*above, left*) — Wrought Flatiron
Stand
From Central Ohio. Simplified to the
point of pure functionalism

Fig. 7 (*above, right*) — Wrought Plate
Stand
From an Amish community in north-
central Ohio. The iron grille rests on
four wooden feet

Fig. 8 (*left*) — Crimping Iron and
Heater
From eastern Ohio. Like most Ohio
ironwork, a seventeenth- or eighteenth-century type carried over into
the nineteenth century. The outer
case, supported on the standard, was
warmed by insertion of the hot iron
tongue, and was then used for fluting
the ruffles of bonnets and caps

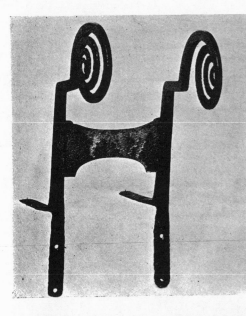

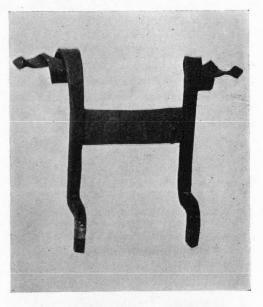

Fig. 9 (*left*) — Wrought Boot
Scraper (*c. 1820–1830*)
From the Quaker settlement of
Mount Pleasant, in eastern Ohio,
where it was fastened close to the
front entrance to the dwelling of
an English-born Quaker who had
lived in Philadelphia before he
migrated westward

Fig. 10 (*right*) — Wrought Boot
Scraper (*1815–1830*)
Found embedded in the step of a
stone house close to the Ohio
River, in a village founded prior
to 1800 by direct French migra-
tion

Fig. 11 (*left*) — Wrought Boot
Scraper (*1830–1840*)
From a doorstep in a Pennsylvania-German settlement in eastern Ohio. Identical or similar
scrapers adorn several contemporary brick houses in the community. The local smithy likewise forged fine hasps and hinges
for the big local barns

Fig. 12 (*right*) — Cast Boot Scraper
(*1825–1840*)
From the doorstep of a Putnam-
Zanesville home. Probably cast
at the Falls of the Licking River,
in the furnace of the Irish pioneer, Dillon

Index

DATE DUE

30 505 JOSTEN'S